THE HERMENEUTICS OF ORIGINAL ARGUMENT

I0892126

Northwestern University
Studies in Phenomenology
and
Existential Philosophy

Founding Editor James M. Edie

General Editors John McCumber
David Michael Levin

Consulting Editors

Robert Bernasconi
Judith P. Butler
David Carr
Edward S. Casey
Stanley Cavell
Roderick M. Chisholm
Hubert L. Dreyfus
Lester E. Embree
Dagfinn Føllesdal
Véronique Fóti
Irene Harvey
Dieter Henrich
Don Ihde
Emmanuel Levinas
Alphonso Lingis
William McBride
J. N. Mohanty
Maurice Natanson
Graeme Nicholson
Frederick Olafson
Paul Ricoeur
Tom Rockmore
George Schrader
Calvin O. Schrag
Thomas Sheehan
Hugh J. Silverman
Robert Sokolowski
Herbert Spiegelberg
Charles Taylor
Samuel J. Todes
Bruce W. Wilshire
David Wood

THE HERMENEUTICS OF ORIGINAL ARGUMENT

Demonstration, Dialectic, Rhetoric

P. Christopher Smith

Northwestern University Press
Evanston, Illinois

Northwestern University Press
625 Colfax Street
Evanston, Illinois 60208-4210

Copyright © 1998 by Northwestern University Press.
Published 1998. All rights reserved.

Printed in the United States of America

ISBN cloth 0-8101-1607-3
paper 0-8101-1608-1

Library of Congress Cataloging-in-Publication Data

Smith, P. Christopher.
The hermeneutics of original arugment : demonstration, dialectic, rhetoric / P. Christopher Smith.
p. cm. — (Northwestern University studies in phenomenology and existential philosophy)
Includes bibliographical references and index.
ISBN 0-8101-1607-3 (alk. paper).—ISBN 0-8101-1608-1 (pbk. : alk. paper)
1. Reasoning—History. 2. Rhetoric—History. 3. Heidegger, Martin, 1889–1976. I. Title II. Series: Northwestern University studies in phenomenology & existential philosophy.
BC177.S64 1998
121'.686—dc21 98-3028
CIP

The paper used in this publication meets the minimum requirements of the American National Standard for Information Sciences—Permanence of Paper for Printed Library Materials, ANSI Z39.48-1984.

Contents

Abbreviations

Frequently cited materials appear as listed here.

DD	Hans-Georg Gadamer, *Dialogue and Dialectic*, trans. P. Christopher Smith (New Haven, 1980)
EM	Martin Heidegger, *Einführung in die Metaphysik* (Tübingen, 1987)
GBAPh	Martin Heidegger, *Grundbegriffe der Aristotelischen Philosophie* (an unpublished transcript of Heidegger's 1924 Summer Semester lecture course at Marburg, in the Marcuse Archiv in the Stadtsbibliotek in Frankfurt a.M.)
GBM	Martin Heidegger, *Grundbegriffe der Metaphysik* (GA 29/30) (Frankfurt a.M, 1983)
GT	Friedrich Nietzsche, *Die Geburt der Tragödie aus dem Geiste der Musik* in KSA 1, pp. 25–156, (Munich, 1988)
GW 3	Hans-Georg Gadamer, *Gesammelte Werke*, vol. 3 (Tübingen, 1987)
HHF	P. Christopher Smith, *Hermeneutics and Human Finitude* (Bronx, N.Y., 1991)
HLR	Heinrich Lausberg, *Handbuch der literarischen Rhetoric* (Munich, 1960)
IGPAPh	Hans-Georg Gadamer, *The Idea of the Good in Platonic Aristotelian Philosophy*, trans. P. Christopher Smith (New Haven, 1986)
KSA 1, 7	Friedrich Nietzsche, *Kritische Studienausgabe*, vols. 1, 7 (Munich, 1988)
PPh	Jacques Derrida, "Plato's Pharmacy," in *Dissemination*, pp. 61–171, trans. Barbara Johnson (Chicago, 1981)

PS	Martin Heidegger, *Platon: Sophistes* (GA 19) (Frankfurt a.M, 1992)
SZ	Martin Heidegger, *Sein und Zeit* (Tübingen, 1960)
VSK	Friedrich Nietzsche, "Versuch einer Selbstkritik," in KSA 1, pp. 11–22, (Munich, 1988)
WM	Hans-Georg Gadamer, *Wahrheit und Methode* (Tübingen, 1965)

1

Introduction: The Hermeneutics of Original Argument

What, precisely, does the word hermeneutics mean? And in just what sense could one speak of the hermeneutics of original argument? As it is used here, the word hermeneutics will have a specific sense derived from Heidegger, and the aim of this book, to provide a hermeneutics of original argument, will be derived from Heidegger's own hermeneutical project. Significantly, Heidegger already appropriates the word "hermeneutics" for the title of one of his earliest lecture courses, *Ontology* (*Hermeneutics of Facticity*), which he gave in Freiburg in the summer semester of 1923, and it was already clear then that he wanted to put his own stamp on it.[1]

In seeking out just the right sense of "hermeneutics" for his endeavor, Heidegger, as is typical of him, goes back behind the Western tradition to Aristotle, whom he considers to be "earlier" and "closer to the origin" (*früher, ursprünglicher*) than Plato, even if he is chronologically later. Heidegger points out that originally, and in Aristotle still, hermeneutics was *the process itself of making things clear in talking about them*: "As such, *logos* or speech," he says, "is privileged insofar as for it alone bringing about *alêtheuein* is possible, i.e., making unhidden what was previously hidden and covered up and putting it 'there,' in the open and at our disposal" (11).

However, this original meaning of hermeneutics gets covered up when hermeneutics becomes the exegesis and translation of biblical texts. For then certain preconditions must be established if the *hermeneuein* or "interpreting" is to be done appropriately (11–12). For instance, in Augustine such things as "the fear of God, piety, the desire to seek only the will of God in scripture, and complete disinterest in disputing the mere meaning of words" become the prerequisite traits of anyone who would interpret validly (12; see *De doctrina christiana* 2.1.1). Once that has happened, says Heidegger, "Hermeneutics is no longer interpretation [*Auslegung*] itself but rather the doctrine of the conditions of interpretion, of its object, of the means for its communication and its practical application" (13), and the path is obvious leading from here to Schleiermacher's definition of hermeneutics as an "art" (*Kunstlehre, ars, technê*) of interpretation, a definition, in fact, that still prevails (13). Now, it is precisely this historical development that Heidegger wishes to undo. In going back to Aristotle he would reverse the shift away from the original sense of hermeneutics and return us to hermeneutics, not as the *art* of interpretion, but as the *act* of interpretation itself.

For Heidegger, then, hermeneutics is not to be thought of as a doctrine of interpretation but as the actual "carrying out of *hermeneuein* or communication" (14), and just this *hermeneuein*, he tells us, will be put into practice in these lectures of 1923, which will be the "interpretive laying out [*Auslegung*] of facticity" or, stated more precisely, the act of "facticity's own interpretive laying out of itself" (14). "Facticity" is the ineluctable "fact that" we are always already "there" in the world, and, he says,

> Hermeneutics has the task of making this being-there [*Dasein*] accessible to itself and communicating to it the character of its own being-there at any given time. Hermeneutics has the task of following up on the self-alienation which has befallen being-there. In hermeneutics just how being-there might come to be, and might actually be, *understanding* of itself for itself, begins to take shape for it. (15)

Hermeneutics, then, is not something superimposed on our being-there from the outside. Rather, hermeneutics is one of being-there's own possibilities: being-there can either make itself clearly understandable to itself, or, in the case of what is already called "averageness" (*Durchscnittlichkeit*) (31) and "everydayness" (*Alltäglichkeit*) (99–100) here, it can abandon itself to saying and doing what "everybody" (*das Man*) says and does (31–32) and thereby fall into self-deception and self-alienation. When this happens, "Being-there speaks about itself and views itself this way or that, but this way of speaking is only a *mask* that it holds up to itself in order not to be frightened of itself" (31). Thus "laying [itself] out interpretively [*das Auslegen*] is itself a possible specific way 'how,' in the character of its being, facticity can be" (15), but a way of being that can be recovered and appropriated only if what hides it from view is first taken down and it is thereby "laid bare" (*freigelegt*).[2]

Four years later, in *Being and Time* Heidegger provides the following account of what hermeneutics means for him, and even if "phenomenology" is now in the foreground, not much else has changed in the meantime: "As for its method," he says,

> phenomenological description means laying something out interpretively [*Auslegung*]. The *logos* in the phenomeno*logy* of being-there [in the world] has the character of a *hermeneuein* by which the proper sense of being, and the basic strutures of being-there's own being, are *made known* in the understanding of being that belongs to being-there itself. Phenomenology of being-there is hermeneutics in that original sense of the word which designates the business of laying something out interpretively. (SZ 37)

And, he continues,

> Philosophy is universal phenomenological ontology starting from a hermeneutics of being-there which, as the analytics of *existence,* has attached the end of the thematic thread of all philosophical questioning to the place out of which this questioning arises and back into which it recoils [namely, being-there itself]. (SZ 38)

Following Heidegger's hermeneutical method, the hermeneutics of original argument or *logos* undertaken here will not be a contribution to the *art* of interpreting. Rather, it will attempt to "lay bare" and "lay out" interpretively what original argument is by penetrating beneath the abstractions that cover it up and conceal it from us. Furthermore, it will not do this from outside our factual experience of argument itself, but from within this factual experience, and "out of it," as Heidegger would say. We will thus abandon from the start any attempt to systematize argument by reducing its various kinds to some sort of explanatory principles, causes, or grounds; and if in our hemeneutics of argument we uncover beneath logical argument, dialectical argument, and beneath dialectical argument, rhetorical argument, we will not pretend to have established some sort of *fundamentum inconcussum* or "unshakeable foundation" on the basis of which all argument could be comprehended (see SZ 24). Rather, our task will be only to disclose and win back what has been buried and forgotten. Following Heidegger's hermeneutical strategies, this book will attempt to "lay bare" and "lay out" interpretively the structure and nature of argument as it originally occurs in our existence "there" in the world, and as it is to be displayed beneath the coverings that a subsequent "metaphysics" of "static presence" has superimposed on it.

In brief, there are three points to be established here. First, argument takes place originally within our experience of what comes to pass, and takes place, accordingly, in a kind of speech that tells the story of how this self-contradictory, "narrative-historical" world is "happening" (see SZ 19 on *Geschichtlichkeit* and *Geschehen*). Put another way, original argument reasons by the "topics," namely "similarity," "difference," "contraries," "the more and the less," "the prior and posterior," "the part and whole," and so forth. Original argument reasons, this is to say, by standard sequences in our speaking, according to which one thing we say naturally tends to "follow upon" another temporally in our speech rather than to "follow from" it necessarily according to logical rules of inference. However, after Plato's revolutionary turn to the permanent essences of things, argument comes more and more to be about what "forms," "classes," or *eidê* of timeless and placeless conceptual things either can or cannot belong to which other "classes." Consequently, it has come more and more to be governed by the logical "laws" of self-identity and noncontradiction. Second, our reasoning with each other by the "topics," and in these standard sequences of speech, is about contingent, temporal, ever self-contradictory things and comes, accordingly, only to likelihoods and inconclusive "conclusions." However, as it has developed from its oral, spoken beginnings, first into dialectic and then into logical demonstration or *apodeixis,* argument has come less and less to be communal deliberation that entertains "contra-dictory" possibilities, one "spoken against" the other out loud, and more and more to be a monological "pointing something out" (*apodeiknunai, demonstrare*) in "necessary" and conclusive inferences drawn, by a single mind, from the logical relationships it envisions among classes of static invariable things. Hence, argument has removed itself from the original circumstance of two or more speaking to each other. Finally, original argument, which is to say, *logos* or speech, was spoken in the voiced word names, the *onomata,* of natural, preconceptual speech, but later, derivative argument has come more and more to be in a language in which univocal signs, *sêmeia,* signifying universal essences, like "2" or "=," have replaced equivocal "talk."

These shifts, which at their core, as we will see, are a shift from orality to writing, have decisive consequences for what were originally a speaker and an audience. Originally, the minds or souls, the *puchai,* of the participants in the *logos,* or argument, were not disconnected from the lived, bodily experience of what they were hearing and undergoing but were, like those dancing to the music they hear, rooted in that bodily experience. From this it follows that, originally, the *logos,* or the sequential reasoning of what was said vocally was inseparable from the bodily *pathos* or feeling which it simultaneously communicated and in which it was set; the *logos* was inseparable, this is to say, from its acoustical "tone" and "voicing" (Heidegger: *Stimmung*). Following the Platonic revolution, however, the "mind" removes itself from the "body," and, correspondingly, the cognitive content is, as in mathematics, purified of any "contamination" by the *pathê* or affects. As we will see, this abstraction would have been as incomprehensible for a Homeric hero, who argues from *thumos* and *phrenes*, from spirited passion and the "gut," as it would have been for the first Christian evangelists, who argue viscerally from *splanchna* and the *kardia*, from "bowels" and the heart. This abstraction, too, it will be our business to "take down" or "destruct" in order to "lay bare" what it covers up.

Thus, our hermeneutical task is also a philological one: on the one hand, we will attempt, in destructive readings of Plato and Aristotle, to "lay bare" the earlier, original kind of argument beneath the layers of abstraction covering it up. (Even Aristotle's term "topic," from *topos* or "place," is the superimposition, as we will see, of a later spatialized, literary rhetoric of reading across a surface, on an original oral/aural speaking over time.) On the other hand, we will endeavor simultaneously to "lay out" hermeneutically original argument as it is thereby disclosed underneath the surface of the texts we will take from Plato and Aristotle.

If, however, this hermeneutics of original argument will require that we turn to these two thinkers of the ancient past, its ultimate, if unelaborated, purpose is nonetheless to speak to our present, modern and postmodern condition, and it is no accident that we can conclude our study with Nietzsche's similarly intended philological appropriations of pre-Platonic experience in his *Birth of Tragedy Out of the Spirit of Music.* To be sure, the object of our concern about modernity and postmodernity is a rather different one from Nietzsche's, namely the contemporary collapse of community, a collapse that has its most obvious manifestation in our inablity any longer to carry on a genuine conversation with each other about what to do. Whereas argument was originally a community of two or more taking counsel with each other, for us today it has degenerated into a litigious conflict of "rival" interests.[3] Consequently, argument now endeavors to put "cogent" demonstrations of individual points of view to one's opponents, and in striving in this way to force them to concede, we have always already forfeited any sense we might have had that we were not contestants to begin with but participants in conjoint elaboration of a shared understanding, of a *sensus communis,* a *consensus.* What is more, since one side can no longer hear and accept what the other has to say, each resorts to asserting its own position while demolishing its opponent's, and thus argument has come to mean a dispute in which "claims" are asserted and either successfully defended against a rival's challenges or defeated by them. The result is what MacIntyre has aptly called "interminable debate." Paraphrasing Clausewitz, we could say that political discussion has become war "with other means," or, with Hobbes, that the "war of all against all" now manifests itself most of all in how we speak to each other.

The underlying thesis here is that this devolution of argument is in fact not just a modern or postmodern phenomenon; rather, like the "metaphysics" that conditions modernity and, quite possibly, postmodernity too, it is something that began with the Greeks' abstraction from original argument and that, in some ways at least, was already consummated by them. Indeed, it is not hard to see how the Greeks' withdrawal from public oral-aural "con-sultation" or communal taking counsel—Aristotle speaks here of *sumbouleuesthai*—to private dialogue and, ultimately, to logic's voiceless demonstrations for no audience and best written down for solitary readers, could provide the perfect argumentative tool for modernity's and postmodernity's communityless "possessive individualism."[4] For in "communicating" logic's demonstration, one insular individual, like a teacher of geometry, only "points out," on some spatial surface, be this an area of sand, of slate, or of a computer monitor, what he or she has envisioned privately in his or her own mind—and points this out for other insular individuals, it should be noted, who are now mere onlookers (*theôretes*) and no longer participants in a public or even dialogical practice (*praxis*). Affect-free "impartiality" and "unassailable" logical demonstration, or at least the feigned appearance of these, thus becomes the ideal fortification with which each individual can shield himself or herself from perceived encroachments of others upon his or her private mental turf.

The only way out of this situation is the way back behind it. Hence, in appropriating another of Heidegger's themes, "Back to the beginning," we will try here to disclose and recover earlier understandings of argument by going back to its origins in Greece. For at the beginning we will find beneath demonstration, dialectic, and beneath dialectic, we will find rhetoric. Put another way, in our hermeneutical exposition, we will uncover beneath logic's monological and private "pointing out" to oneself (*apodeiknusthai*), dialogical conversation (*dialegesthai*). But behind dialectic's dialogical conversation we will uncover rhetoric's public con-sultation or our communal taking counsel with each other (*sumbouleusthai*).

Ostensibly, of course, logic's monological demonstration presents to silent onlookers the inferences to be drawn necessarily from any individual's insights into necessary and certain self-evident truths—see the starting point or *archê* of Jefferson's apparent demonstration, "We hold these truths to be self-evident . . ." In contrast, dialectical conversation, in simultaneously entertaining both of two contrary received opinions, each of which might or might not be so, reaches a mutual understanding concerning the subject matter under discussion. Like dialectic, rhetoric's public taking counsel also proceeds from contrary and uncertain received opinions and moves to a provisional consensus concerning them. But whereas the subject matters of dialectical conversation are still theoretical and existentially disengaged, those about which we take counsel together are practical: they concern our actions with others "there" in the world where we are engaged in shared undertakings. Hence, not only how we see things is to be changed in the course of rhetorical argument, but also how we feel about them and what we are willed to do; we are not merely to come to an opinion as the result of our exchange of *views*, but also to reach a decision (*krisis*) or choice (*prohairesis*) concerning a course of action as the result of *hearing* what the other has said.

There are important consequenses of this difference of rhetoric from both logic and dialectic. To begin with, since consent to an action rather than assent to a proposition is the goal of rhetorical argument, rhetorical argument alone is always addressed to an *audience*: it is addressed to listeners (*akouontes*) who will either hear or not hear what is asked of them, and precisely not to onlookers (*theôretes*) who will either see or not see the point. A rhetorical argument ends in either *pistis* or *apeitheia*, which is to say, either in a conviction involving trust and engagement or in a lack of faith and even disobedience. For, although the response to dialectical and logical argument is merely "Yes, I see it that way" or "No, I do not see it that way," the response to a rhetorical argument is "Yes, I (we) will" or "No, I (we) will not." From this it follows, moreover, that whereas in logic and dialectic the character or *êthos* of the speaker and the feeling or *pathos* communicated about the subject matter are extraneous, in rhetoric *êthos* and *pathos* are indissociable from the communication of the logical content, indissociable from the the *logos* of the argument. For if we are to hear and obey the word that is addressed to us for our volitional consent and not mere intellectual assent, if our *pistis* or trust is to be won by the speaker, it is obvious that how we have come to feel both about him or her and about the matter about which we are to decide and choose are crucial. As a matter of fact, any attempt to substitute logical demonstration for rhetorical conviction only falsifies this circumstance and opens the way for propagandistic manipulation in the guise of "objectivity." (Even Jefferson, whose goal is to win consent to a revolutionary act, finds himself constrained to disguise his rhetorical exhortation and defense as a demonstration seeking only assent to a proposition.)

In following Heidegger's lead and in going back to the origins of argument in Greek rhetorical practice, we will thus expose a gradual *aphairesis* or abstraction, a withdrawal, that is, *from* our original engagement in undertaking actions and getting things done in our being "there" in the world with others and among things at hand, and a withdrawal *to* the stance of a detached *theôretês* or spectator who looks on from above and "sees and knows" (*oide*) the "logic" of events transpiring down below.[5]

The abstract spectator, this is to say, sees the static universal "look," the *eidos,* of each narrative-historical thing that comes to pass in *time,* and establishes the *place* of this new object, the *eidos,* in the system of differences and relations separating it and joining it systematically with the "looks" or *eidê* of other things. Just as "geometry," for example, originally meant the practical activity of surveying land or "measuring the earth," and this for the sake of collective home building on it and getting around, but then comes to mean the theoretical study of the various static and universal "looks" to geo-metrical things, square, circle, triangle, and so forth, in their interrelations and differences, so too in one's experience of all things, one withdraws from the immediate encounter with them to a system of abstract significations of them. Indeed, as Aristotle himself notes critically, one can go so far in this abstraction that one now takes the the *eidos* or "look" of a thing, as this look is given to intellectual intuition, to be "primary being," and the thing itself, as it is given to the senses, to be a secondary and inferior copy. To use a contemporary illustration, the abstraction here would be tantamount to taking the flight schedule that one reads in the airport hall to be prior to, and more real than, the planes themselves that, from the flight deck, one sees and hears coming and going.

With this abstraction and withdrawal communication undergoes a radical change. Whereas we once communicated with each other to get things done together in a community, now, as sources of "information," each individual "points out" to the other, on some anonymous visual space like a monitor screen, the static relationships, the "*states* of affairs," obtaining among signified entities—"US Air Flight #502 to Chicago: (departs) 7:15 P.M., Gate 6A." And whereas we once *heard* the word spoken by another and were thereby joined with him or her as participants in a common undertaking "there" in the world of things coming to pass over time, we now *read* across a space impartial "views" of things stated by unknown people from whom, given our own and their withdrawal from the world, we are entirely disconnected.

But, I should say, *supposedly* impartial views. For, as such diverse critics of modern technological rationality as Nietzsche and Marx have shown in their penetration of the facade of scientific objectivity and their exposure of modernity's self-delusions, we never were the disinterested theoreticians we pretended to be. Like our correspondents on the other side of this communityless communication, each of us was always pursuing what either we or someone ruling over us *wanted* and *willed.* The ruse of the pseudo-demonstration was always only a more subtle way of forcing one's own individual interests sophistically against the individual interests of our ant-agonists in the *agôn* or contest of life. The "demonstration" was always only apparently the transmission of information presented for the intellectual assent of any impartial observer, and always really aimed at getting a specific audience to consent to what the speaker wants.

Indeed, the turn away from the rhetorical to the pseudo-demonstrative emerges not so much as a cause of the withdrawal from community as its effect: after Hobbes and Locke, and given the ascendence of a "perpetual and restless desire of power after power, that ceaseth only in death" over any remaining sense of loyalty and community (see Hobbes, *Leviathan* 1.11), we no longer willed to be in communion with others. We no longer willed to hear and belong; we willed, rather, to see and control. Hence, we "always already" found ourselves disconnected from involvement on the playing field, as it were, and, having become spectators in the stands, we sought to win our bets by a proper "reading" of what was going on below. Our own "pure," rational and scientific discourse, if not that of the Greeks, was thus always for the sake of technological control and always in the pursuit of self-interest.

No wonder, then, that today any supposedly impartial exchange of "theoretical" points of view concerning the common good degenerates rapidly and inevitably into adversarial contention. When the veneer of logical objectivity peels away, it becomes clear for all to see that at heart we have all become partisan, contentious sophists, who realize that the truth, the existence of which we doubt anyway, is not the real issue. Rather, it is victory in the contest with others and the advantage for oneself that comes with that victory, the *opheleia* that comes with *nikê* in the verbal *agôn.* Indeed, in our speaking we are no longer friends and kin in conversation with each other, but antagonists, each of us pitted against each other for the prize. Pseudo-demonstration thus emerges as just the right form of argument for possessive individualism and its competitive, communityless nonsociety. No wonder, then, that its "logic" of inference has completely displaced rhetoric in the standard academic curricula.

But, it might be objected, was not Plato's turn to the eidetic logic of things and to mathematical *apodeixis* or demonstration meant to counter precisely this devolution of human conversation into feral self-assertion? And is it not precisely our capacity for objective reasoning that distinguishes us from Hobbesian "wolves" and frees us from their territorial fights? Was not Plato's call to envision the idea of "the just itself" meant precisely to counter a Thrasymachus's irrational and bestial *pleonexia,* his infinite and wanton pursuit of "having ever more"? Indeed, it was; for, plainly, and as will be made clear here, Plato saw in the genuine objectivity of mathematical theory the possibility of countering the sophistical perversion of rhetoric and public discourse. At least for mathematicians there *is* a truth beyond the opinions that one defends out of self-interest. For them a number or a geometrical figure is what it is in and by itself, and hence it could be investigated and explained publicly, in common, and quite apart from any private motives of the investigators. Could it not be that, similarly, what is just, what is decent, what is good—*to dikaion, to kalon, to agathon*—could be investigated, as these mathematical entities are, in and by themselves, *kath' hauta*? Did not Socrates see what is just and right so clearly that he was immune to all sophistical attempts to make a wrong thing appear to be the right thing to do?[6]

Such, certainly, was the hope: Socratic discussion of ethical and political concerns was to be raised to the level of mathematical objectivity, and the sophists were thus to be deprived of their subject matter. For if we could only see and know what justice is in truth, sophists could neither pass something off for just when it was in truth unjust, nor play upon our emotions to get us to feel and believe that it was just. Given the fact that communal shared beliefs about what was just had collapsed, leaving the sophists a vast field in which to apply their devious and seductive craft, given the absence of any ethical and political consensus, might it not be that the mathematization of ethical and political discourse was the only means of transcending private interest left? Once rhetoric had degenerated into sophism, was not reasoning by mathematical demonstration the only hope?

It seemed so to Plato, or at least to Platonists, and has seemed so to "enlightened" thinkers ever since Plato, but I will try to show in what follows here that the conversion of ethical and political deliberation into mathematic demonstration is in fact impossible and that where it is attempted, which in modernity has been everywhere, it generates what Kant would call a *Blendwerk,* a construct which dazzles us and blinds us to its deceptiveness. For if there is, as I maintain, no such thing as the *eidos* or "look" of justice itself, decency itself, the good itself, or even if, as I think Plato ultimately believed, these *eidê* exist but only for a god and divine reasoning, then any apparently demonstrative human reasoning concerning them is in the end a facade, a rationalization of individual will, and not objective rationality at all.

Not that we have been immune to this appearance of impartial objectivity. How easy it once was for ideologues to make us think that either capitalism or communism were rationally demonstrable forms of a just, decent, and good political order. And how often have supposedly disinterested rational arguments in support of one or the other of these ideologies been used effectively to rationalize and conceal barbarism and brutality in the pursuit of power? No, a pure mathematic rationality cannot provide substitutes for the traditional standards of ethical and political practice that are lost when a community collapses and individuals are thrown back into a Hobbesian belligerence. Here apparent rationality and pseudo-demonstrative "logic" only blind us to the irrational horror of it all.

But what, then, *is* the way back to reasonable communal deliberation? Surely not the abandonment of ethical and political discourse to demogogic manipulators of the passions who, like someone who shouts "Fire!" in a crowded subway, would only plunge individuals into a mobilized mob. And is this not the only alternative now to reasoned, logical argument?

The task here is to show that it is not. To begin with, the splitting off of the "cognitive" from the "emotive" is, as we will see, in fact a function of the abstraction intrinsic to "mathematical" reasoning by demonstration. If, hermeneutically, we work back from reasoning by demonstration, through talking things out theoretically in dialectic, and to our communal, practical taking counsel in rhetoric, we will discover at the origins of argument the original *logos-êthos-pathos* unity in which the validity of what someone says is to be measured not just by the trustworthiness of his or her reasoning but always, conjointly, by the trustworthiness of his or her character and by the trustworthiness of his or her feelings about the matter. Along with asking if there is reason to trust the grounds he or she has advanced for undertaking the action proposed, we must ask simultaneously if he or she is prudent, temperate, honest, or rash, immoderate, and self-deceived, and if he or she speaks out of benevolence and in the spirit of reconciliation—or out of hatred and contentiousness. None of these things can be considered by an audience in separation from the others, and sophism can be exposed, or, conversely, the validity of the argument can be established, only by testing what is said against all three taken together.

One might think, in this regard, of Lincoln's Second Inaugural Address, and of how different it is from the "statements" issued in contemporary political discourse, and, consequently, how much more trustworthy and valid. I cite here only its conclusion:

> Fondly do we hope, fervently do we pray that this mighty scourge of war may speedily pass away. Yet, if God wills that it continue until all the wealth

> piled by the bondsman's two hundred and fifty years of unrequited toil shall be sunk, and until every drop of blood drawn with the lash shall be paid by another drawn with the sword, as was said three thousand years ago, so still it must be said, 'The judgments of the Lord are true and righteous altogether.'
>
> With malice toward none, with charity for all, with firmness in the right as God gives us to see the right, let us strive on to finish the work we are in, to bind up the nation's wounds, to care for him who shall have borne the battle and for his widow and his orphan, to do all which may achieve and cherish a just and lasting peace among ourselves and with all nations.

It is precisely the differences from sophistical argument and the consequent trustworthiness of rhetorical speech like this that I wish to "lay bare" and "lay out" in the hermeneutical exposition of original argument that follows here.

2

Heidegger and the Recovery of Aristotle's *Rhetoric*

The denigration of rhetoric as "mere rhetoric" is nothing new. So strong was the aversion to rhetoric in Greece after the perversion of it by sophism, that even Aristotle, who devoted at least one full book to rhetoric, cannot accept it for what it is but instead must measure it critically against dialectic's syllogisms and, ultimately, against the demonstrative logic of science. Indeed, Aristotle often writes in his own *Rhetoric* as if the whole of it were a concession to the unfortunate fact that sometimes we must deal with simpleminded people who are incapable of following an extended logical argument and who, given their inability to comprehend things rationally, must be "persuaded" by other means, namely abbreviated syllogisms or "enthymemes" and even appeals to the *pathê* or affects. In speaking of why rhetoric's loose reasoning is worth bothering with at all, Aristotle submits that "with some people it is not easy, even if we have the most exact science, to persuade them of something by our speaking. For argument in science is instruction, but [with these people] instruction is impossible" (1355a25–27).

Moreover, he begins his *Rhetoric* by telling us right at the outset that rhetoric is the counterpart (*antistrophos*) of dialectic (1354a1), and the point not only implied but argued for in the remainder of this first chapter is that since dialectic is not concerned with the communication of *pathos* or affect, ideally rhetoric should not be either. Aristotle maintains, accordingly, that the emphasis on the *pathê* in previous treatises on rhetoric is wholly misplaced: just as in dialectic, the emphasis in rhetoric too should be on syllogisms insofar as this is possible given the circumstances. This negative attitude about the tradition of rhetoric, which begins at least with Plato and which, in fact, is only perpetuated by Aristotle, persists through modernity, in which rhetoric would seem, finally and definitively, to have been driven from the field by a purely cognitive reasoning supposedly uncontaminated by rhetoric's emotional appeals.

We need to keep this history in mind in order to appreciate the full radicality of Heidegger's recovery of Aristotle's *Rhetoric* for philosophy as such. Indeed, one of Heidegger's most revolutionary feats might be to have brought the *Rhetoric* back from the extreme periphery of Aristotle's works to which the tradition of philosophy, including even Aristotle himself, had relegated it. But how was this recovery possible? And why was it possible for Heidegger but not for anyone else? It is to these questions that we will turn in this chapter. To answer them we will work our way back from *Being and Time* to the extraordinary 1924 Marburg lectures that preceded it, "Basic Concepts of Aristotelian Philosophy."[1]

2.1 The Place of Aristotle's *Rhetoric* in the Project of *Being and Time*

What is there in Heidegger's thinking that reopens the way to Aristotle's *Rhetoric*? A first answer lies precisely in Heidegger's "hermeneutics of facticity" and in the penetration this "hermeneutics of facticity" makes possible behind the theoretical *logos apophantikos*, the proposition or declarative sentence (*Aussagesatz*), that had become philosophy's exclusive and unquestioned paradigm for all discourse. The task Heidegger had set for himself in *Being and Time* and, in fact, in all the lecture courses leading up to it, was to get beneath the abstractions of "metaphysical philosophy" and to "lay bare" and "lay out" hermeneutically our original being-there in the world. In the "Basic Concepts of Aristotelian Philosophy," for instance, the task was to ground the Aristotelian *Grundbegriffe* or basic concepts in the ground and soil (*Boden*) of concrete human practice, the ground and soil from which they grew and in which they must be rooted again if they are to be properly understood.

As Gadamer has put this (see chapter 1, note 2 above), the "hermeneutics *of* facticity" is in fact "facticity's hermeneutics." The point is that human being-there in the world is to be thought of precisely as the carrying out of interpretation (W 3, 324). However, in laying itself out interpretively facticity "does not bring interpretive concepts to bear on itself, rather its interpretation is a kind of conceptual speaking that wants to hold fast to its origin and, thereby, to its life's breath, when it is translated into the form of a theoretical assertion" (W 3, 421). In accord with this principle, the task in Heidegger's "Basic Concepts of Aristotelian Philosophy" is to reverse the metaphysical abstractions of scholasticism's "Aristotle" and to read Aristotle's own "theoretical assertions" once again as just such a conceptual speaking that is rooted in life's laying itself out hermeneutically.

Similarly, in *Being and Time* Descartes's "world" of extended, measurable objects "present" to some sort of detached thinking "subject" was to be displayed as an abstraction arising from our original "factual" existence "there" in the world and "there" in the midst of an interpreted system of implements for getting on with the projects of our life (see SZ, part 1, chapter 2, "Being-in-the-World as Such as the Basic Constitution [*Grundverfassung*] of Being-There" pp. 52–62 and chapter 3, "The Worldliness of World" pp. 63–113).

To be sure, in *Being and Time* the *ultimate* goal of this reduction was not "ontic," was not, this is to say, to uncover the particular being of human existence at its original levels and to lay this out interpretively. Rather, the goal was "ontological": the task was to uncover, and interpretively lay out, the original meaning of being, and the original concomitance of being and not being and the original conjunction of being and time were to be displayed. Hence, this uncovering of original human being-there in the world was ultimately meant only to exemplify original being as such, being prior to the "metaphysical" conception of being as "beingness" or "static presence." For human existence, human "being," far from being statically present and self-identical, "is" in concomitant being-authentic and not-being-authentic and "is" in the temporal process of becoming what it "is not" yet and, finally, of "not being" any longer in death. So, too, the being of the implements with which human being-there is involved was to be displayed not only in their handiness and usefulness but also precisely in their "not being" what we had in mind for them to be, in their "deficient modes" of withholding themselves from us, namely their recalcitrance in being useless for the task we had in mind, or their never being where we think they are when we want them, or even in being in the way (see SZ 73–74). (Any amateur carpenter knows exactly what Heidegger is talking about here!) Despite Heidegger's wider purpose for his investigations, however, much else is made clear in them besides the character of original being, and made clear, in particular, about the ways we *talk* to each other. This last will be our concern here, a concern considerably more narrow than Heidegger's own.

Now Heidegger had seen early on what philosophy, even Aristotle's "more inceptive" philosophy "closer to the origin," had largely forgotten, namely that theoretical philosophy's *logos apophantikos* was not the original and basic form of talking, but rather that it was somehow derivative and "multiply founded" (*mehrfach fundiert*).[2] He had seen, that is to say, that it was based in a layer of speaking that, in turn, was based in yet another layer of speaking that was its ultimate and original "ground" (*Grund*). This "ground" was not to be thought of as some sort of cause (*aitia, causa*) or explanatory principle (*archê, principium*) that we might get wholly in view and grasp systematically. Rather, it was to be thought of as the *Boden* or "soil," interpretable for us but in the end impenetrable, and on which speech rested but in which it was embedded and from which it "grew."

Thus, Heidegger could reverse Aristotle's own reduction of speech and, with that, he effectively reversed the priorities of all post-Aristotelian philosophy of language: the rhetorical enthymeme was not, as Aristotle had sought, to be based on the dialectical syllogism, which, in turn, was to be based on the demonstrative syllogism built of *logoi apophantikoi* or propositions. On the contrary, as Heidegger saw it, theoretical speech's detached propositions about an objectified reality merely lying on hand before us in static presence were an abstraction from what we say to each other in our engaged, practical taking care of things (*Besorgen*) from *within* in the world in which these things, and other people there with us in the world, meet up with us (*uns begegnen*). As he saw it, science's *apodeixis* or demonstration was an abstraction from dialetic's *dialegesthai* or talking something through theoretically, and dialectic's *dialegesthai* was, in turn, an abstraction from rhetoric's practical *peithein* or convincing. Seen this way, rhetoric's art of convincing is not at all the deficient form of demonstration and instruction, not at all the poor substitute for the strict logical inference, that Aristotle makes it out to be, but rather the reverse: theoretical instruction and demonstration occur only once the art of practical conviction has been suspended. In its expatiations on the *Rhetoric* and in its application of the method of *Destruktion* or "taking down", metaphysical abstractions, the movement in the 1924 "Basic Concepts of Aristotelian Philosophy" is the same in the 1927 *Being and Time,* namely, a movement back *from* a theoretical looking on and looking at things, and back *to* our practical, concerned, and worried being-there in the world with others in the midst of things.

This hermeneutical strategy of Heidegger's will be crucial for our own hermeneutics of argument and speech (*logos*) here, in which we will seek to "ground" demonstration in theoretical dialectic, but, then, to "ground" theoretical dialectic in the "soil" of practical rhetoric. For it makes clear that Aristotle's *logos ousias* arrived at in dialectic, the statement of the *to ti ên einai* or conceptual definition of "what it is (was) to be" a thing, is to be traced to the original *logos* or argument we make to each other in getting things done in our everyday existence, and it is precisely from Aristotle's *Rhetoric* that we learn about this original *logos.* Hence, we can say that as early as 1924 it was Heidegger's project of a "hermeneutics of facticity"—his project elaborated later in *Being and Time* of grounding abstractions in original being as this comes to us "in the world"—that allows him to penetrate the "obvious" primacy of theoretical language and to redeem the "obviously" inferior "mere" rhetoric. And it will allow us to do the same.[3]

But there is another important reason for Heidegger's revolutionary reevaluation of rhetoric. Heidegger, namely, had seen that the divorce of *logos* from *pathos*, of the rational and cognitive from what supposedly is merely ancillary feeling and emotion, was not only an abstraction from our original experience, but also an illusion. Thus, when Heidegger comes to elaborate our being-there in the world within which we carry out our projects, and when he comes to elaborate our knowledge and understanding of that world, he must go behind the usual accounts of the "subjects" of cognition just as he had gone behind the usual accounts of its "objects" (see SZ part 1, chapter 5, "Being-in as Such," pp. 130–80 and chapter 6, "Worry as the Being of Being-There," pp. 180–230). For the uncovering of our original being-there in the world makes clear that all our understanding of things takes place within the setting of a certain tonality or mood that these things have about them, a voicing or *Stimmung*, as Heidegger calls it, and which, unbeknownst to us, has somehow "always already" come over us and them and given a particular tenor to our awareness of things.

In surveying the objectified world theoretically we tend to overlook this feature of our knowing, for in theoretical observations we are, it seems, just looking on detachedly, and emotions, feelings, and the like only seem to cloud our understanding and distort our impartiality. But if, with Heidegger, we acknowledge that this theoretical looking on in "fact" originates in the very world from which it has withdrawn and abstracted, and if, with Heidegger, we acknowledge that our being-there in the world was "always already" conditioned by the way we happen to find ourselves feeling about it, a heretofore inconceivable question becomes unavoidable: We must ask ourselves just what *feeling* it was that made possible our withdrawal and abstraction from that world in the first place. To answer this question Heidegger refers us to Aristotle's *Metaphysics*:

> If, then, it was for the sake of escaping from ignorance that one philosophized, it is plain that they [the first philosophers] pursued scientific knowing for the sake of insight [διὰ τὸ εἰδέναι τὸ ἐπίστασθαι ἐδίωκον] and not for the sake of anything useful. The way things came to pass bears witness to this, for only when all the necessities and everything needed for rest and diversion [πρὸς ῥᾳστώνην καὶ διαγωγήν] were present, did a wisdom of this sort begin to be sought. (982b21–24; see SZ 138, n.1)

Here it emerges that even the most detached and abstract theoretical propositions have their ineliminable setting in a feeling or predisposition which alone makes them possible, namely *rhaistonê* and *diagôgê*, the relief from being harried and the leisure to just pass time with things as an impartial observer of them (SZ 138). Just as theory originates from a "deficient mode" of practice, that is, when for the moment one is *not* concerned with taking care of something, so too the sense of leisure that makes theory possible may be thought of as the "deficent mode" of feeling or *pathos.* But theoretical *dis*passion—and this is Heidegger's point—is very much a passion nonetheless.

A fortiori, if the separation of the cognitive from the affective is an illusion even in those theoretical abstractions where it would seem most evidently to have occurred, we can be sure that it is an illusion everywhere, and consequently we must look at the affects generally as a "condition of the possibility" of all knowledge. Kant's question, "What can I know?" thus becomes inseparable from "How do I *feel* about this?" Here Heidegger has pushed forward to one of his boldest and most unsettling proposals, for if he is right, modernity's goal of attaining dispassionate "objective" knowledge must be rejected as self-deception:

> Existentially-ontologically there is not the slightest justification for suppressing the "evidence" of the feeling in which one finds oneself by measuring it against the demonstrative certainty in theoretical cognition of the pure "present on hand." (SZ 136)

Heidegger's word here for this basic affective underpinning at the ground of all epistemology is the notoriously untranslatable *Befindlichkeit,* "the feeling in which one finds oneself." The sense of this expression, however, is really not so obscure. In a variation of the idiom, a doctor might ask a patient, for instance, *Wie befinden Sie sich heute*? (How are you feeling today?). For Heidegger the point to be stressed here is that, though patients can perhaps name the feeling that conditions their well-being or ill-feeling at that moment, they have no control over that feeling. The feeling is something that they always "find" themselves feeling already; it is the condition in which they "find" themselves. And as a matter of fact, in all one's projects or thrusts forward, one's *Sich-Entwerfen,* one always "finds oneself" already thrust into the situation in a certain affective way. Precisely this uncircumventable passivity in all activity—the "fact" that we are in all things patients even when we are agents—is what Heidegger wants to bring out in conjoining *Befindlichkeit,* or the way one finds oneself feeling, with *Geworfenheit,* one's always already having been thrust into things and one's always already finding oneself with a certain affective predisposition toward them (SZ 136–38). The idea of the conscious "subject" as an agent-self whose "performances" provide a transcendental foundation for all knowedge is thus destroyed; for what

I do is always already conditioned by what has happened to me; my action is always already conditioned by my passion.

Once this "patiency" is recognized, Aristotle's detailed and incisive phenomenological exposition in his *Rhetoric* (2.2–11) of the *pathê*, the affects or feelings we undergo, no longer appears to be just a concession to the orator's practical need to convince simpleminded listeners who cannot follow an extended argument, as even Aristotle himself would sometimes have us believe (see, for instance, the *Rhetoric* 1355a25–27). Rather, the *pathê* and the examination of them emerge as intrinsic and crucial to any account of argument and speech.

For this reason too, then, Aristotle's *Rhetoric* can take on *philosophical* importance for Heidegger that even Aristotle himself seems to have denied it. To be sure, Heidegger restricts himself in *Being and Time* to elaborating only one of those *pathê* to which Aristotle devotes himself, namely fear (see SZ 140 f. and the reference to Aristotle's *Rhetoric*, 1382a20–1383b11, at SZ 140 n.1). For his goal is to move beyond feelings that concern specific things in the world to *the* feeling that discloses the being of the world in its totality, or better said, the feeling that discloses the not-being of the world in its totality, namely *Angst*; in *Angst* not just one thing but every thing is drained of its being and recedes into no-thing-ness, *das Nichts* (SZ 184–89). Heidegger's goal, it must be remembered, was not just to produce a regional phenomenology of human being-there in the world, but a universal ontology of being as such, which would display the original concomitance of being and not-being.

Still, even a cursory look at Aristotle's account of the *pathê*, of the feelings, "voicings" or "Stimmungen" that come over us, suffices to make clear why Heidegger found Aristotle's exposition of all the particular *pathê* fascinating and, more to the point, why he found Aristotle's technique of exposition exemplary for his own phenomenological description. For everywhere in Aristotle's methodical and painstaking investigations of the *pathê* one finds the kind of piece-by-piece phenomenological craftsmanship that Heidegger had learned from the master at such things, Husserl.

For instance, in regard to any particular *pathos*, Aristotle tells us, three things will need to be established, first, the predisposition that disposes someone to have it, second, the kind of people one tends to feel it toward, and, third, what sort of thing one feels it about (*Rhet.* 1378a22–26). To start with the last of these, the occasion for anger, for instance, may be seen to be a slight. A slight, in turn, takes three forms, contempt, spite, and insolence; in the first someone treats us as if we were worthless; in the second someone does things for no other reason than to thwart us; and in the third someone disgraces us in the presence of others (1378a30–1379a9). From this it follows that we get angry at those who ridicule us, at those who belittle the things we value, with those who, having honored us, no longer do, with those who do not return our favors, with those of no value themselves who slight us, with friends who mistreat us, with those who are indifferent to the pain they cause us, with those who listen to others who belittle us, and with anyone who slights us before our rivals, those we admire, those we would like to admire us, those whom we respect, and those who respect us (1379a30–1380a5). And we are disposed to get angry when we are pained—all the *pathê* involve either pleasure or pain—by having been thwarted in the pursuit of something we desire (1379a11–29). In this remarkable phenomenological description, which for the time being we have only briefly summarized, the anger of Achilles, to whom Aristotle often refers, is brought into three-dimensional plasticity before our eyes: he has been thwarted by Agamemnon in his sexual desire for Briseis; by publicly taking Briseis from him Agamemnon has slighted him in all three ways, contempt, spite, and insolence; and, as a supposed friend, not enemy, Agamemnon has dishonored him and shown himself utterly indifferent to the pain he has caused him. (We will return to these matters in chapter 6.)

To be sure, Aristotle's reason for working things out this way is far removed from anything in Heidegger. As we will see, Aristotle is concerned with the effectiveness of *peithein* or conviction, and he recognizes that Achilles would never hear what Odysseus, Phoenix, and Ajax are saying to him and be convinced unless they can displace the *pathos* of anger with another *pathos*, either gentleness, fear, or, what is more likely, pity (see the *Iliad*, book 9). Their *logos* will be lost on him if the *pathos* dominating him is not changed, and for a speaker to change a *pathos* he or she must understand it and know which other *pathê* might drive it out. Still, Heidegger could not fail to be impressed with such a lucid, Husserlian reconstitution of the subject matter as the *Rhetoric*'s account of the *pathê* in these chapters.

What is more, he could not fail, either, to recognize in Aristotle's exposition here of what goes on, as it were, "behind the back" of the conscious subject, an ally in his own resistence to Husserl's drive to ground experience in the "performances" of consciousness. For this reason, too, he could not pass the *Rhetoric* by.

In our efforts to see how Heidegger reopens access to Aristotle's *Rhetoric* we can begin, accordingly, with the specific reference to this work that Heidegger makes in *Being and Time.* "It is no coincidence," he writes there,

> that [in] the first systematically executed interpretation of the affects handed down to us these are not treated in the framework of "psychology."

> Aristotle examines the *pathê* in the second book of his *Rhetoric.* Contrary to the traditional relegation of rhetoric to something like a "discipline," this work must be grasped as the first hermeneutics of the everydayness of [our] being together with one another. Publicness, as the kind of being belonging to the "everybody" [*das Man*], not only has its way of feeling [*Gestimmtheit*] but uses feeling [*Stimmung*] and "peps things up" by creating it for itself. The rhetor speaks into a feeling and speaks out of, and from a feeling. He needs an understanding of the possibilities of feeling in order to awaken it and steer it in the right way. (SZ 138–39)

Let us take as our lead the contention here that Aristotle's *Rhetoric* is to be understood as "the first hermeneutics of the everydayness of [our] being together with one another."[4] In other words, as a hermeneutics or interpretive application the *Rhetoric,* we may assume, uncovers and lays out interpretively the original realm where we, together with each other, are practically engaged in taking care of our tasks in cooperative employment of the interconnected system of implements (*Zeuge*), in and among which we always already find ourselves. And thus the *Rhetoric* takes us first behind the realm of Cartesian objectified "res extensae," behind abstract measurable things for the theoretical observation of some sort of detached "subject" and "consciousness," takes us then behind the "stuff" (*das Zeug*) merely lying around on hand before us (*Vorhandenes*), which "stuff" is the forerunner and precondition of *res extensae,* and takes us, finally, back to the original and basic realm of our practical activity, where we are not yet onlookers, but agents doing things with things. (See in particular, SZ §15, 66 ff., "The being of the beings that meet up [with us] in the world around [us]" and §19, 89 ff., "The determination of 'world' as *res extensa.*") And as a rhetoric the book deals specifically, we may assume, with *rhêmata,* the things we *say* to each other in taking care of things at just this basic level. Thus, in Heidegger's hands Aristotle's *Rhetoric* emerges as a theory of language and speech, *Sprache* and *Rede,* as these occur originally and prior to the abstractions from then, first, in the detached arguments of dialectic and, then, in the theoretical demonstrations of science.

2.2 Reading the *Rhetoric* Hermeneutically in the Light of Heidegger's "Basic Concepts of Aristotelian Philosophy" (The "Lecture Course," Marburg, 1924)

It is striking that we already discover the appropriation of the *Rhetoric* for the purposes of a linguistic "hermeneutics of facticity" in the 1924

"Basic Concepts of Aristotelian Philosophy." For instance, in the lecture of 30 May 1924 we find Heidegger rereading Aristotle's definition of the human being as the *zôion logon echon* in the light of the *Rhetoric*: not the tradition's understanding of "rational animal" is meant by this, he says, but rather a living being-there in the world, whose way of being there is to be engaged in conversation (*Gespräch*) and speech (*Rede*) or *logos.* Thus, the *logos* that this living being or *zôion* has is not the language of science's and dialectic's theoretical syllogisms, but rather the "everyday" speech of our practical exchanges with other, which is to say, precisely that speech which is the concern of rhetoric.

In Aristotle's *Rhetoric,* Heidegger tells us, it is precisely this speech of the life world (*Lebenswelt*), first, that is displayed at foundation of language, second, that is the "basic possibility (*Grundmöglichkeit*) of speaking," and, third, that is "the ground and soil" (*der Boden*) upon which any "theoretical speaking of the things themselves," any theoretical *logos ousias* or statement of the essence of something, any *horismos* or definition, rests (30.5.24). Accordingly, in the next lecture Heidegger adds that the *legein* or speaking in the *Rhetoric* is a "basic determinant [*Grundbestimmung*] of being-there's self in the concrete mode of its being in its everydayness" and that the *Rhetoric* offers us "access to this original [*ursprüngliches*] phenomenon" (2.6.24). Later in the lectures he will say that rhetoric is "the speaking of being-there in the world, feeling the way it finds itself feeling" (*befindliches Reden des Dasein in der Welt*) (7.7.24).

Furthermore, the *logos* and *legein* in the *Rhetoric,* he points out, are to be distinguished from any merely "theoretical observation," precisely insofar as they are *pithanos* or persuasive: "the subject matter of rhetoric," he says, "is our speaking with one another in giving counsel [*beratenderweise*; Aristotle: *sumbouleutikôs*] about things . . . that come to pass every day and usually" (6.6.24). This is to say, first, that rhetoric is prior to any special and more abstract forms of expertise; we read in the *Rhetoric* itself, for instance, that the specific arts each have their technical subject matter: medicine deals with health, geometry with variations in size, arithmentic with numbers, and so forth; as Aristotle himself puts it, "the art of rhetoric seems to be capable, so to speak, of treating theoretically what is persuasive in regard to any given subject. For this reason we say that its techniques are not limited to any specific kind of thing all its own" (*Rhet.* 1355b34–35). Second, as consultative (*sumbouleutikos*; *Rhet.* 1357a1–6), rhetorical speech, Heidegger points out, not only aims to create in the listeners a *doxa* or view (Heidegger: *Ansicht*), which is to say, "a particular way . . . of appropriating what is as it shows itself," but beyond this, to exhort them to an active *krisis* or decision (6.6.24). Indeed, we find Aristotle saying just this: "But it is necessary," he writes,

> that the hearer be either an onlooker or a judge [ἀνάγκη δὲ τον ἀκροατήν ἤ θεωρόν εἶναι ἤ κριτήν], but when a judge, one who decides either about things that have happened or that are about to happen [ἤ τῶν γεγενημένων ἤ τῶν μελλόντων]. For example, the member of the general assembly is one who decides about what will happen, while the judge in a court decides about what has happened. (*Rhet.* 1358b1–3)

The references here are to consultative or *sumbuleutikê* rhetoric when the decision is about future things, and to judicial or *dikanikê* rhetoric when it is about past things. Only "show-off" or *epideiktikê* rhetoric—panegyric—in which not so much the subject matter is to be judged as is the "ability" of the speaker, allows the listener to remain an onlooker (*theôros*) uncommitted to either one side of the issue or the other (see 1358b6: "the one deciding about the rhetor's capabilities is merely an observer").

Rhetoric's need to obtain not only belief but also a decision makes two other "convincers" or *pithana* intrinsic to its *logos pithanos* or convincing argument besides the *logos* itself. First, says Heidegger, there is the "Haltung" or comportment of the one speaking and, second, the *diathesis* or, importantly, as Heidegger translates this, the *Befindlichkeit* induced in the hearer—the way in which he finds himself feeling, or, put another way, *wie er gestimmt ist,* how he feels in regard to the speaker and the matter being spoken of. As Aristotle himself puts this,

> Since rhetoric aims at a decision—for also those taking counsel with each other decide, and the verdict of a court is itself a decision [καὶ γὰρ τάς συμβουλὰς κρίνουσι καὶ ἡ δίκη κρίσις ἐστίν]—it is necessary not only to look at the argument [πρὸς τὸν λόγον] with regard to how demonstrative it will be and convincing, but necessary, also, for the speaker both to present himself, and to predispose the one making the decision, in a certain way. (1377b20–26)

> Now conviction is achieved by the character of the speaker [διὰ μὲν οὖν τοῦ ἤθους] when the argument is spoken in such a way as to make the one speaking worthy of belief and trust [ὥστε ἀξιόπιστον ποιῆσαι τὸν λέγοντα]. For we believe and trust those who are kind more fully and more readily, and this in regard to all things generally but, above all, in regard to those matters where no exactitude is to be had and beliefs go both ways. (1356a4–8)

> Moreover, conviction may be achieved through the listeners whenever they are moved to a feeling by the argument [ὅταν εἰς πάθος ὑπὸ τοῦ λόγου προαχθῶσιν]. For we do not make the same decisions when we

are in pain or feeling hate as when we are enjoying ourselves or feeling friendship. (1356a14–16)

Aristotle's *Rhetoric* thus confirms Heidegger's thesis that our disposition toward things, the way we find ourselves feeling about them, has "always already" conditioned our reasoning about them. Indeed, Heidegger's rediscovery of the *Stimmungen,* the moods or tonal voicings underlying any cognition and constituting it, may, we now discover, owe as much to Aristotle's elaboration of the *pathê* in the *Rhetoric* as to the announced sources for the doctrine of the *Stimmungen* in *Being and Time,* namely Augustine, Pascal, Luther, and Kierkegaard (see SZ 139, n.1, and 190, n.1). For in some crucial ways, at least, *Stimmung* in Heidegger translates *pathos* in Aristotle. Whatever its source for Heidegger might have been, Heidegger's rediscovery of the *Stimmungen* allows *us,* at least, to rediscover the central importance of Aristotle's *Rhetoric* and its elaboration of the *pathê* for any hermeneutics of original argument.

What is more, as in *Being and Time* (SZ 136 ff.), we find in the 1924 lectures that "these *pathê* or affects are not mere psychological conditions. Rather, the concern here is with a way in which a living being finds itself in its world" (6.6.24). The *pathê,* this is to say, are not mere accidents on the surface of one's being but rather the way that "an existent being, as living, is carried along" (30.6.24). One cannot say, for instance, that the "soul" hopes, rather only that the whole human being (*der ganze Mensch*) hopes (id.). In other words, here in Aristotle's *Rhetoric* Heidegger uncovers for us an earlier and more original understanding of human existence prior to the severence of mind and consciousness from the physical corporeal world into which it bodily "ek-sists" or "stands out." He uncovers, that is, an understanding of human existence and being prior to the "apparent question" how consciousness "inside" with its feelings could possibly interact with a world "outside" (see SZ 27–28). For the *Rhetoric's pistis* or convincing, trust-winning argument generates a *pathos* not only as a frame of mind but as a frame of world, as it were, as a tonal setting, namely, in which the world displays itself, and which in "fact" makes this self-display of the world possible in the first place. The *pathos* or "Stimmung," the timbre, tone, and "feel" of things, is an indivisible continuum of self and world within which things come to one's being-there (*dem Dasein begegnen*) and within which the speaker speaks of them. Indeed, far from being a mere mental coloration, the *pathê,* Heidegger points out, are *meta sômatos,* "given through bodiliness" and are "behavior of the full human being with its bodiliness" (7.7.24).

Precisely this centrality of the *pathê* to one's whole psychosomatic being is the reason why the hearer, if he or she is to be persuaded to make the *krisis* or decision that the speaker is advising, must be brought to feel a certain way about the matter at hand and not just to see it in a certain light. This is to say that the rhetorical *logos* must be what Aristotle terms a *logos enhulos,* an embodied speech, that affects and moves the listener physically (1.7.24). Hence, Heidegger speaks of the "fundamental role of the *pathê* in *krinein,*" in *Sich-Entscheiden,* in deciding and resolving to do something, and even of *pathos* as the "ground and soil of the *logos*" (*Boden des logos*) (23.6.24; see 26.6.24). And in the lecture of 15 July 1924 we find "The ground and soil [*Boden*] out of which speaking grows and down into which what has been spoken and expressed grows back is the *pathê.*" Seen this way, dialectic, in which the *pathê* no longer have an explicit role, is already uprooted speech.

For Aristotle, of course, rhetoric, as the "counterpart" of dialectic, shares important features with it (6.5.24). The premises and conclusions of argument in both rhetoric and dialectic are prior to the propositions of demonstrative science insofar as both rhetoric and dialectic reason from *endoxa* or received opinions and reason to *doxa* or new opinions. Their reasoning begins and ends in our "views" about something, in *doxa* or what Heidegger calls *Ansichten.* Thus, the being or reality they speak about is not "being" at all, if by this is meant statically and fully present necessary being. Rather, the subject matter of both rhetoric and dialectic is contingent and indeterminate: "The *endoxon* [received opinion]," writes Heidegger, "is a way of being oriented in regard to the kind of being which also can be otherwise [*anders*]" and that consequently is "subject to revision" (6.6.24). Not *to aei on,* not what is ever and always the same, is the concern here but *to endechomenon allôs echein,* what is susceptible of being otherwise than it is, what "always wavers" and is "not firmly established" (17.6.24; see *Rhet.* 1357a4–7).

Furthermore, in both dialectic and rhetoric the *endoxon* from which one reasons is proposed in a *protasis* or premise, namely that which is "laid before" us (*vorgelegt*), which is "conceded in advance" (*die Vorgabe*), and which "is not up for further discussion." This premise, in turn, has the form of an *erôtêsis endoxos,* "an asking that stays within the circle of that about which there is a firm view" (19.6.24; see *Topics* I, 10–11, 104a2 f.). The key to understanding this strange expression of Aristotle's, as well as Heidegger's no less strange gloss on it, is the "*ara ge*" of the dialectical premise, the "it is so, *is it not*" (Heidegger: *es ist doch wohl*). Like any *erôtêsis* or asking, the dialectical premise is an *apokriseôs aitêsis,* or in Heidegger's translation, "a plea for an answer, a plea for a concession [*Zugeständnis*]." It is a plea for "a concession in advance [*Vorgabe*] of the ground [*Boden*] on which the conversation is to move" (id.; see also *de Interp.* 20b22). Hence, in contrast to the premise of a demonstrative syllogism, which is a *logos apophantikos* or declarative statment of necessary fact, here indeterminacy and contingency show up in the intrinsic questionability of the premise even if, for the purpose of having a conversation at all, it must be conceded ahead of time that the premise will not actually be placed in question. (We will return to this intrinsic questionability in our consideration of the ontology of dialectical and rhetorical reasoning in chapter 3.)

But these important similarities not withstanding, there are some fundamental differences between dialectic and rhetoric to which Heidegger now alerts us. For dialectic's *dialegesthai* or talking something through, is, to use the expression from *Being and Time,* still a "founded" phenomenon, which is to say that even it is an abstraction from "more original" rhetorical, deliberative speech, from *sumbouleuesthai,* or our taking counsel with each other. For dialectic's *dialegesthai,* as Heidegger points out here, concerns itself with that speech "which has no further purpose," with that speech, namely, "which does not result from the natural function of language having a practical intent." Rather, in dialectic speech has the sole function of "exhibiting [*Aufzeigen*] what is being treated in its 'how it is' and 'what it is' ": "the *logos* here," says Heidegger, "is freed from the *prakton*" (19.6.24), freed, this is to say, from anything that "needs to be done."

Thus, dialectic has removed itself from the original "situation at a given time" (*die jeweilige Lage*) in which one existing individual in the world sought, through speaking, to move another to a particular decision (*krisis*).[5] Moreover, as a consequence of this abstraction, dialectic has removed itself *to* a "world" no longer at a time and in a place. Rhetoric deals with the temporal, narrative-historical being of human affairs "there"; in seeking, on specific occasions, decisions from existing individuals in a specific situation, it treats what is "not yet on hand" (and might not be) in its consultative (*sumbouleutikê*) form, what "has already happened" (or might not have) in its judicial (*dikanikê*) form, and what "exists now" (or might not) in its panegyrical, show-off (*epideiktikê*) form (6.6.24; see also 5.6.24 and *Rhet.* 1358a36 ff.). In contrast, the temporality of dialectic's issues, even if these are still "susceptible of being otherwise," has already been reduced to things "present" statically for disengaged onlookers outside any place and beyond the flow of time. These objects of theoretical investigation may indeed turn out to "be" different from what we dialectically reason they "are," but we are, neverless, reasoning here about general matters excerpted from time and place, reasoning about what is "beneficial" or "right" "always" and "on the whole" (*aei, katholou*), for instance, and not reasoning narratively-historically (Heidegger: *geschichtlich*) about local particular happenings

(Heidegger: *Geschehendes*) as they have come to pass, are coming to pass, or will come to pass. We are no longer reasoning, for instance, about whether this will be the beneficial thing to do *next* or whether that was the right and just thing to have done *then.* Hence, rhetoric's concern with the narrative-historical, with what might or might not happen in the future or what might or might not have happened in the past, has been transcended, and practical knowing has become theoretical "knowing at a distance" (Heidegger: *Wissen auf Abstand*). In dialectic, Heidegger shows us, the *logos* itself has become the *praxis* and talking itself, the activity (19.6.24). The art of dialectic, he points out, "is concerned with those *logoi* [arguments] which are not directed to taking care of something [*Besorgen*] but rather to speaking with one another about a theoretical question" (5.6.24).

Furthermore, dialectic has indeed achieved its aim when it has brought the partner in the discussion to an opinion or view (*Ansicht*). But originally, in rhetorical speech between people there in the world taking care of practical concerns, bringing someone to believe something was, as we have already established, only preliminary to calling him or her to decide on, and choose a course of action. *Hairesis,* taking up a course of action, and *phugein,* shunning a course of action, are, Heidegger tells us, "the fundamental possibility of being-there's fundamental ways of being moved" (14.7.24; see *De anima* 3.7). *Prohairesis,* taking up one course of action over another, is, Heidegger says here, "being toward something," specifically, being toward a *prakton agathon* or practical good, and being resolved on it; *prohairesis* is *Entschlossenheit,* resolve (16.6.24; compare SZ 298 on *Entschlossenheit*). Accordingly, the *logos* or speech in rhetoric is the "original" practical *logos* of "worried being-there (*besorgtes Dasein*) in the world and living bodily toward something" (4.7.24). The *logos* here is "the way in which *krinein* [deciding, *Sich-Entschliessen*] is carried out" (4.7.24).

And with that, Heidegger boldly asserts, "the intrinsic connection between *pathos* and *logos* [in rhetoric as opposed to dialectic] has been brought to light" (id.). Why? A first indication is given in the difference between the dialectical syllogism and the enthymeme of the rhetorical *pistis* or convincing argument. Superficially, this difference appears to be only that the enthymeme is usually shorter, having only one premise, whereas the dialectical syllogism has two (see *Rhet.* 1357a17–23). This would appear to follow merely from the enthymeme's being suited to an audience incapable of grasping an extended argument (see *Rhet.* 1357a10–12). But Heidegger radically redirects Aristotle's line of thought here: the enthymeme, he says, correlates with *enthumeisthai* or "taking something to heart [to the *thumos*]," and it is primarily in this, not in the number of its premises, that its *logos* or argument is to be distinguished from the *logos* of a dialectical syllogism.[6] For the task of the latter is only *apophainesthai,* only to let something be seen, to make something visible (*sichtbar*) (5.6.24).

We could say, accordingly, that the dialectical syllogism is already aimed at the intellect of someone now looking on, a *theoretês,* whereas the rhetorical enthymeme is still aimed at the practical will of someone participating in what is happening. The one seeks to bring someone to the point of saying, "Yes, I see that this is so," whereas the other, still engaged as it is in taking care of things (*Besorgen*) in the world, seeks to move someone to the point of saying, "Yes, I will do this."[7] Heidegger's way of putting this is to say that with the enthymeme the *lambanein tas protaseis,* the acceptance of the premises and granting of "concessions" (*Vorgaben*), implies more than the hearer's accepting the beliefs of the speaker (23.6.24); beyond this the hearer's willingness to do what is urged is requisite. Hence, not only how he or she "views" things but how he or she "feels" about them must be changed.

Consequently, says Heidegger, "the feeling [*Stimmung*] of the one spoken to must be taken into account, as must, also, the particular situation at the time [*jeweilige Lage*] and the manner and way one stands on the issue oneself [namely, the speaker himself or herself]" (23.6.24). In dialectic neither the *êthos* of the speaker (Heidegger: *die Haltung*) nor the *diathesis* of the hearer (Heidegger: *die Befindlichkeit*) are important, neither, this is to say, the speaker's own position on the issue and comportment toward the audience, nor how the hearer finds himself or herself feeling about the subject matter. But in rhetoric, as we have seen, both of these things are crucial. For in dialectical speech, in *dialegesthai* as opposed to rhetoric's *sumbouleuesthai,* we are not involved but detached; in theoretically "talking something through" rather than "taking counsel with each other," we have become "objective" onlookers. But it was not this way originally, in rhetorical speech, where not what we see theoretically to be the case, but what each of us is called to do individually, is at stake.

This, then, is the reason why Heidegger, in penetrating even behind Aristotle, stresses the *thumos* in the enthymeme. For in a decision or *krisis* it is the *thumos,* the heart, the seat of the *pathê,* that must be changed and not just one's view of things: "ἔστι δὲ τὰ πάθη δι᾽ ὅσα μεταβάλλοντες διαφέρουσι πρὸς τὰς κρίσεις," says Heidegger, quoting Aristotle: "But it is on account of changing feelings that human beings differ in regard to their decisions" (24.6.24; *Rhet.* 1378a20).[8] Here Heidegger stresses the *metaballein,* the switch or *Umschlagen* from one feeling in which we find ourselves to another; for only this switch makes possible the decision of the existing individual, which rhetoric's original speech is meant to induce. Clearly, Heidegger is on to something here, something that at times seems lost from view in Aristotle but that, even so, always shimmers in the background of what he says.

To be sure, if we trace the word "enthymeme" to *enthumeisthai*, we see that by Aristotle's time the latter had, in fact, come to mean "to take under consideration" and not "to take to heart." Thus, we find, for example, Thucydides' "Pericles" saying in his oration that as Athenenians "ἤτοι κρίνομέν γε ἢ ἐνθυμούμεθα ὀρθως τὰ πράγματα" for which the translation must be "either we decide on actions or we *take them under consideration* properly" (2.40.2; emphasis added). Significantly, there is a linking of *enthumeisthai* with *krinein* here, within which *enthumeisthai* means only the appropriate kind of detached and purely rational consideration that is supposed to precede any *krinein* or deciding to act (see Burnyeat, "Enthymeme," p. 12 and note 6 above). In this use of *enthumeisthai* no trace of the *thumos* and the heartfelt is perceptible any longer, and it often seems as if that is exactly how Aristotle, too, understands the relationship between *enthumeisthai* and making good decisions. Seen this way, the enthymeme is indeed just the reasoning and nothing more, just a logical syllogism, albeit imperfect, that leads, all by itself, to a *krisis* or decision, and in this understanding of the enthymeme the intrinsic relationship of the enthymeme to *pathos* and of *pathos* to any decision is nearly obliterated.

On the other hand, if, in following Aristotle's own frequent acknowledgement of the importance of the *pathê* for any decision, we go behind the separation of the thinking *psychê* from the experiencing *sôma* that Aristotle inherits from Plato—inherits from the *Phaedo*, in particular, as we will see in chapter 6—and if, with Heidegger, we look for an earlier kind of somatically embedded *logos* in the original life world, we quickly discover that Thucydides' and even Aristotle's own evisceration of *enthumeisthai* is indeed a derivative abstraction. For instance, in Aeschylus's *Eumenides*, we find Apollo saying to the chorus leader, "τὰ μὲν γὰρ οἶδα κάρτα σ' ἐνθυμουμένην, / τὰ δ' ἐμφανῶς πράσσουσαν ἡσυξαιτέραν," which must be translated something like this: "In the one regard I know you *to be strongly enraged*, / but in the other, clearly, to be milder in what you do" (222–23; emphasis added); and here we can see that the *enthumeisthai* or "being enraged" which would lead to a decision to do something (*prattein*) is still very much a matter of the *thumos*, of the heart and viscera, and that it is determined by *pathos*. Thus, if we follow Heidegger in his hermeneutical strategy of "laying bare" "earlier" meanings "closer to the origin" that are to be found beneath the subsequent abstractions covering them up, it turns out that he was right about the *enthumêmê* after all.

2.3 Rereading *Being and Time* as a Hermeneutics of Original Argument

These remarkable lectures of 1924 make clear how the later *Being and Time,* particularly §33 (154 f.), and §34 (160 f.), can be applied in recovering Aristotle's rhetoric. In §33, "The Declarative Statement [*Aussage*] as a Derivative Mode of Interpretation," Heidegger obviously intends to "destruct" the declarative statement in order thereafter, in §34, to "lay bare" the "original" mode of speech in which it is grounded and from which it is an abstraction. With the lectures of 1924 more precisely defining our perspective, we can now see that this "original" speech, in which the declarative statement or *logos apophantikos* is to be grounded, is precisely the subject matter of Aristotle's *Rhetoric,* namely, the rhetorical *logos.*

The declarative statement, Heidegger tells us in §33, is three things. First, it implies exhibiting something (*Aufzeigung*). "In this," says Heidegger, "we are holding firmly to the original sense of *logos* as *apophansis* or letting existent things be seen in starting from [*apo*] these themselves" (SZ 154). Furthermore, in the declarative statement "The hammer is too heavy," what is uncovered for sight is not any "meaning" but rather "an existent thing in the way it is ready to hand" (id.). We must be careful, however, not to lose sight of the fact that even this speaking *about Zuhandenes, about* things ready to hand, although "earlier" and "more original" than any representation of things merely "present on hand" before us observers (*Vorhandenes*), *is still derivative,* which is to say, as something to be grounded in something else still "more original" and prior to it.

Second, says Heidegger, the declarative statement is predication: "A 'predicate' is 'stated' of a 'subject'; the latter is *defined* by the former" (id.). "Defining here does not first uncover [what is]; rather, precisely as a mode of pointing something out, it *limits* one's seeing to what is showing itself—'hammer'—as such, and this in order, by an express *limitation* [*horos, horizein*] of one's looking, to make what is plain *expressly* plain in its definiteness" (155). Here *Being and Time* correlates perfectly with the exposition in the "Basic Concepts of Aristotelian Philosophy" of the *horismos* as the "original" "definition" lying beneath the derivative genus/species *definitio* of the Middle Ages, and which, as a *logos,* "speaks to a subject matter in regard to what it is in itself, *kath' hauto,*" and which, as *apophainesthai,* entails "bringing [something] into view" in "speaking to oneself or with someone" (2.5.24). Although "more original" than the *definitio,* predication, too, precisely as definition, is still derivative and, as we will see momentarily, is preceded by something even "more original."

Finally, the declarative statement means sharing and communicating with someone (*Mitteilung*), which entails saying it out loud (*die*

Heraussage). This, Heidegger explains, is letting someone else see too (*Mitsehenlassen*), letting him or her see the "existent being that is pointed out in its definiteness" (id.). Again, we should note that, like exhibiting something and predication, communication too, precisely as a mode of the declarative statement, is to be displayed as a derivative abstraction: "in circumspective taking care of things [*besorgende Umsicht*]," says Heidegger, "there are 'to begin with' no such declarative statements" (157).

Indeed, the statement "The hammer is too heavy" originally showed up as "Too heavy!" and "The other hammer!"—utterances which are not declarative statements at all (id.), and are as near as one can come to the origins of speech in an action performed without anything having been said at all:

> Originally, carrying out an interpretation does not consist in any theoretical declarative sentence [*in einem theoretischen Aussagesatz*], but rather, in circumspective taking care of something, in putting aside the wrong utensil ["Too heavy!"], or, respectively, in exchanging it for another ["The other hammer!"], without saying a word. (SZ 157)

In looking back to Heidegger's exploration of Aristotle's *Rhetoric* in the "Basic Concepts" we can now see that these original utterances "Too heavy!" and "The other hammer!" which are closest to the unspoken action and prior to the statement and declarative sentence are precisely the kind of original utterance that Heidegger found in rhetorical practice. For unlike logical and dialectial *logoi,* they are not made by one impartial "theoretical" onlooker to another but are made instead in the practical context of getting things done by getting ourselves and others to do them. They urge a *krisis* upon the audience, a decision or resolve to act. *Hence, in essence they are imperative, not declarative.* In the words of *Grundebegriffe der Aristotelischen Philosophie,* "In the human being himself lies the possible being of *hupakouein,*" of "listening and obeying [*Gehorschen*]":

> All these forms of our natural speaking with one another [*paraklêsis* or encouragement, *nouthetêsis* or warning, *epitimêsis* or reproach] carry within them the demand that the other not only take cognizance of something but that he take it up, that he follow some command, that he reflect upon something, that he repeat what is said so that in repeating it he listens to what is said. (30.5.24)[9]

This makes clear that in SZ §34, "Being There and Speech [*Rede*]. Language [*Sprache*]," Heidegger is at least in part recurring to the exhortative speech (*die Rede*) in rhetoric, that is, the speech the speaker or orator (*der Redner*) gives. And though language (*Sprache*) is surely a wider concept than speech (*Rede*), without question it is to be as founded in speech; indeed, "The existential-ontological foundation of language is [the] speech [die Rede]" (160). In this way, Heidegger has taken up again and "grounded" the third dimension of the statement, namely, sharing and communicating in speaking out loud: "The understandability of our being in the world, conditioned as it is by the feeling in which we find ourselves, *is spoken out* [loud] *(spricht sich aus) as speech.* The whole meaningfulness of understandability *is put into words,*" and "Speech's being spoken out [loud] is language" (SZ 161; emphasis Heidegger's).

Put another way, as opposed to the declarative statement or *logos apophantikos,* in Heidegger original speech and argument, the original *Rede* or *logos,* is to be taken as *oral and acoustical,* as it is, in fact, throughout Aristotle's *Rhetoric.* This is made evident by Heidegger's recourse here to its necessary counterpart in hearing and keeping quiet, *Hören und Schweigen* (SW 161). For everyone who speaks—in "saying yes or saying no to something, in challenging someone, warning someone, exchanging opinions, conferring with someone, interceding for someone"—there must, he says, be someone who keeps still and listens (id.). Thus, originally *Rede,* speech, is a reciprocal oral-acoustical exchange between two or more of us there in the world together taking care of what needs to be done, and precisely this oral-acoustical realm, it turns out, is the realm of rhetoric.

Of course, not all these verbal exchanges are merely injunctions ending in voiced imperatives that are meant to be heard. Along the way they also do make something clear for us to *see*; they do have a visual component: "A command is issued about something; the wish has its 'what it is about.' Intercession does not lack its 'what it is about.' Speech necessarily has this structural element because it is co-constitutive of the disclosure [*Erschlossenheit*] of being-in-the-world" (SZ 162). There is a charactistic shift here from an acoustically induced *Sich-Entschließen* and *Entschlossenheit,* from a listener's deciding and resolve, to the visual *Erschlossenheit* or disclosure of things for an onlooker. However, as an aspect of the world in which we find ourselves, even the things displayed visually still have a basic "feel" (*Stimmung, pathos*) to them that is fundamentally constitutive of how they are opened up for us. How they "are," this is to say, is communicated and shared within the feeling in which we together find ourselves (*Mitbefindlichkeit*) and within which they meet up with us (*uns begegnen*); and this felt dimension of the disclosure of the world is itself *not* visual and is *not* communicated by speech visually, rather it is acoustical and communicated acoustically. For the *Stimmung* or "feel" of things that conditions how we see them is not so much a visual hue as it is an audible timbre or "voicing" they have about them, a "ring" they have to them, as when we say, for instance, "That does not sound good!"

Hence, as Heidegger points out, the determinant features of speech have to do with how it sounds: "The linguistic index of the announcement of the being-in, determined as it is by the feeling in which we find ourselves, lies in the cadence, the modulation, in the tempo of speech, in the way of speaking" (SZ 162). Or as Heidegger had put it some three years earlier in reference to Aristotle's *Rhetoric* in his *Basic Concepts* lectures (GBAPh),

> Hearing, *akouein,* the hearing which corresponds to speaking, is the most fundamental way of sensing [*des Vernehmens*], the possibility proper of *aisthesis.* To the extent being human means speaking, in hearing I am in communication with other human beings. The [Aristotle's] explicit emphasis on hearing [*Metaphy.* 980b20–25] is remarkable because otherwise *theôrein, horan* [looking on, seeing], is designated by the Greeks as the basic possibility, as existence. (15.5.24)

and

> *Akouein* [hearing] is *aisthesis* [sensing, perception] in the proper sense. Although seeing, in conjunction with *theôrein* [looking on] reveals the world in the proper sense of "reveal," *aisthesis* proper is still hearing. For hearing is the perception of speaking and the possibility of [our] being together with one another. (30.5.24)

With that we have recovered the dimension of rhetoric largely dismissed, as we will see, even by Aristotle, and which fell into complete oblivion once, in France, Descartes's and Port Royal's reasoning *more geometrico* became the norm (see the "Port Royal Logic" [1662]), and once, thereafter, in England, Thomas Sprat's "History of the Royal Society" (1667) and John Wilken's "An Essay towards a Real Character and a Philosophical Language" (1668) had sought to strip words (*verba*) of anything that might distort a pure signification of the things (*res*) themselves—namely diction and delivery or the *way* something is said out loud, in Greek, *lexis* and *hupokrisis,* in Latin, *elocutio* and *pronuntiatio.* For these are precisely a matter of what Heidegger calls "the cadence, the modulation, the tempo" (SZ 162), which is to say, of the tone and rhythm of speech, of how it sounds. It is no accident that these should be at issue in original argument; for if the hearer is to hear, if he or she is to decide and obey the call to him or her, say, "The other hammer!" obviously the tone and rhythm with which this is said are crucial. Indeed, it is not what we think, but what we feel about something that must be changed if we are to obey, our *diathesis* and *pathos*, and this change is brought about by the sound of what we hear. If, as Heidegger says, "Our hearing one another, in which our being-together takes form, has the possible forms of obeying, going along with something, while the privative modes of not-hearing have the possible forms of disobeying, defying, turning away" (SZ 163), whether we hear or not depends on the sound of what is said to us. Surely, as we learned from our parents' "Do you hear me!" the *pathos* required to get us to hear, in this case fear, is communicated acoustically. To take a more felicitous example, perhaps, so, too, the *pathos* of charity needed to get us to hear a word of reconciliation and forgiveness, is communicated in what we *hear* someone say. Our hermeneutics of original argument has already made clear, then, that original argument is spoken, not written.[10]

3

A Hermeneutics of Original Argument Based on Aristotle's *Rhetoric*

We have learned from Heidegger's *Basic Concepts of Aristotelian Philosophy* just how effectively Aristotle can be used to "destruct" or take down Platonist metaphysical abstractions—even Aristotle's own—and used hermeneutically, to "lay bare" and "lay out" beneath these abstractions our original practical experience of taking care of things while being "there" together with each other and being "there" in the world with its nexus of implements (*Zeuge*) ready at hand and ready to be employed in our practices. We have also seen that *Rede* or *logos,* that is, speech, at this original level prior to any detached looking on at "stuff" (*Zeug*) just lying around on hand does not yet consist in apophantic propositions that point things out or "demonstrate" them; rather, it consists in the language of getting things done. Hence, not the declarative but the imperative is its primary grammatical mood. In the terms of Aristotle's *Rhetoric* we can say that original speech consists in either exhortation and dehortation (*protropê, apotropê*) in consultative speech, or accusation and defense (*katêgoria, apologia*) in judicial speech, or praise or blame (*epainos, psogos*) in epideictical speech (see *Rhet.* 1358b7 f.). Accordingly, we may take Heidegger's exhortative "The other hammer!" to be an elementary example of this original speech among people existing "there" in the world with each other and engaged in getting things done.

In this chapter we want to continue in a direction that Heidegger himself abandoned: we want to "lay bare" and "lay out" interpretively the structure and components of this reasoning that is "earlier" and "closer to the origin" (Heidegger: *früher, ursprünglicher*) and that we carry on with each other in our various day-to-day practices and undertakings in the world.[1] Following the young Heidegger's lead, this is to say, we will take Aristotle as a basis and starting point for a hermeneutics of original argument.

We will see, to begin with, that original argument differs *logically* in four ways from demonstration in abstract theoretical speech. First, as opposed to the subject matters of demonstration, the subject matters of original argument are not eternal and static, not always what they are immutably; rather, they are temporal and caught up in the process of becoming. Hence, they are contingent or, to use Aristotle's unique expression, "susceptible of being otherwise" than they are (*endechomena allôs echein*). Second, original argument argues not from intuitively certain first principles or *archai*, as demonstration must ultimately do, but from shared beliefs or *endoxa*, usually tacit, and which, though questionable, we "concede in advance" and do not call into question (see chapter 2 above on Heidegger's rendering of the *protasis* or premise as *die Vorgabe*). Third, as opposed to logical demonstration, original argument always reasons inconclusively, for the logical principles governing it are not those of strict syllogistic inference, and in rhetoric's original argument even the logical laws of noncontradiction and self-identity are suspended. Its reasoning is not definitive, but "likely" (*eikos*) reasoning, and hence the certainty and conclusiveness of "necessary" demonstrative argument, give way here to openendedness and continuing questionability. Fourth, and consequently, original argument does not argue just one side of an argument, that is, not the just the affirmation, "That is so," to the exclusion of the negation, "That is not so," or vice versa, but instead always entertains simultaneously both of two contradictory possibilities even as it argues for one or the other of them.

Finally in regard to rhetorical argument's distinctive logical character, we will see that whereas demonstrations are stated in univocal signs (*sêmeia*), like "2" or "=," that signify previously established conceptual entities or universal classes of things, rhetoric's original argument is phrased in the ordinary, ambiguous names (*onomata*) that we have for particular things. Put another way, in contrast to logical demonstration, rhetoric's original argument will not argue by the inclusion or exclusion of one univocally designated class of universals in another, as do, for example, the standard demonstrative syllogisms "All A are B; all C are A; therefore, all C are B," or "No A are B; all C are A; therefore, no C are B." Rather, rhetoric proceeds by tracing typical speech sequences in our ordinary language of names and naming, namely the standard "topics" or "lines" of argument, the *topoi*.

But demonstration and rhetoric are not just *logically* different. Hence, we will also need to "lay bare" and "lay out" how rhetoric's original argument differs *in purpose* from demonstration. In this regard it is to be noted, first, that original argument seeks not so much to *show* (*deiknunai*) uninvolved observers and onlookers that something is so as it seeks to *move* involved listeners and participants to a decision (*krisis*), the consequences of which will affect them themselves in their existence. Hence, unlike demonstration, it does not try to eliminate the influence of the feelings or *pathê* we undergo, in order that we might "see" and "know" something with detached and impassive objectivity. On the contrary, its task is precisely to communicate the right feeling for the right decision about the thing to be done and in so doing to displace the wrong feeling; to be convinced to act, this is to say, the audience must not only have been made to believe that something is the right, beneficial, and decent thing to do but also have been made to feel like doing it.

Since in large part this change in *pathos* is accomplished by the sound of what is said, that is, by *how* a rhetorical argument is voiced, the style (*lexis*) and delivery (*hupokrisis*) of it, will, in sharp distinction from the purely logical and demonstrative argument, be a crucial consideration. Contrary to argumentation theory after Peter Ramus and Port Royal in France, and the Royal Society in England, style and delivery are, therefore, not to be taken as mere extrinsic ornamentation.[2] As a matter of fact, even the "topics" or logical lines of reasoning used in original argument will turn out to be grounded in what a later, literary "rhetoric" based in reading came to call the "figures" of speech, namely the "tropes" and "schemes," and these "figures," "tropes," and "schemes" are not originally spatial and visual, as the terms—properly, "shapes," "turns," and "forms"—would seem to imply, but temporal and acoustical. Of these we will keep "tropes" since the the metaphorical transference of "turn" from the visual-spatial, say, in to "turn down" or to "turn up" to the acoustical-temporal, in "to turn a phrase" or in "a turn of speech," is easily and even unnoticeably accomplished. At issue here is vocal phrasing, modulations in sound over time, and, as we will see, the so-called "tropes" or "turns of speech" not only provide the speech sequences from which the topics derive but also determine the tone of argument, the "feel" to it, and the feeling that it communicates. Hence, the "tropes" are crucial not only for communication of its *logos* but also of the appropriate *pathos.*

Finally, since a successful rhetorical argument, as opposed to a demonstration, must attain not only the listeners' intellectual assent but also their consent to do what is asked of them, it must not only be logically valid but trustworthy. Indeed, the Greek word *pistos,* from which *pistis,* the name for a rhetorical "proof," derives, means both convincing *and trustworthy.* Consequently, it is also the purpose of original argument to communicate the *êthos* or good character of the speaker who makes that argument. Here, too, style and delivery are the communicators, and thus here, too, *how* something is said, the sound of it achieved by the tropes and schemes employed, is an intrinsic component of original argument indissociable from its *logos* or logic.

3.1 The Kinds of Argument: Demonstration (*apodeixis*) versus Dialectical Conversation (*dialegesthai*) and Rhetorical Consultation (*sumbouleuesthai*)

In the end, Aristotle's *Rhetoric* itself makes all these differences between original rhetorical argument and demonstrative reasoning clear, but before proceeding to this work it is useful, even so, to lay the groundwork for our hermeneutical exposition of original argument by turning to Aristotle's remarkable differentiation of our distinct ways of "getting to the truth" (*aletheuein*) in book 6 of the *Nicomachean Ethics.* For implied in the different ways of getting to the truth are the different forms of argumentation and reasoning appropriate to each of these ways. Thus indirectly, at least, book 6 of the *Ethics* tells us a great deal about the fundamental differences between demonstration and rhetoric's original argument.[3]

Significantly for us, the question addressed in book 6 of the *Ethics* is none other than "What is right argument?" (τίς ἐστὶν ὁ ὀρθὸς λόγος) (1138b34), and the answer to this question, we are told straight away, is to be sought in an analysis of the reasoning part of the soul, the part, that is, which engages in argument or *logos* in all its variations. Aristotle begins his analysis with a basic distinction between two capacities for reasoning and argument, "one in which we consider such things the first principles of which are *not* susceptible of being otherwise than they are [μὴ ἐνδέχονται ἄλλως ἔχειν] and another in which consider things that *are* susceptible [of being otherwise]" (1139a7–9; my emphasis). "The one shall be called scientific," he continues, "and the other, calculative [τὸ μὲν ἐπιστημονικὸν τὸ δὲ λογιστικόν]; for to take counsel and to calculate are the same thing [τὸ γὰρ βουλεύεσθαι καὶ λογίζεσθαι ταυτόν], but no one takes counsel about things not susceptible of being otherwise" (12–15; compare Heidegger, PS 28 f.).

Bouleuesthai and *logizesthai* are nowhere clearly distinguished from each other in Aristotle, and both words are used, apparently interchangeably, in the exposition of reasoning concerning *praxis* or choosing courses of action, which is our principal concern here. However, it would seem that *bouleuesthai,* which originates, as we will see, in *sumbouleuesthai* or taking counsel with others, is often the more appropriate of the two words for reasoning in the communal, practical realm, where choices of what to do have to be made, and that *logizesthai* is often more appropriate in the realm of *technê* and *poiêsis,* where the "logistics" of how to make something, say, a pair of shoes or a healthy body, can be be "figured out" or "reckoned" by oneself. It would follow, furthermore, that *logizesthai* is more closely correlated with *technê*'s *deinotês,* or cleverness in finding the means to an end, and *bouleuesthai* with *phronêsis's euboulia,* or being well-advised in choosing what is good. Whatever the case, this much is clear: both *logizesthai* and *bouleuesthai* have to do exclusively with the kind of reasoning and argument that concerns what is not necessary but, on the contrary, "susceptible of being otherwise than it is." If someone sets out to make something, the outcome can always be different from what he or she had in mind, and the same holds if we choose to pursue or shun a particular course of action.

Aristotle turns first to the practical realm of action and its *prohairesis,* namely the individual's choice or, to be precise, taking up (*hairein*) one course of action instead of (*pro*) the other, and it becomes evident from the start that the kind of reasoning involved here, though sharing with *technê* the concern with the variable and contingent, also differs from *technê* insofar as it has an intrinsic extra-rational dimension, namely *orexis* or our desiderative, volitional "tendency" toward or away from something. When Aristotle says that pursuit of an action and shunning it in our "tendency" correspond to affirmation and negation in our thinking (1139a21–22), and when he says that in making the right choice both the reasoning must be true and the tendency right (24–25), an implicit distinction between choosing the right course of action and finding the right means to make something becomes immediately evident: we can find the right means to make something no matter how we are disposed toward it, for as Aristotle points out later, this time explicitly, any *technê* or art of making something aims at something other than the maker himself or herself (1140b4), be this thing a pair of shoes, a healthy condition in someone else's body, or a wagon. But choosing a course of action "makes" individuals themselves what they are insofar as it always reinforces their tendency to behave in a certain way, and hence, says Aristotle, the aim of choosing well is not something distinct from the act of choosing, rather the aim is choosing well itself (see 1140b5–6). In choosing a course of action we ourselves are involved in the result (see Heidegger, PS 48–49, and Gadamer, WM 299–300). Looked at another way, at any given time we are the history and narrative of our previous choices.

For this reason how we are *already* habitually predisposed by character to choose, what our *orexeis* or "tendencies" *already* are, is also crucial to any taking counsel or deliberation leading to a choice. More to the point, if because of previous wrong choices we already tend to choose wrongly, if we habitually tend in the wrong direction, say, to avoid pain and pursue pleasure above all else, this tendency will have to be changed before we can choose rightly, and for this to happen we will have to be changed at an affective and even visceral level. For in taking counsel about choices of action, it will be remembered, all the true reasoning or *logos* there is will not help us if our tendency is not right. Aristotle, to be sure, was considerably less sanguine than were the early Christian evangelists, for example, that this visceral change could be effected by hearing the spoken word alone, and consequently in the *Ethics* he placed the major emphasis on discipline and habituation. Still, as the *Rhetoric* says explicitly, any taking counsel that would issue in a decision to act must, on some basic level, not only change how we think but also how we are disposed to feel about the matter in question. (Where the *Ethics* speaks of *orexis* the *Rhetoric* will speak of *diathêsis*, predisposition, in this regard.) Thus, when Aristotle says in the *Ethics* that choice is "either an intellection that tends toward something or a tending toward something that thinks things out intellectually" (ἢ ὀρεκτικὸς νοῦς ἡ προαίρεσις ἢ ὄρεξις διανοητική) (1139b5–6), he has not only distinguished practical, ethical reasoning from theoretical reasoning but from *technê* or art as well: "The origin of practical action," he says, "is choice (πράξεως μὲν οὖν ἀρχὴ προαίρεσις)—'origin' here meaning whence the action comes and not the thing for the sake of which it is done. But the origin of choice is [both] a tendency toward something and reasoning to some end" (1139a32–33).

As a matter of fact, Aristotle is only reinforcing a basic point made early on in the *Ethics*, namely that "there exists an unreasonable aspect of the soul that nevertheless participates somehow in reasoning" (φύσις τῆς ψυχῆς ἄλογος εἶναι, μετέχουσα μέντοι πῇ λόγου), and with which ethical reasoning, as opposed, say, to mathematical and even technical reasoning, must be concerned (1102b13–14). "That, in fact, this unreasonable part is somehow convinced by reasoning is indicated by warning as well as every kind of reproach and encouragement [ἡ νουθέτησις καὶ πᾶσα ἐπιτίμησίς τε καὶ παράκλησις]" (1102b35–1103a1). This passage in the *Ethics*, we note again, is the one to which Heidegger refers in his exposition of the *Rhetoric* in the "Basic Concepts of Aristotelian Philosophy" on 30 May 1924 (see above, chapter 2, note 9). Aristotle's way of putting things here makes unmistakably clear that ethical reasoning, *bouleuesthai* or one's taking counsel with oneself, which is the concern of the *Ethics*, originates in the realm of rhetorical conviction and our *sumbouleuesthai* or taking counsel with others, in which we not only see the point of what is said to us but hear it and are made to feel like doing what is urged upon us.

This conjunction in practical reasoning of *orexis,* of our tendency toward or away from something—and even our ethical predisposition (*êthikê hexis*; see 1139a34)—with our *logos* or reasoning about it, figures centrally in our primary consideration here, namely the special kind of rhetorical argumentation that leads up to practical, ethical choice and decision, *sumbouleuesthai* or taking counsel with others. For in any taking counsel, as opposed to logical, and even dialectical reasoning, communication of the *pathê,* or feelings that predispose us in a certain way and that provide the acoustical setting or "voicing" for how we will hear something, will be crucial. Put another way, if *logos* and *orexis* are conjoined, as they are in the *Ethics,* so, implicitly, are *logos* and *pathos.* Thus, even in the *Ethics,* which, in largely withdrawing from the communal origins of our taking counsel together about a decision (*krisis*), and which focuses instead on the individual's private deliberation about an ethical choice (*prohairesis*), we have nonetheless already retreated from the abstract level of demonstrative logic, moved back past dialectic, which remains theoretical and disengaged, and, in essence, returned to rhetoric.

To be sure, beginning at 1139b14 Aristotle makes matters considerably more complicated: he now distinguishes among no less than five ways that the mind or *psuchê* can affirm and negate something, only one of which involves *orexis* or the tendency to move toward something or away from it, to pursue it or shun it. The five are *technê, epistêmê, phronêsis, sophia,* and *nous* or, as we will translate them here, art, science, discernment, wisdom, and intellection. However, though five kinds of reasoning are named, it will emerge that the distinction to be elaborated is still fundamentally among three kinds; for wisdom combines the intellection of first principles (*archai*) with science's demonstrations of new truths from these: "wisdom is both science and intellection of things by nature the most worthy" (1141b3). Hence, the nexus of *sophia-epistêmê-nous* stands over against *technê,* on the one hand, and *phronêsis,* on the other.[4]

Furthermore, in yet another complication, to *phronêsis* Aristotle adds *euboulia* or being well advised, on the one hand, and, on the other, *sunesis, gnômê* and *sungnômê,* and *epieikeia* or, as we will render these, understanding, consideration and forbearance, and clemency (see 1142a32 f. and 1142b35 f.).[5] These last adjunct "intellectual excellences" are essential, it turns out, if *phronêsis* is to be carried over into *dikastê phronêsis,* if "prudence," that is, is to be carried over into "jurisprudence." Hence, they will be essential to us if we are to use this exposition in the *Ethics* to lay out the foundations not only of consultative rhetoric but judicial rhetoric as well.

Now, *epistêmê*, as we have been told ahead of time (1139b18 ff.), is distinguished by the fact that its subject matters are "not susceptible of being otherwise" than they are, which is to say that they are what they are necessarily *(ex anangês)* and that they are "ever" *(aidion)* the same and are not subject to generation or corruption. Here, then, we have always already abstracted and withdrawn from the world of place and time in which we were originally engaged in taking care of variable, contingent things. In other words, even if it is not stated explicitly, we have already become onlookers, *theoretês*, who *with Plato* and not in opposition to him, look over and beyond contingent things to the statically present universals of which these contingent things are now taken to be the mere instantiations.

To be sure, in explaining *epistêmê's* demonstrative reasoning in the *Posterior Analytics*, Aristotle says that

> It is not necessary, then, that, for there to be a demonstration, there exist either ideas or a one along side the many, but it is indeed necessary that one can say in truth that there is a one in the many. For there would be no universal if this were not so, and if there were no universal, there would be no middle term and hence no demonstration either. Hence there must be something one and the same about the many, and not in the sense of these merely having the same name. (77a5–10)

Plato, for his part, distinguishes in his *Philebus* between an earlier, physiological "*epistêmê*," on the one hand, which still "looks at physical things coming to be and being destroyed" (ἐπὶ τὰ γιγνόμενα καὶ ἀπολλύμενα ἀποβπλέπουσα) and, on the other, the true mathematical *epistêmê*, which looks "neither at what comes to be nor at what is destroyed, but beings in and for themselves and ever the same [ἐπὶ τὰ . . . κατὰ ταὐτὰ δὲ καὶ ὡσαύτως ὄντα ἀεί]" (61c).[6] Now, whatever Aristotle's differences with Plato may be concerning the "ideas," in the *Ethics*, book 6, at least, Aristotle himself takes a similar, metaphysical turn in matters of scientific knowing and reasoning: for Aristotle *epistêmê* is reasoning and argumentation not only *from* universals (*sullogismos ek tôn katholou*) (1139b29)—as opposed to contingent beliefs about contingent particulars, *ta kath' hekasta*—but also reasoning and argumentation *about* universals and things that are of necessity (1140b31–32). Accordingly, "*epistêmê* is apodictical or demonstrative in its mode" (ἐπιστήμη ἐστὶν ἕξις ἀποδεικτική) (1139b32). In *epistêmê*, this is to say, we are no longer reasoning inconclusively about "this particular square thing here," for example, but conclusively and with certainty about what the universal concept "square" implies and excludes.

But as Platonic as this characterization of *epistêmê* may seem, it is striking that all this is said about it here in the *Ethics* precisely in order to contrast it with, and thereby to highlight, *phronêsis* or discernment, which guides our reasoning about those human matters (*ta anthrôpina*) with which our taking counsel is concerned (1141b8 ff.). For, writes Aristotle, "Neither is discernment just of things taken on the whole [τῶν καθόλου μόνον], rather it must be knowing particular things each taken singly [τὰ καθ' ἕκαστα γνωρίζειν]; for it is practical but practice concerns particular things" (1141b14–17). Moreover, *phronêsis* or discernment, in contrast to *epistêmê* or science, *is* about what is "susceptible of being otherwise" (1140a1) and is precisely not about what is "of necessity," and hence there is no *apodeixis* or demonstration in the reasoning and argument guided by it:

> Thus, all in all, the one who can take counsel would be discerning [ἂν εἴη φρόνιμος ὁ βουλευτικός]; however, no one takes counsel about things incapable of being otherwise than they are, nor about deeds not susceptible of being done. Thus, since science is by demonstration, but there is no demonstration of things whose first principles are susceptible of being otherwise than they are, everything else about them being susceptible of being otherwise too, and since, moreover, there is no taking counsel [οὐκ ἔστι βουλεύσασθαι] about things that are what they are of necessity, discernment is not science. (1140a31–b2)

Or, as he has said in book 3's earlier considerations of choice and taking counsel,

> There is no counsel [οὐκ ἔστι βουλή] concerning the exactly defined and self-contained fields of the sciences. . . . Rather, we take counsel about such things as happen through our doing but not always in the same way; we take counsel, for instance, in matters of health and doing business, and about navigation more than gymnastics, since navigation is less exactly worked out, and more about the arts than the sciences, for of the former we are uncertain. (1112b1–8)

and

> Taking counsel, on the other hand, occurs in those things that hold for the most part, the outcome of which is not clear, and in indeterminate matters in regard to the greatest of which we bring in consultants [συμβούλους δὲ παραλαμβάνομεν] since we do not consider ourselves adequate to sort them out. (8–12)

Obviously, then, deliberative argument, the process of taking counsel leading to a choice that either pursues or shuns a course of action, will have a very different structure from demonstrative argument and reasoning as practiced in the mathematical sciences. Aristotle's way of putting this is to say that "All counseling is inquiry" (ἡ δὲ βούλευσις πᾶσα ζήτησις) (24), inquiry, that is, about whether something is to be done *or* is not to be done. Important here is that both of two contradictory possibilities will be left hanging in the balance. In other words, instead of starting with a clearly defined and self-evident declarative sentence that either affirms or denies that something is so, deliberative argument will start by entertaining simultaneously both sides of the question whether something is so or whether it is not.

Moreover—and most important for us since we, in distinction from Heidegger, are seeking to "lay bare" and "lay out" the ultimate *communal* origins of argument—instead of reasoning, as in science's monological demonstration, by oneself and from a premise self-evident to oneself, deliberative argument asks and weighs these contradictory possibilities in consultation with others. Salient in this regard is the often repeated *bouleuometha* in this passage or "*we* take counsel." Indeed, deliberation, as opposed to demonstration, is to begin with a communal undertaking *with* others: as we have just heard, in deliberation we bring in *sum-bouleutikoi*, con-sultants. Deliberation is *the* communal undertaking, in fact, that will be exposited in the *Rhetoric* as *rhêtorikê sumbouleutikê*, which is to say, rhetoric with counselors, or what we have called consultative rhetoric.[7] Thus, if taking counsel in the *Ethics* sometimes seems to us now to be something individuals originally do by themselves, this appearance turns out to be a retrojection from the position of modern individualism, which measures all argument against the paradigm of monological demonstration. For in Aristotle any deliberations that I carry on with myself will be in the language I have learned first in deliberations with others. In the end, *my* taking counsel with myself privately will thus be a secondary internalization of *our* having taken counsel with each other in public rhetoric. In Aristotle, as the ultimate joining of ethics and politics makes plain, the *zôion logon echon* and the *zôion politikon*, the animal possessing rational argument and the political animal, are one and the same.[8]

But let us now focus on the decisive difference between argument in science and argument governed by discernment, namely that, as opposed to science's dispassionate demonstrations, discernment's deliberations are affectively preconditioned.[9] This difference between the kinds of argumentation corresponds to the conjunction we have already established of *logos* with *orexis* in practical reasoning, of argument with our underlying volitional tendencies and predispositions. In this regard it is useful to consider Aristotle's remarkable and well-known linking in the *Ethics* of *phronêsis* with *sôphrosunê,* the latter meaning temperance (Latin: *sobrietas*) but, above all, keeping one's wits about one even when one is subjected to intense feelings of fear, desire, and the like.

Having shown what *phronêsis* or discernment is not, Aristotle goes on to say,

> It remains, therefore, that it [discernment] is a mode of practical truth along with reasoning and argument [μετὰ λόγου] that concerns things good and bad for the human being. On account of this we believe Pericles and other such people to be discerning since it is possible for them to envision what is good and bad for themselves and human beings generally. . . . Whence comes our use of the word *sôphrosunê* meaning to keep one's discernment intact [σῴζουσαν τὴν φρόνησιν]. And discernment, in turn, keeps intact just this sort of assumption [σῴζει δὲ τὴν τοιαύτην ὑπόληψιν] concerning what is good and bad. For pleasure and pain do not corrupt or pervert all assumptions, for instance, neither the assumption that the three angles of a triangle are equal to two right angles nor the assumption that they are not, rather pleasure and pain corrupt and pervert assumptions concerning what is to be done. The starting points for reasoning about actions are the things for the sake of which they are done, but for people corrupted by pleasure or pain, neither is this starting point immediately evident nor is it evident that they ought to choose and do everything on account of this starting point and for its sake. For vice is destructive of the starting point. (1140b6–19)

We can see from this account that in practical taking counsel under the guidance of discernment the *archai* or starting points are not only *ontologically* and *logically* different from what they are in *epistêmê.* We can see, this is to say, that they are not only different because they are all "susceptible of being otherwise" and hence are never intuited certainties but always simply assumptions (*hupolepseis*). (The *Rhetoric,* as we know, will call them *endoxa* or received opinions.) For beyond this ontological and logical difference lies a crucial fact: unlike our comprehension of mathematical truth, our understanding of the truth concerning what is good or bad, as well as the validity of our reasoning and argument about it, depends, first, on our character or *êthos,* and, second, on our feeling or *pathos* about the matter in question. It depends above all, this is to say, on whether we possess *aretê* or *kakia,* excellence or badness, in regard to our feelings and, especially, in regard to the desire for pleasure and the aversion to pain. For as the *Ethics* has pointed out earlier, all our feelings, desire, anger, fear, envy, friendliness, jealousy, and so forth are bound up with pleasure and pain (1105b21–24), and this underscores that, as opposed to arguments in *epistêmê* where character and affect play no role, in practical matters an argument made in taking counsel with ourselves or with others will not succeed if either bad character or a wrong feeling is left unchanged by it. The *logos* of any practical, deliberative argument is tied inextricably to the communication of the right *pathos.*

More precisely, it is a wrong relationship to pleasure and pain that distorts our relationship to all the other feelings we undergo and thus undermines any of our deliberations about what to do (see 1104b4 ff.). For in the end there are, as Aristotle has made clear in book 2, three considerations in our taking a course of action or shunning it: what is noble and decent (*to kalon*) or, conversely, what is shameful and ugly (*to aischron*), what is beneficial or, conversely, what is harmful, and what is pleasant or, conversely, what is painful (1104b30–33). The difficulty comes when a wrong relationship to pleasure and pain, and hence to the other feelings, corrupts our reasoning, for then we choose the pleasant course of action even if it is indecent and shameful and, in fact, as in the case of addictions, even if it is harmful to us: "In regard to all these things the good person chooses correctly and the bad person misses the mark, but most of all in regard to pleasure" (33–34).

To be sure, no conclusion for argument as such is drawn here; nevertheless it would follow that if someone is to be convinced to choose the noble and decent course of action, or even the beneficial one, the argument advanced to him or her will fail if it fails to bring about any correction needed on this fundamental affective level. Just how it might succeed in effecting a change here will concern us subsequently. For now we note only that the noble or decent in contrast to the shameful and ugly, and the beneficial in contrast to the harmful, are, respectively, the principal concerns of two of the three fields of rhetoric, the principal concerns, namely, of epideictic rhetoric, which treats the decent and shameful, and of consultative rhetoric, which treats the beneficial and harmful.

But what about judicial rhetoric, whose principal concern is with the right and wrong, the just and the unjust (see *Rhet.* 1358b25)? Has Aristotle's analysis of the different intellectual excellences in book 6 of the *Ethics* "laid bare" and "laied out" hermeneutically anything basic to original judicial argument? And what, if anything, does it teach us about the relationships of *logos, ethos,* and *pathos* here?

We have already learned from Heidegger that, as opposed to science's demonstration about timeless subject matters, all rhetorical argument, insofar as it takes counsel and deliberates, will be about temporal subject matters, about *Sein* that is *Zeit,* being that is time. We have seen that, in fact, taking counsel in practical matters, be these ethical or political, is concerned with what might or might not be done in the future: in the *Rhetoric* Aristotle states specifically that the future, what is about to happen, is the province of consultative or *sumbouleutikê* rhetoric (1358b13–15). On the other hand, judicial rhetoric, he tells us there, is about what has happened in the past (1358b15–17). Does the *Ethics,* concerned as it is with ethical and political deliberations, tell us anything about judicial reasoning and argument?

As a matter of fact, it does tell us a great deal, for it is precisely here where the aforementioned intellectual excellences of *sunesis, gnômê, sungnômê,* and *epieikeia,* or, as we have translated these, understanding, consideration, forbearance, and clemency, come into play (see 1142b35 ff.). Now, like discernment, *sunesis,* or understanding, we are told, is not concerned with those things that "are forever or are unmoved, neither is it concerned with all the things that happen, rather it is concerned only with the things about which one puzzles and takes counsel" (1143a5–7). But, Aristotle continues, "discernment gives orders, since its end is what we ought to do or ought not to do, whereas understanding only passes judgments [ἡ δὲ σύνεσις κριτικὴ μόνον]" (8–10). Here "giving orders" stands for making choices concerning our actions, and it is discernment, along with *euboulia,* or being well advised (see 1141a2 ff.), that guides the process of taking counsel leading up to these choices. Discernment, then, guides deliberations about our own actions, actions still to be taken in the future; and these deliberations will turn out to be precisely the province of consultative rhetoric. But—and this is the point here in the *Ethics*—we also take counsel about the actions someone else has already chosen in the past. And in these deliberations that come, not to a choice about a course of action we should take in the future, but to a decision (*krisis*) about an action someone else has taken in the past, we are guided by understanding:

> Understanding means neither the possession nor the acquisition of discernment; rather, as "to understand" means "to comprehend" whenever the word is used in science, so too is "understanding" appropriate in our use of opinion for passing judgment—and doing so fairly—*when another person is speaking* about those things with which discernment is concerned. (1143a13–16; emphasis added)

In other words, understanding relates to discernment among the intellectual excellences much as pity relates to fear among the affects: it is the way we ourselves experience what another went through, affectively in the case of pity, intellectually in the case of understanding (see *Rhet.*

1385b11 ff.). Only with understanding can we judge fairly the course of action another person chose—chose either rightly, having used discernment to guide his or her deliberations, or wrongly, having succumbed to immoderate passions and not "saved" or "kept" his or her discernment. And with the introduction of *krinein,* here in the sense of rendering a decision with regard to the actions of someone else, we have indeed entered the realm of judicial rhetoric and argument.

That we have is further underscored by the interweaving of consideration, forbearance, and clemency, which follows directly upon Aristotle's account of understanding; for these, along with understanding, he tells us, are prerequisite for rendering a right legal decision (*krisis*):

> What is called consideration, in regard to which we say that a person assesses things considerately and well and that he displays forbearance, is a right judgment of what the clement thing to do is [ἡ τοῦ ἐπιεικοῦς ἐστὶ κρίσις ὀρθή]. A sign of this is that we say the clement person is most forbearing of all and clemency is showing forbearance in regard to some things. But forbearance is correct, considerate judgment of what the clement thing is [γνώμη ἐστὶ κριτικὴ τοῦ ἐπιεικοῦς ὀρθή]. (1143a19–24)

Now, though it is not stated explicitly here, we note that *all these intellectal excellences essential for rendering a right decision are embedded in the affects.* Indeed, the analogy of understanding with pity was not in the least coincidental: to have this understanding for others and, especially, the forbearance and clemency that goes with it one must be disposed to sympathize, to feel with these others, to feel for them. Looking ahead, we might say that with clemency or *epieikeia*—which literally means "letting up" or "easing off" from implacability—Aristotle comes as close as he ever does to the Jewish-Christian idea of *chesed-eleos,* meaning not so much pity, as *eleos* does in Aristotle, as it means forgiveness and mercy; and looked at this way it is clear that *epieikeia* presupposes an affective shift from hatred to kindness in the person who shows it, a change in the "voicing," as it were, within which she or he hears and understands what the other says.

3.2 The *Rhetoric*'s Exposition of the *Logos* of Original Argument: The Example and the Enthymeme

With this background from the *Nicomachean Ethics* in place, let us turn now to the treatment of deliberative reasoning in the *Rhetoric* itself. The use of convincing arguments (*pithanoi logoi*), says Aristotle at 1391b7, is to attain a decision or *krisis*, and this not only in accusing or defending someone in judicial argument but also, in consultative argument, in exhorting someone to do, or disuading someone from doing, some action (9–11) and even in praising or blaming someone in epideictic argument (15).[10] For in each case the audience is addressed as a judge or *kritês* in the wide sense of someone who renders a decision even if strictly speaking someone is a "judge" only in legal matters. The point is that in any convincing argument something is put to us not just for us to assent to intellectually but for us to decide about (*krinein*). *Krisis*, then, is to be taken not just in the narrow sense of "judgment" but also in the wide sense of "decision" or existential "resolve"—Heidegger translates it as *Entschluß*—and thus it can be seen to overlap with what the *Ethics* calls *prohairesis*, or the choice of one course of action instead of another. Indeed, what results from taking counsel about a course of action is called a *prohairesis* in the *Ethics* but called a *krisis* in the *Rhetoric*. The only difference would seem to be that a private taking counsel with oneself is more the concern of the *Ethics* whereas public taking counsel with others is more the concern of rhetoric, in particular, of *sumbouleutikê* or consultative rhetoric. However, we have already seen that any taking counsel with oneself originates in taking counsel with others: the deliberation or *bouleusthai* of the *Ethics* is, in fact, grounded in the codeliberation or *sumbouleuesthai* of the *Rhetoric*.

Furthermore, all of rhetoric, says Aristotle, and not just consultative rhetoric, treats those things about which we take counsel (*peri hôn bouleuometha*) (1357a1), namely those contingent things which "could go either way in the future, could be either way in the present, or could have been either way in the past" (5–7). Rhetoric employs precisely that kind of argument and reasoning, which leads to either a choice of what to do oneself or a decision regarding how another tends to act now or regarding what she or he has done in the past. Hence, in specifying just how we reason and argue in these matters the *Rhetoric* is in fact elaborating the conclusions drawn in the *Ethics* about the kinds of intellectual excellences required to carry on this reasoning, in particular, *phronêsis* or discernment, and its adjuncts, understanding, consideration, forbearance, and clemency.

In showing us how public taking counsel originally works, the *Rhetoric* will thus provide us with a hermeneutics of original argument. It will "lay out" interpretively how we reason, not each with himself or herself alone, as in the *Ethics*, but how we reason to begin with, namely with each other, communally, in our practical day-to-day taking care of things; it will "lay out" how we reason originally in our being together with others (*Mitsein*) "there" in the world of temporal, local things as they happen. (See SZ §26, 117–25 and 116: "The clarification of being-in-the-world showed that, to begin with, there is never given, and there never 'is,' a mere subject without world. And, in the end, just as little is there given, to begin with, an isolated 'I' without others.") Our exposition of the *Rhetoric* will thus display what argument is like prior to any theoretical abstraction or withdrawal to detached and isolated observation of static being, placeless and ever present, and prior to any monological demonstration about such static being. Just what, then, does original argument turn out to be once we have taken down the layers of abstraction and withdrawal subsequently superimposed on it and thereby "laid bare" its original structure? This is the question we must now address.

First, like dialectic, and unlike science and art (see 1357a1), rhetoric, says Aristotle, is a faculty of furnishing arguments (*porisai logous*) about no specifically defined field (1356a33). And, again like dialectic, rhetoric gets its material, he tells us, from among such things that require argument (*ek tôn logou deomenôn*) (1356b37) but that already tend to be the subject matters of taking counsel (*ek tôn bouleuesthai eiôthotôn*), which is to say, from things that "could go either way" (1357a5) and precisely not from "what is incapable of having happened otherwise than it did, or of being otherwise than it is in the future, or of being otherwise than it is now, for nobody takes counsel about these things" (1357a5–7). Furthermore, its arguments will be constructed, he tells us, either out of examples (*paradeigmata*) or enthymemes (*enthumêmata*), with the example corresponding to induction (*epagôgê*) in dialectic—but not, we may assume, to the induction that provides demonstration with its first principles—and with the enthymeme corresponding to the dialectical syllogism (1357a15).[11]

In beginning with the example, we note that as opposed to scientific induction, argument based on the rhetorical example reasons neither from the part to the whole, nor from the whole to the part, nor from the whole to the whole, rather it reasons from the part to the part and from "like to like" (1357b26–29). This is to say that in argument by example we do not shift ontological levels from temporal, local, particular beings to static universal forms or classes of things. In fact, we do not even shift from things, each taken as particulars (*kath' hekasta*), to things taken in general or "on the whole" (*katholou*). Rather, in reasoning by similarity and difference we move from one temporal, local, particular thing to a different thing that is nonetheless in some respect like it. Here, then, there is no abstraction and withdrawal yet from contingent things in the world as these either did or did not come to pass someplace in the past, either come to pass or do not someplace in the present, and either will come to pass or will not someplace in the future. On the contrary, says Aristotle, "Whenever both things are of the same kind and one is better known than the other, that is an example" (29–30).

Just how this reasoning works is illustrated in book 2, chapter 20, 1393a23 ff. Reasoning by example, says Aristotle, is of two kinds, one based on telling things which actually did happen, and the other on telling things that have been made up. The fictional kind of example, moreover, has two variations, the parallel (*parabolê*) and the tale (*logos*) (1393a28–31). In reasoning from past fact one reasons from a thing that happened in the past to a similar or analogous thing that is likely to happen in the future. Thus, one might argue, for instance, that Darius crossed the Aegean having seized Egypt, and so did Xerxes; therefore the present king of Persia is also likely to cross the Aegean and invade Greece if he seizes Egypt (1393a32–b3).

In the case of the fictional parallel, one argues, as Socrates did, for instance, that selecting public officials by lot is like selecting athletes by lot; therefore let us not select our public officials by lot. Here, too, in another instance of consultative rhetoric, the reasoning proceeds from like to like even if the "thing better known" of the two is in this case fictional and never happened. And, again, the reasoning is temporal: one reasons from what might happen now to what might happen in the future, and one does so without recourse to universal truths. It is this way, too, with the tale, Aesop's fable, for instance, of the fox covered with fleas who refused the hedgehog's offer to remove them, saying that they, at least, were now full and slow to bite, whereas the empty ones that would surely come in their place would attack him voraciously; therefore, exhorted Aesop, do not put your present leader, who has already amassed his wealth, to death (1393b23–1394a1).

We find Aristotle's most specific accounts of the enthymeme, on the other hand, in book 1, chapter 1, 1355a3 ff. and chapter 2, 1357b13 ff.[12] In the first of these passages he tells us that rhetoric is a methodological approach to the *pistis*, or convincing argument and, moreover, that the *pistis* should be an *apodeixis* or demonstration of a kind since we are convinced most of all (*pisteomen malista*) whenever anything has been demonstrated for us (1355a2–6). The proper rhetorical form of demonstration is what Aristotle here calls the enthymeme. But the enthymeme, in turn, is a sort of syllogism (6–8); so, he continues, that person will be best at finding enthymemes who knows, first, what the materials of a syllogism are, but, also, how the materials of enthymemes *differ* from the materials of the "syllogisms of logic" (8–14). These differences are not yet specified, but we may assume that they have something to do with the distinction Aristotle appends here between what is true (*to alêthes*) and what is "like the truth" or verisimilar (*to homoion tôi alêthei*) (15). Moreover, in elaborating the difference between enthymemes and the "syllogisms of logic" Aristotle adds that the ability to hit upon *endoxa* or received opinions and the ability to hit upon the truth (*hê alêtheia*) are alike (*homoios*) (17–18), which is to say, similar but not the same, and this would seem to imply that *endoxa* are similar to, but not the same as, the truth. As the materials out of which enthymemes are to be constructed, these *endoxa* or received opinions, we may conclude, are not "true" in the strict logical sense but only "like the truth."

The exegesis here is ellipitical and all the more difficult to reconstruct because it harbors within itself some characteristic ambivalences on Aristotle's part. For obvious, on the one hand, is his very Platonic prediliction for demonstration or *apodeixis*, which in its strict, logical form, at least, argues conclusively from what is really true and does not argue inconclusively from what is only "like the truth" and always capable of being otherwise than it seems. Seen this way, rhetorical and even dialectical arguments, which start not from intuitively certain first principles but mere received opinions, are a second best, and, wherever possible, they should be reduced to demonstration in the form of the "syllogisms of logic."

Nevertheless, at the same time that Aristotle embraces the Platonic paradigm, he retreats from it. For there is also a clear acknowledgment here of the inappropriateness of demonstration and the "syllogisms of logic" for argument about the kinds of practical matters with which rhetoric is concerned, matters about which noetic insights into certain, first principles are unavailable, and for which the enthymeme based on received opinions is indeed the best kind of argument and is to be thought of in no way as second best to anything else. Hence, we find only a little further on,

> There are few necessary things that provide the subject matters out of which rhetorical syllogisms are constructed since most of what decisions and inquiries are concerned with is susceptible of being otherwise. For it is about deeds that one takes counsel and inquires, but all deeds are the kind of thing that is susceptible of being otherwise, and we can very nearly say that none of them occur of necessity. But things that happen for the most part and are susceptible [of being otherwise] must be reasoned to from other things of the same sort [ἐκ τοιούτων ἀνάγκε ἑτέρων συλλογίζεσθαι], just as necessary things are reasoned to from necessary things. . . . It is plain, then, that though some of the materials out of which enthymemes are said to be constructed will be necessary, the vast majority will be what is so for the most part. Enthymemes will be drawn,

> correspondingly, either from likelihoods or signs, the necessary ones from signs, but the others from likelihoods. (1357a23–33)

The likely (*to eikos*), Aristotle goes on to say, is what happens for the most part (*epi to polu*) and, beyond this, it is, as Aristotle characteristically puts it, "susceptible of being otherwise" (34–35).

We should note too that the enthymeme is now said to differ from the "primary syllogism" insofar as it often has fewer parts (1357a16–17). If, for instance, one wants to argue that (1) Dorieus has won in the Olympic games, that (2) in the Olympic games the prize is a crown, and, therefore, that (3) Dorieus has won in games in which the prize is a crown, the major premise (2) is superfluous since it is not necessary to state what everybody already knows (17–21)—and we might add, with Heidegger, what everybody "takes for granted."

Contrary to the opinion of some, this is no incidental point.[13] For this omission of the major premise implies that in rhetorical reasoning by enthymemes we will generally start from a *tacit* consensus, which is to say, from an *endoxon* or received opinion that, questionable though it may be, we share and implicitly agree not to call into question. It is precisely this dimension of original argument that Heidegger has elicited for us with his translation of *protasis* not as premise but as *Vorgabe* or what is "conceded in advance" (see chapter 2 above). Without this concession the argumentation would become an interminable digging for grounds for the grounds for the grounds, *ad infinitum*, in which the bottom would drop out, as it often does in contentious arguments with sophists, who, like children bent on disobedience to any authority, keep on asking of every reason advanced, "But why?" Aristotle is implying here that scientific demonstrations way of stopping this infinite regress is not available in original rhetorical argumentation, and in fact not even desirable: in rhetoric there is no getting back to an intuitively certain and self-grounding first principle, at which one can stop the search for grounds and from which one can then start to reason apodictically. (Contrast *An. Post.* 72a7–8: "The first principle of a demonstration is an immediate premise, 'immediate' meaning no other premise prior to it.")

In rhetorical argument, then, we cannot proceed unless we have some measure of community with each other to begin with and have always already tacitly agreed to agree about some things. If, say, with Thomas Jefferson, we try to evade this fact by arguing in a pseudo-demonstration beginning from supposedly "self-evident" truths concerning everyone's right to life, liberty, and the pursuit of happiness, truths supposedly available to a private individual in complete isolation from any communal tradition, then we only open the door to the eristic sceptic who, in challenging their self-evidence, says, "Yes, but what reason do you really have for saying that, and what reason for that reason," and so forth. With that we are plunged into the cacaphony of "interminable debate" among communityless antagonists.[14] Far from eliminating the "logical deficiencies" of reasoning by the enthymeme, recourse to the demonstrative paradigm in such matters actually results in a subjectivistic subversion of any sound communal deliberation.

Now, insofar as the enthymeme and the example correspond, respectively, to the syllogism and the induction in dialectic, and these, we may presume, in some way to the syllogism and the induction in logical demonstration (see 1356a35 ff.), we could expect Aristotle to draw a clear distinction between reasoning by enthymeme and reasoning by example. For in logical demonstration, at least, reasoning *from* first principles by demonstration is very different from reasoning *to* first principles by induction (compare the *Posterior Analytics*, book 1, chapter 1, and book 2, chapter 19). Indeed, Aristotle often does proceed as if there were some such clear distinction between rhetorical reasoning by enthymemes and rhetorical reasoning by examples. For instance, he says at 1394a9 ff. that it is generally best, first, to provide enthymemes in the *pistis* or convincing argument, and then, second, to support these with argument by examples—as if the difference were plain.

But, in fact, any real distinction between reasoning by enthymemes and reasoning by examples collapses, and not surprisingly. For after all, argument by example in the *Rhetoric* never has the function that induction has in the *Posterior Analytics*, namely to guide the intellect to intellection of an immediate first principle from which we can then construct the chain of our demonstrations. In rhetorical argument—and in dialectical argument too, for that matter—we do not reason from intuitively certain first principles (*archai*) but from received opinions (*endoxa*). Indeed, the example's chief role in the *Rhetoric*, namely as support for enthememes previously provided, makes clear that the enthymeme is not founded in the example, as demonstration is in induction, but, often, only subsequently backed up by it. The example, then, is just another kind of argument besides the enthymeme and, like the enthymeme, the example too will reason—*sunlogizesthai*—by putting one *logos* or utterance together with (*sun*) another, and drawing the second *logos* as a conclusion from the first.

This ultimate conflation of reasoning by examples and reasoning by enthymemes is made evident, too, in Aristotle's treatment of induction (*epagôgê*), to which reasoning by example is supposed to correspond, as one of the rhetorical *topoi* or topics (*Rhet.* 1398a33 ff.); for the topics are "places," where one might look for appropriate enthymemes much as one goes to certain "places" in a spice rack or apothecary to find appropriate herbs. Here, in other words, inductive reasoning is even presented as one kind of enthymeme. Let us remember, furthermore, that in rhetoric, argument by induction means argument by example, and as a matter of fact, the illustrative arguments given for enthymemes based on the topic of induction at 1398a33 ff. are precisely the sort of thing used to illustrate the example at 2.20.1393a22 ff. To be sure, here in book 2, chapter 23's discussion of the topic of induction, not just one example is provided, rather two or more are always given: for instance, "If we do not give our horses to people who have abused others' horses," so the argument may be summarized, "*nor* our ships to people who have wrecked others' ships, then we should not put our security in the hands of those who have failed to insure the security of others" (see 1398b6–10). And from this number of parallel instances it might seem that a universal principle is to be derived. Thus, the movement here would seem to be not from a part to another part, as in the case of the example (compare *Rhet.* 1357b27 f.), but from parts to the whole (compare *Top.* 105a13–19). However, it must be kept in mind that what we have so far is not yet the entire argument, but only one premise of the speech writer Theodectes' hypothetical enthymeme, which is to be used to urge a particular decision upon a particular audience, a premise to which must be added another, tacit premise, "We don't do these things with our horses and ships," and a conclusion, "Therefore, let us not put our security in the hands of X." Once the full argument is stated, we can see that though there are two "parts," horses and ships, we do not so much move from part to whole here as from two particular actions to a third similar but different particular action. Put another way, we note that no major term, say, "putting things in the care of those who abuse them," is invoked here.[15]

As a matter of fact, we will see in our examination of the topics that the distinguishing structural feature of all rhetorical argument, be this argument either by examples *or enthymemes,* is that, for the most part, it proceeds neither by deduction from, nor by induction to, static universal concepts under which temporal and local particulars may be classified, but rather proceeds according to accepted beliefs and speech patterns regarding *the similarities and differences of one temporal and local particular to another*—be these similarities and differences in opposite qualities, in degrees of more and less, or in priority and posteriority in time. Hence, the distinction Aristotle makes between enthymemes and examples in saying that, in contrast to reasoning by enthymemes, reasoning by examples reasons neither from part to whole nor from whole to part but from part to part (1357b26–28) is misleading; for *like* examples, most enthymemes, in reasoning by similarity and difference, reason *kata meros,* that is, according to the particular and from one part to another, and they do this without recourse to what is "on the whole" (*katholou*), to say nothing of a universal class of things. We must keep in mind, therefore, that in contrasting enthymemes with examples Aristotle is speaking here primarily of those few enthymemes based on signs or indications (*sêmeia*) and not the vast majority of enthymemes that are based on likelihoods (*ex eikotôn*) (see 1357a32).

Here is the point: as opposed to the induction of the *Posterior Analytics,* 99b15 ff., *there is no ontological shift here to a timeless, intuitively certain and necessary universal truth.* All rhetorical reasoning, by enthymeme as well as example, is at its basis reasoning from the similarities to each other, and differences from each other, of imaginable particular things. Thus, in the *Rhetoric* reasoning by examples and reasoning by induction amount to the same thing. We may say, accordingly, that the "topic of induction" shows us how in rhetoric reasoning from examples may be used not only to supplement a given enthymeme but also to construct one in the first place. Reasoning by enthymemes and reasoning by examples are fully interwoven. Both reason from the similarity and differences of particular, temporal experiences in the world, and we need not make any systematic effort to distinguish between them.

3.3 Original Argument as Reasoning by the Topics

It is, in fact, just this fusion of reasoning by ethymemes and reasoning by examples that we wish to exposit hermeneutically here, and this, with respect to the inescapable contingency and questionability in both, but also, following Heidegger's conjunction of being and time, specifically with respect to their particularity, locality, and temporality, as these are characteristic of our original argumentation while "being-there," "in-the-world," and "taking care" (*besorgen*) of particular things there and then, here and now. Temporality is the "horizon" of all rhetorical argument, be it by enthymemes or by examples, and this is made evident from the start by Aristotle's initial treatment of the rhetorical topics under the headings of "future possibility and impossibility" at 2.19.1392a8 ff., of "past fact" or "what has happened or has not happened" at 1392b15 ff., and of "future fact" or "what will be the case or what will not be" at 1393a1 ff. For, in effect, what he does in these passages is display the temporality of all the basic topics, namely "similarity and "difference," "opposites," "the part and the whole," "the more and the less," and "the prior and posterior," by distributing these over their applications to the past in judicial rhetoric, to the present in epideictic rhetoric and to the future in consultative rhetoric. Hence, not only the "susceptibility of being otherwise," the "Is it or is it not?" questionablility of the premises and conclusions of all original argument is underscored, not only, that is, the "original concomitance of being and not being" (Heidegger: *die Gleichursprünglichkeit des Seins und des Nichts*), but also their original and basic temporality (Heidegger: *Zeitlichkeit*). Thus, in the *Rhetoric*'s topical reasoning, unlike the topical reasoning of dialectic, we are dealing with particular matters in particular places and at particular times and not with statically present universals.

In this section it is our task, then, to lay out interpretively reasoning by these basic topics by showing how they aid in the "invention" (*heuresis*) of original arguments from within our being-there at a particular place in the world, and on a particular occasion in time. There is no set way that the rhetorical tradition has organized its exposition of the topics, and Aristotle's own treatment of them in the *Topics* is for the most part even more distressingly haphazard than it is in the *Rhetoric.*[16] To be sure, in the *Rhetoric,* as we have just mentioned, they are sometimes grouped with regard to their specific application in each of the three fields of rhetoric, consultative, judicial, and epideictic, and hence according to the different temporality of each of these. This not withstanding, in book 2, chapter 23, Aristotle reverts to providing a random list of twenty-eight topics with no discernible order at all. Following Heidegger's cue and, in fact, Aristotle's own principle of division of the three fields of rhetoric into speech about the future, speech about the past, and speech about the present, we will attempt to lay out the basic general topics in regard to their temporality: we will, this is to say, treat "similarity and difference," "opposites," "the part and the whole," "the more and the less," and "the prior and posterior" as each of these deals with the past, present, and future. In the end, it will be clear that whatever tense or tenses they appear in, all of rhetoric's original arguments by the topics deal not with things statically present but with contingent local particulars as these "happen to have happened" over time, with *sumbebêkota* or "accidents." Even the dialectical use of the topics, it will emerge, does not display the pervasive temporality of rhetoric's use of them, and insofar as dialectic treats its subject matters, instead, as statically present to mind and divorced from any particulary place and time, it already proves to be a derivative abstraction from original rhetorical argument.

3.3.1 "Similarity" (*homoiotês*)

Significantly, given our concern with the temporality of the *Rhetoric*'s topical reasoning, it is the discussion of the consultative topics of "future possibility" that provides the occasion in the *Rhetoric* for Aristotle to introduce the most basic topic of all, "similarity" (*homoiotês*) or "the like" (*to homoion*). For instance, at 1392a12 we find "If something is possible, then what is like that thing is [will be] possible," an argument that, we remark, could be cast in the past as well, "If something was possible then, it is possible now," and vice versa. However, since the *Rhetoric* does not further elaborate this basic topic of "similarity" as such, we must, with the caveats previously noted about dialectical reasoning, turn to the *Topics*, 108a7 ff. for specifics. There, where things are not treated temporally but as static presence, similarity is explained as an analogy whose terms belong in different genera of things (*en heterois genesin*), as in the case, for example, of "As science is related to the thing known scientifically, so, likewise, is perception related to the thing perceived," or "As sight is in the eye, so too intellect is in the soul" and "As calm is in the ocean, so is stillness of the wind in the air" (108a9–13).

As is characteristic of the dialectical reasoning with which the *Topics* is concerned, these examples presuppose, to be sure, an abstraction from particular, local, and temporal contingency that is not possible for rhetorical reasoning, whose defining characteristic is temporality. Still, an obvious correlation with reasoning in rhetoric is present here. As is made clear by the well-known saying in the *Poetics* at 1459a7, "for to find good metaphors is to see the similar" [τὸ γὰρ εὖ μεταφέρειν τὸ τὸ ὅμοιον θεωρεῖν]" in any reasoning by the topic of similarity, be this either dialectical or rhetorical, we are dealing with that original and basic kind of reasoning that finds metaphors. Indeed, in book 2, chapter 20, of the *Rhetoric* Aristotle, in contrasting the invention of fictional examples with the discovery of actual examples, comments that it is "hard *to find similar things* that have actually come to pass" [πράγματα μὲν εὑρεῖν ὅμοια γεγενημένα χαλεπόν], but easy to find fables; for, as with parallels, one needs to make them up assuming that "one can *see the similarity*" [ἄν τις δύνηται τό ὅμοιον ὁρᾶν] (1394a2–5; emphasis added). Hence, despite the *Topics*' reference to the "genus" or conceptual class of things in its discussion of similarity (see also 108a15), this kind of reasoning, as the *Rhetoric* shows, is originally preconceptual: originally, this is to say, it moves not from conceived essence to conceived essence, not from one abstract genus of things to another class—a species (*eidos*)—contained or not contained in the first class, but rather from a concretely experienced, named quality. To take the illustration from the *Topics*, it moves from the calm of the sea, to a different but nonetheless in some way similar, concretely experienced, named quality, the stillness of the wind (108a12–13).[17]

Moreover, this original preconceptual dimension of reasoning by similarity can still be ascertained even when Aristotle raises the level of logical abstraction by substituting "the same" or "the identical" (*to auton*) for "the like" at 103a6 f. Here Aristotle maintains that things can be "the same" in several senses: in the first place, they can be numerically the same, and this in three ways, that is, (1) by being one and the same thing by definition as a cloak is the "same" as a mantel, (2) by having one and the same property as being able to acquire knowledge is the "same" thing as being a human being, *but also,* and most important for us, (3) by sharing several accidents (*sumbebêkota*) as when "the one talking" and "the one sitting" both "happen to be" the "same" person (103a25–39).

To be sure, Aristotle has also said just before this that we speak of things as the "same" when they do not differ in species, as one human being does not differ from another, and, finally, that we speak of things as the "same" when they fall under the same genus, as do human beings and horses (under "animal") (103a11–19). But if the characteristic move to definition by genus/species here reveals the amount of Platonic theoretical abstraction from practical experience that has already taken place in Aristotle's thinking, the reference to "accidents" that follows, to *sumbebêkota* or what "has happened to happen with" something accidentally, reveals at the same time Aristotle's equally characteristic reluctance to abandon completely argumentation about the temporal and local particulars of our day-to-day experience for a purely logical reasoning about timeless universal essences. Indeed, the *original* "similarity" of particular things may be said to be precisely in regard to what can be predicated of them accidentally and in regard to their accidental appearances. Put another way, the original "categories" or questions to be put to the things "accused" here, *ta katêgoroumena,* are "Where?" "How?" or "As how much?" they "have happened to happen" (*sumbebêkasin*), or "In relation to what?" or "As doing what?" or "As undergoing what?" The original "categories" are, this is to say, precisely not "What are they in essence?" or "What are they by definition?"[18] (Compare *Metaphy.* 5.9.1017b29 ff. and 10.3154a20 ff. on likeness and identity.)

This rootedness, in preconceptual experience of temporal and local particulars, of all original argument by the topic of similarity is perhaps best illustrated by Androcles' argument, cited at 1400a5 ff., in the *Rhetoric*'s random list of topics for constructing enthymemes: when asked to justify his improbable assertion that a law will be needed to set the failure of the laws right, Androcles replied that when cooked, fish, which live in salt water, need salt, and olive cakes need olive oil, as unlikely as this might seem. The reasoning here has the basic structure of all rhetorical reasoning: it is reasoning neither from particular to universal nor from universal to particular but by analogy, from one experience of particular temporal things to another.

Remarkably, this instance, too, of a topic for reasoning by enthymemes is best explained in Aristotle's account of reasoning by one kind of example; see 1393b8 ff. on the fictional parallel and the similar inadvisability of choosing athletes and public officers by lot. Once again, the line separating enthymemes from examples is erased, and erased precisely insofar as both proceed from the similarity of one particular thing to another.

We note, finally, that the topic of similarity also occurs implicitly in the random list of book 2, chapter 23, as a variation on the arguments by the topic of the "more and the less," namely as an argument neither *a fortiori* nor *a minori* but *ex paribus,* which is to say, by what is "neither more nor less" but on a par (1397b20 ff.), as in, roughly, "You feel pity for your father who has lost his sons, so have you no pity for Oineus who has lost his son?" That this argument, indirectly exhorting its audience to a decision by an *erôtêma* or "rhetorical question," is taken from a drama, evidently about Meleager, is obvious, and this allows us to partially reconstruct its inherent particular and local and temporal occasion; this much, at least, is clear: someone is rebuking someone else at a particular place and on a particular occasion. Not agreement about universal classes of things is sought here, but consent to a particular action, and as Robb has pointed out, its reasoning by similarity of particulars is typical of oral, preliterate, preconceptual argument (see above, n.15). For our part we will say that it is typical of original argument "there," "in-the-world," typical of rhetorical speech.

3.3.2 Three variations on "difference" (*heterotês*), namely "opposites" (*antitheseis*) as (1) "contraries" (*enantia*), (2) "contradiction" (*antiphasis*), and (3) "lacking and having"(*sterêsis kai hexis*)

Since similarity can be established only between things that are somehow different and, conversely, difference can be established only between things that are somehow similar, our exposition of the topic of similarity leads us naturally to the exposition of the equally basic and equally original (Heidegger: *gleichursprünglich*) topic of "difference." Indeed, as we will now see, difference—in being, quality, quantity, relation, potentiality, actuality, place, time—underlies all the topics remaining for our consideration (see the *Topics*' introduction of the categegories at 103b20 ff.).[19]

1. We will begin our investigation of difference with the topic of "contraries" or things opposed to each other in their contrary being, as in temperance/licentiousness, peace/war, love/hate, or in their contrary

qualities, as in hot/cold, loud/soft, sweet/bitter, and so forth. Significantly for us, insofar as we are emphasizing the temporality of original, topical argument, Aristotle begins his elaboration of the topics for consultative rhetoric at 2.18.1392a8–11 by applying "the topic of contraries" (*enantia*) within the discussion of what is "possible and impossible" in the future. The premise for an enthymeme to be found at this *topos*, or "place" in the apothecary of arguments has the hypothetical form of "If something is possible in the future, then the contrary of that thing is possible," or, to take Aristotle's example, "If a person can get well, he or she can also fall sick." Now, though this argument by contraries is applied here only in regard to future possibility it is clear that it applies equally to past possibility, for example, in the form "If a person got well, he or she fell sick," and to a blend of past fact with future possibility, for example, in the form "If she got well, she can fall sick again."

The inherent temporality of this topic is, however, not as obvious in the version of it we find at 1397a6 ff. heading up book 2, chapter 23's random list. Here it is argued that opposites have opposite qualities, that, for example, if temperance is beneficial, licentiousness is harmful, or if war is harmful, peace is beneficial, or if those who do wrong unintentionally deserve our anger, those who do good unintentionally do not deserve our thanks, or if liars are often believed, those telling the truth are often not believed. Still, if these samples taken out of context seem to belong to the tenseless theoretical arguments of dialectic, with the exception of the first, they clearly emerge as temporal when a possible rhetorical or dramatic context is reconstructed for them. For unlike the first, the last three, we note, are all taken from either specific dramas or speeches, and, as a matter of fact, none of these last three is proposing something for someone's theoretical assent, rather each of them is urging a decision upon someone, a decision which is about either a particular present or future matter and which is to be based on either particular present or past matters. For instance, these arguments might be recontextualized in the following ways: "We are at war now, so let us sue for peace," or "We have been angry at those who did us wrong unintentionally, so let us not be grateful to these who do us good unintentionally," or "Let us believe this man, for what he said may well be true despite our disbelief."

Now, as Aristotle points out in the *Topics*—in regard to dialectic, to be sure, but not without relevance to rhetoric, which is, of course, the "counterpart" to dialectic (see 13541a1)—"contraries" (*enantia*) are, in fact, only one of four kinds of opposites (*antitheseis*). Besides "contraries" he names "contradiction" (*antiphasis*), "lacking and having" a natural attribute (*sterêsis* and *hexis*), such as being blind and having sight, and "correlatives" (*ta pros ti*) (*Top.* 113b15 ff.). Since "correlatives," in which the existence of one of the correlatives implies the existence of the other, obviously can be taken as the matrix that engenders the crucial topics of "the part and the whole," "the more and less," and the "prior and posterior," we will postpone our consideration of this topic until the next subsection and devote ourselves in the rest of this subsection first to "contradiction" and then to "lacking and having."

2. Contradiction, of course, is the one topic that seems to have been preserved in logical demonstration, for generally it is applied in falsifying invalid reasoning by classes of things. It is a contradiction, for instance, to say that the class of A belongs to the class of C and, at the same time, that the class of A belongs to the class of B and none of the class of B belong to the class C; it is a contradiction to say, that is, that Socrates is an immortal being, and at the same time that Socrates is a human being, but no human being is an immortal being. We note that in such reasoning as this even "Socrates" is not taken as a temporal and local particular but as a statically present being or class of one, an *infima species*; after all, we do not say this Socrates "was" or "will be" but only that he "is." However, the logical-demonstrative use of contradiction is, as Aristotle's *Rhetoric* makes clear, an abstraction for its original use in speech, "there" and "in-the-world" where we are taking care of things over a time. Indeed, the reduction in demonstration of all the rhetorical topics of difference to logical contradiction (A•~A) reveals the same degree of abstraction as demonstration's reduction of the rhetorical topic of similarity to logical identity (A = A).

However, argument by contradiction, pointing out that what someone is now saying (*dicet*) goes against (*contra*) what he or she has said (*dixit*) before, was not originally the abstract thing it has become in demonstration, and this Aristotle's *Rhetoric* makes patent. To be sure, in the random list of book 2, chapter 23, Aristotle does not speak of contradiction but of "disagreement": "Another refutation," he says, "consists in looking for disagreements [τὸ τὰ ἀνομολογούμενα σκοπεῖν], and if these disagreements can be taken from *place and time and deed and words*" (1400a15–17; emphasis added). However, as the examples given make clear, we are talking here about the original kind of argument from which the topic contradiction derives: "He says he is fond of you people, but he *swore* allegiance [συνώμοσεν] to the Thirty Tyrants" and "He says that I am litigious, but he cannot point to a single case where I *have pursued* [δεδικασμένον] litigation" (17–20; emphasis added). We note that, in contrast to the contradictions of logical demonstration, the disagreements or contradictions here are indeed between different particular actions and words done and said over a time, in one place and in another place, done and said there then as opposed to done and said here now. This particularity, locality, and, above all, temporality of original argument by contradiction is even more obvious in an earlier topic in the random list at 1397b30–33: "Another topic results from looking at time," says Aristotle:

> For example, Iphicrates in his speech against Harmodius argued, "Had I demanded a statue in the event my undertaking was successful before I undertook it, you people would have given me one, and now, after the task has been completed, you won't give me one?"

(We note, in addition, that though it is basic to rhetorical argument, which always allows that the *contradictory* position might be valid, the *erôtêma* or "rhetorical question" here is in sharp contrast to anything in demonstration, in which the logical law of noncontradiction obtains, questions are not entertained, and questionability—"It is, is it not?"—has been eliminated. See below, chapter 6 on the law of noncontradiction.)

Also from book 2, chapter 23 might be added here the consultative and futural argument by the topic of contradiction that "If when fleeing our land we fought to return, then having returned, we should not flee to order not to fight," for, Aristotle comments, "the one time [ὁτε μὲν] they chose to remain at home rather than fight, but the other time [ὁτε δὲ], not to fight rather than not to remain at home" (1399b16–19). Far from being purely logical, the contradiction here is in particular deeds, namely choices made at a place and at a time. Indeed, as Aristotle points out (1399b15), and as we will see momentarily, this use of the topic also involves a variation of the topic of temporal sequence, "prior/posterior" (*proteron/husteron*).

3. Since the *Rhetoric* gives us precious little to go on in regard to the topic of "lacking and having," we are once again constrained to turn to the *Topics*. At 114a9–10 we find the example that "if being sensate follows upon sight, being insensate follows upon blindness, for sensation is opposed to not being sensate as having is to lacking." True to the nature of dialectical resoning, the "follows upon" here is conceived of logically, and not temporally. The *Rhetoric*, however, gives us a hint that this was not always the case with arguments by lacking and having, for, significantly, the sample argument there that comes closest to this topic is fused with reasoning from what is posterior in time and at a place to what is prior in time and at a place: at 1392b17–18 we find that "if what tends to happen afterward [τὸ ὕστερον εἰωθὸς γίγνεσθαι] has happened, then that which tends to happen before [τὸ πρότερον] has happened; for example, if someone has forgotten something, he or she once learned it also." Thus, we see argument by the topic of "lacking/having," too, has an

original, particular, local, temporal form, from which the dialectical use of this topic is an abstraction. Here, too, the *Rhetoric* reveals the dialectical, theoretical reasoning of the *Topics* to be a withdrawal from our original "taking care" of practical matters, there and then, "in-the-world" even if the level of abstraction is not yet as great as it is in logical demonstration.

3.3.3 Four more variations on "difference": (1) "correlatives" (*ta pros ti*), (2) "the more and the less," (*to mallon kai hêtton*), (3) "the part and the whole" (*to meros kai to holos*), and (4) "The prior and the posterior" (*to proteron kai to husteron*)

1. Significantly, the topic of correlatives first shows up in the *Rhetoric* in book 2, chapter 19, under the heading of "possibility," which would seem to indicate that it has to do with contingent particular things that might or might not have happened in the past, might or might not be happening now, or might or might not happen in the future. The example given, however, is from mathematics and disappoints our expectations in this regard: "If double is possible, so is half and vice versa" (1392a27–b5); for here, obviously, we are dealing with abstract, conceptual universals with no past and no future and which exist in static presence, ever (*aei*) the same. There are, however, other applications of this topic in the random list in the *Rhetoric*, book 2, chapter 23, and these do in fact display the particularity, locality, and temporality of its original use. Indeed, the first set of these plainly falls under judicial argument about past time, namely the publican Diomedon's argument that "If it is no disgrace for you to sell [to have sold] the rights to collect taxes, it is no disgrace for us to buy [to have bought] them" (1397a25–27), in which buying and selling are the correlatives, and Demonsthenes' argment that since those who killed Nicanor were thought to have done so justly, it was thought that he was killed justly (1397b6–8), in which killing and being killed are the correlatives. On the other hand, Iphicrates' argument by the topic of correlatives falls equally plainly under consultative argument about future time, namely that "If you declare tall boys to be men, then you will have to declare short men to be boys" (1399a35–38).

The three remaining topics for our consideration, "the part and the whole," "the more and the less," and "the prior and the posterior," are not only variations on the basic topic of difference but, more specifically, variations on correlatives. For a part cannot exist without a whole, more of something without less of something else, and something prior without something else posterior, and conversely in each case. Even so, each of these topics is distinctive and deserves to be treated in its own right.

2. We know "the part and the whole" best, of course, in its Platonic transfomation into demonstrative argument by genus and species. For instance, the species (*eidos*) Love, as we will see in our investigation of the *Phaedrus*'s transformation of original argument in the next chapter, can be thought of either as a part of the whole genus (*genos*) of Irrational Desire or as a part of the whole genus of Divine Madness. In each case we are conceiving of what Love is logically, and, unlike the Lysias of the *Phaedrus* dialogue, we are not designing a particular proposal of love, that is to say, non-love, respectively, to be made to a particular person at a place and time. To be sure, this Platonic tendency to transform argument by particular contingent parts and wholes into a dialectic of collection into a genus and division into species might seem at first glance to predominate, too, in Aristotle's *Rhetoric*, but on closer scrutiny it becomes evident that it does not and that here, at least, Aristotle is thinking of part and whole in "earlier" ways "closer to the origin" of argument. Indeed, even *genos* and *eidos*, which must be taken here not as genus and species but as kind and sort, appear in the *Rhetoric* under the heading of past and future possibility and have to do not with statically present conceptual classes of things but with kinds and sorts that come to pass: "If the whole kind of *things that can happen* [εἰ τὸ γένος ὅλον τῶν δυνατῶν γενέσθαι] [is or was possible], so too [is or was] the sort, and if the sort, then also the kind" (1392a31–b2; emphasis added).[20] That the argument here is still about concrete particulars that "happen" at a place and time is further underscored by the example of argument by the part and the whole given just before: if the parts are possible, says Aristotle, so is the whole, "For if the slit, the toepiece and the uppers can come to be [δύναται γενέσθαι], so can sandals, and if sandals, then the slit, the toepiece and the uppers too" (1392a27–31).

3. Aristotle first introduces the basic topic of "the more and the less" (*to mallon kai hetton*) under the topic of "future possibility," or, here summarized, "If the more difficult of two things is possible, so is [will be] the less difficult and easier" (see 1392a12–13). This topic, however, receives its full elaboration in its past, present, and future temporality in the *Rhetoric* 2.23.1397b13 ff., where he provides three variations in the hypothetical premise for an enthymeme to be located here: (1) the argument *a fortiori*, "If the the more likely thing does *not* [did not, will not] obtain, then plainly neither does [did, will] the less likely," as in "If the gods do not know everything, then it can hardly be that human beings do" (see 1397b12–14); (2) the argument *a minori*, "If the less likely thing does [did, will] obtain, then so does [did, will] the more likely," as in, "If he strikes [struck, will strike] his father, then he strikes [struck, will strike] his neighbor" (see 16–18); and (3) the argument *paria ex paribus*,

"If one of a pair of equally likely things is [was] so, then so is [was, will be] the other" as in "If if was right for Hector to kill Patroclus, then it was right for Paris to kill Achilles" (see 19–29). (This last use of the topic we have already treated under similarity.)

To these three variations, the *Topics* adds a fourth (see 114b37 ff.): "If x is y, then more of x is more of y," as in "If committing an injustice is evil, then committing a greater injustice is a greater evil still" (see *Top.* 114b38–115a2). As is typical of the theoretical, dialectical reasoning it is explicating, the *Topics* treats this subject matter "at a distance" (Heidegger: *auf Abstand*) and from the point of view of a detached onlooker, not an engaged participant "in the world." This argument, unlike those in the *Rhetoric,* this is to say, is not urging a particular decision upon a particular audience on a particular occasion, and its concern is not with any particular action taken in the past, action being taken now, or action to be taken in the future; instead, it seeks only to engender a belief about things in general. But the conversion of this topic from a dialectical use to a rhetorical use on a given occasion and at a place and time is easily executed; for example, we could say, "If the injustice of stealing from his neighbor *was* (or will be) evil, then the greater injustice of stealing from his father *was* (will be) a greater evil."

Again, the point to be stressed is the particularization of times and tenses in the premises in rhetoric, for in this and any original kind of *logos* or argument we are arguing from within the world as it is happening, and within which we always already find ourselves under way as we proceed from the past through the present into the future. We are not yet, in other words, abstract observers of some static systematic construct of forms (*eidê*), some "schedule" as it were, that we have superimposed on what comes to pass in the temporal flow of events. Rather, as our *Destruktion* of any such eidetic constructs, and our hermeneutical "laying bare" and "laying out" of original argument beneath them makes clear, originally we are reasoners, who in urging decisions upon each other and trying to get things done are still within the temporal flow of narrative-history and caught up in it. Hence, the argumentation and reasoning by the topic of "the more and the less" in any of its three variations may in fact proceed (1) from a past possibility to another past possibility as in the judicial reasoning "He struck his father, so he very likely is guilty of having struck his neighbor, and is to be condemned," (2) from past possibility to future possibility as in consultative reasoning, "He struck his father, so watch out; he will very likely strike his neighbor," or (3) from present possibility to present possibility, as in the epideictic reasoning, "He is vicious enough to strike his father, so very likely he is vicious enough to strike his neighbor and is worthy of our contempt."

4. This temporality of original argument is most obvious, however, in the topic of *proteron/husteron* or, as it has commonly come to be called, in logical demonstration's abstract detemporalization of it, "antecedent/consequence." "Prior/posterior," however, would be closest to its original temporal sense. As we might expect, the discussion of possibility in book 2, chapter 19, provides a number of variations of this topic in the context of both future possibility for consultative rhetoric and past fact for judicial rhetoric. For example, "If what is later [τὸ ὕστερον], either in essence or in coming to pass, happens to be possible, then too, what is earlier [τὸ πρότερον] is possible" and vice versa: for instance, "If a man can come into being, so can a boy . . . and if a boy, so can a man" (see 1392a19–22); "If the beginning is possible, so is the end" (see 18–19); "If what tends to happen later [τὸ ὕστερον] has happened, then so has what has happened before [τὸ πρότερον], for instance, if someone forgot something, he once learned it" (b17–18) (see above on "lacking/having"); "If such things as naturally happen later, or such things as happen for the sake of something else have happened, then either that which happened first has happened or that for the sake of which they happened; for instance, if it thundered, there was lightening" (28–30); and "If the prerequisites for something have come to be, then so too will that thing come to be, for example, if the foundation, then the house" (1393a6–8).

To be sure, this list indiscriminately mixes original, preconceptual senses of the prior and the posterior with derivative, more abstract senses. In the *Metaphysics*, at 1018b9 f., however, Aristotle carefully distinguishes among various senses of prior and posterior, and, conveniently, his way of sorting things out allows us to sort out the original uses of these words from their later, derivative uses. In the first group of meanings he elaborates, things are said to be prior or posterior (1) in a locative sense of nearer to, and further away from some place (1018b11–15), (2) in a temporal sense of being nearer to the present in either the past or future or being further from the present (14–19), (3) in regard to motion, being either prior in the sense of nearer to the first in a sequence of motions, or later and further along (20–22), or (4) in regard to power and choice (*dunamis kai prohairesis*), where who has the power and makes the choice is prior and determines what comes later (22–26). (The "motivation" topics in the *Rhetoric*, book 2, chapter 19 would seem to fit here, for example, "if someone was able to do something and wanted to do it, then [subsequently] he did it" [1392a19–20].) In addition, things are said to be prior or posterior (5) in regard to the ordering (*taxis*) of things as the next to the lowest string is prior to the lowest in the octachord (27–29). Significantly, in all these cases so far, and consequently in all *logoi* or arguments drawing upon them as topics, we are still dealing with the world of things ready at hand and ready to be used in taking care of practical tasks. We have not yet, that is to say, set ourselves at a remove from the temporal-local world in which we originally find ourselves under way.

This is not true, however, for the meanings of prior/posterior, which now follow. For instance, at 1018b30 f., a distinction is introduced between what is prior *logically* (*kata ton logon*), namely universals or *ta katholou*—here clearly in an abstract sense going beyond particular things "taken on the whole"—and what is prior in regard to perception (*kata tên aisthesin*), namely particular things or *ta kath' hekasta*—here still in the preconceptual sense of "things each taken singly" (31–34). Aristotle's mathematical examples make clear the level of abstraction here: following out the logical side of his distinction, he goes on to say that "straightness" is prior to "planeness" because "staighthness" is an attribute of a line whereas "planeness" is an attribute of a surface, and a line is prior to a surface (1018b39–1019a2). Finally, he submits that some things are prior or posterior in regard to their nature and essential being (*kata phusin kai ousian*). Here, in such purely logical considerations, the locative-temporal sense of *proteron* and *husteron* as regards things in the world reached "before" and "after" other things falls away completely (1019a2–4).

3.3.4 "The prior and the posterior" and reasoning by "causality"

Since the topic of "the prior and the posterior" is closely related to explanation by "cause and effect," this is perhaps the place to ask what level of abstraction is implied in causal explanation, as it is used, for instance, in the argument "that something exists if the cause [*aitia*] is present, and if the cause is not present, it does not exist" and vice versa (*Rhet.* 2.23.1400a30–31). For viewed in terms of Heidegger's "hermeneutics of facticity," causal explanation, we can say, is a "founded" (*fundiertes*) phenomenon, the ground and soil (*Boden*) from which it derives being our original speech to one another while we are "there," "in the world," "taking care" of what needs to be done. Put another way, there is a clear shift in our intention from the practical to the theoretical when we stop asking each other *whether to do something* and stop exhorting each other to a decision to do it or not to do it, and begin, instead, to ask and tell each other, in a recounting of something that has become an impartial accounting for it, *why something happens.*

Indeed, as no less an observer than David Hume has pointed out, "cause and effect" originates in our temporal experience of the prior and posterior.[21] The concern for us, however, is rather different from Hume's: it is not our task to call the claims of causal explanation into question, rather we must establish just how much withdrawal and abstraction from that temporal experience is involved in reasoning by cause and effect. We must establish, this is to say, just how much a turn is implied away from the temporal sequence of things happening around us in the practical world and toward the static logic of things statically present (Heidegger: *ständig anwesend*), "placed in view before us" (Heidegger: *vorgestellt*), and merely "on hand" (Heidegger: *vorhanden*). Thus, for us the fact that cause-and-effect explanation originates in an earlier, temporal experience of things is made inescapably obvious not so much by Hume's reduction of abstract ideas to experience as by the very words such explanation uses: for example, causal connections in English, just as in the Greek *hoti* and German *da*, are often stated with temporal words like "since," meaning "afterward" or "hence," meaning "subsequently" or "therefore," meaning "from that time and place on." Turns of speech like "It follows that . . ." did not, this is to say, originally establish the purely logical relationship of "if the class of x, then the class of y," but rather a temporal sequence of "When a particular thing has happened, then (thereafter) another particular thing usually follows." (Compare the German, *Wenn . . . , dann.*)

An indication of the varying degrees of abstraction in causal explanation is to be found in the *Posterior Analytics*, where this kind of "argument" is made fundamental for Aristotle's demonstrative science or *epistêmê*. Near the beginning of this work we find the following:

> We believe ourselves to know each particular thing scientifically in the strict sense [ἐπιστασθαι . . . ἕκαστον ἁπλῶς] as opposed to knowing it in the sophistical way, namely in regard only to what has happened to happen accicentally [κατὰ συμβεβηκός], whenever we believe ourselves also to recognize the cause [τὴν τ′ αἰτίαν] on account of which the thing exists, to recognize that this is the cause of this thing, and to recognize that this thing is not susceptible of being otherwise than it is. (71b9–13)

Here, at least, it is clear that reasoning from the cause, as the defining characteristic of *epistêmê*, involves a high degree of abstraction from the world of temporal things that have just "happened to happen," *kata sumbebêkos*, and a high degree, too, of abstraction to the realm of timeless beings statically present and insusceptible of being otherwise than they are.

But it is not always this way with explanation from the cause in Aristotle, and, surprisingly, not even in his *Posterior Analytics*, which focuses upon the role of the cause in logical science's necessary demonstration and in which, accordingly, we might expect Aristotle to be most consistent in this matter. For instance, at 94a20 ff., in treating the construction of syllogisms, Aristotle begins again, to be sure, with the assertion the "we believe ourselves to know *scientifically* whenever we have seen what the cause is" (20–21: emphasis added). But he then proceeds to differentiate among the four kinds of cause, namely (1) the quiddity or "what it meant to be" the thing, (2) the necessary logical preconditions for a thing to exist, (3) what set in motion the process leading to the thing, and (4) that for the sake of which the thing exists. He goes on to contend that all four are displayed in the middle term of a syllogism (21–24).

Of course, the obvious changes from the standard doctrine of the four causes in the *Physics* (194b24 ff.) are to be explained by the shift here in the *Analytics* from a concern with the concrete physical world as it happens in time to a concern with the abstract logical structure of demonstrative reasoning. In particular, we note that in the *Posterior Analytics* the *Physics*' matter "out of which" the thing came to be (*to ex hou*; 194b24) has been replaced with *logical* preconditions. The exemplification of this cause in the *Posterior Analytics* is, accordingly, purely abstract-mathematical, with no physical dimension remaining: the question to be answered here by giving this cause is "Why is a triangle drawn on the diagonal of a semicircle necessarily a right triangle?" (see 94a28–34). Thus, undeniably, what had been reasoning from the concrete and perceptible material ground in the *Physics* has been transformed here into reasoning by abstract and intelligible logical preconditions and, in effect, has been assimilated to reasoning from the quiddity or what something is in essence. Furthermore, and as the *Metaphysics* also makes clear (987a30 ff.), reasoning from the guiddity or "whatness" of a thing was always abstract theoretical reasoning by *genos/eidos*, or, as this is meant here, by the inclusion of conceptual classes in, or exclusion from, each other, and not by the concrete parts and whole of some imaginable thing, say, the slit, toepiece, and uppers of sandals. Indeed, we have here the basis of *epistêmê*'s abstract demonstration: If all A are the kind of thing that has x as a property, and if B is a form of A, then B has the property x. Or: If no B are a form of A, and if C is a form of B, then C is not a form of A. (See *An. Post.* 2.10.93b29 ff. on the definition [*horismos*].) And the cause essential for "knowing scientifically" would seem to be precisely this one, the "formal" cause.

But, remarkably, even in the *Posterior Analytics* the "first-mover" cause and the cause "for the sake of which" *are* left on the concrete level of practical affairs and historical events, events over time and at a place, and thus, though theoretical, they remain much closer to our original practical argument with each other "there" "in the world." The first-mover cause is illustrated with the following syllogism:

> Those who had committed aggression are those who had war made upon them;
> The Athenians are those who committed aggression;
> therefore, the Athenians had war made upon them.

The middle term and first-mover cause here is "those who have committ*ed* aggression" (see 94a36–b9), and we note, beyond the temporality of this argument, that nothing here is necessary, nothing not susceptible of being otherwise than it was. This, then, is an argument obviously excerpted from an originally rhetorical situation and, even in its uprooted form here, an argument made without recourse to any timeless logic of static essences behind what has just happened to happen accidentally. Ontologically, there is nothing different about it from the rhetorical reasoning by example, investigated above, in which the likelihood of the present king of Persia invading Greece is foreseen in the event he should first invade Egypt. Both arguments are temporal-local, the only difference between them being that the temporality of the first is entirely past time whereas the temporality of the second is from past to future time. Clearly, then, in the first-mover argument we are still under way within the temporal, contingent world even if a decision, say, not to commit aggression, is no longer at issue.

And the same must be said for the fourth cause, that "for the sake of which" something happens, or is done. In answer to the question why one should take a walk after dinner we get the following syllogism:

> Taking a walk after dinner is an act for the sake of normal digestion;
> an act for the sake of normal digestion is a thing conducive to good health;
> therefore, taking a walk after dinner is a thing conducive to good health.
> (see 94b8–26)

Here, though the obvious rhetorical conclusion "So, take a walk after dinner!" has been deleted, the very practical consideration "an act for the sake of normal digestion" is still the "cause" and middle term, not any abstract essence or logical class of things. We note, beyond this, that the premises in this syllogism are not seen with certainty to be so necessarily but "believed to hold good" (see the *dokei gar huparchein* at 16–17).

Moreover, in the "first-mover cause" and the "cause for the sake of which," the word "cause," or *aitia*, continues to display traces of its original judicial-rhetorical and very practical meaning: originally, when we assign the *aitia,* the cause or ground for something having happened, we are assigning responsibility, that is, "blame" for it, as we do, for instance, when we answer the question "Who is the idiot who blocked my driveway with his car?" Obviously, in "explaining" this there will be no recourse to an abstract set of timeless laws governing the relationships to each other of immutable essences beyond the world of local temporal things "ready at hand" (Heidegger: *zuhanden*)—or in this case, not ready at hand. (See *Being and Time* on the deficient modes of *Zuhandenheit,* among these *Aufsässigkeit* or the obtrusiveness of what "lies in the way" [SZ 73–74].)

3.4 The Origin of Topical Argument in the "Prior Accomplishments" (Gadamer: *Vorausleistungen*) of Speech: The Tropes or "Turns" of Speech

In our hermeneutics of the original temporal-local structure of argument from the topics, we have not yet had occasion to deal with the rootedness of the topics in the ground and soil (Heidegger: *Boden*) of ordinary, preconceptual speech. Indeed, we might now say, with Kant, that the "condition of the possibility" for any argument by the topics is in fact the particular natural phrasing according to which these topics are formulated in the first place, for they all follow standard speech modulations and sequences. The fact that they do is made uncircumventable for us by the topics based on nothing but speech, topics like *ptôsis* or "inflection," which until now we have left untreated. Thus, our task in this section will be to "lay bare" and "lay out" hermeneutically just how original argument from the topics is "grounded" in the tropes or "turns" of speech, which is to say, in the ways natural speech phrases things. We will consequently be looking not only at what is said but also at how it said, or, with Cicero, not only at the *quid* but also at its origins in the *quo modo.*

3.4.1 The topic of inflection (*ptôsis*) and the proliferation of *onomata* or word names by the metonymic tropes of "polyptoton," "prosopoeia," "synechdoche," "eponymy," "metaphora," "periphrasis," "eironeia," "hyperbole," "litotes," "catachresis," and "oxymoron"

We may begin with the topic *apo tês ptôseôs* or argument "from inflection," which, significantly, correlates with one of the fundamental tropes, namely "polyptoton" or "multiple inflection," in which the proliferation of a word from one sense, and even one part of speech to another, is accomplished by a modulation of the beginning, middle, or end of it (see *Poetics* 1457a18–23 and Lausberg, HLR, §§640–48). Thus, in the Authorized Version of the New Testament (King James) we have, for instance, "When he ascended upon high he led *captivity captive* and *gave gifts* to men" (Ephesians 4:8). The capacity of speech to spread out this way from "captivity" to "captive" or from "gave" to "gift" provides a key topic in Aristotle's random list in the *Rhetoric*, book 2, chpater 23, where he says,

> Another topic is to be derived from the similar inflections of words [ἐκ τῶν ὁμοίων πτώσεων], for the same thing ought to hold or not hold for words similarly inflected. For instance, it can be argued that the just thing is not in every case good, for otherwise what happens just*ly* would always be good, but to die, even if it is to die justly, is not chosen as a good. (1397a20–23)

Similarly, we find in the *Topics* that in looking for premises for arguments one must see,

> whether like inflections in a defining phrase fit together with like inflections of the word being so defined. For instance, if "beneficial" means "what makes for health," we must see whether "beneficial*ly*" means "what happens *in such a way* as to make for health," and if "having benefit*ed*" means "what *has* made for health." (*Top.* 148a10–13; see also 114a26–b5)

and, again,

> one must take a look at inflections. For if "just*ly*" is said in more ways than one, then so too will "just" be spoken in more than one sense; for corresponding to each "just*ly*" there is a "just." For instance, if "just*ly*" is said in the sense of "judging according to one's own opinion and as one ought," then "just" will be said in similar senses. . . . And so it is in regard to other words: whenever they are said in more than one way, so too will the inflection of them be uttered in more than one sense, and whenever the inflection, then the word itself too. (106b29–107a2)

We should add here that argument by inflection is not just a matter of arguing from within previously established speech modulations, as if these were somehow fixed and static. Rather, inflection is the principal way a word name, or *onoma*, proliferates metonymically into new uses and senses and comes to name different but similar things. Shakespeare, for one, makes frequent use of this seminal capacity of speech in the trope of polyptoton or multiple inflection, as in King Lear's "The thunder would not peace at my bidding" (*King Lear* IV.vi.103). Here the noun "peace" modulates into the verb "to peace." An even more striking example of this metonymic capicity of speech is Capulet's "Thank me no more thankings nor proud me no more prouds" (*Romeo and Juliet* III.v.153).

From these examples we learn that inflection is not so much a way of finding arguments as one of the basic ways that original speech enables us to construe our world in the first place. As Heidegger puts it, "Speech is the house of being."[22] He means by this that, to begin with, it is speech that gives us the ability to interpret and understand things as what they are. Indeed, nothing could be what it is for us without our finding the word to name it: "There be no thing where the word breaks down."[23]

It follows that in the use of words for our original reasoning we do not move from one prelinguistic fact or entity to another but rather, as in polyptoton and the other metonymic tropes, across the web of speech from one word name to another. Words, then, are originally much more than *sêmeia* or signs like "2" and "3" that designate previously envisioned essences in their logical relationships to each other, in the case of "2" and "3," relationships within the series of numbers. Words, this is to say, are not at all mere signs for things that already "are" prior to our convening upon the signs with which to signify them. Rather, originally words are names, *onomata*, that give not only people but things their being in the first place precisely by naming them as, for example, in "And they shall call his name Immanuel, which interpreted [ὅ ἐστιν μεθερμηνευόμενον], means God with us" (Matthew 1:23; see Isaiah 7:14).

Hence, there is a great deal more than folklore reflected in the topic *nomen et omen* ("name and omen"): "Another topic," says Aristotle, "is derived from the name [ἀπὸ τοῦ ὀνόματος] as in Sophocles' 'Plainly, Steely you are as you bear the name' [σαφῶς Σιδηρὼ καὶ φοροῦσα τοὔνομα]" (*Rhet.* 1400b17–18). Indeed, an earlier understanding of original speech is discoverable here, for, as Eric Havelock points out, it is characteristic of earlier oral and preliterate speech to make naming universal and thus to extend it far beyond the naming of people.[24] In oral speech the phenomena of the world were not yet construed in terms of some invisible static, necessary laws of cause and effect behind them, but rather as a narrative sequence of actions and births and deaths, as these have happened to happen over time. Hence, they were to be accounted for only in attributing them to, or "blaming" them on, personified agents, like the "wrath" of Achilles, who "did" them. (See 3.3.4 above on the original sense of *aitia* as blame.) Now, in original speech these personified agent things *are* what they were named to be. Thus, the trope of *prosopoeia* or personification is not just the artistic device that it became once speech had been reduced to a language of signs signifying preexistent objects. On the contrary, its naming is the basic trope, the wellspring of original speech itself.

Now, despite his Platonic tendency to reduce names to signs wherever possible, even Aristotle himself extends this earlier onomatic or nominative understanding of speech well beyond the naming of persons. For instance, in the *Topics* he suggests that it is sometimes useful to refer the *onoma* or word name back to the descriptive phrase (*logos*) from which it derives rather than to take the word in the currently established meaning for it. For example, *eu-psuchos*, the established meaning for which is "courageous," might better be understood, he suggests, as being "well" disposed in one's "soul" and, likewise, *eu-daimon* or happy, as "in good spirits" (*Top.* 112a33–39). This tracing of the word name to its original components—a strategy often employed by Heidegger, incidentally—tells us how the name originally names the thing in question, much as Herodicus's tracing the name "Thrasymachus" to its components, *thrasus* or bold in the *machê* or fight, tells us how the name originally names the person (see *Rhet.* 1400b20–21). With Heidegger, we could say the spoken name tells us how speech originally lets the thing be what it is.

In the end, even the topic derived from definition, *ex horismou*, is based in this same kind of nomination (*Rhet.* 1398a15 ff.). To be sure, the example given here is Socrates' defense based on "what" the spiritual or *to daimonion* is said to be, and we might well expect that, accordingly, an essential *to ti ên einai*, a "what [in essence] it meant to be the thing" would be introduced. But that expectation goes noticeably unfulfilled: "You say," so the argument might be approximately restated, "that I do not believe that gods exist, however, you allow that I do believe in the spiritual. But is not the spiritual either itself a god or at least the work of a god? And even if one only believes that the work of a god exists, then, of necessity, one believes that gods exist" (see 1398a15–17). If we look closely, we see that, in fact, the "definition" here is not attained by reducing the word name to a sign and then establishing the static logical order of *eidê* or forms governing the thing "in itself" (*kath' hauto*) which the sign signifies. In other words, the definition here is not attained in the way that the definition of a mathematical entity is attained, say, a number, like 2 or 3, or a geometrical element, like a point, line, plane figure, or solid. Nor, if viewed ontologically, is the "division" (*dihairesis*) of *to daimonion* into either "a god" or "the work of a god" anything like the abstract genus/species division of straight-sided plane figures into three-sided, four-sided, five-sided figures, and so forth, where insight into the intelligible *eidos* or conceptual "look" of the thing is prerequisite.

Rather, the definition of *to daimonion* here, of "the spiritual," is based entirely on listening to the reverberations of speech that lead us to how the word name is said on various occasions, be this in just one sense or be this in multiple senses as is "sharp," which when said of a note is the contrary of "flat," and when said of a knife is the contrary of "dull" (see *Top.* 106a9 ff.).

Indeed, even the topic in the *Rhetoric* specifically derived from "division" (*ek dihaireseôs*; 1398a30 f.) is, despite the Platonic tradition's appropriation of this term for classification by abstract universals, quite far removed from the division of such universals that we know from Plato's dialogues, say, of the genus numbers into the species odd and even (see the *Phaedo*, 103e f). Indeed, here in the *Rhetoric* it is simply a matter of practical (judicial) elimination: "Everyone commits injustice for the sake of three things, that is, for the sake of this, this, or that. But of these three, two are impossible and the third not even they themselves allege" (see 1398a30–33; originally the references would have been to specific concrete ends).

Besides polyptoton there are other, even more basic, ways, however, that original, onomatic speech proliferates and, in so doing, provides the ground and soil for reasoning from the topics. Although speech proliferates in polyptoton through the inflection of a word name, in other metonymic tropes speech proliferates, either by the substitution of one word name for another as in the paradigmatic "synechdoche," which renames the whole by "taking out" a part, as in "All *hands* on deck!" and vice versa, or by "eponymy" or "naming after" something. These are such basic forms of a word name's proliferiation that Aristotle simply calls them both *metaphor* or "carry over" as such (see *Poetics* 1457b6 ff.). Metaphor, he says, consists in "transposition" (*epiphora*) of a name to some other thing which is now taken in a sense that initially was foreign to it, for instance, when (1) the general kind (*genos*) is transferred to a specific sort (*eidos*) of that kind, (2) the specific sort to the general kind, (3) one specific form to another, or when (4) a proportional analogy is drawn in which one of the two terms on one side of the equation is transferred to one of the two terms on the other side.

Aristotle's examples make clear that here *genos* and *eidos* still have their original sense of "kind" and "form" and that we are not yet moving "demonstratively" from one abstract class to another but still within the realm of imaginable concrete experiences: for (1), the transferrence of *genos* to *eidos*, he takes "There *stands* my ship" (*Odyssey* 1.185), where the general kind of thing, "standing" is substituted for the specific form of that kind, "lying at anchor." For (2), the transferrence of *eidos* to *genos*, he takes "Indeed, *ten thousand* brave deeds Odysseus has done" (*Iliad*

2.272), where the *eidos* or specific form of something is "ten thousand" and the *genos* or general kind, "many." (As we will see, "ten thousand" is also the metonymic trope "hyperbole.") And for (3), the transference from specific form to specific form, he takes the phrase "*drawing off* from his soul with bronze," where one specific form of something, "drawing off," is substituted for another, "cutting off," and where both are specific forms of the general kind, "taking away" (see 1457b9–26). (We might add that "bronze" here is the metonymic trope "periphrasis" or "circumlocution," which is to say, the substitution of a description for a name, as in *polumechanos,* or man "of many devices" for Odysseus, whose name, of course, was a description to begin with, the "hated one" (see *Odyssey* 19.406–9 and chapter 4 below).

For (4) or analogy, Aristotle gives the following example: since old age is to life as evening is to the day, evening can be called "the old age of the day," as it is in Empedocles (Aristotle, *Poet.* 1457b23–26). With Heidegger, we might say that this renaming or metonymy, too, is "apophantic" insofar as saying it lets the thing spoken of appear (*apophainesthai*) in a new light and gives it new being it had not had before (see SZ 32–34). It would be more appropriate for us, however, to say that any metonymy lets us *hear* about the thing named in new ways.

"Eironeia," "hyperbole," and "litotes," or irony, exaggeration, and understatement, are still other metonymic tropes by which word names can proliferate into new senses, and as such they too are important in the discovery of premises in original argument by the topics. Here the speaker, generally by intonation, says word names in such a way that they name the contrary of what they usually do. For instance, in the case of irony, "Wonderful!" if voiced appropriately comes to mean "awful," or "terrific" can even revert to its original sense of "terrible." Similar in this regard are "litotes," or understatement, as in Paul's "I am . . . a citizen of no insignificant city" (Acts 21:39), and its opposite, "hyperbole," as in Virgil's lovely "Illa vel intactae segetis per summa volaret / Gramina nec terneras cursu laesisset aristas" (She would have flown over the top of uncut blades / neither would have hurt the grain's tender ears in her course) (*Aeneid* 7.808–9; cited by Quintilian, *Inst. Or.* 8.6.69). These, too, are ways, dramatic ways, in fact, in which spoken word names continue to proliferate by renaming different but similar things.

Finally in this category of metonymic tropes, we come to their most radical form, "catechresis" and "oxymoron." In catechresis or deliberate "misuse"—the Latin rhetoricians even called it *abusio*—word names, usually adjectives, acquire new meaning by being conjoined with other word names in ways prohibited by the canons of standard usage, as in "cold comfort," "green wounds," "white sustenance," and "dark brightness." This last is also an oxymoron, or, as the metonymy by which this topic is named indicates—literally, "sharp-witted fool"—a self-contradictory conjunction of contraries. The oxymoron, then, is not only a way that speech proliferates but, more basically, a way that original speech says and "lets be" the original temporal world of unstable, contradictory being. For if being and time are fused as they are originally, whatever *is, is* only in simultaneously not being any longer what it is but being already the opposite of itself: with Heraclitus, dark is always already no longer dark but already bright. Hence, when Shakespeare has Romeo say

> O brawling love! O loving hate!
> O anything of nothing first create!
> O heavy lightness, serious vanity!
> Misshapen chaos of well-seeming forms!
> Feather of lead, bright smoke, cold fire, sick health
> still-waking sleep, that is not what it is! (*Romeo and Juliet* I.i.174–79),

this startling violation of demonstrative logic's first principle that "It is impossible that at the same time something both hold and not hold for the same thing and in the same respect" in fact "tells it the way it is," the way it "is," this is to say, in our original experience of being as temporal-local coming to pass (compare Aristotle, *Metaphy.* 1005b19–21; see chapter 4 below).[25]

(As none other than Yogi Berra put it, when asked about playing in the shadows at Yankee Stadium, "It gets late early around here." One might not expect to find in a baseball player such ontological genius for "telling it the way it is" in violation of demonstrative logic's laws of noncontradiction and self-identity, but no end of such bon mots are attributed to him, among them his comment on a New York restaurant, "Nobody goes there anymore; it's too crowded." Perhaps a more acceptable example for standard academic discourse would be Mark Twain's comment on Wagner's music, "It's not as bad as it sounds!")

3.4.2 Temporal/acoustical phrasing, in the diachronic tropes of "symphony" (parallelism) and "antiphony" (antithesis), as the ground of the topic of "sameness," and of the topic of "difference" in its forms of "opposites" and "correlatives"

Having passed the metonymic tropes in review let us treat now to the diachronic tropes, which establish the temporal sequence in which spoken words are voiced diachronically or "over time." We will begin with the two basic diachronic tropes that underlie virtually all reasoning by the topics, namely what a later literary and visio-spatially oriented "rhetoric" of reading words on a surface has called "parallelism" and "antithesis," literally, "along side each other" and "placed opposite." To preserve their basis in audio-temporality of original orality we, however, will call them "symphony" and "antiphony." In the phrasing of symphony a number of like phrasings are repeated one after the other as, for example, in Lincoln's "government of the people, by the people, for the people," each part of which would, we can presume, receive the same accentuation and intonation. In the phrasing of antiphony, on the other hand, one phrase is voiced in contrast to another different from it as in St. Paul's "Charity never faileth, but whether there be prophecies, they shall fail" (1. Corinthians 13:8), where, in English, for example, the rising intonation of "prophesies" in the second phrase would counter the lower pitch of "charity" in the first. In Western rhetoric the origins of symphony lie in the Greek "*te* . . . *kai*" or "both this . . . and also this" phrasing, and of antiphony, in the Greek "*men* . . . *de*" or "on the one hand, this, . . . on the other, that." (It is worth noting, in this regard, that our modern "literary" translations of Paul and, with the exception of African-American churches and the Evangelical churches influenced by them, even the readings of these translations aloud, do not take such considerations of original orality into account.)

In our hermeneutical "laying bare" of original argument we have now penetrated to something even more basic to argument than the proliferation of language through the metonymic tropes; indeed, we have penetrated to something that the metonymic tropes in fact presuppose. For each time a word proliferates into a new sense, be this metonymy or "renaming" by polyptoton, personification, or irony, it carries itself over into a meaning that in some ways sounds *like* the original meaning but in some ways sounds *different*. With that we have uncovered the core originative function of the spoken word.

Gadamer, who has broken the ground for us here, puts it this way:

> If someone carries out the transference of an expression from one thing to a different thing, he does so with regard to something both things have in common, *but this in no way has to be the universality of a genus*. On the contrary, he is following his ever widening experience, which takes note of similarities, be these the similarities of the things as they appear or be they similarities in their meaningfulness for us. The ingeniousness of our speech-consciousness lies in its knowing how to express such similarities. We call this the basic "metaphorics" of speech, and we must recognize that when the metaphorical sense of a word is dismissed as an improper use, this only expresses the prejudice of a logical theory foreign to our actual experience of speech. (WM 406; emphasis added)

He continues,

> It goes without saying that the special nature of our experience of speech, which is manifested in just such a *transference [or metapherein], is in no way the fruit of any process of concept formation by abstraction. . . . Classificatory logic starts with the prior logical accomplishment [die logische Vorausleistung] that speech has already performed for it.* (id.; emphasis added)

Extending this thought, we can say that demonstration's inference by one class of things's inclusion in, or exclusion from, another class of things, as in "All A are B" or "No P are Q," is an abstraction from our original reasoning by the phrasings "both this and this" and "on the one hand, this, on the other, that." Demonstration's inference, this is to say, is an abstraction from original reasoning by the topics of similarity and difference, topics that are based in the diachronic tropes of symphony and antiphony.

As an illustration of this metaphorical power of speech to reason from one thing to another similar but different thing, Gadamer cites Speusippus's reasoning by proportional analogy, for example, "As wings are to birds so fins are to fish" (407), and to trace this way of arguing back to Aristotle's "To transfer well is to recognize what is in common" (407; see *Poetics* 22.1459a8: τὸ γὰρ εὖ μεταφέρειν το τὸ ὅμοιον θεωρεῖν ἐστιν), with which we are already familiar, albeit in a somewhat different translation from Gadamer's (see 3.3.1 above). And, indeed, in our own examination of Aristotle's treatment of analogy in the *Poetics* (1457b17 ff.) we have already seen the justification for precisely this connection of metaphoric transferrence and reasoning by analogy. However, what we now see, in going beyond Gadamer, is that this "metaphorics" of speech derives from the *way in which—quo modo*—words are phrased when they are spoken. It derives, this is to say, from the diachronic tropes employed in diction and delivery. For viewed logically, the two fundamental diachronic tropes from which the primary topics of similarity and difference are engendered are precisely symphony, whose phrasing links similar but different things, and antiphony, whose phrasing contrasts different but similar things. Thus, *these two tropes are phrasings which make reasoning by the primary topics of similarity and difference possible in the first place.*

Even the topics of the opposites, namely contraries, contradiction, and lacking, and of the correlatives and the more and the less, the part and the whole, and the prior and posterior, are, it turns out, rooted in these two basic diachronic tropes, for in being either opposite poles of the same thing, more or less of the same thing, parts of the same whole, or earlier or later than something similar, they are all variations of difference in what is similar. Hence, in extending Gadamer, we can say that these two diachronic tropes, symphony and antiphony, in all the variations of these which we are about to explore, are the origin of the "prior accomplishment" that speech has always already performed for us whenever we set about finding the premises for an argument at the basic "places," or *topoi* of similarity and difference, the latter in its forms of opposites, the more and the less, the part and the whole, and the prior and the posterior. With the abstractions of logic's reasoning by classes of things, by abstract *genos* and *eidos*, taken down, and with the diachonic tropes of symphony and antiphony thus "laid bare," or better, made audible beneath them, these diachronic tropes can now be "layed out" hermeneutically as the originative turns of speech at the ground of all original argument by the topics.

Can there be any doubt, for example, that beneath Plato's dialectic of the *eidê* or abstract conceptual "looks" to things, beneath his collection into a *genos* and division into *eidê*, lies the *audible phrasing* of the Greek diachronic tropes of *te . . . kai* and *men . . . de*, of "both this . . . and also this," and "on the one hand, this, . . . on the other, that"? Can there be any doubt that it is these Greek ways of phrasing things acoustically that generates his optical dialectic of the ideas? For it is surely no coincidence that when first elaborating the hierarchies of the ideas in the *Phaedo*, Plato uses acoustical language: "If, however, someone should attack the hypothesis itself, you would," he says, "let that pass and not answer until you had examined whether the things that follow from it seem to you *consonant* with each other or *dissonant* [εἴ σοι ἀλλέλοις συμφωνεῖ ἢ διαφωνεῖ]" (101d; emphasis added). Although the examples which follow, for instance, the collection of the different species under a common genus "Number" and, in turn, the division of "Number" back into the species of "Odd" and "Even," make clear that Plato always had in mind the *eidos* or conceptual "look" to something (see 103e f.), even he starts from *phônê*, from the voice and sound of the spoken word (see chapter 4 below on the *Phaedo* and *Symposium*).

3.4.3 The communication of *pathos* in original argument; the diachronic tropes of tone, tempo, and rhythm: "anaphora," "asyndeton," "ellipsis," "epistrophe," "alliteration," "assonance," and "asterismos"

In our consideration of the metonymic and diachronic tropes up to now, our concern has been with the fundamental role played by these turns of speech in finding *logoi* or arguments from the topics. We have, accordingly, been focusing exclusively on the ground of the "logical" dimension of argument, the *logos* itself. But in the end, as even Aristotle himself allows, even this is still an abstraction from what really goes on in original argument, and we need to take it down.

Indeed, in the *Rhetoric,* book 1, chapter 2, Aristotle tells us that there are, in fact, not one but three ways for an argument to achieve conviction and trust—*pistis,* it will be recalled means both conviction and trust. One way, he tells us, consists "in the character of the one speaking [ἐν τῷ ἔθει τοῦ λέγοντος], another, in disposing the listener in a certain way [ἐν τῷ τὸ ἀκροατὴν διαθεῖναί πως], and yet another, in the argument itself [ἐν αὐτῷ τῷ λόγῳ] by which something is shown or appears to be shown" (1356a1–4). "Disposing the listener," we note, has to do with getting him or her to feel a certain way, with putting him or her in a certain mental "tenor" (Heidegger: *Stimmung*) and disposition (Aristotle: *diathesis*; Heidegger: *Befindlichkeit*). Hence, the *pathos* or feeling engendered by the speech is the concern (see 1356a14).

Just what are we to make of this? To begin with, Aristotle has made it clear here that in rhetorical conviction the argument or *logos* itself does not stand on its own; on the contrary, in any successful rhetorical argument it is conjoined with *êthos* and *pathos,* with the character of the speaker and the appropriate feelings or *pathê* that are to be communicated in the argument or *logos.* Consequently we, who are uncovering and explicating the structure of argument as it originally takes place in rhetoric, can no longer be concerned solely with what is "shown" in the argument, with what its language brings into the open for us to *see,* rather we must consider what the argument gives us to *hear.* From now on, and, in particular, in continuing our consideration of the the diachronic tropes, we must pay attention to the tone of what is said, for *êthos* and *pathos* are both communicated acoustically.

Put another way, for us diction and delivery, *lexis* and *hupokrisis,* under which consideration of the diachronic tropes is largely to be subsumed, cannot be separated from the logic of an argument and relegated to mere ornamentation as they were for Peter Ramus, Port Royal, and the Royal Society. In maintaining that they cannot, we will, of course, be contesting the entire logical tradition since Port Royal and the Royal Society, a tradition that sees in mathematical demonstration the essence of all valid argument, and that, accordingly, would banish diction and delivery to mere "rhetoric." And, to be sure, there is, on the face of it, something to be said for the "Royal Society." No one, it seems, cares about the character of someone who would demonstrate the Pythagorean theorem, nor about the feelings we might have about right triangles, and hence the diction and delivery by which *êthos* and *pathos* are communicated would seem to be entirely extrinsic concerns here.

But as Heidegger has pointed out for us in reference to Aristotle's *Metaphysics*, 982b22–23, a very specific kind of feeling is in fact presupposed and absolutely indispensable for the effectiveness of even such a theoretical argument as a mathematical demonstration, namely, in this case, the detachment of *rhastonê* or ease and the disengagement of *diagôgê* or just passing time; one must be "in the mood" for mathematics and "feel like" doing it (see SZ 138 and 2.1 above). It follows that even mathematical argumentation has, despite what its proponents claim, its own prerequisite and proper *dis*passionate diction and delivery, a monotonic diction and delivery so "toned down" as to approximate in speech silent reading, and which today provides the paradigm for all academic elocution.[26] Accordingly, we will maintain, against the modern tradition of "logic and critical reasoning," that diction and delivery are indeed an intrinsic component of the process of *all* argumentative conviction and indissociable from it.

At this point, then, we will need, once again, to go beyond Gadamer in our analysis, beyond, this is to say, consideration of the merely "logical" function of the tropes. For given the indissoluble fusion of the *logos* of original argument with *êthos* and *pathos*, our concern cannot any longer be just with what these "turns" of speech have "accomplished" logically. Rather, our concern now must also be with the way in which they also predispose the listener to either trust or mistrust the character (*êthos*) of the speaker and, by the very sound of them, dispose the listener to have a certain feeling (*pathos*) about the subject matter. Accordingly, we need to look at the diachronic tropes of "symphony" and "antiphony" again, and this time in a new way. We shall consider, first, the communication of feelings by the sound of what is said when these tropes are employed and, second, their role in the communication of the character of the speaker.

What we have called symphony and the literary tradition, parallelism, consists, as we have said, in a number of similarly intoned phrasings that express variations of the same thing. Symphony occurs, for instance, at the conclusion of Lincoln's Gettysburg Address:

> It is rather for us to be here dedicated to the great task remaining before us—that from these honored dead we take increased devotion to that cause for which they gave the last full measure of devotion; that we here highly resolve that these dead shall not have died in vain; that this nation, under God, shall have a new birth of freedom; and that government of the people, by the people, for the people, shall not perish from the earth.

One instance of symphony here consists in the temporal sequence of four "that . . ." phrases which specify four similar yet different tasks remaining to be carried out. Another is present in the strict equality or *isocolon* within the last of these "that . . ." phrases, in the "of the people, by the people, for the people." Taking a purely logical perspective—the silent reader's—we can *see* why the visual "schema" or "figure" of "parallelism" would be called "enumeratio" by the Latin rhetoricians; indeed, today, when an affective neutrality prerequisite for "rational" discourse is the norm, when hearing the temporal sound of what is said has fallen into disregard and envisioning its logical content spatially is everything, we would very likely "itemize" this figure diagrammatically on a page or screen with a "bulleted" "first, . . . , second, . . . , third, and so forth." Moreover, we have a clear illustation here of the logical capacity of speech to gather what is similar and analogous into a whole and yet, at the same time, to divide what is different into parts, the capacity of speech which, as Gadamer has shown us, both precedes and makes possible abstract logic's classification by genus and species. Lincoln, then, is able to find the premises for his exhortation to his audience by tracing out the different branches of speech that stem from a common origin.

But for Lincoln, who is not concerned to demomstrate something for dispassionate spectators, but rather to convince his listeners to choose a course of action, the sound of what he says *is* a conscious and crucial consideration, crucial, that is, for getting his audience to feel a certain way about the cause that he is exhorting them to carry on. It is not by accident, for example, that he begins this speech with the solemn-sounding "assonance" and "alliteration" of "f*our* s*core* and *s*even" rather than with "87." Hence, we find within the overall trope of symphony, on the one hand, diachronic tropes that by their phrasing effect over time a particular tempo, rhythm, and stress and, on the other, diachronic tropes that effect a particular sonority by variations in volume, pitch, and timbre. We note that these, the first primarily temporal, the second primarily tonal, are the musical materials with which any acoustical art must work, *including the art of rhetorical conviction.*[27]

With regard to tempo, rhythm, and stress, we note that the repetition of the same word "that" at the beginning of each of the symphonic phrases—a trope known as "anaphora" or "carry-over"—marks off the pulse in a stately and regular rhythm, the urgent tempo of which is nevertheless sustained by "asyndeton," or the "lack of conjunctions" between these phrases, and which is even accelerated by the asyndeton of the climactic "government of the people, by the people, for the people," and by the "ellipsis" or "dropping out" of "government" in the second and third elements of this second instance of "symphony." Here the "epistrophe," or "turning out" of the same word "people" at the end, further propels the phrase toward its cadenced resolution and the release of its building tension in the concluding "shall not perish from the earth."

The trope of epistrophe is also present at the beginning in the doubling of "devotion" at the ends of its opening and closing phrases: "that . . . we take increased *devotion* to that cause to which they gave the last full measure of *devotion*." Here, however, antiphony (antithesis) is present as well, for the difference in these two "devotions" is more the point than their similarity: one is to be taken, "that we *take* . . . ," whereas the other has been given, "they *gave*," and one is to be "increased devotion," whereas the other was the "last full measure of devotion." To be sure, this counterpoint plays an important *logical* role insofar as the topics of correlatives and the more and the less derive from what this antiphonal speech sequence "accomplishes." But it is also of the greatest acoustical and, hence, affective importance: as in music's antiphon, one phrase answers the other thus providing both metric and tonal symmetry and stability. If, like an actor, a *hupokritês*, we were to consider the delivery of this passage, its *hupokrisis* or *pronuntiatio*, if we were to consider how to say it out loud and phrase it vocally, we could surmise that in Lincoln's delivery the raised pitch and stress on "take" would very likely correspond to the raised pitch and stress on "gave," and the raised pitch and stress on "increased," to the raised pitch and stress on "measure."

Of this last we cannot be sure, of course, for the oratorical tradition of how Lincoln actually spoke this written text has long since broken off, and we are left with something like the mere written score of a piece of music for which a tradition of performance no longer exists. This circumstance tells us a great deal: after Ramus, Port Royal, and the Royal Society, we have been so fixated on the "pure" logical content of what we say and so convinced that the only appropriate passion for understanding it is the dispassion of mathematical rationality, that we have become wholly oblivious to the sound of how we say it. As a matter of fact, today one would have to study musical performance or acting to get even a hint of the central importance of phrasing and enunciation for the interpretation of a text. The eviscerated and monotonic Bible translations of today are one indication of the huge loss here, for, in fact, there is no way to say them aloud and make them sound like anything at all. Even here, where it would seem most obvious, we seem to have forgotten that, as opposed to reading the voiceless written word silently and dispassionately, *hearing* the spoken word is not just a matter of cognition but also of volition and that we must not only be brought to see that something is so but moved by the sound of what we hear to do what we are called upon to do. Even the uninterpreted written text of the Gettysburg Address that we have, however, makes clear that Lincoln himself did not forget the sound of what is said. For in addition to its metric, rhythmic, and cadenced phrasing we can read and see—if not hear—frequent and considered use of the diachronic tropes of pitch and timbre, in particular "alliteration," which repeats or varies consonants, and "assonance," which repeats or varies vowels.

For a starting point in our hermeneutical explication of these tropes of pitch and timbre we may turn again to Aristotle's *Poetics.* In chapter 20, 1456b22 ff., he distinguishes among the basic elements or *stoicheia* of diction. It is wrong to call these elements "letters," which, of course, are written, for Aristotle specifically says that they are voiced sounds, *phônai,* of which there are three sorts, the vowel, half-vowel, and mute, the *phônêen, hêmiphônon,* and *aphônon*: "the vowel," he continues,

> has an audible voice [ἔχον φωνὴν ἀκουστήν] without the resistance [of lips, throat, teeth, or tongue]; a half-vowel, such as S and R, has an audible voice along with such resistance; and a mute, such as G or D, as just this resistance by itself, has no voice at all but acquires an audible voice [if uttered] along with elements that do have one. (1456b26–31)

Among the mutes, which is to say, consonants, that are voiced only in conjunction with vowels or half-vowels, English speakers may distinguish gutterals like c, k, or g, labials like b and p, and dentals like d and t, all of which stop the sound more or less abruptly if they are at the end of a syllable or punctuate the sound more or less sharply if they are at the beginning. In contrast, the half-vowels such as l, m, n, r, and s, which we would call consonants too but also liquids, let the sound continue. With Aristotle we might also add aspiration with h, as in ch, ph (f), th, and sh, and before vowels (see 1456b33), which softens the sound. (In English, like Greek, the liquid s can also be hardened by combination with a dental or gutteral, as in z [ds] or x [ks].) What Aristotle, as well as the entire subsequent science of phonetics, has failed to tell us, however, is *what role these various voicings play in the communication of a pathos or affect.* For beginning with Aristotle these voiced sounds are considered only in regard to their ultimate contribution in signfying (*sêmainein*) propositional content or "states of affairs": the spoken sounds and the syllables composed of these are each taken to be an as yet insignificant (*asêmos*) component of what will be significant words; the word made up of them is "a significant compound voiced sound" [φωνὴ συνθετὴ σημαντική] (145712). Even so, from Heidegger's exploitation of conjunction of "voicing" and feeling in the German word *Stimmung* we may conclude that originally the role of voiced sounds in communication of the affects must have been central.

That it was is further confirmed by the tropes of timbre we find in this passage of Lincoln's address. Striking, in this regard, are the alliterations in the d's of "*d*edicate*d*," "*d*ea*d*," "*d*evotion," "*d*ie*d*," and in the p's of "*p*eo*p*le, . . . *p*eo*p*le, . . . *p*eo*p*le, . . . *p*erish." With these alliterations of dentals and labials Lincoln artfully interweaves assonances by modulating the vowel colors of "d*ea*d," "d*ie*d," "v*ai*n" and "p*eo*ple," "p*e*rish," "*ea*rth." In this way he achieves a euphony appropriate to the panegyric for the fallen soldiers which he has built into his consultative exhortation to keep on with the war. In largely avoiding cacaphonous and abrasive gutterals like k and sharp concluding dentals like t, and, further, in choosing the aspirated and softened sh of "perish" and th of "earth," for example, and in his frequent use of concluding liquids as in "fu*ll* measu*r*e of devotio*n*," Lincoln achives a gentle yet impressive tone suitable for voicing the feeling of solemn awe in which his praise and ultimate exhortation is embedded. In contrast, Macbeth's depiction of life as a "player tha*t* *s*tru*ts* and fre*ts* i*ts* hour upon the *st*age" and a "*t*ale *t*ol*d* by an i*d*io*t*" (*Macbeth* V.v.20–29) shows, for instance, how a harsh and caphonous voicing communicates despair and disgust. And even the assonance of the vowel modulation here in "fr*e*ts *i*ts h*ou*r *u*pon" is ugly.[28]

We have noted that, taken logically, the diachronic tropes of symphony and antiphony are correlates: whereas symphony conveys the likeness of different things, antiphony stresses the difference of like things. We have noted, too, that antiphony is especially natural to Greek with its basic and frequent *men . . . de* constructions, or "On the one hand, this; on the other hand, that," and that the trope antiphony is precisely the "prior accomplishment" of speech which underlies the Greek thinkers' ability to argue dialectically from the topic of contraries: "Some say this, but we, in contrast, say the opposite." The capacity of Greek to generate this dialectical kind of argument is operative even in Saint Paul, for instance, in 1 Corinthians 13, cited here in the King James version, which for the most part renders Paul's Greek diction accurately:

> Charity never faileth: but whether there be prophecies [ἔιτε δὲ προφητεῖαι], they shall fail, whether there be tongues, they shall cease; whether there be knowledge, it shall vanish away. For now we know in part, and we prophesy in part. But when [ὅταν δὲ] that which is perfect is come, then that which is in part shall be done away. When I was a child, I spake as a child, I understood as a child, I thought as a child: but when I became a man I put away childish things. For now we see through a glass, darkly; but then [τότε δὲ], face to face: now I know in part; but then [τότε δὲ] shall I know even as also I am known. And now [νυνὶ δὲ]

abideth faith, hope, charity, these three; but the greatest of these [μείζων δὲ τούτον] is charity. (8–13)

There are antiphonies here, first, in the contraries of "never faileth" versus the "shall fail," "shall cease," and "shall vanish away"; second, in the "in part" versus "that which is perfect"; third, in the "that which is perfect is come" versus "that which is in part shall be done away"; fourth, in the then "a child" versus the now "a man"; fifth, in the "now through a glass darkly" versus "then face to face"; and, finally, in the "now I know in part" versus the "then I shall know as I am known." (The "through a glass, darkly," if something of a mistranslation, renders Paul's *anastrophe* or "inversion" and "pleonism," δι' ἐσόπτρου ἐν αἰνίγματι, nicely.)

But as was the case with the symphonies in Lincoln's address, the antiphonies here obviously have more than logical importance: they create the balanced antiphonic phrasing which is appropriate to the dignity and weight of Paul's homiletic *parainesis* or exhortation, and which the King James version, largely following Paul's Greek, enhances with a number of other diachronic tropes. We find, for example, anaphora, or "carry-over" of the first word, in the "whether there be . . . , whether there be . . . , whether there be . . ." We find epistrophe, or making the phrases "result" in the same word at the end, in the " . . . in part; . . . in part" and in the "as a child . . . as a child . . . as a child. And we find, of course, the metonymic trope of polyptoton in the "child . . . childish" and the "know . . . known," but here its function is metric and primarily syntactical. The building tension of the sequence of antiphonies comes to a cadenced resolution in a concluding symphony: To the "now we see through a glass darkly" Paul, employing "asyndeton" or the "lack of conjunctions," adds, "And now abideth faith, hope, charity, these three." The "these three" is an "asterismos"—an asterisk or "namely, . . . ," which in retarding the accelerating forward impulse brings the whole passage to its actual conclusion. For the "but the greatest of these is charity," though perpetuating the antithetical structure, serves at the same time as a segue into the next thought, "Follow after charity . . ." (14:1).

Notable precisely for their absence here are other diachronic tropes that often accompany antiphony but that would have disturbed the measured and regular pace of Paul's lesson had he employed them, namely the "ellipsis," which effects a syncopated rhythm by "dropping out" something, sometimes even the "but" of an antithesis, as in Shakespeare's "he, in twelve, found truth in all but one; I, in twelve thousand, none" (see *Richard II*, IV i 170), and the *chiasmus* or "crisscross," which even makes the phrasing unsteady and giddy, as in Samuel Johnson's "By day the frolic and the dance by night" (see Corbett, *Classical Rhetoric*, 443).

Again, the point here is that the diachronic tropes are not merely pleasant decoration and ingratiating displays of the speaker's urbanity. In setting the tone of what is said they do not merely "sweeten something up" in order to get the listener to swallow it, as the origins of the Latin *persuadere* in *suavis* or "sweet" would seem to indicate, and as Royal Society logicians would have us believe. Rather, they are primarily communicants of the auditory affective setting, of the proper "voicing" or *Stimmung* in which alone the message can be heard and received, and without which no conviction can be brought about. What Heidegger has achieved in getting behind the apparent severance of "cognition" from "emotion" in a pure, mathematical logic and in showing the embeddedness of original practical understanding, and, in fact, even abstract theoretical cognition, in a prerequisite feeling or *pathos*, makes clear to us that the sound and phrasing of what is said, far from being a mere ornament, is intrinsic to its communication. The diachronic tropes display for us, in other words, the indissociability of *logos* and *pathos*.

3.4.4 The communication of *êthos* in original argument by the diachronically disruptive tropes of parenthesis, apostrophe, epanorthosis, and asiopesis

But what about Aristotole's third *pithonon* or "convincer," *êthos*? (see *Rhet.* 1.2.1355b26). What role do the diachronic tropes play here? Thus far we have been considering the diachronic tropes, first, with regard to their correlation with topics, which is to say, with regard to their *logos*, and then, second, with regard to their role in the communication of the affects, which is to say, their *pathos*. But, we now must ask, finally, about their role in the communication of the character of the speaker. After all, as even Aristotle himself maintains that

> it is not true, as some of the experts on the art of rhetoric say in their handbooks, that the clemency of the one speaking [τὴν ἐπιείκειαν τοῦ λέγοντος] adds nothing to the convincingness of an argument, rather character has, we might say, virtually the greatest power of conviction of all [κυριωτάτην ἔχει πίστιν τὸ ἦθος]. (*Rhet.* 1356a11–14)

This crucial assertion, to which we will often have occasion to return, brings to light another important difference between the Latin *persuasio* and the Greek *pistis, peithô,* and *peithein.* As we have noted, *pistis* implies a faith and trust in someone that goes beyond merely having been brought to believe that something is so. Thus, the very word *pistis* takes us back before the abstraction from the practical world in which we were engaged with other people, each one more or less trustworthy, in getting things done. It takes us back *before* our having become uninvolved onlookers looking on at states of affairs "on hand before us" (Heidegger: *vorhanden*), and back *before* our arriving at impartial and disengaged insight in our arguments with each other, that something is or is not so. It takes us back *to* our convincing each other what to do or what not to do, and here the character of the speakers is decisive.[29]

Indeed, in the *Rhetoric*, 2.1.1378a7 ff., Aristotle goes on to say that speakers are found trustworthy and convincing—like the noun *pistis*, the adjective here, *pistos*, means both—for three reasons: their *phronêsis*, their *aretê*, their *eunoia*, which is to say, their good sense and discernment, their ethical excellence, and their being well-intentioned toward the audience:

> For in what they talk or give counsel about [περὶ ὧν λέγουσιν ἢ συμβουλεύουσιν], they can be deceptive for all of these reasons or just one of them: if they lack good sense and discernment they arrive at wrong beliefs; or, if their beliefs are right, out of moral turpitude they do not say what they believe; or, if they have discernment and clemency but bad intentions, it is possible that they know what is best but still do not counsel it. (1378a9–13)

We note the emphasis here on *logos* or argument as a process of convincing someone of something in the practical realm where, in taking and giving counsel, we bring each other to decide upon (*krinein*) a course of action. Thus, as opposed to the theoretical realm where, as observers, the speaker and the audience are not engaged any longer in getting things done, in this practical realm both speaker and audience *are* engaged in getting things done. For this reason we are not so much concerned here with the speakers' capacity for abstract intellection as with their ability, first, to discern, from within a present situation, its similiarities with, and differences from, past situations and, then, to counsel a wise course of action. Moreover, we need to trust that they are honest and well intentioned enough to counsel what they believe to be best not for themselves but for us, and that they will not deceive and mislead us. For in this realm of our original speaking to each other we ourselves will be affected for better or for worse by the decision we make at a speaker's urging. Here, then, where argument is still a matter of convincing someone rather than demonstrating something, *who* is speaking is crucial.

But how do we hear who this is in what (*quid*) he or she has to say, and, more to the point, how do we hear it in the way (*quo modo*) he or she says it?

Four diachronic tropes are central here, "parenthesis," "apostrophe," "epanorthosis," and "aposiopesis." Were they not employed deliberately, they all would remind us of the Freudian slip, for in all of them the surface of the *logos* or logical line of argument is interrupted, and in the breach something of the character of the speaker, of the *êthos* underneath the *logos* and sustaining it, becomes audible.

In the parenthesis or "putting along side" (again, a misleading visual-spatial term from "literary" rhetoric), a kind of commentary revealing the speaker's own attitude about something is injected into the course of the argument, as in Saint Paul's "But wherein any man is bold—I am speaking foolishly—I also am bold . . ." (2 Corinthians 11). Similarly, in apostrophe the logical flow is broken when one "turns aside" to address someone not present. Quintilian, not one to spare us the gory, illustrates this with another vivid, if utterly repugnant, quotation from Virgil: "And then the four horse span, driven apart, / pulled Metus to pieces—but that you had remained true to your words, Alban!—and Tullus carried off the innards of that medacious man" (see *Inst. Or.* 9.3.26).

In epanorthosis, or "setting right," one thinks better of what one has said and qualifies it or even takes it back, as in Augustine's classic "Give me chastity and continence—but not yet" (*Confessions* 8.7). Epanorthosis is particularly revealing of the character of the speaker, in this case, of an untrustworthy soul divided against itself and given even more to self-deception than to deception of others. Finally, aposiopesis, or "falling silent," radicalizes epanorthosis insofar as it does not just interrupt the logical line of thought, but breaks it off altogether. In this turn of speech the speaker reveals a reaction so strong that he or she simply cannot go on with the thought, as in Lear's "I will have revenges on you both / That all the world shall—I will do such things" (*King Lear* II.iv.304–5).

Aposiopesis makes clear that *êthos* is not only indissociable from the *logos* of any *pistis* but indissociable from its *pathos* as well. For in addition to breaking the linear logic of the argument and showing us that in a *pistis* more things are going on than one, this diachronic trope, in particular, communicates powerfully to the audience a background feeling and tonal setting within which alone the argument can be heard and received. Thus, we see, once again, that as opposed to the demonstration, in which *êthos* and *pathos* are apparently extrinsic and dispensable, in the rhetorical *pistis*, at least, *logos*, *pathos*, and *êthos* are intrinsic structural components inextricably interconnected with each other. Such, then, is the "ground and soil" (Heidegger: Boden) that our hermeneutics of original argument has "laid bare" beneath superimposed layers of abstraction and that it has "laid out" interpretively.

4

Demonstration, Dialectic, and Rhetoric in Plato

We must now ask how it came about that the ground of argument in rhetorical speech, a ground which Aristotle's *Rhetoric* still can "lay bare" and "lay out" hermeneutically, came to be covered up in the first place. The turning point in the abstraction from rhetoric to theoretical dialectic and, then, the further abstraction from dialectic to demonstration is, one might think, to be located in Plato, for whom mathematical argument in the form of demonstration from secured starting points or *archai* would appear to be the remedy against sophism's perversion of rhetorical argument. And, indeed, all of Plato, the early, middle, and even the late dialogues, can be read as a response to sophism's corruption and destruction of reasonable *sumbouleuesthai*, of our deliberating and taking counsel with each other concerning the good, the right, and the decent thing to do. Even the *Sophist*, for instance, which introduces the purely theoretical and ontological themes that so fascinated Heidegger, truth as *alêtheia*, being and not being, and so forth, is, as the very title tells us, still concerned with defending to an impressionable audience the philosopher's life against the charms of sophism's deceitful speech.[1] Plato's primary task, we might say, was to immunize audiences against sophism's techniques of passing off the contraries of these three, the good, the right, and the decent, for the real thing, and even his concern with the guidance of the soul and care for it (*psuchagôgia, therapeia*) is at its root a concern with shielding the soul from the harmful effects of sophistical arguments, be these made to the soul by someone else, or, what is worse, perhaps, made by the soul to itself. For these sophistical arguments, in "feeding and watering the passions," subvert the soul's *phronêsis*, its ethical discernment, and seduce the soul into a ruinous life of insatiable self-aggrandizement. Instead of *sôphrosune*, namely, saving one's *phronêsis*, keeping one's wits about one and making reasonable choices, the soul that listens to sophistical arguments falls for *pleonexia*, the tyrannical compulsion to seek, endlessly, ever more. What is more, in wrecking any sense of *philia* or kinship these arguments plunge the community, the *polis*, into the war of every individual against every other.

Thus, it is Plato's primary philosophical endeavor to achieve for ethical and political deliberations, for the realm of rhetoric, that is, the same sort of immunity to sophistical arguments displayed by mathematicians: his proposal is that just as mathematicians have seen and know what the area of a square and the area of a circle are in and by themselves (*kath' hauta*) and hence cannot be "persuaded" by any appearances produced by drawings that a square can be constructed equal in area to a given circle, so too might someone who has seen and knows what the good, right and decent are "in and by themselves," in essence, be made immune to the play on the ambiguity of mere *onomata* or word names for things that makes a bad, wrong, and indecent thing seem like a good, right, and decent thing to do. And just as a mathematician infers unassailable conclusions demonstratively from stabilized insights into the "forms" or "looks" (*eidê*) of what a square and circular area are, so too would ethical and political deliberation and counsel concerning the good, right, and decent thing to do be converted into demonstration from insight into what these are, "in and by themselves."

However, even in the proposal of such a project a discrepancy is obvious; for, unlike rhetoric's deliberation and taking counsel, demonstration concludes not with an action chosen but only with a further insight. Someone who has followed the logic of a demonstration responds with intellectual assent, not voluntary consent, responds with "Yes, I see," not "Yes, I will." Put another way, whereas deliberation and taking counsel is for engaged listeners (*akounontes*) who either hear and obey or do not, demonstration is for detached spectatators and onlookers (*theôretes*) who either see the point or do not. For this reason the ideal of mathematical demonstration, to which Plato, in his effort to defeat sophism's seduction, would seemingly recur, ultimately proves inappropriate for the rhetorical exhortation he would make to his audience to decide against sophism and for the good, right, and decent life. As we will see in our examination of the *Phaedo* and *Phaedrus* dialogues here, *Plato knows this full well.* Thus, in the end it is not Plato himself but only the subsequent tradition of mathematically oriented Platonist metaphysics that takes his demonstrative project seriously and abandons inconclusive deliberation for apparently conclusive demonstration. We in the West, with our own paradigm of argument by "logical" inference, are thus the products not so much of Plato as of this Platonist tradition. It is our shadow, so to speak, which even such a radical critic of it as Derrida, as I will try to display in the third part of this chapter, is unable to leap over. A careful reading of Plato, however, one that uncovers and retrieves the elements of an earlier, rhetorical form of argument that persist in Plato himself, just might make a leap over this shadow possible. That, at least, is the intention of what will follow here.

4.1 Demonstration, Dialectic, and Rhetorical Conviction in the *Phaedo*

In this section we will see that Plato, despite his apparent privileging of mathematical *apodeixis* or demonstration in the *Phaedo,* actually never abandons standard rhetorical conviction. Put another way, if viewed in retrospect from Aristotle's *Rhetoric,* the *Phaedo*'s arguments ultimately remain convincing speeches, *pithanoi logoi,* urging an audience to a *prohairesis tou biou* or choice of life the opposite of sophism's. They are, this is to say, a singular blend of theoretical instruction, on the one hand, and rhetorical exhortation, on the other. As Plato contrives it, Socrates' interlocutors here, Cebes and Simmias, are students of Philolaus and mathematicians of the Pythagorean school (see 61d) and, like many of their contempories, have also been sufficiently exposed to sophistical confutation to mistrust any nonmathematical argument (see 89c on *misologoi* or "haters of argument").[2] From this selection of *dramatis personae* for the *Phaedo* we can see why Plato sees himself constrained to explore critically the possibility of founding rhetorical argumentation in a form of argument beyond the inescapable controvertability of all rhetoric: since mathematicians display the kind of invulnerability to sophism that his audience seeks, the argumentative paradigm, which he tries out for this foundational role, becomes mathematics' *apodeixis* or demonstration, a kind of argument whose nature and even presumed superiority are, as we will see in the next chapter, exposited later in Aristotle's *Prior* and *Posterior Analytics.*

To review the differences between demonstrative and rhetorical argument, the tension between which drives the *Phaedo* dialogue, we may say in outline that, on the one hand, there are arguments which infer, deduce, prove that something is necessarily so. As in geometry or number theory, for instance, these arguments either start, themselves, from self-evident, noetically intuited first principles (*archai*) or start from the conclusions of other arguments that do (*An. Post.* 72a7 ff.), and proceeding by conceptual incompatibility or compatibility, they reach necessary conclusions *about which there is no further question.* Such arguments Aristotle calls *apodeiknusthai haplôs* or demonstrating in the strict sense (see, for example, *An. Post.* 72b26, passim).

Opposed to these are dialectical and rhetorical arguments, which, as Heidegger has pointed our for us in his *Basic Concepts of Aristotelian Philosophy*, begin from what Aristotle variously calls an *erôtêsis endoxos* or an *erôtêsis antiphaseôs*—expressions not easily translated (*Top.* 104a9, *An. Pr.* 24b1). Literally, the first means a "questioning that is generally accepted and believed"; let us call it a "belief in question." The second would be something like a "questioning of a contradiction" or more felicitously, perhaps, "a contradiction in question." The point of both expressions is that though generally believed (*endoxos*), the premises of dialectical-rhetorical argument are always still open to question. Hence, as we have noted in chapter 2, they will have the form "X is so, *is it not* [*ara ge*]?" (*Top.* 101b30, 32). This kind of argument will proceed not by necessary logical inference according to one class of things's inclusion in, or exclusion from, another class but by the topics or standard speech patterns of argument, in the *Phaedo* primarily similarity and difference, or the more and the less, and it will arrive at only provisional, inconclusive "conclusions." In short, its procedure is dialogical and discursive, and its form is *dialegesthai* or "talking" something "through"; contraries are entertained simultaneously, and the question of which of them is so remains open at the end. Hence, here there is *apodeixis* or demonstration only in a loose sense, and as in rhetoric, if not dialectic, the *apodeixis* is absorbed in a *pistis* or "convincer," whose results are not necessary truths at all, but likelihoods. The *logos* here is thus only an *eikos logos* or likely argument.

Finally, contrary to demonstration in the strict sense, the goal of this kind of argument, at least in its rhetorical application, is, as we have noted, not to bring some theoretical onlooker to an insight (*mathêma*) of which he or she says, "Yes, I see." Rather, it is to induce a choice or decision (*prohairesis, krisis*) in a listener expressed in "Yes, I will." And since not intellectual assent but voluntary consent is sought here, it follows that communication of the *logos* or logic of the argument per se must be based in rhetoric's communication of *pathos* and *êthos*, that is to say, of the affective disposition (*diathesis;* Heidegger: *Befindlichkeit*) to be induced in the audience, and of the character of the speaker. For not only how someone sees something but how he or she feels about it must be changed (see *Rhet.* 1356a1–20).

4.1.1 The *Phaedo*'s dialectical-rhetorical arguments by the topics of similarity, difference, contraries, and the more and the less

The tension in Plato between the demonstrative and the dialectical-rhetorical is displayed best of all, perhaps, in the *Phaedo*, for if any dialogue is focused on argument as such, surely it is this one. Indeed, we may take as an announcement of its theme the statement at 63a that "Cebes is always tracking down some argument or other [λόγους τινὰς ἀνερευνᾷ] and is not in the least wont to let himself be convinced [πείθεσθαι] by what someone just happens to say" (*Phaedo* 63a).

It will emerge in our investigations of the *Phaedo* that Plato's proposal of an apodictical, demonstrative foundation for all argument, whatever hopes it might have held out to mathematicians like Cebes and Simmias for securing argument against sophistic word twisting, ultimately fails. In the end, Plato himself makes clear that any *apodeiknusthai* or demonstrating by conceptual compatibility or, in the case of the *Phaedo,* incompatibility—Aristotle's second syllogism, "No A are B; C is A; therefore C is not B"—must give way again to the very rhetorical *peithein* or conviction that it was meant to replace. In the end, the point that Plato makes to his mathematically inclined audience is that conviction and trust, *pistis,* will be achieved only in talking through our received opinions (*endoxa*) and taking counsel with each other about them—in *dialegesthai* and rhetoric's *sumbouleuesthai.* Hence, the only security against sophism will be in the genuineness of the *pathos* communicated and choice and decision (*prohairesis, krisis*) of the speaker, namely, to which sort of existence, either *pleonexia* or *sôphrosunê,* he or she, in this case Plato's "Socrates," has committed himself. In other words, the only security against sophism will be rhetorical, not demonstrative.[3]

This can scarcely be surprising, for we must, of course, keep in mind the setting of the *Phaedo* as the third part of a trilogy preceded by the *Apology* and the *Crito,* and in the latter a life-and-death existential decision was at stake: either to accept the offer to escape from the execution of an unjustly imposed penalty of death or to submit to it. Which of these, it is asked there, is the good, right, and decent *thing to do?* It is only in the light of the decision Socrates has made in the *Crito* that the *Phaedo* can then move on to a correlative and, as the affective involvement of its participants displays, only apparently more theoretical issue: whether death is to be feared and avoided or not. Choices and decisions about such matters as these, obviously, are the subject matter for rhetorical, deliberative argument, for people taking counsel with each other about what to do, and are not the subject matter of any *apodeiknunai* or "pointing something out" to an impartial audience.

Obviously Simmias and Cebes are uncomfortable arguing about such existential questions. As stand-ins for a young mathematically trained audience already fed up with sophistical confutation and grown jaded and sceptical about the possibility of any reasonable ethical argument at all, they would prefer to stay with the proper subject matters of demonstration. Not only the allusion to the danger of becoming *misologoi* or haters of argument (89d) speaks to their attitude but also the very pointed indication of their indifference to their teacher Philolaus's teachings on the ethical question of suicide (61d; see DD 23).

Indeed, Cebes is even portrayed as the "human being most strongly disposed to distrust and remain unconvinced by arguments [ἀπιστεῖν τοῖς λόγοις]" (77a), and, as a matter of fact, he has mastered enough of the sophists' techniques of confutation himself to apparently demolish Socrates' best argument for the imperishability of the soul with his own counterargument, by the topic of similarity, of the long-lasting but nevertheless perishable cloak: "We had been," narrates Phaedo, "strongly convinced by the previous argument [of Socrates] but seemed now to have been plunged into turmoil again and thrown into distrust and disbelief [εἰς ἀπιστίαν καταβαλεῖν] not only about the arguments made before but also about those still to be made" (88c). And, characteristically, it is Cebes who at the very beginning of the dialogue exposes a contradiction in Socrates' preliminary argument against suicide (62c ff.) and who, in so doing, sets up the *rhetorical* situation of the discussion: "For I think you and Simmias are saying," responds Socrates, "that I must defend myself against these things [πρὸς ταῦτα ἀπολογήσασθαι] as if were were in a court of law" (63b).

As it turns out, the first of the real arguments that Plato gives us in the *Phaedo* (63e-69e), namely that one who has lived well should die willingly, is said explicitly to be rhetorical insofar as it is called an *apologia*, or "defense," that, it is hoped, will be more convincing than the one Socrates had made to his judges (see 63b). This would seem to place it in the second of the major divisions of rhetoric specified by Aristotle (*Rhet.* 1.2.1358a35 ff.), namely *logoi dikanikoi* or judicial arguments, whose principal concerns are the right and the wrong, and whose subject matter is actions taken in the past. Clearly the concern here, however, is much more a matter of the "beneficial and harmful," and with actions to be taken in the future, albeit in Socrates' case here, a very immediate future. Hence, properly speaking, this argument will not be an *apologia* at all but ultimately a *protrepsis* or exhortation characteristic of what Aristotle terms *logoi sumbouleutikoi* or consultative arguments. But whatever the case may be, we *are* in the realm of rhetoric here and in a form of rhetoric that, unlike Aristotle's third division, epideictical or "display" argument, clearly urges a *krisis*, an existential decision upon those listening. The aim here is thus not to get us to see from a distance how things stand but to get us to hear and obey the call to a certain kind of life. Consequently, the argument will be a *pistis* or inducement of conviction, whose task is to convince its audience to choose a certain way—this as opposed to a demonstration, which aims at instructing to a mere insight (*mathêma*). In this first argument, then, the issue is not so much the theoretical one of whether death is to be feared or not, but rather the very practical one of whether or not we should choose a life such that we will not have to fear it.

We note, too, that precisely as *sumbouleutikos* or consultative, the argument's subject matter must be ontologically different from the subject matter of any demonstration. For it will consider things that, far from being necessarily what they are, are "susceptible of being otherwise"; as we have heard, "No one," says Aristotle, "takes counsel [*bouleuetai*] about things that he holds to be incapable of either having been otherwise, being otherwise in the future, or being otherwise now" (*Rhet.* 1357a5–7). Consequently, the argument here cannot "prove" what must necessarily be true, but will only "show," by an *eikos logos* or "likely argument," what is likely to be so but might not be. The task of any such argument as this can only be to inquire "if things do likely stand thus or if they do not" (εἴτε εἰκὸς οὕτως ἔχειν εἴτε μή) (70b). Consequently, any *apodeiknusthai* or demonstrating here will be in the loose sense only of "talking through" received opinions.[4] This means, of course, that the argument will always be open to a counterargument that things were not, will not be, are not, as they have been presented. And indeed, as we will see, precisely this vulnerability to confutation is not denied but expressly confirmed by what occurs in the *Phaedo.*

Now, if, to begin with, we focus on the *logos* itself here, and not yet on the *êthos* and *pathos* that are, as Aristotle emphasizes, indispensable "convincers" [*pithana*] in any such consultative argument (*Rhet.* 1356a1 ff.), we see right away that contrary to demonstration, which proceeds by necessary logical entailment, this *logos* proceeds by topical reasoning, in particular, by "similarity" (see *Top.* 114b25 ff. and *Rhet.* 1363b ff.). As the separation of the mind from the body, death is *like* the practice of philosophy. For philosophy abandons care for the adornment of the body (64d ff.); philosophy purifies itself of the body's influences (65a ff.) in order—*like* mathematics, it is implied—to arrive at undistorted insight into its objects, the right (*dikaion*), the decent (*kalon*), and the good (*agathon*) (65d), and to obtain the life of discernment (*phronêsis*) (66a), and courage, temperance, and justness (*andreia, sôphrosunê, dikaiosunê*) (68d ff.). These things, the philosophers find, are to be decided for and chosen, and in this they have only been preparing for a death they welcome.

We note, first, that, as always in the *Phaedo,* the background argument beneath the surface thesis, here, that death is not to be feared by those who have led their life aright, is a rhetorical epideictic *praise* of philosophy and a rhetorical consultative *exhortation* to decide for, and choose the life of philosophy over the pursuit of sensual gratification. (See the *Rhetoric*, 1358a36 ff., for the rhetorical modes of epideictic and consultative rhetoric, praise or condemnation, and exhortation and dehortation, respectively.) In characterizing the form of this *logos* we should also note that, quite in contrast to the mathematical *logos apodeiktikos*, we have actually begun not, as in demonstration, from an incontestable first principle or intuited *archê* (see *An. Post.* 2.19, on the intuition of such certain starting points), but from an *erôtêsis endoxos* or received opinion still very much in question, namely that "death is the separation of the soul from the body" (64c). Furthemore, since the premises here, unlike the premises of a mathematical argument, are "susceptible of being otherwise," the conclusion drawn will also be open to question and, like the premises, implicitly has the interrogative, not declarative, form "Death, then, is to be hoped for, is it not?" (Compare, for example, the "is it not" in "But purification, is, is it not [ἆρα οὐ], . . . most of all separating the soul from the body" [67c].) Obviously, then, this argument, like all arguments by the topic of similarity, remains open to further question and subject to controversion.

Indeed, Socrates implicitly grants this possibility and, at 69e, he allows that consequently the *peithein* or conviction sought may not have been achieved: "If, then, I am more convincing to you [ὑμῖν πιθανώτερός εἰμι] in this apology," says Socrates, "than I was to the Athenian judges, all is well," to which the ever skeptical Cebes responds, "In the other matters you seem to me to have spoken well, but what you said about the soul generates great distrust and disbelief in human beings [πολλὴν ἀπιστίαν παρέχει τοῖς ἀνθρώποις]" (70a). Hence, this argument must be buttressed by others, which follow immediately upon it: "Indeed, no small amount of encouragement and convincing is needed [οὐκ ὀλίγης παραμυθίας δεῖται καὶ πίστεως] that the human soul is immortal" (70b). Importantly, however, these next arguments, too, are intended only to convince the audience of a likelihood and not at all to demonstrate an insight. *Peithein* and not *apodeiknusthai* is the task: again, "Is it your will," Socrates asks, "that in our recounting of things to the end we pursue whether things do *likely* stand thus or whether they do not [εἴτε εἰκὸς οὕτως ἔχειν εἴτε μή]?" (70b; emphasis added).

The first of these corroborative arguments (70c–72a) is clearly dialectical-rhetorical too and would not demonstrate something for us by inference from a secured starting point but, rather, by employing the topics of similarity (*homoiotês*) and contraries (*enantia*) (see *Top.* 112b26 f. and above 3.3.1 and 3.3.2), convince us that the soul is not scattered at death but remains to generate new life. Strikingly, the topic of contraries as such is first introduced here with examples taken from the epideictic and judicial fields of rhetoric, namely the decent and despicable (*kalon* and *aischron*) and the right and wrong (*dikaion* and *adikon*) (70e). These are word names, the shifting senses of which sophism notoriously exploits to make an indecent thing seem decent and a wrong thing, right, but here, in contrast to Socrates' opening "defense," there is no indication given of the project of stabilizing the meanings of these word names "mathematically" by founding them in an insight into static form or "look" of what each of them is "in and by itself." Indeed, sophistic exploitation of contrariety and equivocation is not at issue; rather, like all dialectical and rhetorical argument, this argument remains explicitly on the level of *genesis*, or coming to pass, and continues to employ the unstable word names we use to speak of it: as, in general, less *comes from* more, and vice versa, so, similarly, slower *comes from* quicker, worse from better, heating from cooling, combining from separation, generation from corruption, and the other way around. So too with sleeping and waking, and so too, *similarly*, with life and death (70e–71d). And if life comes from death, the *psuchê*, or life and soul of the person, must have continued to live somewhere so that new life might arise from it (72a).

The second corroborative argument is equally dialectical-rhetorical in also arguing by the topics of similarity and contraries and, hence, in remaining in the world of coming to pass. Despite the introductory reference to circles and staight lines (72b)—the engagement of Plato's mathematical audience must be insured, after all—there is no abstraction yet to the mathematician's statically present conceptual realities. Indeed, like the previous one, this argument remains in the form of precisely those naturalistic and "physiological" arguments that the "Socrates" of this dialogue will claim to have abandoned later on (see 96a ff.): Just as there would be no one awake now if, like Endymion, no one ever awoke from sleep, and just as all things would still be one chaotic mix if separation did not come out of combination, so, *similarly*, there would be no one alive now if life did not come from death (72b–d).

However, the third corroborative argument, from "being reminded" or *anamnêsis* (72e–76e), does come close to a demonstration. Indeed, Simmias specifically asks at 73a, "Of what sort were the demonstrations of these things?" (ποῖαι τούτων αἱ ἀποδείξεις), and, as we will see, he will affirm at 92d that the argument made here was a strict *apodeixis ex hupotheseôs* in the geometrical mode and thus very much to his liking. In syllogistic form it might be restated as follows: Let it be the case that any new insight entails being reminded of a previous insight in the soul; previous insight in the soul entails preexistence of the soul. Therefore, *by logical inference*, the soul preexists.

To be sure, the ensuing argument (73a–75b) for the first premise here is not in the least demonstrative; rather, it reverts to a pure *eikos logos* by the dialectical-rhetorical topic of similarity: In response to Cebes' obvious allusion to the *anamnêsis* that Socrates' "questioning" induced in Meno's household servant concerning the mathematical problem of doubling of the area of a given square (73a; see *Meno* 82b ff.), Socrates proceeds here by *drawing an extended analogy* between being reminded of a conceptual insight by physical things and being reminded of a physical thing by other similar or even dissimilar physical things, for instance, of a beloved by his lyre or cloak, of a man by a picture of a horse, of Cebes by a picture of Simmias, or of Simmias by a picture of Simmias (73d–e): "From all these instances it follows, does it not [ἆρ' οὖν], that being reminded is induced by what is similar but also by what is dissimilar [μὲν ἀφ' ὁμοίων . . . δὲ ἀπὸ ἀνομοίων]?" (74a). Reasoning by the similarity and dissimilarity of one physical experience to another has not yet given way to demonstrative reasoning by the inclusion or exclusion of one class of thing by another.

However, we should note that the similarity and dissimilarity which Socrates establishes next between being reminded of a physical thing by another physical thing and being reminded of a conceptual mathematical thing by physical things, that is, of equality itself (*auto to ison*) by two seemingly equal stones or sticks (74a), does prefigure the very mathematical-ontological transition from the physiological and empirical to the conceptual, which Socrates will try out later in his attempt at securing the foundations of argument against sophistical controversion by making argument demonstrative—as do also, clearly, the references "regarding the decent itself, the good itself and right and and holy" (περὶ αὐτοῦ τοῦ καλοῦ, καὶ αὐτοῦ τοῦ ἀγαθοῦ καὶ δικαίου καὶ ὁσίου) (75d). As we can see, the proposal already emerging at this point is to put rhetorical argument about these "goods" to be chosen on the same foundation as demonstrative argument about mathematical equality.

Nevertheless, an indication of troubles to come for this proposal is already given too, for the rhetorical task of conviction, which, as rhetorical, involves not only convincing the listener by the *logos* of the argument but also by changing his or her *pathos* or feeling—here from fear of dying to hope—has obviously not been accomplished. Simmias remains, as we have already heard, most emphatically distrustful, *apistos*, of arguments (77b). His *apistia*, or failure to be convinced, is not so much an intellectual lack of belief as it is a basic distrust, an attitude or *diathesis*, namely, which, as Socrates later observes, could easily potentiate into hatred of arguments (89d). Hence, a fourth fortification of the original thesis that death is not to be feared, and which responds to that feeling of fear, must now be advanced: "Try to convince us, said Cebes laughing, as if we were indeed afraid, or, better, as if, not we were afraid, but perhaps some child in us too, who has these fears. Let us try to convince him not to be afraid of death as some kind of spook" (77e). We note, too, that it is Socrates alone whom Cebes, despite his prevailing attitude of mistrust, thinks might en*chant* and *sing* away (*epaidein, exepaidein*) this fear (77e). In other words, the affective change from fear to confidence prerequisite for winning conviction in these matters, the change in the *Stimmung* or voicing, will not come as a result of what a demonstration gives us to *see* but only from *hearing* the tone of voice of someone we trust. (See 7.2 below on Nietzsche and the "birth of argument from the spirit of music.")

But even viewed logically, the argument that now follows (78b–84b) has the form not of a demonstration but of a rhetorical *eikos logos*, here by the dialectical-rhetorical topic of sameness and difference, and even if its subargument once again privileges the mathematical, the main argument itself, in resuming the "defense" of 63b–69e and arguing by the topic of similarity, is clearly intended as a rhetorical *pistis* and not as an *apodeixis*: There are, so it runs, perceived visible things that change by composition and decomposition, and there are conceived invisible things, like "the equal itself," that do not change at all. The soul is more like (*homoioteron* [79b, 79e]) the invisible and more different from the visible, so, *very likely*, the soul is neither composed nor does it decompose. Hence, death is not to be feared. Or: The divine rules and is immortal; the soul is like the divine and rules; therefore it is likely, is it not, that the soul is immortal (79b–80b). So—and here we have the exhortative *muthos* or tale of the requisite *paramuthia* and the *diamuthologomen*, the "encouragement" and "let us recount" at 70b—

> This soul, then, invisible and on its way to another place which, like itself, is worthy and pure and invisible, on its way as if to the true Hades with the good and sage god, the true Hades to which, if God wills, my soul is soon to go—is it ours to say, as most do of this soul, that being of such kind and such nature, it is blown away forthwith and destroyed when it is separated from the body? Far from it my dear Cebes and Simmias! (80d)

Once the protreptical "defense" has been resumed, it emerges that the conclusion of the three previous arguments, namely that the soul exists after death, was really only a premise for the main rhetorical argument: The soul exists after death, so choose the life of purity now that will assure that its existence then will be with "the good god," and flee the life of sophistical *pleonexia*. As powerful as this exhortation is, however, it fails as a *pistis*; for it fails to convince (*peithein*). And precisely this is what Plato's brilliant dramatization here—the dead silence, then the murmuring, the doubts expressed, and, later at 87b ff., the transitional switch to the narrator, Phaedo—is meant to bring home.[5] Again, Simmias: "In regard to such matters, it seems to me, as perhaps it does to you, that clear knowledge is either something impossible in this life or something exceedingly difficult" (85c).

Even so, Simmias, every bit the hound on the trace of arguments that Cebes is, is anxious to go on. If, he says,

> it is impossible either to gain insight into [μαθεῖν], or to find out how, these matters stand, one should take the best of human arguments [τὸν γοῦν βέλτιστον τῶν ἀνθρωπίνων λόγων], the one most difficult to refute, and borne along on it as on a raft, risk navigating one's life—if, that is, one cannot sail across more securely and less perilously borne on a more unshakeable carrier, some divine argument [ἐπὶ βεβαιοτέρου ὀχήματος, λόγου θείου τινός]. (85c–d)

In this proposal we have the entire dialogue in a nutshell: only "divine arguments" based on "unshakeable" insights or *mathêmata* would be entirely secure against sophism's counter argumentive strategies and its ability to destroy any position. Ideally, then, we should make these "divine arguments" the foundation of our ethical arguments, just as mathematicians have done for their mathematical arguments. But in matters of life and death, in questions of just what the good, right, and decent life is which we are supposed to choose, these infallible "divine arguments" are in fact not available to us. Risking instability and confutation, we must therefore rely on the best of "human arguments," those that we have put to the test and subjected to refutation, those that have proven strongest so far.

In keeping with this principle Simmias and Cebes now proceed to put Socrates' "human arguments" for the immortality of the soul to the test (85e–88b). Simmias's counter argument, like the arguments it would refute, is by the topic of similarity, for all one needs to do to counter an argument by similarity is change the analogy: If the soul is to the body as the harmony is to the lyre, he submits, then just as the harmony ceases to exist when the lyre does, so too will the soul cease to exist when the body does (see 85e–86d), to which Socrates responds, "He is right to say this, Simmias is" (86d). And so too with Cebes: "It seems as if I, just like Simmias, am in need of a likeness," he says. If the soul *is like* a cloak that lasts longer than the body, it will perish eventually, even if it outlasts a number of bodies in the meantime (see 87a–88b). And, "if indeed it is this way," he concludes,

> it befits no one to face death with confidence—lest he be confident foolishly—who cannot demonstrate first [ἀποδεῖξαι] that the soul is altogether immortal and indestructible. If this cannot be done, however, the one about to die must necessarily always fear for his soul that, at the moment when the body goes to pieces, it will be altogether destroyed. (88b)

(We cannot overlook the background anguish this mathematician feels, who is beginning to sense that the cultivated affective neutrality of his preferred argumentative form, demonstration, is peculiarly misplaced in arguments about these ultimate existential concerns of life and death, and that a *logos* without the communication of the right *pathos* and trustworthy *êthos* will not suffice.)

As the reflective interlude between Phaedo and Echechrates now drives home, Plato's obvious meta-argumentative point here is that *any* dialectical or rhetorical argument can be refuted since it reasons only from questionable belief, not from secured starting points, and reaches its conclusions by the topics, not by necessary logical inference. And thus he has skillfully led us to the crux of the dialogue: "In what argument, then, shall we still put our trust?" (τίνι οὖν ἔτιπιστεύσομεν λόγῳ) asks Echecrates. "For the argument Socrates argued was powerfully convincing [σφόδρα πιθανὸς ὤν]," says Phaedo, "but now has collapsed into mistrust and disbelief [εἰς ἀπιστίαν]" (88d).

4.1.2 The trial and failure of demonstration (*apodeixis*) as a paradigm for argument

In response to this apparent impasse there follows a remarkable interlude (89b–91c) in which Socrates' *êthos* of complete self-possession in the face of turmoil is again vividly displayed—see also Plato's carefully constructed mise-en-scène before at 60a–61d—and in which the danger of mistrust of arguments turning into hatred of them is confronted with a standard topical argument by the similarity of arguments to human acquaintances, and this despite the acknowledged untrustworthiness of such merely "likely" arguments. It is only after this interlude that Plato gives us a first indication of another kind of argument that might really seem trustworthy to these mathematicians amid all their mistrust. For regarding the argument from *anamnêsis*, namely "Being reminded implies having known before; the soul's having known before implies its preexistence; therefore, being reminded implies the soul's preexistence," Cebes is now made to say "I was wonderfully convinced [ἔπεσθεν] by it—more than by any other argument—and remain so," in which opinion Simmias wholeheartedly concurs (91e–92a). And when Simmias is pressed to choose between this argument from *anamnêsis* and his own harmony argument advanced against the separate existence of the soul, it is said specifically why he concurs with Cebes in his preference for the former: the harmony argument, he says, was *aneu apodeixeôs* and *meta eikotos,* without demonstration and by likelihood, and, he continues,

> I know full well that arguments making their "demonstrations" by means of likelihoods are deceptive, and, should one not guard oneself against these, one might well be fooled—in geometry and in all other matters. But the argument about being reminded and understanding was demonstrated by means of a worthy hypothesis [δι' ὑποθέσεως ἀξίας ἀποδέξασθαι]. (92c–d)

The reference to geometry makes clear that "demonstrations" by likelihood are not demonstrations in the strict sense. But demonstrations by means of a hypothesis, as in geometry, are real demonstrations, and only these are immune to sophistical refutation. Indeed, we know from the *Theaetetus* that mathematicians were challenged by sophistical counter arguments based on appearances, for instance, that the circle *could* be squared, and that they were immune to these arguments' deceptiveness.[6] Simmias tells us here what the basis of their immunity was. Their demonstrations were from a "worthy hypothesis" in the form of "Let X be Y," and they proceeded not by means of topics based on apparent likenesses and differences but by means of logical entailment and contradiction, which is to say, by means of conceptual compatibility and incompatibility: Let X be Y, Y implies Z, therefore X implies Z. Or, negatively: Let X be Y; Y implies Z, but X excludes Z, therefore X is not Y (see *An. Post.* 87a7–12 on the *apodeixis eis to adunaton* or demonstration by impossibility).

Significantly, precisely the latter is the form of Socrates' first arguments in response to Simmias's harmony argument: Let Soul be Harmony; Harmony implies Contemporaneousness with the thing harmonized, but Soul, as preexisting the body (the result of the *anamnêsis* demonstration), excludes Contemporaneousness with the body; therefore, Soul is not Harmony (92a–c). Or, Let Soul be Harmony. Harmony implies More or Less, but Soul excludes More or Less. Therefore Soul is not Harmony (93b–94b). Thus, it emerges that the argument based on the "hypothesis . . . that the soul is a harmony" (94b) has been demonstrated, in the strict sense, to be false and that the hypothesis must be rejected. With that we are prepared for the grand meta-argumentative excursus (95e–105b) that will develop the theory of a *logos* by an *apodeixis ex hupotheseôs*, an interlude occasioned by Cebes' "cloak" argument. The exemplary problem to be addressed here is whether Soul implies Destructibility or excludes Destructibility.

To be sure, in order to lead his readers up to the theory of an *apodeixis ex hupotheseôs* Plato, again with great pedagogical skill, has Socrates begin with a very different kind of *logos*, namely a variation on an argument by the topics of contraries and prior/posterior characteristic of the "physiological" explanations of the time. In this *logos*, as in the previous argument for the immortality of the soul, the subject matter is stated in terms of a sequential process between contraries: prior to things becoming what they are now, they were the contrary. Having been cold before, they "then" come to be hot; having been small before, they "then" come to be large. (As we observed in 3.3.4, the "then" here hovers between its original concrete sense indicating only a temporal sequence and its later abstract sense indicating a cause-and-effect relationship.) And all this coming into being and passing away, it is proposed, is to be accounted for in terms of a Heraclitian process "down" which is to be thought of as combination, or addition, and process "up" which is to be thought of as separation, or division and substraction. The point is that, as stated, all such *logoi* are vulnerable to sophistic confutation: On the one hand, "two" is said to result from combination or addition of what before were separate, of one thing with another. But this is contradicted when "two" is said to result from the opposite, namely separation or division of one thing into two. By such sophistical conundrums one's mind is thrown into confusion: "and oftentimes," says Socrates, "I was thrown around, up, down, investigating the likes of these things" (96b). Precisely this dismay epitomizes the mathematician's reaction to a sophistic word twisting that makes one seem to have said the opposite of what one did say. How then are we to defend arguments against sophists making our heads swim in this way? Certainly not on the sophists' own level of rhetoric and arguments by the topics, as the demise of the previous arguments in this dialogue have made definitively clear.

Hence, Plato now has Socrates take another run at it, so to speak, the famous "second voyage" (τὸν δεύτερον πλοῦν) (99d) "fleeing into arguments" (εἰς τοὺς λόγους καταφυγόντα) (99e). Here it is proposed that the refuge from sophism sought by his mathematical audience might be found at last in argumentative theory as such:

> I hypothesize each time an assertion [ὑποθέμενος ἑκάστοτε λόγον] that I judge to be strongest, and the things that seem to me to be consonant with it I posit as true, be this in regard to causal explanations [περὶ

> αἰτίας] or all manner of other things. And what is not consonant with my hypothesis, I posit as not true. (100a)

Furthermore, he says to Simmias and Cebes in language they would surely understand,

> holding on to that secure foothold of your hypothesis, you would answer in this way. And should someone attack your hypothesis itself, you would first let that go, and not answer him until you had investigated the things that follow from it in regard to which of these, in your view, are consonant with each other and which, dissonant. And when you are constrained to provide an argument [διδόναι λόγον] for the hypothesis itself, you would posit another hypothesis that appears to be the best of those above it until you came to the one that was sufficient. (101d–e)

All this, it should be noted, is said in opposition precisely to the "wiser ones," the *sophoteroi* (101a), who "delight in themselves when they, in their wisdom [ὑπὸ σοφίας], are able to conflate everything" (101e).

In short, to defend against sophism, *eikoi logoi* or merely likely arguments by the standard topics will be shunned and recourse will be had to arguments by conceptual compatibility and incompatibility, for which the mathematical demonstration from a hypothesis provides the paradigm. To use the example given here (101b–c), if we argue about "two," the argument will be about what, exactly, "two" is and what the concept or "two itself" logically entails and excludes; it will not be about how "two things" came to be. Loose talk about any temporal sequence of "combination" and "separation" of things will be abandoned for the number theory behind addition and subtraction, multiplication and division. This is a proposal guaranteed to find favor with this "Socrates' "—and Plato's—audience of mathematicians.

However, the question Plato now poses to this very audience is whether in fact this method of founding and securing argument can be universalized and extended to matters like *auto to kalon*, namely beauty itself, if we are speaking aesthetically as we seem to be here (see 100d), or the fair, noble, and decent itself, which is the object of our ethical and political *sumbouleuesthai*, our deliberating and taking counsel with each other about what is the good, right, and decent thing to do. Can this method be paradigmatic, that is, not only for *logoi* as accounts and explanations in the mathematical realm, where things are necessarily what they are, but for *logoi* as consultative arguments given in support of an ethical choice and decision, where things are "susceptible of being otherwise"? As a matter of fact, the preliminary answer seems to be "yes"; *apodeiknusthai,* demonstrating, appears to become the paradigm for rhetoric's deliberations about what to do, and with that a theory of argumentation as logical inference is established that continues to prevail even today.

Before proceeding any futher with Plato's own critique of this proposal we should note, as the dialogue itself does at 102a–b, that a decisive reversal in the relationship of language and things would be required if ethical argument were really to be converted into demonstration, a reversal that the Pythagorean mathematicians Simmias and Cebes have already executed even if it is only now that they are made explicitly aware of it. To have demonstration in the strict sense, *onomata* must have become what Plato here calls *eponuma* and Aristotle will call *sêmeia*; word names must have become eponyms and signs. The shift here is crucial. Before, in Homer, for instance, nothing had its being for the poet and for his listeners until he had found just the right word name by which to call it.[7] Now, however, word names that lend a thing its meaning and being in the very naming of it, much as personal names tell us who someone is, must have become signs designating exactly a thing whose being "in and by itself" has already been seen before we find the right word to say it. *Onomata,* that is to say, must have become *eponumiai,* eponyms named after, and named afterwards for, the *eidos* or "visible" form of the thing. We note that it is none other than Phaedo, the narrator nearest to the voice of the author of dialogue, who inserts in his recounting of what transpired:

> *Once this had been granted to him and it was agreed that any and each "what" of the visible forms exists* [εἶναί τι ἕκαστον τῶν εἰδῶν], *and that other things taking part in these visible forms get their eponyms from these themselves,* Socrates then went on to ask, "But if you say this, then whenever you say that Simmias is larger than Socrates but smaller that Phaedo you are saying, are you not [ἆρ' οὐχ'], that in Simmias there is both Largeness and Smallness?" (102b; emphasis added)

The mathematical terms Largeness and Smallness are readily grasped examples of this reversed relationship of name and thing (and of the demonstrative transformation of topical argument by the more and the less), for any mathematician sees "what" each of these is, sees its *ti estin,* before assigning a name to it and sees, too, that though these visible forms as such exclude each other, there is, despite sophistical attempts to make it seem otherwise, no contradiction at all in saying that a physical particular like Simmias participates in both (102b–c). And so it is with every mathematical term, with one, two, three, even, odd, and so forth, to cite the examples used here. (We note, however, that even in this meta-argumentative discussion of such fully determinate and static forms as Largenesss and Smallness the interrogative language of inderterminacy continues: with the ". . . are you not?" Plato maintains even here the dialectical-rhetorical priority of the question over any conclusive answer, as, ultimately, he will in the dialogue as a whole.)

Now, the potential advantage for securing arguments of this reversal in naming is obvious. For if arguments could be couched in such eponyms signifying what is already seen clearly and distinctly to be what it is, they would indeed be immune to the sophists' exploitation of the power of word names to confound us. Plays on a word name's ambiguity will not impress a mathematician, who sees precisely what it is that "one" or "two" are "named after" and signify, and none of these clearly and distinctly discerned entities can be made any longer to look like the opposite of itself by some twisting of the word we use for it. For "what" it is and "what" it is not have always already been stabilized.

This, then, is the strategy Plato proposes in order to rob sophistic controversialists, the "*antilogikoi*" of 90c, of their foothold: to the unknown person objecting that before contraries *were* said to come from contraries (103a), Socrates responds,

> Then, my friend, we were speaking of things that have contrary qualities, naming the former after the latter with the eponym of the latter [ἐπονομάζοντες αὐτὰ τῇ ἐκείνων ἐπωνυμίᾳ]. But now we are speaking of these contraries themselves, by the indwelling of which the things named get their eponyms [ἔχει τὴν ἐπωνυμίαν τὰ ὀνομαζόενα]." (103b)[8]

A particular large thing could come to pass out of a smaller thing, for instance, but Large itself could never come to pass out of Small itself. For once we have seen precisely what it is that the eponym "large" is named after, once we have seen Large itself for *what* it is, no twisting of the word we use to designate it can talk us into believing that it itself is somehow the contrary of itself. In this way the fear "that a contrary argument [ἐναντίος λόγος] might come your way" (101a) has been successfully banished.

To show how all this might work Socrates now exemplifies how one should reason on this new foundation for argument. Beginning with contraries in physical processes, heat and cold, fire and snow (103c ff.), he shifts adroitly to a mathematical contraries argument that his audience will readily comprehend: once we have seen what the pairs of things we call "three" and "five," and "two" and "four," are in themselves we could never be seduced into thinking that either of the first could be conflated with either of the second (103e ff.). But not only is Triplicity incompatible with Duality; each of these, in turn, is incompatible with the "next highest hypothesis" above the other one; each is incompatible, that is, with the other's genus; Triplicity is incompatible with Even and Duality is incompatible with Odd. And now the method of argument by *apodeixis ex hupotheseôs*, demonstration from a hypothesis, is clear for all to see: we will set down, hypothesize, a genus or kind (*genos*) whose being we have clearly and distinctly discerned *without words for it*, and, again without words, we will infer from what this genus itself is, which species or forms (*eidê*) may be combined with it and predicated of it without contradiction, and which may not. Specifically, when our hypothesis that Soul excludes Death has been attacked, we will recur to the next hypothesis above Soul, namely Life. (The word name *psuchê* means life, after all; hence, unlike argument in number theory, this argument still depends, more than Plato lets on here, on following a trace of what a given word name makes audible in the first place.) And having clearly seen what Life itself is, we will set down the genus Life, knowing that as such it excludes its opposite, Death as such. Soul itself, we will then infer, excludes Death itself (105b ff.). And if this proposed argumentative strategy actually works, and if word names like "just," "decent," and "good" can be converted into eponyms for concepts of things whose nature we have also discerned clearly and distinctly, then we have indeed found an argument immune to sophistic controversion by opposites. That is the proposal.

However, Plato now gives us a clear indication that even for things like "soul" this method does *not* work, let alone for protreptical exhortative argument about the "just," "decent" and "good." For no irrefutable "divine" *logos* about a particular soul, mine or yours, has been provided, as Plato specifically has Simmias point out: "Despite what has been said," says Simmias, "holding human weakness in such contempt [τὴν ἀθρωπίνην ἀσθένειαν ἀτιμάζων], I am constrained by the vast dimensions of the subject matter which these arguments have treated, still to harbor distrust and be unconvinced [ἀπιστίαν ἔτι ἔχειν] regarding what has been argued"; to which Socrates responds, "You have said it well, o Simmias" (107b). It is clear that the attempt to secure the foundations for a merely "human argument" about the kind of life we ought to choose by some sort of apodictical "divine argument" that demonstrates the immortality of the soul from a hypothesis has, in fact, miscarried.[9]

For, in fact, not even the premise has been secured for the main argument, namely that, *since the soul is immortal,* one ought to care for it by leading a decent, righteous, and good life. Hence, this main argument must now be reformulated: "If indeed the soul is immortal, then it ought to be cared for not only in the time we call life but for all time. For if we leave it uncared for the danger appears terrible" (107c). Here the premise "the soul is immortal" is neither hypothesized as a stabilized first principle, nor is it demonstrated from such an *archê*; rather, it is left pending precisely as what Aristotle calls an *erôtêsis endoxos*, a question generally believed to be answered in one way, but not definitively answered. It is left, in other words, as an *erôtêsis antiphaseôs* or contradiction still in question. Both sides of this contradiction, namely the assertions that "Yes, the soul is immortal" and "No, the soul is not immortal," continue to be entertained, and the decision between them remains undecided.

Accordingly, in the argument now built upon this "contradiction in question" there is no trace of necessary, conclusive demonstration left (107d ff.). Instead, we have reverted to pure rhetorical *peithein* or conviction concerning a question that, viewed logically, could go either way. And, once again, the argument is made, not from a firmly secured *archê* or "starting point," but by the admittedly "shaky" topic of similarity, here in the grand *eikotês* or likeness of the "the true heaven, the true light and the true earth" (109e–110a), as opposed to the underworld of Tartarus (112a ff.). The former offers hopes, which the "orderly and reasonable soul" (108a) might aspire to fulfill, but the latter, terrors, to which the soul "full of desires of the body" (*id.*) must fear to be condemned (see 113e ff.). Whereas Plato refers to this account as a tale or *muthos* (110b), Aristotle would call it an argument by example or *paradigma* in the form, specifically, of the invented "fable" (*logos*) (see *Rhet.* 1393b 8f. and 3.2 above), and, as we might expect, the conclusion drawn at 114c, the "moral of the story," so to speak, is not really a declarative statement of fact at all, but has the implicit form of a pure rhetorical *protrepsis* or exhortation. We note that from the beginning of this tale telling Plato has turned back to oral-acoustical speech for listeners: "If, indeed, it is proper to tell a tale, Simmias, it is worth hearing [ἄξιον ἀκοῦσαι] what sort the things on the earth and under the heavens happen to be," to which Simmias responds, "but of course, Socrates; we would gladly hear this tale [τούτου τοῦ μύθου ἡδέως ἂν ἀκούσαιμεν]." The reason for this reversion to tale telling is made plain at the end of the story, for not an insight to be seen is at stake here but rather an admonition to be heard: "On account of these things which we have worked our way through, Simmias, it is necessary to go to any lengths in order that in our lives we partake of excellence and discernment [ὥστε ἀρετῆς καὶ φρονήσεως ἐν τῷ βίῳ μετασχεῖν] for the prize is fair [καλὸν γὰρ τὸ ἆθλον] and the hope, great" (114c)." Here we are called upon to flee the shameful life to which sophism's perversion of rhetorical conviction would seduce us, and to decide for, and choose, the fair and decent life instead. (See Aristotle's *Rhetoric* 1358b20 ff. on the the *aischron* and *kalon* as the special subject matters of epideictic rhetoric.)

This turning back from demonstration to rhetorical conviction at the conclusion of Socrates' argument shows us that Plato himself never expected to escape sophism's confutational skills by founding all argument in mathematical demonstration. Indeed, we see now that in the *Phaedo,* as in so many other dialogues, he has actually only run a characteristic aporetic thought experiment specially designed, in this case, for his mathematically inclined audience. As do so many of the other dialogues, this one, too, ends in logical perplexity and indeterminacy, with no definitive answer given to the theoretical questions it raises. Viewed logically, this is to say, it ends with what Gadamer calls the continuing priority of the question over the answer (see WM 344 ff.).

But more to the point that concerns us, it ends with a return not just from the demonstrative to the dialectical but, beyond that, from the dialectical to the rhetorical: *the theoretical aporia or impasse reached is preparatory for our hearing the practical exhortation.* Thus, with Heidegger, we could say that here all derivative, abstract, theoretical argument "at a distance" for onlookers is taken down and grounded in the "soil" of practical speech for hearers "there," "in the world" in which they must decide upon one course of action over another.

The result of our investigation of the *Phaedo* is remarkable: in the end Plato agrees with Aristotle that the only difference between sophistical and rhetorical argument is in the *prohairesis tou biou,* the choice of life, that the speaker has always already made. Consequently, the only available way to secure a *logos* that would convince an audience to decide for the good, right, and decent life is through changing the *pathos* and *diathesis* of that audience, through changing, this is to say, its feeling and disposition from mistrust and fear to trust and confidence. This means, in turn, establishing with the audience the good, righteous and decent *êthos* or character of the speaker who makes that *logos* and the genuineness of the feeling he would communicate. As Aristotle puts it,

> There are three means of convicing someone [τῶν . . . πίστεων] provided by the argument. These are based, respectively, either in the character of the speaker [ἐν τῷ ἤθει τοῦ λέγοντος], or in the way in which the audience has been disposed, or in the argument itself by its showing, or apparently showing, something to be so. Convincing is accomplished by character [διὰ μὲ οὖν τοῦ ἤθος] whenever the argument is so spoken that it makes the speaker worthy of trust and convincing [ἀξιόπιστον ποιῆσαι τὸν λέγοντα]. Those who are good people we trust and are convinced by [πιστεύομεν] more and sooner, and this strictly speaking in

all things, but most of all where opinions go in contrary directions. (*Rhet.* 1356a5–13)

In ethical matters, then, in questions of what is the good, right, and decent thing to do, there is for us human beings no divine argument, no *theos logos* after all but only human argument, only *ho anthropinos logos* (compare HHF 188–209 on the unavailability of mathematical *eidê* for ethical reasoning). Here "in the world" of our taking care of things with each other there is no transformation of questionable belief into some unshakeable mathematical insight regarding what each of these is "itself," no *eidos* "after which" these words might be "named." Consequently opinions about these will always be divided and "go in contrary directions," and here most of all the *êthos* of the speaker and the *pathos* he or she communicates are decisive. It is not by coincidence, then, that Plato concludes his rhetorical and exhortative speech to his audience with Phaedo saying of Socrates, "This was the end, Echecrates, of our companion, a man, as we might say, who of all those we encountered then was the best, most reasonable and most righteous" (118a).

4.2 Dialogue and Dialectic in the *Phaedrus*

It would, of course, be quite wrong to say that, having shown in the *Phaedo* the inadequacy of mathematical demonstration for ethical subject, Plato had once and for all abandoned it. For in fact, the possibility that demonstration holds out for countering sophism's corruption of rhetoric continues to fascinate him. In turning to the *Phaedrus*, we will now explore other dimensions of the tension generated by this ambivalence, a tension, however, that is found throughout Plato's dialogues.[10] For, on the one hand, insofar as they continue to take mathematics as their model and would instruct the learner in the way that mathematics does, they presuppose that "what really is," *to ontôs on*, is the kind of being characteristic of mathematical entities such as numbers or geometrical forms, namely being that "is" as fully disclosed and ever present to consciousness, with no "no longer but past" and no "not yet but coming" attaching to it. And such an understanding of what "is" presupposes, in turn, that writing in visual word signs (*sêmeia*) has begun to displace speaking in audible word names (*onomata*) as the appropriate mode of communication.[11] On the other hand, the dialogues, even as they would call rhetoric into question and replace it with the real "art" of dialectic, the *dialectikê technê*, remain persuasive speeches (*logoi*) to be enacted out loud and heard, and to this extent, at least, the older being as what "is" in coming to pass (*gignesthai*) and told orally in the narrative historical tale, still prevails in them.[12]

Stated another way, Plato, as the *Phaedrus* will make clear to us, has followed through after all on the very project he found wanting in the *Phaedo,* and in part, at least, he himself has converted consultative *dialegesthai,* or "talking through" what is the good, right, and decent thing to do, here, "in the world," into *dialegesthai* as "sorting out," theoretically and "at a distance," envisioned *eidê* or "looks" to things, for instance, love into a "left," opposite a "right" love (see the *Phaedrus* 265e ff.). And for this new *dialegesthai* as "dialectic" rather than dialogue, writing, which distributes characters spatially for a silent reader who sees their relationships, is obviously the most appropriate means of communication. This not withstanding, however, consultative *dialegesthai,* oral dialogue leading to conviction and an existential decision, remains central to Plato's task. For in the end, an actor, reenacting to himself or herself the parts out loud, is meant not so much to *see* the point demonstrated as to *hear* the exhortation to a *prohairesis tou biou,* to the choice of one way of life over another, namely the philosophical over the sophistical.[13]

4.2.1 From dialogue to diagram: rewriting sophistical written speech

What is the source of this tension in Plato between instructional "pointing something out" and rhetorical convincing, a tension that we have displayed in the *Phaedo* and that shows up anew in the *Phaedrus* in the opposition of writing and orality? In the *Phaedrus* the answer is clearly indicated right at the beginning when Phaedrus explains his fascination with Lysias's speech on love: "For Lysias," says Phaedrus, "has, in fact, written that one of the beautiful youths is being tempted, not, however, by a lover, and in just this consists the subtlety of it all: for he says that one should gratify the non-lover rather than the lover" (227c). The point here is that Lysias has been able to take something, namely love, the received opinion or *endoxon* about which holds that it is a good thing, and, by playing with the ambiguity of word names, *onomata,* make it seem to be, and in fact convince the listener that it really is, a bad thing. One need only compare the *Symposium*'s sequence of panegyrics on love to see why Phaedrus would be so impressed with Lysias's standing the norm on its head in this way. He marvels at Lysias's rhetorical prowess in inventing an epideictic speech that does not praise love but censures it. (See Aristotle's *Rhetoric,* 1358b12–13, on praise and censure [*epainos* and *psogos*] as the special tasks of epideictic or "showoff" rhetoric.)

At issue for Plato, of course, is not love specifically but the principal concerns of rhetoric in what Aristotle was later to define as its three branches: namely with *ta dikaia*, or what is just and right, in judicial *(dikanikê)* rhetoric; with *ta sumphera* or what is beneficial, in consultative (*sumbouleutikê*) rhetoric (Plato speaks instead of *ta agatha* or what is good); and, above all, with *ta kala*, or what is decent, noble, fair in "show off" (*epideiktikê*) rhetoric (see Aristotle's *Rhetoric*, 1358a36 ff. and the *Phaedrus* 263b). "Love" serves here as an example of the "weakness of word names" (*Epist.* 7.342e), their inherent equivocalness, and consequent susceptibility to sophists' techniques of making a word seem to mean the opposite of itself, specifically, what is "wrong" seem "right," what is "bad" seem "good," and, above all, what is "ignoble," "indecent," and "despicable" seem "decent." Indeed, precisely by playing upon the multiple and contradictory meanings of the word name "love," Lysias's speech has made it seem that it is "right," "beneficial," and "decent" to gratify the non-lover and has thereby implicitly twisted the meaning of each of these word names, too, into its opposite.[14]

As it was in the *Phaedo*, then, Plato's primary concern in the *Phaedrus* is with countering just this sophistical sleight of hand. It is to this end, in fact, that Plato advances the "doctrine" of the forms in the first place and that he elaborates in the *Phaedrus* the new idea of *dialegesthai*, no longer as "talking through" an existential question about what to do, but now as "sorting out" the conceptual "looks" or forms of things by "collecting" many forms into to one kind of thing, by "collecting," that is to say, many species or *eidê* into one genus or *genos*, and by "dividing," in turn, the one kind into its specific number of forms. The hope remains this: If, as the *Phaedo* proposed, one could found word names, as these are employed by traditional rhetorical argumentation, in univocal word signs designating forms, and if, as a consequence of this founding, one could found argument by the standard rhetorical "topics" of similarity and difference, the more and the less, the part and the whole, the prior and posterior, and so forth, in the dialectic of the forms, then one would have made oneself immune to sophistical twisting of a word name's meaning into the opposite of itself.

Later on in the *Phaedrus* we find an even more specific indication of the issue here: "It is not necessary," says Phaedrus, in restating the contemporary belief about rhetoric, "for the aspiring rhetor to learn what is right and just in reality [τὰ τῷ ὄντι δίκαια μανθάνειν] but rather only what seems so to the crowd, whichever crowd it is that is passing judgment, and not what is really good and decent [τὰ ὄντως ἀγαθὰ ἢ καλά] but only such things as seem to be [ὅσα δόξει]" (259e–260a). The point is that by reasoning in unstable, equivocal word names rhetors can make a thing seem (*dokei*) to be one thing and then seem to be its contrary. Thus, they only persuade to belief, the mental state corresponding to appearance—*doxa,* we note, means both belief and appearance—and they do not instruct to an insight or *mathêma* into what a thing really is "in itself." The older understanding of language as word names that give things their being in the first place by naming them[15] has no way of countering this sophistical exploitation of the weakness of word names, no way of countering the sophists' "knack" making a thing usually named "wrong" seem "right," a thing named "bad" seem "good," and a thing named "despicable" seem "decent." How, then, *is* this sophistical exploitation of a word name's instability to be countered?

As we have already seen in our investigations of the *Phaedo,* mathematics, with its true learning or *manthanein,* offers a model here, for mathematicians are invulnerable to sophistical attempts to make it seem, for instance, that a square can be constructed equal in area to a given circle.[16] The reason is this: unlike word names, their words, circle or square, or, better yet, 2 or 3^2, are what Plato, in still deferring to the traditional idea or the word as a name, calls *eponuma,* and Aristotle, *sêmeia* or signs (see the analysis of the *Phaedo,* 102b ff., in the previous section). These "eponyms," we have noted, are "named after" something already existent and fully present to consciousness, a form or conceptual "look" to something (*eidos*) that mathematicians have in view *before* convening upon a word for it. Mathematicians, then, know the thing "itself" that the eponym is "named after"; they know the *ti estin,* the "what it is" to be a circle. Hence, mathematicians do not get drawn into plays on representations of the thing itself, be these in words or in drawings, that treat the representations as if these were the real thing, the thing itself "really" (*ontôs*) and "in reality" (*tôi onti*). Put another way, they know the "truth" of the matter as opposed to its appearance in representations.

Now, despite the inadequacies of this attempt at a mathematical founding of rhetoric displayed in the *Phaedo,* the hope continues to be held out that the same sort of stable, static being which the mere eponyms "circle" and "2" designate can be "learned" mathematically for the assumed eponyms "the right," "the good," and "the decent," the principal subject matters of rhetorical speech. For once these are no longer taken as word names but as eponyms named after the things in themselves, *ta dikaia auta, ta agatha auta, ta kala auta,* and once one has the static universal beings themselves fully present in view, one could no longer be misled by plays on re-presentations of them any more than a mathematician could be misled into thinking six things were nine by someone turning "6" upside down and trying to pass it off as "9." In sum, as in the *Phaedo,* a shift from the understanding of speech as word names to an understanding of speech as re-presentations of something already present to the mind of the speaker is to become once again in the *Phaedrus* the new basis for the oral rhetorical process of taking counsel and conviction concerning the right, the good, and the decent. At least, that is Plato's proposal. Of course, it remains to be seen in the *Phaedrus,* too, just how far he is willing to go with it.

New in the *Phaedrus,* however, is the explicit opposition of writing and orality, and it is the tension here on which we now need to focus. Lysias's speech, for which the impressionable "Phaedrus" character expresses such enthusiasm and which establishes the theme of rhetoric for the entire dialogue, is a consummate example of writing that is only oral speech written down—"Do you believe," Phaedrus asks, "that any other of the Greeks could *speak* [εἰπεῖν] better on this same subject and more fully?" (234e; emphasis added). Its oral syntax according to what were only in a later literary rhetoric to be called the "schemata" of "parallelism" and "antithesis," and its argument by "topics" based on this oral syntax, principally, as we are about to see, by "similarity and difference" and "the prior and posterior," both make clear that, even though this speech is written and put forward precisely as an example of speech writing, the technology of writing has not yet influenced its composition in any definitive way.[17] The same, however, cannot be said of either of Socrates' speeches, and just this is the point. If Plato condemns a kind of writing in the *Phaedrus* it is not the "writing" behind Socrates' speeches, the "writing in the soul" (see 276a and 278a), but only the "writing down" of oral speech.[18]

In this regard we note, to begin with, that Lysias's "written" speech is organized according to precisely that standard oral form of *taxis* or "arrangement" which is condemned later on in the dialogue's critique of traditional rhetorical theory (see 266d ff.). It still has, if sometimes only in vestigial form, a *prooimion* or "introduction" to ingratiate the speaker with the audience (see HLR §§263–88 on the *exordium*), a *diêgesis,* or "narration" of the circumstances surrounding the argument (see HLR §§289–347 on the *narratio*), a *pistis* or "confirmation" in which the case is made for the speaker's claim (see HLR §§348–430 on the *argumentatio*), a *lusis* or "refutation" in which opposed arguments are anticipated and countered (see HLR §430 on the *refutatio*), and a *protrepsis* or "peroration" in which the argument is recapitulated and the point driven home (see HLR §§431–42 on the *peroratio*).

To be sure, the "introduction" and "narration" are fused, and both thereby nearly suppressed, in a brief recapitulation of the circumstances and the claim of the argument: "You know how things stand with me and you have heard how I consider it to our advantage that these things come to pass: for I am worthy that you not refuse me in what I ask in as much as I happen not to be your lover" (230e-31a). The speech then moves quickly and even abruptly into the "confirmation" itself (231a ff.), which contains, by my count, twelve arguments from premises mostly derived from the "topics" of "similarity and difference" and "the prior and posterior," and which for the most part is composed, accordingly, with the diachronic trope of antiphony (antithesis), "*men . . . de*," which is to say, "On the one hand, this . . . (whereas) on the other hand, that." Thus we find (1) lovers repent once their passion ceases (topic: prior/posterior), whereas (trope: antiphony) non-lovers do not (topic: difference); (2) lovers later take into acount the losses they once incurred and benefits they once granted (topic: prior/posterior), whereas (trope: antiphony) non-lovers do not (topic: difference); (3) if lovers once incurred the enmity of a former love to win their new love, they will later incur the enmity of their present love to win a new love (topic: prior/posterior); (4) lovers are like madmen to whom no one entrusts serious matters (topic: similarity); (5) lovers who were once mad will, when they have later become sane, regret what they have done (topic: prior/posterior); (6) if you choose from among lovers the choice will be small, whereas (trope: antiphony) if you choose from among non-lovers, it will be large (topic: difference; also contraries); (7) lovers boast of their success, whereas (trope: antiphony) non-lovers do not (topic: difference); (8) people will see lovers and gossip about them, whereas (trope: antiphony) no one pays any attention to non-lovers (topic: difference); (9) when lovers quarrel, the damage to the beloved is greater than to the lover (topic: more/less), whereas (trope: antiphony) when non-lovers quarrel the damage to both is equal (topic: difference); (10) lovers feel threatened and are hence(forth) possessive (topic: prior/posterior), whereas (trope: antiphony) non-lovers do not and are not (topic: difference); (11) lovers are first blinded by physical desire; hence, later (topic: prior/posterior) when they have sobered up, they will not wish to remain friends, but (trope: antiphony) non-lovers will always be friends (topic: difference); and (12) I, the non-lover, will not praise you indiscriminately, whereas (trope: antiphony) a lover will (topic: difference).

This last argument contains a misplaced "peroration," misplaced technically, at least, since the "refutation" is still to come:

> If you let me persuade you, I will consort with you out of concern not only for present pleasure but also for future advantage; for, love has not subdued me, but I having mastered myself, will not be suddenly seized with strong hatred on account of small matters but will slowly build small anger on account of great matters, forgiving what is unintentional and trying to prevent what is intentional. (233b–c)

It is precisely this kind of typically oral, pleonastic, and antiphonal phrasing of contraries that Phaedrus finds so compelling here—"present pleasure" versus "future advantage," love has not "subdued me" versus I have "mastered myself," "suddenly seized" versus "slowly build," "strong hatred" versus "small matters" crisscrossed (diachronic trope: "chiasmus") with "small anger" versus "great matters." At 234c Phaedrus comments approvingly, "Is it [the speech] not marvelously florid [ὑπερφυῶς], in everything else, to be sure, but especially in its speaking with the words it does [τοῖς ὀνόμασιν εἰρῆσθαι]?" And to Socrates' critical assessment that the speech is repetitive—only writing, we note with Havelock, which obviates the need for memorization, could afford not to be—and to his objection that it should be praised not because "each of the words [ἕκαστα τῶν ὀνόματῶν] is clear, rounded and precisely turned" but only if it has said what it ought to (234e), Phaedrus responds, "You are speaking nonsense, Socrates, for what is best about the speech consists in just that. . . . No one could say anything else more full and fully worthy of the subject [πλείω καὶ πλείονος ἄξια]" (234b).

We note, finally, the oral, "appositive" syntax of this "confirmation."[19] The whole section lacks subordinating causal inferences, such as "because," "therefore," "hence," and so forth. Instead, it is "stitched together" in a merely temporal sequence with coordinating conjunctions like "and furthermore" and "moreover" (*kai men de, eti de*). One utterance, this is to say, simply follows narratively, in time, upon another as "this . . . and then this . . . and then this," and so forth, with no timeless *logical* connections discernible beneath what is spoken over time. (As we will see momentarily, in Socrates' first speech Plato will use the syntax of writing to make revisions in just this regard too.)

There follows next at 233c ff. a kind of "refutation" in which counterarguments are anticipated: (1) if you say that kinship (*philia*) cannot be as strong if the partners are not in love, consider that, then, we would value neither our children, nor our fathers and mothers, as we do, and that we would not have the many trusted friends we do; and (2) if it is said that one ought above all to gratify those who plead most ardently, then in all other matters we should gratify those most in need too, for instance, by inviting beggars to a banquet. The *reductio ad absurdum* here is a variation on the topic of "difference," namely, an argument by "contradiction."[20] A later, formal logic would put it this way, "If A, then B; but not B; therefore, not A," but this would be an abstraction from the concrete argument here, which is based on *endoxa* or received opinions about the usual train of events "in the world," and not on insight into universals.

If we turn now to the objections advanced against this speech, it becomes immediately evident that, despite the dialogue's own notorious criticisms of writing (274b ff.), this speech is being measured against a *literary*, architechtonic standard: the crucial objection is that it is not *structured* properly.[21] Already at 235a it is said that its author seems to have trouble saying many things about one and the same thing in an organized fashion, and this objection becomes the core of the criticisms made later at 263d ff.: Lysias did not require us to take love as "some one thing among existent things [ἕν τι τῶν ὄντων]" and consequently did not "put together" his speech properly (see the *suntaxamenos* at 263e); on the contrary, its various thoughts seem to have been just "tossed in" without rhyme or reason (264 b). As we have seen, the speech does follow, albeit if loosely, the *taxis* or "arrangement" traditionally appropriate for *oral* rhetoric. However, as precisely as a written (*graphemenos*) speech it does not measure up; indeed, it is expressely said that it lacks "any logo*graphical* necessity" (τινὰ ἀνάγκην λογογραφικήν) (id.; emphasis added), and "every speech," we read, "ought to be put together [συνεστάναι] like a living thing having a sort of body of its own such that it lacks neither a head nor feet but has a middle and extremities written [γεγραμμένα] as is fitting in relation to each other and the whole" (264c).

Thus, it is not so much in the "invention" (*heuresis*) of arguments where fault is to be found as in their "positioning" (*diathesis*) (see 235e–236a). The proposal, accordingly, is to replace the merely temporal sequence of traditional oral rhetoric with the spatial logographical "positioning" of collection into a one and division into many (265d ff.).[22] In failing to do anything like this, Lysias demonstrates no more knowledge of the proper structural principles for the composition of speeches than do the writers of the standard handbooks on rhetoric. To be sure, these writers speak of the elements of speeches and even of the "positioning" of these elements, beginning, first, with an "introduction" followed, second by a "narration," third by "proofs," fourth by "likelihoods" (266e), and, in conclusion, some kind of "recapitulation" (267d). Moreover, they speak of "refutation" and "further refutation" as these are to be employed in judicial rhetoric's "accusation" and "defense" (267a). And in telling us of such "subtleties of the art" (τὰ κομψὰ τῆς τέχνης) (266d), for which, incidentally, Phaedrus was so enthusiastic—see his *kekompseutai,* or "[it] has been finely wrought," at 227c in description of Lysias's speech—they go on to broach matters of "insinuation," "indirect praise," "indirect censure," the proper length, "duplication," "sententiousness," "speaking in likenesses," "right speaking," and the like (267a–c).

But all these things, it is concluded, are mere knacks and preliminaries and not part of a *technê* or art at all, for any art implies knowledge of the structural principles underlying the thing, in this case the speech, which it would "put together."[23] Indeed, the practice and teachings of contemporary rhetoric appear ridiculous when measured against those real arts that do know the proper structural form of the thing they are putting together of which the *Phaedrus* names three: the art of medicine, which knows the right form of the body and, hence, not just how, but why and when to induce a change its condition and bring that right form about; the art of composing of tragedy, which knows the right form of the whole and, hence, not just how, but when and why to make long and short declamations; and harmony and the art of composing of music, which knows the right form of the whole piece, and, hence, not just how, but when and why to strike high and low notes (268a–269a).

In all these cases the true practitioners of the art must have envisioned and "read" ahead of time a static dia*gram*, a written chart of the particular narrative historical subject matter on which they are working. Thus, an ontological shift is presupposed here: the true *technitês* or artisan must "look away from" (*apoblepein*) beings that come to pass in the temporal world, and look "to" (*pros*) the static being or conceptual "look," the *eidos*, behind what he or she is dealing with. Put another way, he or she must transcend the world, the tale of which is told orally and *heard*, and must now *see* its underlying structure. In effect, reading what is written over space has displaced listening to what is spoken over time.

How, then, is this transition from, and transcendence of, the narrative historical world to be accomplished in rhetoric? How can what has heretofore been only an empirical "knack" (*empeiria, tribê*) be raised to a true art? As is expressly stated at 264e ff., "Socrates'," that is, Plato's, rewriting of Lysias's speech shows us the strategy to be employed, namely, "Seeing together [συνορῶντα] and bringing under one idea things dispersed in all directions in order that whatever one wishes to instruct about [περὶ οὗ ἂν ἀεὶ δοδάσκειν ἐθέλῃ] may, in being defined, be made plain" (265d) and, second, "being able, in turn, to sever according to species and forms [κατ' εἴδη], and at the natural joints" (265e).

Put another way, "it is necessary to have seen and to know [εἰδέναι] what the counsel [ἡ βουλή] is about" (237c). Seeing and knowing such fully determinate subject matter requires, however, that both the being of that subject matter and the method of arguing about it be radically transformed; for, ordinarily, rhetorical taking counsel (*sumbouleuesthai*) is, as Aristotle tells us, about precisely that kind of being which "*is* susceptible of being otherwise" than it is (*Rhet.* 1357a4–7), and, consequently, rhetorical argument cannot have the form of demonstration in the strict sense (*apodeixis haplôs*), which treats only being that "*is not* susceptible of being otherwise" (*An. Post.* 71b12–13; emphasis added). But all this is now to be changed by Plato's proposal to put rhetoric on a new foundation: Behind the indeterminate narrative historical being of the things we take counsel about, indeterminate things that, as Heidegger would say, always "keep to themselves" and partially "hide themselves" from our view, there will now be uncovered a necessary, statically present being, fully in view, that always is what it is and cannot be otherwise. And having thus stripped the content of rhetorical argument of all its questionability, of any "Is it or isn't it?" it will no longer have even the residual dialogical form that simultaneously entertains two possible contradictory claims in both a "confirmation" and a "refutation"—"Yes, it is" and "No, it is not." Instead, it will now become demonstration (*apodeixis*), which is to say, logical inference from one indisputable declarative statement to the next. In other words, we are back to where the *Phaedo* had left off. Let us now turn to "Socrates' " first speech to see just how this transformation of content and argumentative form actually works.

We note that, strikingly, right from the beginning the mode of discourse has switched from *peithein* to *didaskein*, from persuading to instruction.[24] Indeed, there is no longer any standard rhetorical "introduction" at all, by which the speaker might ingratiate himself with his audience, but rather a statement of argumentative method! For an argument to succeed, it is declared, it must begin with a definition of the subject matter (see 237c f.). In other words, the task the speaker has set for himself is no longer the rhetorical one of getting the listener to hear and follow an exhortation to a particular choice and decision but, instead, is now the didactic one of getting an onlooker to see and understand something: "It is necessary to see intellectually [δεῖ δὴ νοῆσαι]" we are told, "that there are in each of us some two forms [ἰδέα] of what rules and drives us" (237d). We are to see, this is to say, the logical structure of unity and multiplicity obtaining behind the particular case of what we are talking about and keep "looking at it" (εἰς τοῦτο ἀποβλέποντες) (id.).

It is not surprising, accordingly, that this speech has an obvious visual, dia*grammatic*, that is, written structure underlying it and is easily schematized or "outlined" spatially (see Figure 1).

Beyond its lack of a true rhetorical "introduction" and its diagrammatical format there are three further important indications of the didactic and apodictical intent of this "speech." The first is the omission of a "refutation," for in treating its subject matter as static, necessary being that is precisely "not susceptible of being otherwise than it is," the argument here obviously cannot follow the form of the "earlier," "more original" (Heidegger: *früher, ursprünglicher*) dialectic and rhetoric. For by nature these entertain both sides of an argument (see *Top.* 101a35–36 and *Rhet.* 1355a29–30), and, in presupposing that both sides of that contradiction could be true, pursue a "questioning of a contradiction" (*erôtêsis antiphaseôs*) (see *An. Pr.* 24a–25). Rather, precisely as demonstration, this argument must state premises and conclusions drawn from them in an unbroken logical chain of declarative sentences.

Figure 1

Introduction: Exposition of the appropriate method.

(I) "Diagrammatic" definition of what love is by collection into a one and division into a many:

(A) "forms of what rules and drives us,"

(A) (1) "an inborn desire for pleasure,"

(1) (a) "temperance" (*sôphrosunê*) when the desire is under the guidance of reason,

(1) (b) "wantonness" (*hubris*) when it is irrational:

(b) (i) the wanton desire for food or "gluttony,"

(b) (ii) the wanton desire for drink,

(b) (iii) the wanton desire for the pleasure of the beautiful or "love."

(A) (2) "an acquired opinion aimed at what is best";

(II) Effects that follow from love being what it is:

(A) while the lover is still in love,

(1) he will be injurious to the beloved

(a) intellectually (b) physically (c) socially/materially

(B) and when the lover is no longer in love,

(1) he will welsh on his promises,

(2) he will force the beloved to chase after him.

Conclusion: the argument summarized in reverse.

The second indication is the "speech's" affective neutrality. Because the task is to "point out" (*apodeiknunai*) something to a spectator and not to move a hearer to a decision, there is no need to change how an audience feels about something, no need to change their *diathesis*, or, with Heidegger, how they "find themselves feeling about it."[25] Indeed, it is presupposed from the start that the interlocutors will be *theoretically* disposed, that they will "feel like" looking at things dispassionately. We note, in this regard, the carefully crafted pastoral setting which Plato contrives for their exchange, namely the gentle and verdant slopes of the Ilissus, where the interlocutors can repose in peace (*hesuchia*; 229a) and at their leisure (*scholê*; see 229e and also 258e).[26]

Third, and in keeping with the "speech's" affective neutrality, is the drastically reduced and even perfunctory "peroration." There is, to be sure, a sort of exhortation to an audience here, but it is so pat as to make the claim of near dithyrambic inspiration at 241e utterly ironic.

It is clear, then, that this "speech" is not meant so much to be heard and acted upon practically, as it is meant to "point out," *apodeiknunai*, something for us to see as spectators and onlookers (*theôretes*). Hence, not the temporal acoustical sequence and tone of what is said is important, rather, the static spatial structure that the writer constructs for himself prior to speaking out loud. The "speech's" purpose, in other words, is to let us see, too, the writer's overview and chart of the subject matter, and for that, it might best be read silently by the one for whom it is intended.

It is in regard specifically to wantonness, however, that Plato most obviously tips his hand concerning the overall strategy here: "Wantonness is many-named [πολυώνυμον]," his "Socrates" is made to say, "for it is of many parts and many forms [πολυμελὲς γὰρ καὶ πολυειδές] and the most outstanding of these forms [τούτων τῶν ἰδεῶν], whichever this happens to be, provides an eponym [ἐπωνυμίαν] of its own for the man possessing it and so named [ὀνομζόμενον]" (237a).

The deeper point of this apparently incidental observation is best explained by the *Phaedo*.[27] As we have already seen in section 2.2, in that dialogue the word name is converted into an "after-name," an *eponuma*, named "after" the preexistent idea and form, and signifing it. As such, this word is then predicated of particular things exemplifying the idea and form, in the case of the *Phaedrus*'s "wantonness," for example, predicated of a man who is said to be wanton, or, more "specifically," to be a glutton, drunk, or eroticist, for these are the many forms or species (*eidê*) into which the one kind or genus (*genos*) of "wanton" is to be divided. In the *Phaedrus* we now learn that once this change in the understanding of word names occurs, the next step is to uncover behind word names and the things to which they are applied the lattice-like differential structure of interrelated forms or "looks" things have about them and remain focused on it (βλέποντες δὲ πρὸς αὐτό) (238e).

We now also learn in the *Phaedrus* that when Plato proceeds, as he does here, from the definition of love according to this lattice-like eidetic structure, to reasoning by cause and effect, he has also radically altered the topic of prior/posterior and deleted its essential temporality and narrative historicality. In contrast to Lysias's speech in which connections between the prior and the posterior were nothing but temporal, the "causal" sequence in Socrates' first speech is entirely timeless and purely logical. To apply Aristotle's terminology, we have here neither efficient, material, nor final causality, all of which preserve the original temporal sequence of the topic, the prior and the posterior, but only formal causality, which is completely atemporal: Love being by definition "what it *is*," it "follows" (that is, it can be inferred logically) that the lover *is* deleterious, *is* disagreeable, and so forth. Far from telling the narrative of something's coming to pass, the "is" here states a static logical relationship that holds always (*aei*) regardless of time and place.[28] In this respect, too, then, we have moved away from hearing the oral tale and turned to reading the eidetic chart posited behind it, and it is for this reason that what might count as a "narration"—"Now once there *was* [ἦν] a young boy . . ." (237b)—falls outside of the "speech" proper and belongs, in fact, to the rhetorical exhortation of the *Phaedrus* dialogue as a whole.

The art of "positioning" on which the new rhetoric is to be founded thus amounts to this: Before, in invention or *heuresis*, we merely "hit upon" or "came across" arguments by ransacking our memory, or, as a later, literary "rhetoric" was to put it, by turning, randomly and unsystematically, to the various *topoi* or "places" in the "apothecary" of standard arguments and fishing out a premise based on what were later to be called the "topics" of "similarity and difference," the "more and the less," "the prior and posterior," "the whole and the part." Now, however, we are to first organize our "speech" according to collection into a one, a genus (*genos*) and division into species (*eidê*). Before, the speaker traced, in "topical" arguments, the way that speech presents the narrative historical world in its naming of things according to the diachronic tropes of symphony (*te . . . kai*; "both this . . . and this") and antiphony (*men . . . de*; "one the one hand, this . . . on the other, that") and the metonymic tropes of synechdoche and metaphor. Now, however, he or she first "sorts out," in dialectic, the static forms of things into classes and then argues in eponyms "named after" these classes of things and draws inferences according to which of these forms or classes is included in, or excluded from, which other ones: "All A are B, all C are A; therefore all A are C," and so on. In this way *dialegesthai* as "talking things through," in narrative historical speech and telling about them as they come to pass, is converted into *dialegesthai* as "sorting things out" dialectically in words that are now taken to be, not a presentation of the thing in itself, but a secondary re-presentation, in signs, of the classes or forms of things. The critique of Lysias's speech and Plato's rewriting of it thus make clear, on the one hand, an ontological shift from being that is understood as narrative historical coming to pass, to being that is understood as static presence, and, on the other, a consequent logical shift from reasoning by the natural topics to reasoning by *apodeixis*, demonstration.

Moreover, we note that with these ontological and logical shifts argument is stripped of all traces of its original dialogical form, even those merely residual traces evidenced in traditional rhetoric's inclusion of a "refutation" of opposed arguments. The reason is clear: the new universal being in which the particular case is to be founded, *to ontôs on,* "being that really is," has no more questionablity or indeterminacy about it. With Aristotle we could say that, unlike contingent practical matters, the subject matter now is "necessary" being and is "not susceptible of being otherwise" than it is. Therefore, it will be spoken about or, better yet, written about, not in interrogative, but in declarative, sentences, *logoi apophantikoi,* one "following" logically and necessarily from the next. Phaedrus, consequently, has nothing to object to in the actual argument of Socrates' first speech but only something to say about its supposed "inspirational" quality; for that is all he is asked about, and most ironically, at that, given the speech's complete sterility: "Well, does it not seem to you, dear Phaedrus, that I have been undergoing some sort of divine experience?" (238c).

4.2.2 The *Phaedrus*'s return from instruction (*didaskalia*) to conviction (*peithô*)

The fact, however, that monological argument is so uncharacteristic of Plato gives us a clear indication that this proposed revision of rhetoric and conversion of it into demonstration can hardly be the whole story here. Indeed, the account we have given so far would be entirely inadequate, not only to explain the whole of Plato's work, in which no other "set" speeches constructed according to the principles of the newly proposed dialectical "art" are to be found, but also to explain the *Phaedrus* dialogue itself, and even to explain "Socrates' " second speech, which in large part reverts from instructional demonstration to an oral and persuasive form. Just why the second speech does revert to the older orality can be discerned at least in part in Plato's account of the second feature of the true art of rhetoric he is proposing: in addition to knowing the differential system of the forms for the things it speaks about, it must also know the differential system of the forms of the souls *it would guide.* For ultimately the task of even this new art of rhetoric is not just getting someone to see how things stand, but still *psuchagôgia,* guidance of the soul to a decision and choice of life. In other words, its task remains, after all, conviction and persuasion, getting someone to hear.

Hence, as we learn at 269e ff., there is another deficiency in the non-art of traditional rhetoric that must be remedied besides its lack of organizational principles: it is completely without this knowledge of the souls or personalities on which it works, and consequently it engenders its effects on these only haphazardly, without rhyme or reason. Indeed, it arouses *pathê* or feelings in the soul in much the ridiculous way that a non-doctor might arouse motions in the body, namely with no idea of the right order for its object, affective or physiological, respectively, and of how the *pathê* or motions induced might contribute to that order.[29] In fact, however, "The same thing holds for the art of healing as for the rhetorical art. . . . In both it is necessary to sort things out, in the body, on the one hand, and in the soul, on the other, if you would proceed not merely by knack and experience but by art" (270b).

To be sure, the new rhetorical art will therefore require a dialectical foundation for its guidance of souls just as it does for its composition of speeches. Souls too, that is, must be classified "structurally" according to genus and species, and "if it [soul] has more forms than one [ἐὰν δὲ πλείω εἴδη ἔχῃ], these must be enumerated" (270d). Thus, once again our experience of particular things at a place and time, in this case souls, must be charted and founded in a static typology. However, something else is now introduced into the notion of an art here: not only must it know the *phusis* or essential nature of a thing in regard to its forms, but it must also know the *phusis* or natural potential (*dunamis*) of the thing in regard to what it can do and undergo over time (270d). In being tied to *dunamis* here, *phusis* preserves its earlier narrative historical sense.[30]

Furthermore, in considering what the soul does and undergoes we are not in the least abandoning practical persuasion for theoretical observation and demonstration:

> When he [the student of the art] is sufficiently able to tell which sort of man is convinced by which sort of speeches, and, coming across such a man, is able to recognize him and prove to himself that this is that man and that this is the nature to which the speeches pertained and to which, a soul of this nature now being in fact present, these speeches must be applied if the end of convincing it in such matters is to be accomplished—possessing all this, and having added to it the right times to speak and refrain from speaking in a brief style and pitiful style and forceful style, and having learned each of the forms, for each of which he knows the appropriate and inappropriate time—only then has the art been nobly worked out to its completion. (271e–72b)

Here any theoretical considerations are merely preliminary to the practical applications and not the other way around; here persuasion to an existential decision, not just by dialectical logic but through communication of *êthos* and *pathos*, is the goal; and here, consequently, the stylistic devices previously discarded as "merely rhetorical," for instance, being "brief," "pitiful," "forceful," are reincorporated—as the grand periodic style of this very passage itself makes clear.

Hence, in still attending to practical *peithô*, persuasion and conviction, and not yet turning fully to *didaskalia*, instruction, Plato has by no means abstracted from the temporal, local, physical world in which particular human beings interact with each other. With Heidegger, we might say that, on the contrary, he is still concerned with how, in our taking care of things "in the world," we human beings affect one another, through speech, and in what we do and undergo in speaking to each other. And here the patent tension in the *Phaedrus* and, in fact in the whole of Plato's dialogues, confronts us once again: at the same time that they are theoretical and would redirect the mind's eye to the static chart of forms that is said to underlie and found our experience in the world, they would, like any consultative or *sumbouleutikê* rhetoric, exhort a particular audience, at a particular time and place, to a practical, existential decision and choice. Thus, though they *can* be read theoretically for their doctrinal content by disengaged readers, they are meant ultimately to be heard by listeners who reenact out loud the parts of "Socrates" and his interlocutor, in this case, "Phaedrus," and who hear the exhortation.[31] What we have at this point in the *Phaedrus*, where the "guidance of souls" is at issue, is, as it were, the theory of the actual rhetorical practice of the dialogues: Plato himself is, in fact, always "matching" speeches with the souls of his particular audience in order to persuade that audience to an existential decision for the life of philosophy.[32]

It is scarcely surprising, then, that even this theoretical and "methodological" section of the dialogue on the art and non-art of rhetoric ends in a kind of rhetorical *protrepsis* and "peroration" of its own, in an exhortation and "turning" of the soul (see 274a). At issue is whether, as Tisias says, rhetors should trade in what is merely likely (*to eikos*) and convincing (*to pithanon*) or should abide by the truth (*alêtheia*) (272e), and though it is proposed again that one who knows the truth will be most effective in convincing people of what is like the truth but false—this is the promise with which "Phaedrus" had been drawn in (see 261e ff.)—the reason given now for choosing the way of truth is quite another. Indeed, it becomes clear now that if one knew the truth, one would no longer be the least interested in exploiting this knowledge to pass off the false verisimilitude for the truth. For if one knows the truth, one will be concerned only with "being able to say what is pleasing to the gods," pleasing to one's "good masters," that is, and not to one's "fellow slaves" (273e–74a). Thus, this "Phaedrus," who, like "Cebes" and "Simmias" in the *Phaedo*, stands in for the audience of a rhetorical drama, has himself been systematically misled. "Socrates," having baited him with the lure of rhetorical prowess, has now, in this exhortation, switched goals on him: "if the way is long and roundabout," Socrates admonishes, "do not be astonished, for it was necessary to traverse it for the sake of greater things, and not those you have in mind" (274a). Whereas before the issue had been the theoretical one of how best to mislead someone else (see 262a: "the one about to deceive another and not be deceived himself must see exactly what the likenesses and differences among things are") the issue has now become the existential one of "how you [Phaedrus] might please God most in acting and speaking in regard to speeches" (274b).

And as a matter of fact, "Socrates' " second speech had already displayed some of the tensions between instruction and conviction that have come to the fore here. For one thing, there is its notably incongruous blending of different modes of argument. For instance, we have the obviously facetious "division" of "divine madness," bad punning on *manikê* and *oiêsis* and all, and the definition of love (244a–45c) followed then by the abruptly different, cut-and-dry demonstrative reasoning about the immortality of "Soul" (245c–46a),[33] and then, finally, by the equally abrupt shift to the rhetorical, merely "likely argument" (*eikos logos*) by the topic of "similarity" and by example (*paradeigma*). What is more, the example employed, namely the "chariot" of the soul with which the remaining, and by far largest, part of the speech (246a–57a) is concerned, is based not on "past events" but "fabricated" by the speaker (see *Rhet.* 1393a23 ff., on the three kinds of example); thus ultimately the argument rests on the metonymic trope of metaphor. Viewed in retrospect from the proposals made afterward for founding traditional "knacks" of rhetoric in the "art" of dialectic (265d ff.), this speech patently fails to measure up. Indeed, its beginning is obviously tongue in cheek and only parodies the "art" of dialectic, much as does the definition of the sophist in the dialogue of that name (see *Sophist* 218b ff.). Even its abruptly inserted demonstration of the immortality of the soul (245c–46a) is based more on "nature" as "potential" than on collection into a genus and division into species (see n.33), and the bulk of the speech argues by the very "likelihoods" and "likenesses" forsworn at 267a and has no dialectical founding whatsoever. (See the "what it [the soul] is like" [ᾧ δὲ ἔοικεν] at 246a.) Obviously, then, if this speech is to be justified at all, it can only be by the second standard of the new rhetorical art, namely the systematic "guidance of souls" and the matching of speeches with their particular audience, *not to instruct the latter, but to guide him or her to the existential decision advocated by the speaker.* In the end, this "Phaedrus" and any intended audience for the dialogue are meant not to see how things stand but to hear; they are to be persuaded to choose the life of philosophy even by such indirectly hortatory passages of the speech as this:

> Now when the better parts of thought, that lead to an ordered regimen and philosophy, win out, they [the lovers] lead a blessed and concordant life here on earth, being empowered over themselves and orderly, and having subjected that part in which the evils of the soul were spawned while having liberated that part in which virtue developed. (256a–b)

(We note this "Socrates' " own adroit use of the diachronic trope of antiphony in the way he, just like "Lysias," phrases contraries: first, "subjected . . . evils," and then, in response, "liberated . . . virtue.")

However, Plato's dialogue as a whole is the real rhetorical "speech" here, and, hence, the real exhortation to a *prohairesis tou biou* or "choice of life" falls outside "Socrates' " second speech proper and into the dialogue itself:

> And if, in the previous speech, Phaedrus and I have spoken anything coarse to you [Love], blame Lysias, the father of that speech, make him desist from such speeches and, as his brother Polemarchus has turned, turn him to philosophy so that his lover here [Phaedrus] might no longer vacillate between both possibilities, as he does now, but rather aim his life simply at Love along with philosophical speeches. (256b)

As we know, crucial for success here in convincing the audience to decide is obviously not the logic of the argument, for that logic could only instruct someone in how things stand. Rather, it is the *êthos* or character of the speaker and the *pathos* or feeling about the issue that the speaker is able to communicate to his or her audience. This accounts for the deliberately passionless, trite, and thoroughly unconvincing exhortation at the end of "Socrates' " first speech (241d), and for Plato's having his "Socrates" recite the whole thing with his head covered (237a), which, given the noonday heat of the place, is a remarkable dramatic device to say the least. The point is that "Socrates," having precisely the *axiopiston*, convincing/trustworthy, character he does (see *Rhet.* 1356a5), cannot possibly invest this devious and disingenuous speech with anything of himself; he cannot possibly stand behind it. (Note the introductory comment before the speech begins: "Among these was a suitor no less in love than any of them, but who had made the youth believe he was not" [237b].) This discrepancy between the *êthos* of the speaker and the *logos* of what he says is not at all present in this second speech, however. Indeed, who this "Socrates" is and how he feels about the subject matter of this speech is decisive for the conviction Plato wants to achieve with it.[34]

Where, then, does that leave us with regard to writing and speech? The point is this: If all good speeches were really demonstrative and not rhetorical, if good speeches were meant to instruct to an insight and not win conviction to decide on an existential choice, and if, consequently, rhetorical speeches were to be made good speeches by founding them in the art of dialectic, then writing would be the appropriate medium for them. For, in the first place, dialectic, as we have seen, is dia*grammatic*, and instead of "talking things through" in the original sense of *dialegesthai* it "sorts things out" in Plato's new sense of that word. In other words it "writes things out"; it distributes them over space. Hence, letters, *grammata*, marks written on a surface, would be the most congenial mode for communication of any dialectic and of whatever "speech" might be founded in it. Second, precisely as marks on a surface, writing communicates relationships for sight. Hence, if, once again, the task were intruction and not conviction, if one were supposed to see how things stand rather than to hear an exhortation to decide on a course of action, then writing would be the appropriate medium of communication, just as it plainly is, for instance, in the mathematical sciences. From this it follows, third, that since the only *pathos* to be communicated would be the affective neutrality prerequisite for theoretical insight, writing's affectively neutral marks rather than voiced intonation would be the proper communicator. Finally, if the communication were really communication of the fully present and static, lattice-like structure of the *eidê* or conceptual "looks" of things, then not spoken words that are heard as they come to pass over time and fade away, but marks that stay where they are, in view, as we read them, would be appropriate.

So why, then, does Plato seem to condemn writing and to turn back to orality, as a majority of scholars, most notably Jacques Derrida, conclude he has?[35] We will have more to say about this question in the next section, but in the end, the answer to it can only be because writing kills off the protreptical, exhortative dimension of speech that Plato, despite his apparent turn away from conviction to instruction, wishes to preserve. Put another way, as toneless, affectively neutral marks distributed over a surface, writing cannot communicate the *êthos* and *pathos* of the speaker and consequently cannot get an audience to hear an exhortation to an existential decision. Contrary to Derrida, it is in just this sense that written speeches are "fatherless" and need their "father" to come to their assistance and say what he has to say *out loud* (see 275e, but also 256b, cited above, "Lysias, the father of that speech . . ."), and not because without him they become disruptive of the semantical status quo. After all, as we have noted before and see again as the dialogue nears its conclusion at 276c, ultimately it is not a "science's" theoretical objects that we are concerned with in making speeches; rather, even if the verb *epistasthai* occurs here, it is the three major existential issues for the decisions that rhetoric would induce, namely what is right, what is decent, what is good (*ta dikaia, ta kala, ta agatha*). Obviously the speaker on these subjects cannot seek mere insight, but must instead exhort to an existential choice; he or she is not just a teacher but an orator, and the communicative task is not to get someone to see by instruction what these three are "in themselves," but, by conviction to get someone to decide to live according to them. For this to happen, as Plato well knows, how the speaker comports himself or herself in regard to them, and how he or she feels about them, must be communicated, and for that, orality is necessary. (It follows that the reenactment of the dialogue must include a reenactment of "Socrates' " part as well as a reenactment of the part of his interlocutor, as I think Plato clearly intended; see note 31 above.)

To be sure, this is not at all the argument that Plato advances for orality in the *Phaedrus*. In the story narrated (!) of Thamus and Theuth (274c ff.)—this too is an argument by a fictional *paradeigma*, and we note again just how "unscientific" and traditionally rhetorical Plato's arguments can be—it is said that by increasing our capacity for memorialization (*hupomnêsis*) writing will only diminish our capacity for "being reminded" (*anamneskesthai*) of the truth: people will read, but "without instruction" (*aneu didachês*) they will only seem to know the things they have read (275a).

However, we note that although the instruction here and even the "art of dialectic" itself are communicated in words "that instruct for the sake of learning," words presumably intended to bring about *insight into* the conceptual relationships obtaining among "what is right, decent, and good" (278a) and not to bring about a *decision for* a right, decent, and good life, the form of communication still turns out to be the earlier oral *dialegesthai* and not some kind of logical demonstration founded on a dialectical "sorting out" of the conceptual "looks" to things: only by "talking things through" *in question and answer*, it is said, can the insight be induced (see 275e and 277e). Thus, even if the interlocutor's relation to them is theoretical and not practical/existential, the realities with which this instruction is concerned, the right, decent, and good, can scarcely be the "necessary" kind of being about which no questions can arise. Rather, they must be that questionable indeterminate being which is "susceptible of being otherwise" than it is, and which withholds itself from our awareness. This much is clear: whatever its aim, any "instruction" here cannot be in regard to a stabilized, static *eidos* fully present to mind and beyond all questionability.[36]

More to the point, however, thus far the consideration of oral "instruction" here has, perforce, treated only the demonstrative dimension of the founded "art of rhetoric" and has omitted its second dimension, the "guidance of souls." But once again, at 277b–c, the demonstrative dimension of the true rhetoric is conjoined with its second, psychagogical dimension, namely inducing right existential decisions by properly correlating each kind of speech with the appropriate kind of soul and

> so ordering and adorning the speech that it gives to the variegated soul variegated and thoroughly harmonized speeches, and to simple souls, simple speeches—and this whether it be something to the end of instruction *or something to the end of conviction* [οὔτε τι πρὸς τὸ διδάξαι οὔτε τι πρὸς τὸ πεῖσαι]. (277b–c; emphasis added)

To be sure, any tension between these two purposes of theoretical instruction, on the one hand, and practical conviction, on the other, would seem here to be definitively resolved in favor of theoretical instruction at 277e: anything "said without questioning and instruction and merely for the sake of convincing [ἄνευ ἀνακρίσεως καὶ διδαχῆς πειθοῦς ἕνεκα ἐλέχθησαν]" is, we are told, not to be taken seriously (277e). Despite this assertion, however, it must be remembered that at issue here are not at all theoretical things like "square," "diagonal," and "double area," from which the listener is existentially disengaged (see n.36 above on the *Meno*), but those practical things for which or against which he or she must decide in his or her own existence, namely what is right, decent, and good. And obviously the written word comes up short in regard to these, not only, and not even primarily, because it substitues memorialization for recollection of what these are in essence, but because, lacking the *êthos* and *pathos* of a speaker "there" "in the world" "with others," as Heidegger might say, it cannot convince any audience, cannot move any soul, to decide for the just, decent, and good life.

Hence, it is hardly surprising that, even if in the theory the dialogue proposes instruction has apparently predominated over conviction, in its actual practice the dialogue does not end with anything like a logical conclusion, drawn at the end of a purely demonstrative argument, and stated in a declarative sentence, but, instead, with a *prayer*: "Grant that I may become fair within and that such things without as I possess may be friends to my inner self. May I consider the wise man rich. May I have such an amount of wealth as no one other than the temperate could bear and handle" (279 b–c).[37]

This prayer is no idle literary flourish on Plato's part; rather, it is something entirely consistent with the rhetorical language of orality that has, despite appearances to the contrary, actually prevailed in the dialogue. In displaying the character and passion, the *êthos* and *pathos*, of the speaker it is, in fact, far more than a prayer. It is a call to all those in the audience who might hear and obey what is being urged here: as in the *Phaedo,* the reenactors of this dialogue are exhorted to take up the life for which this "Socrates" character stands, the right, decent, and good life of philosophy rather than the sophistic life of *pleonexia,* wanting insatiably ever more.

4.3 Writing in the *Phaedrus*: The *Pharmakon* Revisited

In our investigation of the tension between orality and writing in the *Phaedrus* we must turn now to the author who has contributed most to our awareness of the issues here. We want to make the case that as arbitrary and far-fetched as it might seem, and consequently repellent to traditional classicists, Jacques Derrida's "Plato's Pharmacy" is a crucial, indispensable, and uncircumventable contribution to Plato interpretation.[38] For as no other, this work, in a deconstructive variation, brings to bear on Plato Heidegger's radical *Destruktion* of Plato's and metaphysics' privileging of timeless, statically present being over the being that happens in time, the privileging of *ousia* over *genesis.* It brings to bear on Plato, this is to say, Heidegger's revolutionary recovery of an "earlier" unity of being and time in an "inceptive" thought "closer to the origin."[39]

In Derrida's hands, to be sure, this privileging of static presence over temporal flux becomes the privileging of voiced speech over writing, and in what follows we will continue to maintain that, in fact, the privileging of static presence implies just the opposite, namely a privileging of spatial, visual writing, of *graphein* and *grammata,* of the graphic and diagrammatical, over temporal, acoustical voice, a thesis, as we have seen, for which considerable support is to be found in Eric Havelock.[40] Still, it is Derrida who is the real provocateur here and the one who confronts us squarely with the pivotal ontological and grammatological questions: namely, how do voiced speech and writing figure in Plato's privileging of static presence over concomitant presence and absence? And just what is the relationship of voiced speech to writing in Plato?

Or better, just what *are* the relationship*s* of voiced speech to writing? For following Derrida's own deconstructive strategies, we can show that Plato is seminally self-contradictory in regard to the apparent priority he gives to speaking over writing in the *Phaedrus.* Prodded, even by some of Derrida's most extreme interpretations, among them his "tracing" of *pharmakon* or drug, to *pharmakos* or prisoner-scapegoat, we will see in our further investigation of the *Phaedrus* that Plato wavers indecisively on the border between the older oral, dramatic tradition and the newer literate, mathematical one, sometimes pushing forward into the new and other times pulling back into the old.

Our approach will be as follows: in part 1 of this section we will try to clarify carefully the interpretive principles of Derrida's deconstruction of the *Phaedrus* and to display how these principles are applied with expositions of Derrida's readings of specific passages in the Platonic opus. Then, in part 2, we will go back to the source of these interpretive principles in Heidegger's penetration behind the metaphysical privileging of static presence and in his uncovering of the original concomitance of any being's showing itself and withholding itself—much as at sea, still indeterminate shapes are ever emerging from the fog even as they are, at the same time, lapsing back into it. Having asked just what Heidegger's *Destruktion* of the metaphysical superstructure of static presence with no absence might mean for the relationships to each other of hearing and seeing, listening and reading, speaking and writing, we will turn to the *Phaedrus* again. But this time we will proceed more by Heidegger's *Destruktion* than by Derrida's deconstruction, which is to say that instead of seeking out those places, in the interstices of his argument about speech and writing, where Plato contradicts himself, and instead of taking down the hierarchical ordering that seems to give priority to one pole of these "binary oppositions" over the other, we will look for persistent remnants of an "earlier" experience "closer to the origins" of thought that still shimmer through the layers of later metaphysical thought beginning to cover them up. We will, in other words, continue with our hermeneutical project of first "laying bare" and then "laying out" hermeneutically the original *logos,* the original form of argument or "discourse," as Derrida would say, beneath derivative abstractions from it. In this way we will be able to see, finally, where Derrida's bold initiatives eventually went wrong.

For Derrida is right: Plato *is* thoroughly contradictory in his arguments about writing and speech. But Derrida is wrong: in the end Plato does not privilege speech over writing. Indeed, the speeches "written in a soul" (*Phaedrus* 278a), of which Derrida rightly makes so much, are not the means of communication for some vocal and acoustical experience underlying them. Rather, according to Plato they are the primary semantical expression of the visual dia-*grammatical genos/eidos* structure of timeless metaphysical being, a system of signs that like letters are statically present and distributed within mental space. *Logos* or speech has come to mean "reasoning" here and is now precisely *aneu phones,* without voice (see the *Sophist* 263e). The acoustical has been eliminated, and we are in the realm of what is to be seen and known (*eidenai*) according to the "look" of it (*to eidos*). Hence it is most of all when Plato falls back on voiced speech, or *legein* and *logos* in the senses of $_{(F)}$*erein* (cf. *verbum*) and $_{(F)}$*epos*, of "to speak" and "tale," that he contradicts himself, and not when he recurs to writing.[41]

4.3.1 The *pharmakon* and Derrida's deconstruction

Reserving criticism for later, let us first explicate Derrida's deconstructive strategy in its own terms. To begin with, and contrary to appearances, the text to be read, in this case the *Phaedrus*, is, he says, not to be taken as a self-contained unity entirely in view and completely present to the interpreter. In other words, unlike any static "metaphysical" being fully present to consciousness, the text is to be read as a crisscrossing of "tracks" and "traces" of what is precisely not in view but absent: the text thus withholds itself from us even as it shows itself to us. Hence, we who would pick up and follow the track of these traces, traces in particular of the word *pharmakon*, are inevitably led across the semantic field of this word's linguistic associations to other uses of it and related words. These tracks and traces lead us, this is to say, to uses and related words not only elsewhere within the the text itself but in the Platonic opus as a whole and, then, in what will eventually become an infinite pursuit, even to uses and words outside this *opus*. In this way we are led beyond the horizons of the "present" text to what is "absent" and outside it, to be sure, but present and inside it too precisely by being unsaid. Thus, *pharmakon*, a word that means an alien substance both in the sense of a "remedy" and a "toxin," and that Plato's Theuth uses to characterize writing in the *Phaedrus* (274e), is to be traced as it "defers" to *pharmakeia* or adminstration of a drug, to *pharmakeus* or the one administering the drug, and then even outside Plato's dialogues to *pharmakos*, the disruptive alien from outside the city walls introduced inside and kept in prison there to serve as a whipping boy in times of disaster. For, writes Derrida, "we do not believe that there exists, in all rigor, a Platonic text, closed upon itself, complete with its inside and its outside. . . . Rather one should simply be able to untangle the hidden forces of attraction linking a present word with and absent word in the text of Plato" (PPh 130).

Crucial here is that any word, of which we would pick up the track, not be taken as a univocal sign signifying some different kind of static essential being ever identical with itself. Unlike "2" which supposedly, at least, signifies univocally the self-identical mathematical *eidos* of duality, *pharmakon* is a sign or indication that in its multivocality points us only to other signs, which in turn point us to still others ad infinitum. Unlike "2," *pharmakon*, in its differing with itself unstably, in its meaning not one thing but now "remedy" and now the contrary "poison," thus continually propels us beyond itself and refers us to equally ambivalent uses of other neighboring words.

Thus, without calling the understanding of words as signs or *semeia* into question, Derrida nevertheless succeeds in undoing the entire Platonic response to sophism's techniques of exploiting the equivocalness of ordinary word names, *onomata.*[42] The meaning of words cannot be secured by converting them into *eponuma* "named after" a static *eidos,* for there is no static *eidos* for them to be named after in the first place. Once the fictional metaphysical superstructure of stablized eidetic essences is "deconstructed," once, that is, the "ontological difference" between the variable signifier and the invariable signified "truth" is taken down and taken away, we are plunged, all over again, into the very same radical instability and chaos of meaning Plato had tried to escape. With no *eidos* to stabilize it, the meaning of *pharmakon,* to take Derrida's well-chosen example, shifts and "slips" from one contrary to the other. If it was Plato's aim to put an end to this "slippage" and its exploitation by sophistical word twisters, by going beyond the physical acounts of the first philosophers and, in fleeing into the *logoi* or arguments themselves, to found these arguments in the hypothesis of the metaphysical *eidê* (see section 4.1 above and the *Phaedo* 99d–102a), Derrida would move in the opposite direction. By subverting the superstructure of static ideas he would set free again the "aneidetic" play and oscillation of *pharmakon's* self-contradictory senses.

Why? And why choose the sign *pharmakon* for this deconstructive liberation? First, because it is writing that is called a *pharmakon* in the *Phaedrus* (274e), and Derrida's ultimate concern here is to subvert the dominance of voice over writing that, in his view, characterizes metaphysics and, indeed, all "hegemonic" structures from Plato on. As voice has been moved to the center, he maintains, writing has been driven out to the margins and beyond. Like the *pharmakos* or alien prisoner and whipping boy, the *pharmakon* of writing is treated as a disruptive alien substance introduced to the inside from outside and best expelled, were it not for the fact that the inside can define itself only in relationship to this outsider that it would both ostracize and incorporate within itself. It is in the *Phaedrus*'s treatment of writing as a *pharmakon-pharmakos,* Derrida argues, that the issue of writing is most obviously joined and where metaphysics of presence and "phonocentrism"—he takes *s'entendre parler,* hearing oneself speaking, to be metaphysics' paradigm of consciousness's full presence to itself—have best displayed their self-contradictory origins. What better place than the *Phaedrus* could there be, then, to apply a "deconstruction" and to dissolve in each other such supposedly distinct "binary oppositions" as "inside/outside," and to show that the text ultimately says the opposite of what it purports to say?

But *pharmakon* is also chosen for a different if related reason: Derrida's deconstructive strategy is also to show that if we were to follow Plato in moving back from what is assumed to be only a copy, a substitute and "supplement" to what the copy is supposedly a copy of, we would end not at all where Plato seems to think we will, namely at the direct intuition of some sort of originary form, static and ever identical with itself, and which itself is not a copy of, a substitute for, and supplement to, anything else but, instead, is what it is "in reality" and "in truth." If, for instance, we were to attempt to trace writing back to the *logos* or speech of which it is said to be the copy, and then speech or *logos* back to the "pure audibility" of one's own speech in full presence to oneself, we would discover that we actually end not at such a "pure audibility" of speech after all but only at more writing, save that this time the writing is the "writing in the soul," which is to say, the communicative system of expression that differentiates and relates a multiplicity of signs to each other—a *grammar*, as it were. In other words, far from penetrating to some primary ground and bottom of what our signification expresses and communicates, we always still find ourselves only at what we mistakenly take to secondary expression and communication, the primary origin of which continues to withhold itself from presence to consciousness and which, like the idea of the good itself, *auto to agathon*, remains *epekeina tês ousias* or beyond presence. But as a matter of fact, in this pursuit we were chasing after a metaphysical phantom that never existed except as a "hypothesis." (See section 4.1 above on the hypothesis of the *eidos* in the *Phaedo*.) Save in our postulations of it, there never was a superior static, stabilized essence, an *archê* or origin above and behind the supposedly inferior supplement or sign substituting for it. *There were always only signs "deferring," infinitely, to other signs in the system.* If we look "behind" writing we see only more writing. The hierarchical structure rising to the *archê* and origin thus collapses, leaving the web of signs across which we move only laterally. To use another metaphor, this means that metaphysics and its *logos* are in fact floating in an abyss: there is no getting down to some stable basis at the bottom of their semantical activity. At any apparent bottom to which one penetrates there is only the aneidetic and variable sign always in contradiction with itself and never the self-identical static thing in itself which the sign is supposed to signify. Ultimately metaphysics and its *logos* rest unstably in the aneidetic oscillations of the universal *pharmakeia*, the "pharmacy" and pharmaceutical brew of all binary oppositions ever collapsing into each other.

Pharmakon is thus in Derrida also a synechdoche, specifically, the turn of speech in which a part becomes a name for the whole of something. Like the "hands" in "All hands on deck!" *pharmakon,* in its oscillations between the opposite senses of remedy and poison, comes to stand for the whole nonground of the aneidetic and equivocal. *Pharmakon* stands for a nonground (Heidegger: *Abgrund*) down to which philosophy and its privileged *logos* are to be deconstructed, namely the bottomless "pharmacy" at the bottom of things. "If the *pharmakon* is 'ambivalent,' " writes Derrida,

> it is because it constitutes the medium in which opposites are opposed, the movement and the play that links them among themselves, reverses them or makes one side cross over into the other (soul/body, good/evil, inside/outside, memory/forgetfulness, speech/writing, etc.). . . . The *pharmakon* is the movement, the locus and the play: (the production of) difference. (PPh 127)

And, Derrida continues, "It is also this store of deep background that we are calling Plato's *pharmacy*" (PPh 128), hence the title of his essay, "Plato's Pharmacy."

It comes as no surprise, then, that Derrida begins his crisscrossing of the web of *pharmakon* in the *Phaedrus* with the initial "little stitch" of the myth of Pharmacia, of *Pharmakeia,* who personifies the administration of drugs: Orithyia, so goes the tale, was carried off by Boreas and cast to her death *while she was playing with Pharmacia* (PPh 69–70; *Phaedrus* 229d). Why, asks Derrida, is this here? By accident? Or is it, he suggests, no accident at all that here "through her games, Pharmacia has dragged down to death a virginal purity and an unpenetrated interior" (PPh 70)? Such an extravagant interpretation might be dismissed were it not for the fact that there follows almost directly upon this passage a reference to the *pharmakon* as a means of seduction from one's general, natural, habitual paths and laws: "You seem," says Socrates, "to have discovered a drug [*pharmakon*] for getting me out [of the city]" (PPh 70; *Phaedrus* 230d). Significantly, this drug that penetrates the inside and brings it outside is here specified as *logoi en bibliois,* words and speeches written in books; for not the spoken word but only such "rolled up," "deferred, reserved" words, says Derrida, can seduce (PPh 71). Furthermore, this association of *pharmakon* and writing is reinforced at 268c, where merely picking up the use of a couple of drugs (*pharmaka*) *out of a book* is contrasted unfavorably with the real science of medicine. Here, too, writing emerges as the external, invasive, alien other that, once internalized, corrupts pure interiority. Hence, it comes as no surprise when writing is explicitly called a *pharmakon* at 274e (PPh 73); the semantic web requisite for this assertion has long since been woven.

There is, Derrida maintains, a hierarchy assumed that dominates the discourse here and that governs the whole issue of speech writing, *logographein*, from its initial thematization at 257d. At the beginning or origin—*archê*—there is posited a pure presense of eidetic truth to the self of the speaker in what Husserl will later call an *Anschauung* and *Gegenwärtigung*, namely the intuition and presentation to oneself of what is self-evident. In descending from this originary "truth" there follows, so the assumption goes, precisely that interior *logos* or speech of the self to itself which Husserl will call *Vergegenwärtigung* or representation, then speech as it is uttered to someone else in communication, and then, last, furthest from the origin, and most derivative, this uttered speech as it is written down and recorded. According to this hierarchy the written speech is a replacement for the spoken speech, which has its origin in the speech of the speaker to himself or herself and, ultimately in his or her immediate intuition of the truth.

Moreover, in the *Phaedrus* the speech *writers* are said to dissociate themselves from their progeny, which now becomes an errant, subversive, and even patricidal orphan disconnected from the truth initially present to its author. Accordingly, says Derrida, speech writing is held in disrepute because the "father" of the *logos* or speech, having abandoned it, is no longer there to stand by and aid his speech, which, after all, is to be read by someone else. Consequently its words, now untied from the insight that alone would give them stable meaning, slip unstably from one meaning to its opposite and can only persuade, now to one side of a contradiction, now to the other, but never instruct in the truth of the matter.

Traces of this condemnation of writing, traces to be tracked "outside" the "text" of the *Phaedrus* itself, persist, Derrida finds, in the very naming of the inventor of writing as Theuth in the myth at 274c–75b. For Theuth, the god of writing is a *replacement* for the sun god, Thamus, Ammon, Ra, just as the moon is replacement for the sun; and as such he begins operating on his own, with "this process of substitution . . . not lacking in violence" (PPh 89), and "his every act marked by unstable ambivalence" (PPh 93). For the deconstructive reader this "outside" background is indissociable from the "inside" myth of Theuth's presentation of the *pharmakon* of writing to Thamus. For crucial to this story is the radical instability of the word *pharmakon*: for Theuth it is a "remedy" for the deficiencies of memory, but for Thamus, whose reign is threatened by it, it is a narcotic "poison" that invades and debilitates the interior life of the mind.

The task for the deconstructive reader is thus to avoid any translation of *pharmakon*, say as remedy (Robin: *remède*), that would eliminate its inherent ambivalence and self-contradiction and shut down the unstable oscillation between its contrary senses. For if the word appears in its positive sense in Theuth's presentation of writing to Thamus, the king, it must nonetheless be read "anagrammatically," that is, as a rewriting and reinscription of the word as it appears elsewhere in other senses. To keep the oscillating play of contrary senses in play a deconstructive interpretation must resist "Platonism," must resist, that is to say, the will to master the play and close it off by imposing one self-identical, noncontradictory sense on the word (see PPh 98).

The *Timaeus*, 89a–d, provides the locus at which to observe best this intrinsic oscillation in the sense of *pharmakon*, its tipping back and forth from meaning something good to meaning something bad, for in arguing against the administration of drugs and pharmaceutical therapies, against *pharmakeia*, pharmacy, Plato contends there that remedies or medicines, once introduced into the living organism from outside, only disrupt its native constitution and aggravate the illness (see PPh 100–101). Pharmaceutical treatment implies the aggression of an alien element to which the living being responds with "metastatic allergic reactions"; hence, the "perfection of a living being would consist in its having no relation at all with any outside" (PPh 101). With this passage in mind, we can now see that in the *Phaedrus* precisely this same "system of features" operates in Thamus's response to Theuth's proposed *pharmakon* of writing:

> by trusting in writing they [the readers] will be reminded from outside by means of characters alien to themselves [ἔξοθεν ὑπ' ἀλλοτρίων τύπων], and will not remember internally by themselves [οὐκ ἔνδοθεν αὐτοὺς ὑφ' αὑτῶν ἀναμιμνῃσκομένους]. So you have found a pharmakon not of memory but of reminding [οὔκουν μνήμης ἀλλ' ὑπομνήσεως]. (*Phaedrus* 275a; cf. PPh 102)

And thus, Derrida adds,

> If writing, according to the king and under the sun, produces the opposite effect from what is expected, if the *pharmakon* is pernicious, it is because, like the one in the *Timaeus*, it doesn't come from around here: It comes from afar, it is external or alien to the living, which is the right-here of the inside, to *logos* as the *zoon* it claims to assist or relieve. (PPh 104)

Mental degeneracy will be the inevitable result of the introduction of this *pharmakon* of writing:

> Confident of the permanence and independence of its types (*tupoi*), memory will fall asleep, will not keep itself up, will no longer keep to keeping itself alert, present, as close as possible to the truth of what is. (PPh 105)

Writing, that is to say, destroys the pure presence to self in the pure audibility of the soul's *s'entendre parler*, its listening to its own *logos* or speech—or so Plato's theory goes.

For in reality, Derrida notes, there is no memory without a sign, no *mnêmê* without *hupomnêsis* or a reminder; but Plato projects a pure presence to self in which no reminder of anything absent, no representation (Husserl: *Vergegenwärtigung*), is needed since everything is fully present (*gegenwärtig*) and nothing is absent or deferred.[43] Ultimately, however, this pure cognition would no longer even be memory, which always presupposes the mediated recovery of what is not yet there, but simply *nous*, direct immediate intuition (Husserl: *Anschauung*) of the self-evident truth (see PPh 109 for the reference to *Republic* 533b on the an-hypothetical intelligibility of the truth). It is the experience of our hearing our own *logos* that gives the appearance of coming closest to this immediacy, Derrida argues, the moment of *s'entendre parler*, and that deludes us into thinking that we could even pass through the experience of our own voice to intuition of the unrepresented truth itself. And deluded in this way, we assume that writing, as a represention of voice, moves us in the opposite direction away from the truth. We take writing to be the *pharmakon*-supplement, the sign of a sign, the signifier of a phonic signifier (PPh 109–10), a dangerous, penetrating supplement "that breaks into the very thing that would like to do without it yet lets itself at once be breached, roughed up, fulfilled and replaced" (PPh 110).

Yet Plato cannot do without the *pharmakon*. The sophists, Gorgias in particular (see PPh 115–16), know that *logos* itself, speech, is a *pharmakon*, and against this *pharmakon* of sophistics Plato advances the *alexipharmakon*, the counter-*pharmakon*, of Socratic dialetics. Like the sophists, Socrates, a stingray, a gadfly, a bee, is a *pharmakeus* too, but one whose *pharmakon*, in casting its spell upon the audience, wards off (*alexei*) the bad *pharmakon* of sophism (see PPh 119–21). The counter-*pharmakon* thus restores the purity of the inside by "bringing charges" against exteriority as a supplement: "It is thus necessary to put the outside back in its place. To keep the outside out" (PPh 128). The dialectical cure by Socratic *logos*, by cross-examination or *elenchos*, will thus exorcize writing.

With that we are again led "outside" the traces we have been tracking of *pharmakeia, pharmakon, pharmakeus* within the *Phaedrus* and the Platonic opus as a whole: we are led to *pharmakos*, the prisoner-scapegoat, which is present precisely in being absent from the Platonic texts, "inside," in being "outside." In the Thargelion, the rite of civic purification occurs by beating *pharmakoi* to death and driving the "evil" from their bodies:

> The city's body *proper* thus reconstitutes its unity, closes around the security of its inner courts, gives back to itself the word that links it with itself within the confines of the agora, by violently excluding from its territory the representative of an external threat or aggression. That representative represents the otherness of the evil that comes to affect or infect the inside by unpredictably breaking into it. Yet the representative of the outside is nonetheless *constituted*, regularly granted its place by the community, chosen, kept, fed, etc., in the very heart of the inside. (PPh 133)

And just so it is with the *pharmakon* of sophistical speech writing that Socrates subjects to cross-examination in the *Phaedrus*. This exterior writing, which invades and disrupts the interior pure presence to self in one's *s'entendre parler*, in hearing and understanding one's own speech, is, even so, indispensable for, and constitutive of, the interior it disrupts. As with the *pharmakos*, the *extra muros* is *intra muros* and vice versa (see PPh 133).

Hence, the *pharmakon* of writing *also* turns up as an internal, good thing: we find in the *Laws*, for example, "of all these [forms of speech, *logoi*] the clear test will be the writings of the lawgiver [τὰ τοῦ νομοθέτου γράμματα], which it is necessary that he possess in himself as counterpotions to ward off those other speeches [ἃ δεῖ κεκτημένον ἐν αὑτῷ, καθάπερ ἀλεξιφάρμακα τῶν ἄλλων λόγων]" (957d; cf. PPh 121). *This* writing, internal writing, good writing, or what the *Phaedrus* will call "writing in the soul of the learner" (276a), is recovered not in "hypomnesic" sophistics, which would only remind us with external signs, but in "anamnesic dialectics," whose object is the internal *eidos*, never differing from itself but always the same as itself (see PPH 123 and the *Phaedo* 78c, e). Hence, it is to be contrasted with *hupomnêsis* by external writing, which is a supplement to *anamesis* and which "only intervenes when a subject of knowledge already possesses the signifieds" (PPh 135). Still, what is crucial here is that the good inside, *logos*, can only be understood in terms of the bad outside, *graphê*, which, like the *pharmakos* or whipping boy, is indispensable for, and constitutive of, the inside; the good writing can be designated only through the metaphor of the bad (PPh 149).

Thus, with writing too we are involved in constant shuttling between the contradictory poles of binary oppositions: on the one side we have knowledge and memory and, on the other, nonknowledge as rememoration. On the one side we have a good repetition of truth that presents and exposes the *eidos* and, on the other, a bad repetition that does not present the *eidos,* but re-presents a presentation, repeats a repetition (PPh 135). Opposite the good writing within the soul we have the bad writing that "displaces its model, provides no image of it, violently wrests out of its element the animate interiority of speech" and that "estranges itself immensely from the truth of the thing itself, from the truth of speech" (PPh 137). Bad writing is the fatherless illegitimate orphan, "uprooted, anonymous, unattached to any house or country" (PPh 144), a signifier freed from *logos* (PPh 145), "a moribund, ignorant, external, mute artifice for the senses," whereas the good writing, of noble lineage (*genesios*) and "written in the soul of the learner," is "natural, living, knowledgeable, intelligible, internal, speaking" (PPh 149). But the good writing is "writing" nonetheless.

Writing in what sense? The clue here is that the *tupoi,* the types or characters condemned as alien external reminders in the *Phaedrus,* 275a, are also the paradigm for the archetypes or forms (*eidê*) (see *Rep.* 402d and PPh 112–13, 159): The grammatological system of the letters' relation to, and difference from, each other is the "metaphor" for the collection of the *eidê* into genera and division into species. How this works is spelled out explicitly in the *Philebus,* where Theuth, the god of writing, reappears, but this time as the one who sorts out and sytematizes the unlimited number of voiced sounds (*phonai*) by uncovering the limited number of kinds (*eidê*) of voiced sound, vowels, consonants, and mutes, and by articulating the system of how these elements (*stoicheia*) of sound relate to, and differ from, each other, that is, the system of which elements can and which cannot combine with each other, or what the *Sophist* dialogue will call the "weave of the forms (*sumplôkê tôn eidôn*)" (259e; PPh 165). Importantly, in the *Philebus* this knowledge is called the art of letters (*technê grammatikê*) and the one who possesses it is called lettered (*grammatikos*). Hence, in acquiring it he has moved behind the acoustical "elements" or *stoicheia* to graphic "letters" or *grammata* (see *Philebus* 18b–d and PPh 162–63). As we already know, precisely this move from the acoustical to the graphic, from the undifferentiated flow of sensation to the dia*grammatic genos/eidos* structure behind it and prior to it, is in Plato's own view prerequisite for any science and art. Put another way, before any voiced word can become significant this graphic structure of differences and relations must be in place, and just this is what Derrida means when *he* says that contrary to the "logocentric" prejudices of the metaphysical tradition, *graphê* precedes *logos,* writing precedes speech. (As a matter of fact, then, Plato is a lot closer to Derrida's position then Derrida recognizes.)

Ostensibly this grammatical science, Derrida maintains, is to be distinguished from dialectics and taken merely as a metaphor for it, since dialectics should have as its object the *eidos* itself as it is immediately present to mind without any re-presention in signs. But in fact, he points out, there is never this immediate presence to mind of the "truth," rather only a graphic re-presentation and expression of the ever absent *eidos* itself; hence, the distinction between grammatics and dialectics collapses (PPh 166). The "face" always withdraws (PPh 167); its presence is always deferred, and the origin (*archê*) escapes, leaving only the "pharmacy," the oscillations and conflations of contrary significances in signs that are but traces and tracks leading only to other signs not present. We thus are left with the *fond sans fond*, the wellspring without bottom, ground, foundation (see PPh 127).

4.3.2 Deconstruction and *Destruktion*: reading the written and hearing the spoken

To evaluate this extraordinary thrust by Derrida we need to go back to the ontology behind his strategy of reading with an eye to what is "present" and inside the text precisely by its being "absent" and outside. We need to go back, that is, to Heidegger's *Destruktion* of a metaphysical ontology that privileges the timeless, tenseless being of what is present statically, *ständige Anwesenheit, ousia, einai,* over the being of what comes to pass in time, *Geschehen, genesis, gignesthai.* For Heidegger's precise point is that whatever comes to pass in time *is* presenting itself all the while it is withholding itself. Hence, it is not statically present, rather, its *prae(s)ens* or being there "before" us (*prae*) entails its *ab(s)ens* or being "away from" us (*ab*); in Heidegger's later language, its *Anwesen* entails *Abwesen,* its "fading in," we might say, its simultaneous "fading away." Any "is" is thus embedded in a concomitant "is not" of the past's "is not any longer" and the future's "is not yet."

There is really nothing mysterious about this, and Heidegger provides ample exemplification of what he means. In *Being and Time,* for instance, he points out that human existence, our finite being "there" in the world, is just such a being as this that cannot be construed in terms of being that is statically ever present.[44] Indeed, a faithful phenomenological description of our existence would display that we experience ourselves as having come to be out of a past time beyond the horizons of our consciousness and when we did not exist, all the while we are passing into a time beyond the horizons of our consciousness when we will no longer exist. As human beings our being is not fully present to us but always in part withheld from us and absent. But not only our own existence but also the existence of things of our world, of shoes, pitchers, artworks, dwellings, has this same temporal being of coming to pass. They are present in our awareness only in having arisen from beyond it and in already having faded away out of it.[45] They are neither statically ever present nor fully present. Indeed, in their withholding themselves from us there is always a certain opacity about them and impenetrablility: they are present in concomitantly being absent; they are there in simultaneously being no longer there and not yet there. Consequently, their "truth" is not at all the steady presence of a "look" or *eidos* of the thing "itself" given to the view (*thea*) of some onlooker and beholder (*theôretês*), not, for instance, *auto to dikaion* or *auto to kalon*, the right and just itself, the noble and decent itself, rather only a partial emergence from obscurity, an *a-lêtheia* or disconcealment (*Unverborgenheit*) in which oblivion and concealment (*lethê, Verborgenheit*) are never eliminated.

But Platonic metaphysics, Heidegger maintains, sets out precisely to eliminate this opacity and impenetrability of things.[46] This is why it must abstract from the being of what comes to pass and posit a being which "really" is, *to ontôs on*, and which, in standing and staying statically in view, is fully and ever present to our awareness. In the place of the appearance-disappearance concomitance of what comes to pass, with its fading in even as it is fading out, metaphysics posits the "look" or *eidos*, the static form of what always is. Hence, Heidegger's hermeneutical task becomes that of disclosing the original conjunction of being and time by razing the structure of Platonic metaphysics which the tradition has superimposed upon it.

Now, before returning to the *Phaedrus* to assess critically Derrida's deconstructive reading of it, we must address two questions arising out of this Heideggerian *Destruktion* of Platonic metaphysics: first, how, exactly, do oral and literary expression, respectively, figure in Plato's metaphysical abstraction to the *eidos*? And, second, is it by returning to writing from the priority given to orality that one can take down the edifice of metaphysical constructs and "lay bare," as Heidegger would say, the original being of coming to pass that these metaphysical constructs have covered over? *Or is it not rather by returning to orality from the priority given to writing*? For, in opposition to Derrida and in agreement with Havelock, we can say that in the end Plato and Platonic metaphysics are not attacking writing as secondary to speaking, rather, as our own investigations of the *Phaedo* and *Phaedrus* have already made clear, attacking speaking and the oral tradition by turning to the paradigm of mathematics. And in mathematics the voiced word name was in fact always entirely secondary to the written sign, the sound "two," for instance, always entirely secondary to the visual mark "2" that we read silently.

Our investigation of the *Phaedo* has already shown us that Plato proposes this turn to the mathematical to combat sophism's exploitation of the "weakness" of spoken word names, but the *Phaedrus*, particulary in Derrida's provocative reading of it, gives us indications that there is something more fundamental at stake here, namely the contest of the new literacy with the older oral culture. To understand fully why Platonic philosophy, if not Plato himself, takes this turn to the mathematical we therefore need to distinguish between the two experiences of the being of the word, the one, oral-auditory and the other, literary-visual.

In the oral-auditory experience of the word, what is expressed comes to pass; it "is" as *genesis* or *gignesthai* in time. For as we experience it, a voiced word arises out of previous word or previous silence only then to fade into a subsequent word or silence. Each voiced word displaces either a previous word or, if it is the first word, silence, all the while it momentarily defers what is yet to come and defers to it, be this the next word or silence. The being of a voiced word is thus experienced as a self-contradictory conjunction of being and not being: it *is* all the while it is re-ferring, carrying the listeners back, to what is no longer, and pro-(f)-ferring, carrying the listeners forward, to what is yet to come.

An accurate phenomenological description displays that our experience of the being of written words is quite different. First, as marks on a surface, as things written, as *grammata*, written words stand steadily at a place in space. Even if the letters and markings on this surface were put there at some time and will fade at some time into illegibility, and even if our *reading* of them always implies retention of what we are no longer reading and projection of what we have not yet read, we do not experience their own temporality as readers of them. Even if, as readers, *we* must pass in time from one set of letters to the next, we experience the letters themselves as *spatial and not temporal* being. For we know that we can always go back to *where* they are *at any time* and they will *always* be there. We experience them as always being accessible "above" and "below" where we are presently reading. Moreover, as our own "reading" of the speeches in the *Phaedrus* has already made clear, we can always diagram the whole of any written "text" in some sort of overview of it and "synopsis." This is to say that, even if the significances of written words are traces of significances we can never come to the end of, we can always bring written words themselves into view, or, as Heidegger would put it, *wir können sie vor uns stellen und verfügbar machen.* We can put the written words themselves in front of us and put them at our disposal, and unlike spoken words, we then do not undergo their coming to pass. (Derrida, in taking Husserl's *vorstellen* as synonymous with *vergegenwärtigen* and translating it as "to represent," misses the element of control and even violence done to our experience that Heidegger's splitting the word into *Vor-stellen*, putting-in-front, elicits.)

Granted, the full significance of a written sign, *pharmakon,* for instance, is always deferred too. Where it is present, *pharmakon,* as we have seen, is a trace of words that are absent, of words that are not there, but somewhere else. And one could say, therefore, that it is only at some other *time* that *we* can come across them. But a closer examination of this "differ*a*nce" reveals that the experience of it is primarily spatial, not temporal: the deferred words themselves, which are absent from the text, and to which the words present are to be traced, *are always* where they are in other texts; unlike words that we hear, we do not experience the words themselves that we see and read as coming into being at a time and passing away.

We must ask, accordingly, if the *Phaedrus*'s treatment of writing must be understood quite differently from the way Derrida has understood it. For in the end, is it not writing rather than speaking that *is* statically? And is it not writing, therefore, that might best express static metaphysical being? Precisely because it is, I suggest, the *Phaedrus* actually privileges writing over speaking; for only static writing could articulate dia*gramma*tically the universal and timeless differences from each other and relations to each other of the *eidê.* Orality, on the other hand, keeps us at the level of what is in the conjoint coming forth and lapsing back, fading in and fading out, the level of what is coming to pass. Hence, it keeps at the level of what in Plato's view remains ultimately indeterminate and unknowable. The turn to mathematics and its written signs now assumes wider dimensions: Not merely is sophism to be countered, but, beyond this, the foundations for any *epistêmê,* any scientific knowledge, are to be laid down.

But if this is correct, if it is really the contest of the new literacy with the older orality that is being fought out here, why is it precisely not orality but writing that at the very beginning of the *Phaedrus*'s account of it is linked to the enemy sophism and singled out for criticism (see 257d)? Must it not be the written word, after all, that is unstable, as Derrida maintains, and not the spoken word? And do not oral words become unstable and subversive only once they are written down, abandoned by their "fathers," and cut off from their supposedly stable origin in speech?

To evaluate Derrida's contention here, we might best take Gadamer's rather than Derrida's approach: we might ask, that is, just what the question is which this linking of writing to sophism in Plato is meant to answer.[47] And to find this out we need to resume our inquiry into the three speeches, the one of Lysias's and the two of Socrates'. For, as we have seen, and as the *Symposium* also confirms, these three speeches in the *Phaedrus* are clearly intended as samples of oral speech making in general, samples whose particular subject matter provided a frequent and customary theme for exercises in epideictic or "showoff" rhetoric: in praising love (*erôs*), promising rhetors could learn to "strut their stuff" and, like Agathon in the *Symposium*, best their competitors. We saw, accordingly, that love was never the actual focus of the *Phaedrus* dialogue, but rather speeches, *logoi*, as such, and that what so impresses the all too impressionable Phaedrus about Lysias's speech is that in reversing the standard themes of epideictic rhetoric, *to kalon* and *to aischron*, it is able to make even such a canonically *kalos* or decent thing as love seem *aischros* or despicable and ugly: "in just this," says Phaedrus at 227c, consists its ingeniousness." With that statement the issue for the entire dialogue was joined: How are we best to defend against sophistical exploitation of any ordinary word's inherent potential to mean opposite things? How are we to defend against a sophistical word twisting that makes a good thing seem bad or, what is worse, a bad thing seem good? How can we best stabilize the meanings of words so that this does not happen?

If anything, Derrida's deconstructive interpretation at least makes clear that Plato has a double and inconsistent answer here. At first glance, the attack on writing as a *pharmakon*-poison that deadens our powers of recollection makes it appear that the defense against sophistical deception could only be live discussion; it could only be *dialegesthai* as talking things through, putting sophistical inversions of the truth to the test in Socratic oral cross-examination, and exposing them for what they are. For this to occur the written word would have to be converted back into the voiced word, of which the written word is only the notation. But the speech writer, it seems, evades the Socratic *elenchos* by passing the written speech onto others, who, when they recite it, just read it off, as Phaedrus just reads off Lysias's speech, and who are themselves unable to invest it with new dialogical life. Indeed, Phaedrus, charmed as he is by the speech's rhetorical devices, its copiousness and well-turned phrases, is completely unable to enter into a discussion of the thesis it proposes. Hence, there is little point in putting any questions to him about its subject matter, and since its author Lysias is, after all, not available, the speech stands unchallengeable. This, and not the supposed disruptiveness of a "fatherless" speech, is obviously the point of Socrates' comparison of the written word to paintings at 275d: "if one questions them, he says, "they solemnly keep an utter silence."

Thus, Socrates does not even attempt to engage Phaedrus in live discussion of the speech he has merely read off. Instead, he provides two speeches of his own, speeches, we now observe, that the dialogue presents as extensions, albeit in part written, of an oral tradition—"I have heard [ἀκήκοα] some things from the beautiful Sappho or the wise Anacreon or some prose writers [συγγραφέων] or other" (235c)—but which, of course, Plato himself *writes* for us to read. And with that a remarkable tension and contradiction is introduced in Plato's account of writing, to which Derrida has alerted us but which, contrary to Derrida, goes back to Plato's ambivalence not in regard to writing but in regard to the oral tradition.

For Plato views sophism as an outgrowth of that oral tradition, and this most of all in its writing, which he considers merely a notation for orality. To be sure, he would in part counter sophism's perversion of orality with Socratic oral dialectic. So far, then, Derrida would seem to be right: to prevent seduction by it, the written word must, Plato seems to be saying, be brought back to live speaking. But to note only this is to overlook the fact, already made evident to us by the *Phaedo*, that despite his perpetuation of Socratic dialogue as an antidote to sophism, Plato is also a Pythagorean who sees in Pythagorean mathematics, in its theories of harmony, numbers, and geometrical forms, another, perhaps even more effective, counter to sophism. For the knowledge Pythagorean mathematicians have of their subject matter makes them immune to sophistical confutation: to one who knows a thing mathematically, that thing cannot be passed off for what it is not.

Now, as opposed to Socrates' language, the language with which Pythagoreans make their irrefutable demonstrations is not at all the language of orality and, as Derrida himself rightly points out, is not even based in orality but rather in writing.[48] For as we have noted, the voiced sound that one makes for "2" is entirely secondary to the written mark "2" and, in fact, twice removed from the *eidos* or "look" of duality in the system of numbers that one sees and reads in the "writing in the soul." Here the mark, the *grammê* "2," is the sign most closely approximating the archetype, not the voiced "two."

And with that a question is posed for Plato, which he never clearly decides: How indeed might one best defeat sophism and, in particular, sophism in its best defensed form of oral speech written down? With Socrates' oral dialectic of question and answer? Or should we, like Pythagorean mathematicians, be made immune to its distortions from the start by clear insight into what it is that speech is about, by a clear vision of the *eidos* or "look" of the thing and its place in the diagrammatic system of differences and relations establishing what it combines with and what it does not, say, "2" with "Even" but not with "Odd," "Soul" with "Life" but not with "Death" (see section 4.1.2 above and the *Phaedo*, 104a ff.), and, presumably, "Love" with *Kalos* but not with *Aischros*? If the latter, then *dialegesthai* as Socratic talking things through in time must be transformed into the new *dialegesthai* of a spatialized and systematic "bringing together" or *sunagôgê* of what is related, and a "taking apart" or *dihairesis* of what is different. Dialectic as spoken dialogue, we now see, must become the dia*gramm*ing that Plato refers to as the "writing in the soul" (*Phaedrus* 276a, 278a). Indeed, the possibility that Plato holds out is that, like *duas* or "two," the voiced phonemes *dikaion, kalon, agathon,* which name the three principal topics of rhetorical conviction, are really acoustical signs of mental insights into the "look" or *eidos* of these, a "look" that is primarily signified not vocally at all but graphically, in "writing," which is to say, in some distribution of marks in space just as 2 has its *place* in the series of odd and even numbers, 1, 2, 3, 4, 5, etc.

And just why would recourse to this "good" writing shield us from the dangers of the "bad" writing that merely writes down oral speech? Because recourse to the "writing in the soul," to the diagrammatic system of the *eidê* in their differences and relations, would stabilize the meaning of words, which now would be eponyms and signs for what a thing is seen to be clearly and distinctly. With someone who has seen and knows, *oide,* the *eidos* or "look" of something that "2" signifies, sophists have no chance to make "2" mean something it does not, and the hope, as we have seen, is that the same univocity could be achieved for the rhetorical topics of the *to dikaion, to kalon,* and *to agathon* and that the signs designating these could thereby be made invulnerable to sophistic word twisting. To achieve exactly this is the project of Platonism and metaphysics that comes to its perfection in the Enlightenment's dismissal of rhetoric and turn to mathematical logic, a project that is based in writing and that consequently all but eliminates oral declamation (*hupokrisis, pronuntiatio*) as a concern.

The fact of the matter is that in the *Phaedrus* Plato shifts, albeit incompletely, from taking the Socratic oral response to sophism to taking the Pythagorean written one, and from Socratic dialectic as talking things through in time to a mathematic or instructional *(mathematikê)* dialectic that sorts things out spatially and diagrammatically. Indeed, directly contrary to Derrida, we can say that it is not the attack on writing that characterizes this dialogue but the attack on orality: the only writing it attacks is the one that represents oral speech.

The issue, joined at 258d, is, after all, in just what *kalos graphein* as opposed to *aischrôs te kai kakôs graphein* consists, that is, writing in a noble way, like Lycurgus or Solon, as opposed to writing in a despicable and bad way (compare PPh 121–22 on the good writing of the lawgivers). And the answer is already given away at 259e: Of both *legein te kai graphein,* speaking and writing, it is asked, "Must it not hold for things stated well and nobly that the one saying them must have seen and known in thought the truth of the things that he would speak about?"

The key words here are *dianoia,* thought or discursive intellection, and *eiduia,* the participle of *eidenai* or to have seen and to know. For already here the translation of the auditory into the visual is obvious; *dia-legesthai* or talking something through in Socratic question and answer and listening to the voice of one's partner in the discussion has given way to *dia-noein*, sorting things through intellectually once one has seen the truth of them. In other words, writing nobly presupposes founding the mere *appearances* named in voiced speech, in what is seen to *be*: the vocal sounds we make and write down for others to reinvoke must be founded in an envisioning of what is statically ever present to the intellection or *noein* envisioning it. Even someone who would deceive the audience would, if the deception is to be done "well," have to have seen and known the truth, for "the one who has not seen and known the truth [ὁ τὴν ἀλήθειαν μὴ εἰδώς], but instead chases after beliefs in the apparent, will produce, so it seems, some sort of ridiculous art of speaking that is no art at all" (262c).

To make his point Plato now develops the hypothetical case of one who would persuade his audience artfully and "well," if not "nobly," of something that is not so, and he proceeds to test Lysias's speech to see if it is an example of just such an artful deception founded in a vision of the truth or if it is not rather an instance of the mere knack of producing nice-sounding words about appearances in complete ignorance of the truth. It emerges that Lysias has simply written down what he has heard, namely an acoustical flow of *onomata* or oral, audible word names. There is—and just this is the point—no envisionable structure to his speech at all. In other words, it lacks the *sustasis* or spatial composition of writing (see 268d).

In this regard Lysias's speech provides the perfect foil for Socrates' two speeches, for both of these *are* founded in a prior envisionable dia-grammatic organization. As we have already learned, they are both organized according to the visual-spatial foundational principles of, first,

> seeing synoptically and bringing together under one idea the things dispersed over many places [εἰς μίαν τε ἰδέαν συνορῶντα ἄγειν τά πολλαχῇ δεσπαρμένα], so that by being visually delimited [ὁριζόμενος], each thing, whichever it may be that one wishes to teach about, may be made plain

and, second,

> being able to go back and cut up [this one idea] according to the "looks" [κατ' εἴδη] [of things contained in it]—at the joints and in accord with its natural development—and able to endeavor not to smash any part in the manner of a bad carver. Rather, one must proceed in the manner of

> the two speeches just now. For "irrationality of thought" they assumed one "look of it" in common [ἕν τι κοινῇ εἶδος]; and as out of the body, which is one, two parts with the same name [arm, leg, and so forth] have developed naturally and are called left and right, so also the two speeches took "being out of one's senses" to have in us, by nature, one "look of it" [ἓν ἐν ἡμῖν πεφυκὸς εἶδος]. From this, the one speech cut off the left part and did not cease to go on cutting off parts until it found in these a so-called left love on which it rightly heaped abuse, whereas, the other speech led us into the right-hand parts of madness and found, in turn, a love of the same name but divine, which it proffered and praised as the cause of the greatest goods. (265d–66b)

In particular, we note now the visualization and spatialization here of the *logos* or speech that, as voiced, had been acoustical and temporal. We note now, that is, the transformation of the original *dialegesthai* or talking something through orally in time to the new *dialegesthai* of dialectic, the dia-*gramma*tical bringing together (*sunagôgê*) and taking apart (*dihairesis*) of things marked off and distributed in space—here, as "left" and "right." The prerequisite for this transformation of *dialegesthai,* we also note, is the reconversion of *logos* as audible oral speech into *logos* as visual calculation (see note 41 above).

According to this passage, if a speech is to be written well, the spoken words to be recited by the speaker and heard by an audience over a length of time must be based in a diagrammatical structure envisionable in space, must be based, that is to say, in "the writing in the soul" which, being without voice (*aneu phonês*), was never heard but was always seen and read silently. Measured against this standard, Lysias, as we have already seen, merely perpetuates in what he has written down the oral-auditory tradition of rhetoric, which, like him, is concerned simply with the temporal duration (*mêkos*), be it long or short (see 267b), and the temporal sequence of what the audience will hear, that is, first the introduction, second the narration, third the certain proofs, fourth the likelihoods (266e), and last a da capo to remind the listeners (*hupomnesai . . . tous akouontas*) of what they had heard before but might have forgotten since (267e). Lysias is not in the least concerned with founding this acoustical temporal flow in a visual, spatial diagram. For Plato, Lysias, like all the writers of treatises on the so-called *rhetorikê technê* or rhetorical art, remains caught in the oral tradition and is therefore incapable of the new visual-spatial *dialegesthai,* of "bringing together" dispersed parts and then "taking them apart" again according to their natural divisions. He and they are incapable, that is, of organizing a whole that can be taken in *at a glance* (see 269a–c).

Still, Plato, drawn as he is in the opposite directions of the Socratic oral, and Pythagorean mathematical *logos*, is strikingly inconsistent about all this, and beginning at 274c we now *read* what Plato has *written* about what Socrates has *heard* about writing: "But," Phaedrus enjoins, "do tell what you say you have heard" (ἀλλ' ἃ φῂς ἀκηκοέναι, λέγε). And Plato's literary character "Socrates" then responds with the oral legend (*akoê*) of Theuth and Thamus. In regard to this legend we must note, first, that, as opposed to Husserl, whom Derrida consistently reads into the *Phaedrus* (see PPh 135 n.61, 166 n.82), in Plato there is neither here nor anywhere else mention of some sort of primary internal experience of hearing one's own voice, of hearing oneself speak. Indeed, as *dianoia* or thinking something out, even the dialogue (*dialogos*) of the soul with itself is specifically said in the *Sophist*, at 263e, to be without voice, *aneu phones*. And with good reason, for far from being a two-voiced conversation—the word here is not *dua*logue but *dia*logue—this voiceless thinking consists in the new *dialegesthai*, which does not "talk things through" but "reasons things out" with the spatializing, visualizing *dialectikê technê* of "bringing things *together*"—at a place—and "taking things *apart*," and all this according to the "look" of them, their *eidos*. The *logos* of this *dialogos* is no longer Socratic speech but already the Pythagorean and Euclidean reasoning of graphic diagrammatical mathematics; as Latin translations will make clear, *logos* has now reverted to its computational sense of *ratio* and no longer means *verbum* or *oratio*. And in the *Phaedrus*, too, the internal experience said to be invaded and disrupted by the external *pharmakon* of written characters *is never called oral-acoustical*.

Furthermore, we must keep in mind that the injurious *pharmakon* of *hupomnesis* condemned by Thamus, namely the use of prompts as reminders, was originally an oral-auditory, not literary, device (see *Phaedrus* 267e), and the use of written reminders of what to say, even complete texts, is therefore to be taken only as an extension of oral-auditory mnemonic devices such as meters, repetitions, stock phrases, and so forth.[49] Hence, when Plato contrasts *anamnêsis* with mere *hupomnêsis* here, he is not challenging writing as such but only the appropriation of writing by a continuing oral tradition. Indeed, as the *Meno*'s example of doubling the area of a square makes clear (82b ff.), *anamnêsis* itself is conceived of starting from the graphic and diagrammatic and not at all from the oral and auditory: *anamnêsis* is not at all the mind's recovery of something it has once *heard* but rather of something it has once *seen*. By *anamnêsis* one comes to see and know (*eidenai*) again the interrelations obtaining among the "looks" of things (*eidê*) arrayed for one's envisioning, in this case, Double, Square, Diagonal, and so forth. Thus we find in the *Phaedrus* at 249c: "This, then is remembrance [ἀνάμνησις] of those things which our soul once *saw* [εἶδεν]" (emphasis added).[50]

Still, as it did in the *Phaedo,* the question remains open in the *Phaedrus* whether this anamnesic envisioning of eidetic relationships can be made foundational for the traditional subject matters of oral political and ethical rhetoric, namely "the right and the wrong, and the bad and the good" (277d), and hence, whether in these matters such an oral-auditory manner of talking things through as Socrates' can be founded after all in a diagrammatic visualization of the *eidê,* in "bringing things together" under one idea and then "taking them apart" again according to their natural structure. Indeed, the conclusion drawn in regard to these subject matters is most notable for its inconclusiveness and ambivalence—as well as, remarkably, for the *sound* of its exemplary Greek perodic phrasing with its building tension and climactic release:

> The one, however, who holds that in written speech about each of these there is necessarily much that is playful, and who holds that no speech, be it written or spoken, in meter or without, is worth serious effect, no speech, for example, which, in being sung by a rhapsodist, is spoken without any questioning and instruction and solely for the sake of persuasion [ἄνευ ἀνακρίσεως καὶ διδαχῆς πειθοῦς ἕνεκα ἐλέχθησαν], but who holds instead that in reality the best of speeches have been only a reminder of things already seen and known [τοὺς βελτίστους εἰδότων ὑπόμνησιν γεγονέναι]; the one who holds that, on the contrary, there is something vivid, perfect, and worthy of serious effort only in those things taught and said for the sake of instruction and that in reality are written in the soul about what is just and noble and good; the one who holds that only such speeches ought to be called his genuine legitimate children, so to speak, as, first, the speech within himself, if he finds it existing within him, and, then, [the speeches in others] if some of its progeny and brothers have sprung up at the same time in the souls of others in worthy fashion, and who dismisses the other speeches—such a man as this, I venture to say, o Phaedrus, is such as I and you might pray that you and I might become. (277e–78)

It is striking that in this text so near the end of this dialogue in which the new *dialectikê technê* of "bringing together" and "taking apart" has been introduced, *logos,* as the use of the plural *logoi* makes clear, still has the sense of oral speech, and Socratic oral *dialegesthai,* talking something through in a dialogue of question and answer, is still being advanced as the *alexipharmakon* to ward off the merely persuasive sophistical *makros logos* or long speech, be this "written or spoken, in meter or without," or even "sung by a rhapsodist." (As we will see momentarily in conclusion to this chapter, Plato's skillful juxtaposition in the *Symposium* of Agathon's lyrical and sometimes even metrical panegyric [194e–97e] with Socrates' matter-of-fact questioning [199b ff.] is most instructive in regard to this oral response to the oral tradition.)

Of course, one might say, and rightly, too, that Socratic oral *dialegesthai* about the right, decent, and good is eventually supposed to be reconstituted as instruction (*didaskein*) and teaching (*mathêsis*), the model for which is the anamnesic "dialogue" in the *Meno* concerning diagrammatic relations "*written* in the soul," relations among the *eidê* of Square, Double, Diagonal, and so forth. And, accordingly, one might even say that the "Socratically" induced sprouting of the seeds planted orally in the soul of the listener consists precisely in his or her soul's translation of the oral and acoustical *logos* into the "written" eidetic structure behind it. But there is an obvious disparity here of which Plato continues to be very much aware: the instruction concerning how to double the area of a square is complete when the diagrammatical structure of the relationships among the eidetic elements concerned has been conclusively *demonstrated*. Squares built on the Diagonal of another Square belong "under" the *eidos* of Double Areas; this Square belongs "under" the *eidos* of Squares built on the Diagonal of another Square; therefore this Square belongs "under" the *eidos* of Double Areas—*quod erat demonstrandum*. In the human, intrinsically undecidable matters of what is right, decent, and good, however, this decisive sorting out can never be completed. Hence, here the *dialegesthai* remains inconclusive, which is to say that the reduction of the oral-auditory to the diagrammatic-visual is never accomplished. For we never get the picture of what the "look" of these is; even if it is indeed written someplace in the soul, we can never quite bring it into view. Put another way, this means that in these matters oral *dialegesthai* as talking something through *in time* can never be converted into *dialegesthai* as "bringing together" and "taking apart" species, or forms, diagrammatically *in space*. As we learned from the *Phaedo*, Socratic audible discussion of these thus never becomes Pythagorean visual *apodeixis*, or "pointing something out" for an onlooker, and an earlier orality thus persists even within the turn to writing.

Plato makes this very clear in the *Phaedrus* too when he has Socrates say that for serious speakers on these subjects the word "wise" is too grand and appropriate for God alone, and that "philosopher" or "lover of wisdom" would therefore be the fitting word to use (278d). This is to say that we human beings seek after wisdom in these matters but never reach it; we never escape having to *talk* these things through indefinitely.

4.4 Orality and Writing, the Acoustical and the Visual in Plato: The Diction (*lexis*) of Diotima's "Speech" in the *Symposium*

Where, then, does all this leave us with regard to writing and Platonism's "metaphysical" reductions of otherness to presence to self, and of openness of meaning to closure and univocity? Is it writing, as Derrida contends, that subverts Plato's project of "right reasoning," *ho orthos logos*, and must therefore be suppressed and excluded? Or is it not rather precisely orality that Plato sees as the danger? Our study of the *Phaedo* and *Phaedrus* dialogues has made clear that, in fact, Plato sees not writing but the oral tradition, particularly in its potential for sophistical exploitation, as the real threat. But in what sense could the spoken word, far more than the written, be so radically disruptive that he would seek to counter it, albeit inconsistently, with recourse to voiceless writing?

First, and contrary to Derrida, as Plato very likely recognized, it is not the written word that invades one's self-presence and disrupts one's *autarkeia* or self-sufficiency but rather the spoken word. Derrida does not see this because his phenomenological exposition of hearing the spoken word goes back only to the secondary and derivative phenomenon of hearing oneself speak, *s'entendre parler.* Clearly, however, our original experience of the spoken word begins with, and is grounded in, hearing someone other than oneself speak. Put in terms of our hermeneutics of original argument, we might say that, as we have seen in Aristotle, any *bouleuesthai* or taking counsel with oneself originates in *sumbouleuesthai*, our taking counsel with each other (see chapter 3, note 7 above). For we do not think up the vocal word, the *voca*bulary of our speech, by ourselves; rather, we first hear it spoken to us, and, more often than not, precisely when we wanted and expected it least. Much more than the being of the written word, the being of a voiced word is otherness and alterity, for it is the voiced word, the word that we hear from another, that comes over us from outside us and beyond the horizons of our awareness, draws us listeners into its resonance, only then to withdraw and fade out of hearing. We are not the center, not the agent, in this event, rather, as patients, we undergo something coming from a source other than ourselves and outside our grasp and comprehension. (Even Plato himself speaks in this regard of the *pathos tôn logôn*, our undergoing the words we speak [*Philebus* 15d].) This alterity of the spoken word is crucial. For, in contrast to the original spoken word that we hear from someone other than ourselves, any given written word, even if it is only a trace that constantly defers to words not present, is, for the one who would read it, in view and at the disposal of the reader, who, precisely as a reader or one looking on, can maintain a sovereign theoretical detachment in regard to it, and, if need be, even look away from it—possibilities not available to a listener. Indeed, with Havelock we could argue that it is the displacement of orality by writing that makes the project of pure *theôria*, the pure intellect's unmoved "looking on" at the timeless ideas, possible in the first place; for as long as one remained a listener to tales being sung aloud, one remained captivated by them and drawn into the passions of the protagonists.[51] In this regard we can cite the *Ion*'s critique of the rhapsodist, who, precisely because he sings what he has heard, *cannot* see and know what he is talking about (533c–35a).

Hence, if with Derrida and contrary to Plato, a deconstruction and *Destruktion* of presence to self is the goal, one might better advance an oral, and not literary, tradition. We might turn here to an oral tradition unknown to Plato, to be sure, but perhaps the oral tradition most disruptive of later Platonism, namely the Judeo-Christian tradition of the homiletical, pro-phetic word, the word "spoken forth" and that we hear spoken, not by ourselves to ourselves, but spoken to us by someone decidely *other* than ourselves. As an example of this we might take the "You are the one!" of 2 Samuel 12:7, which Nathan attaches to his story of the rich man who stole from a poor man and which, precisely in coming from "outside" David's self-presence, shatters his detachment from the people with whose lives he had been scheming—schematizing, "diagramming"—and draws him back into good faith. It is Kierkegaard, the apostate Lutheran, who perhaps best understood the existential need for converting such *scriptural* passages as this, that one might *read* dispassionately, back into the surprising spoken word that one either *hears* or does not: "He who has ears to hear, let him hear" (ὁ ἔχων ὦτα ἀκούειν ἀκουέτω) (Luke 8:8). (See section 6.4 below on "embodied argument" and chapter 6, note 1 on the New Testament's "revisceration" of Greek rhetoric.)

Second, the spoken word, as we have seen, is not static but temporary and temporal in its coming to pass, and precisely this inconstancy makes it dangerous for the knowledge that Platonic metaphysics would secure. For if the stabilized truth that we see expressed and articulated diagrammatically were to be drawn back into expression in the mere voiced word that we hear, as this comes into audibility only to fade into inaudibility, it would be undermined and lost. What had seemed to be definitively clear and distinct for us, who could survey it and signify it, would relapse into its infinite questionability. After all, the voiced word originates in the unstable Heraclitian world of audible sensations, where what things are and what they are not are never clearly established, but instead things continue to fade into their opposites, and the voiced word perpetuates the indeterminacy of this origin. It follows that if the *Destruktion* of Platonism is to be at the same time the recovery of the original openness and undecidability of meaning, not the priority of writing but the original orality beneath the layers of literary culture suppressing it must be restored. Not writing is the ramrod with which to breach the fortress of static metaphysical thought, rather, orality.

Indeed, contrary to Derrida's contention, it is the spoken word we hear from another, not the written word we read by ourselves, that is least transparent and least conducive to some sort of illusory reduction of it to a univocal sign designating some sort of static *eidos* behind it. It is the spoken word, therefore, not the written, that remains most open to shifts in meaning. For the spoken word, if it has not yet been converted, for example, into a conventional sign for the written sign "2," but is still part of a premathematical, preliterate *voca*bulary, is not an *eponuma* or eponym named after something else and, even less, a *sêmeion* or sign representing something else, rather, it is an *onoma* or word name that in naming something lets that thing be temporarily and ambiguously what it is—as in Achilles, Achilleus, from *achos* and *laos,* that is, "grief to the people."[52] A written sign such as "2" signifies univocally a function in a system of signs in the "writing in the soul," and other written signs, such as "*to dikaiaon*" or "*to kalon,*" can give the appearance, at least, of analogously designating some sort of *eidos* univocally to which they are completely transparent. But, as Plato recognized and feared, voiced names, *onomata,* which are heard, do not allow this sort of envisioning, rather, they draw us into an event in which the meaning they put to us is constantly becoming new and different.[53]

We see, then, that the graphic and diagrammatical systematization of differences and relations, which Derrida calls *archê*-writing and which Plato calls the "writing in the soul," is in fact not prior to voiced speech and not presupposed by it. Indeed, such a stuctural "grammar" is presupposed only once *onomata* have been recast as *eponuma* and *sêmeia,* and once the temporal event of voiced audible speech has, in subsequent reflection, been stopped, spatialized, and envisioned, and made present to oneself. After all, *grammars* are not produced by native *speakers,* and it was the Romans who first produced grammars of Greek. Derrida, in perpetuating optical metaphysics rather than taking it down, continues to presuppose the priority of visual written signification over audible voiced naming. But he got this wrong: A Heideggerian *Destruktion* of metaphysic's static presence that "lays bare," and then "lays out" hermeneutically, our original ways of speaking with each other makes clear that Homer and the great speeches of his oral tale precede Pythagoras's demonstrations and

Plato's "dialectical art," both of which are abstractions from our original acoustical involvement in being and time.

Even Plato himself makes this clear: for despite all his attacks on Homer and the oral tradition and all his probing of Pythagorean demonstrative logic as an alternative to Socratic orality, Plato himself never abandons orality; rather, it remains for a later Platonic tradition to take this step. We have already seen in a number of majestically styled passages from the dialogues that, as a matter of fact, Plato is acutely conscious of how what he has written will sound when it is acted out and converted back into the voiced word. Perhaps most striking of all in this regard, however, is Diotima's narration in the *Symposium* of the final stages through which the initiate into the mysteries of love will pass, and this not only because of the beauty of its sound but, pardoxically, because it is about the *vision* of beauty itself—"Suddenly he will *see* . . ." (ἐξαίφνης κατόψεταί) (*Symp.* 210e).

To fully appreciate the rhetorical *and acoustical* significance of this passage we need to see how it is situated in the *Symposium* dialogue as a whole. First, Socrates' speech on love follows Agathon's (that is, Plato's) florid and dramatic panegyric, which, in true epideictic style, "shows off" Agathon's prize-winning skills as a dramatist and orator. It is laced with diachronic turns of speech, all adroitly employed for maximum pathetical effect. In addition to displaying the speaker's urbanity, the rolling conclusion at 197d–e, for example, achieves urgency in the accelerando, first, of its antiphonies and epistrophes, that is, phrases answering one another and repetitions of the same sound at the end of each phrase, as in

> polite*ness* contr*iving*, moroseness outdr*iving*; kind giver of am*ity*, giving no enm*ity*; . . . coveted of such as share him *not*, treasured of such as good share have *got*; . . . careful of the good, careless of the bad [πρᾳότετα μὲν πορίζων, ἀγριότετα δ' ἐξορίζων· . . . φιλόδωρος εὐμενείας, ἄδωρος δυσμενείας· . . . ἐπιμελὴς ἀγαθῶν, ἀμελὴς κακῶν]

and, second, of its climactic asydeton, that is, its omission of conjunctions, as in

> in toil, in fear, in drink, in word, helmsman, boatswain, champion and best deliverer [ἐν πόνῳ, ἐν φόβῳ, ἐν πότῳ, ἐν λόγῳ κυβερνήτες, ἐπιβάτης, παραστάτης τε καὶ σωτὴρ ἄριστος].[54]

(The "and" or *te kai* introduced only in the last unit of this sequence begins the rallentando needed to bring the cadence to a graceful end.)

Now, to all of this, Socrates' dry question-and-answer dialectic (199b ff.) in search of just what love is, its *ti estin*, seems, indeed, a very sober antidote—*alexipharmakon*, we might say—and even Diotima's "talking through" love begins in this same, affectively neutral vein (see 201e ff.). One might think, then, that Plato's breach with the stylistic "knacks" he so mocked in the *Phaedrus* was complete. Everything changes, however, at 203b, when Plato has his "Diotima" switch from this *dialogos* form back to the form of precisely that *makros logos* or grand rhetorical speech that we saw illustrated by Agathon. The initial transition occurs when Socrates recounts her response, "That, she said, would be a longer tale to narrate, but I will tell it to you even so." There is, to be sure, a brief return to instruction and question and answer dialectic at 204b ff.—"Now all this too did she teach me [ἐδίδασκέ με]" (207a)—but this modulates more and more into Diotima's telling her tale to her audience, and at 210a the transition back to the *makros logos* form is complete. Indeed, the wording of her exposition even begins now to mingle with the priestess's language of initiation into the mysteries, and when, at 210e–11b, we are to be guided to the holy of holies, *auto to kalon*, the beautiful and decent itself, and where, accordingly, not just the logic of an argument is to be demonstrated, but also the *pathos* of awe requisite for attaining conviction is to be communicated by voice, we find combined, to masterful climactic effect, the diachronic tropes of anaphora, or the repetition of the first word at the beginning of each phrase, and epistrophe in

> [*n*]*ot* coming into be*ing*, *not* passing out of be*ing*; *not* wax*ing*, *not* wan*ing* [οὔτε γιγνόμενον οὔτε ἀπολλύμενον, οὔτε αὐξανόμενον οὔτε φθῖνον],

anaphora and antiphony (*men* . . . *de*) in

> not *in one way* beautiful but *in one way* ugly; not beautiful *at one time* but *at one time* not [οὐ τῇ μέν καλόν, τῇ δ' αἰσχρόν, οὐ τοτὲ μέν, τοτὲ δ' οὐ],

anaphora and antiphony (*men* . . . *de*) in

> *not* beautiful relative to one thing *but* ugly relative to another thing, *not* beautiful in one place *but* ugly in another place, being *to some* beautiful, being *to some* ugly [οὐδὲ πρὸς μὲν καλόν, πρὸς δὲ αἰσχρόν, οὐδ' ἔνθα μὲν καλόν, ἔνθα δὲ αἰσχρόν, ὡς τισὶ μὲν ὂν καλόν τισὶ δὲ αἰσχρόν],

anaphora in

> [*n*]*ot some* word, *not some* science, *not* being somewhere in something else [οὐδέ τις λόγος οὐδὲ τις ἐπιστήμη, οὐδε που ὂν ἐν ἑτέρῳ],

polysyndeton, anaphora, and assonance (repetition of the vowel sound ῳ with modulation to η and ῃ)

> as in an animal *or* on the earth *or* in the sky *or* in some other thing [οἶον ἐν ζῴῳ ἢ ἐν γῇ ἢ ἐν οὐρανῷ ἢ ἐν τῳ ἄλλῳ],

and, after an antithetical "ἄλλα" or "rather" that resolves the building tension of this phrase in a cadence, the assonances of the repeated *au, o,* and *ei* sounds in the αὐτὸ καθ' αὐτὸ μεθ' αὐτοῦ μονοειδὲς ἀεὶ ὄν.

Even Lamb succumbs to a doctrinal and terminological reading here, and consequently his translation, like most others—"existing ever in singularity of form independent by itself"—falls completely flat. But if one does in fact listen to the acoustical dimension of this passage, its voicing in sound, it becomes obvious that the stylistic devices it employs are much more than than dispensable ornamentation for some logical, theoretical insight to be taught to an observer for his or her intellectual *assent.* Contrary to what the literary tradition after Ramus, Port Royal, and the Royal Society would teach us, this extroadinary style is not some sort of extrinsic pleasantry added on in order to palliate a difficult doctrine that, were the learner up to it, might best be explained in writing. On the contrary, its intrinsic function is to create the proper affective setting and tone, the "voicing" or *Stimmung*, as Heidegger calls it, in which alone the force of the argument can be communicated viscerally and without which the conviction and *consent* of an audience cannot be obtained. For not "Yes, I see" is the response this priestess wants, but "Yes, I will."

Can, then, the "significance" here really be divorced from Plato's diction, what is said from how it is said, the conventional indices or signs from the voiced sound of the word names? In the end, Plato knew that it could not. If we seek, as all original argument does, not to demonstrate something to an onlooker but to exhort someone to a decision or *krisis* for one kind of action and one kind of life rather than another, all these divisions between the cognitive and the emotive fuse again in the one whole of our concrete speaking to each other.

5

Traces of Original Argument in Aristotle's Logical Theory: A *Destruktion* of the *Posterior Analytics* and *Topics*

The question for us now is to what extent Aristotle preserves and perpetuates the "original" dialogical/rhetorical dimension of Plato's writing and to what extent, on the contrary, he becomes part of the mathematically oriented tradition of Platonic demonstrative reasoning. For in some ways Aristotle remains an "earlier" thinker, "closer" to the origins of argument, but in others, he contributes to the abstraction from original argument begun in Plato.

In this chapter we will set in abeyance our concern with the origins of argument in rhetoric and proceed no further in our hermeneutical *Destruktion* of demonstrative logic than to "lay bare" and "lay out" interpretively in Aristotle the layer of dialectic immediately beneath it. For the time being, consequently, rhetoric's *pathos* and *êthos* will not concern us, rather, our focus will be solely on the *logos* or logical dimension of argument, and our task to disclose beneath the abstractions of Aristotle's demonstrative logic the features of the more original *logos* of dialectic.

In so doing we will apply to Aristotle Heidegger's method of probing for traces of an earlier kind of thinking about being, traces of an *anfängliches Denken* or "inceptive thinking" at the inception of thought about what "is." In many ways Heidegger has already done this himself. Our concern here, however, will not be with Aristotle's *De Interpretatione, Metaphysics*, and *Physics*, to which, as we will see, Heidegger has already explicitly directed us in this regard, but rather with Aristotle's logical theory as it is elaborated in the *Posterior Analytics* and *Topics*, texts that Heidegger largely neglects.

The discussion will have two stages. Briefly stated, in the first we will see in what sense the question that we are putting to Aristotle is indeed a Heideggerian one, and, in the second, we will proceed with an application of this question to the *Posterior Analytics* and *Topics*. We will try to display that in these texts Aristotle, even when he is elaborating the theory of scientific *apodeixis* or demonstration, does indeed perpetuate an earlier sense of argument, and that he thus extends Plato's mathematical paradigm yet, at the same time, rejects it and in large part reverses Plato's abstractions from the lived world.

5.1 Heidegger's Treatment of Logic

From early on a central concern of Heidegger's has been to get behind traditional logic, which he takes to be one of the three derivative fields of philosophy—logic, physics, ethics—and to get back to a doctrine of the *logos* at the inception (*Anfang*) of thinking before its delimitation into these fields. We now have available his lectures from 1925, *Logik*; from 1929–30, *Die Grundbegriffe der Metaphysik* (GBM) (see, in particular, §§8, 69, 72, and 73 on the *logos*); and from 1943 and 1944, *Heraklit* (see, in particular, "Logik: Heraklits Lehre vom *Logos*," pp. 185–387).[1] These provide considerable insight into the development of Heidegger's thinking about logic before, during, and after the so-called *Kehre* or turning.

Not that there is any sort of radical break here.[2] Indeed, from the beginning Heidegger's questioning about logic and the *logos* had been about what the *logos* displays and hides in opening up the world of beings for us while simultaneously concealing and withholding these beings from us. Hence, logic for him has always had to do with truth, but not the truth of the correspondence of our "propositions" to an external reality and not the formal truth of "logical" validity either, rather with a truth "before" these that makes them possible in the first place. This truth, a truth prior to any *Satzwahrheit* or propositional truth, Heidegger describes as the concomitance of *alêtheia-lêthê*, *Entborgenheit-Verborgenheit*, unhiddenness and hiddenness, in which beings first display themselves as what they are. Seen this way, says Heidegger, "the traditional logic of the schools is the externalized, uprooted, and thereby rigidified content of an original philosophical *questioning such as was still alive in Plato and Aristotle*, a questioning completely suffocated by the scholastic rigidification of it" (*Logik*, p. 13; emphasis added).

The basic thought here is not as obscure as it might seem: before we can have states of affairs about which we can make true or false statements, existent things must have "come into their own," as it were. Beings, be these *Dasein* or human existence, *Zeuge* or everyday use-items, a *Kunstwerk* or work of art like a Greek temple, must have displayed themselves to us as what they are. But they do this only in also keeping to themselves and witholding themselves from us. For example, we are never fully present to ourselves; a hammer often is not where we thought it was or good for what we thought it was; an artwork always has more meanings than any one of us can find in it. Hence, when each of these shows itself "in truth," its disclosure of itself is always at the same time its closing itself off to complete disclosure. Its partial coming to light from impenetrable obscurity is always accompanied by its partial lapsing back into impenetrable obscurity. A thing's coming near and presenting itself to us is thus inevitably conjoined with its falling away and absenting itself from us, its "fading in" or *Anwesen*, as Heidegger would say, with its "fading out" or *Abwesen*. Accordingly, the original *logos*, the "inceptive," narrative historical language which told the tale of, and said, this local, temporal concomitance of being and not being, could not yet *be* logic's language of full and static presence to our consciousness. It could not yet *be* logic's placeless, timeless "All A *are* B; C *is* A; therefore C *is* B," from which any historical narrative "no longer" being here now and "not yet" being here now have been purged. (After all, in demonstrative logic one does not say, "Once upon a time in the land of Q, all A were B.")

Now, despite his turn to the language of demonstrative logic, traces of this original prelogical *logos* still abound in Aristotle. For instance, and as we have already observed in our elaboration of Heidegger's 1924 *Basic Concepts of Aristotelian Philosophy* (GBAPh), in dialectic's *dialegesthai* or "talking things through" the premises or *protaseis* are precisely not propositions or declarative sentences but questions "put forward" and "pro-posed" for inquiry, questions that leave "It is so, isn't it?" and "It is not so, isn't it?" hanging in the balance (see section 2.2 above on Heidegger's analysis of the *protasis*). We will see here in our own investigation of the *Topics* that, consequently, the conclusions drawn from them are inconclusive and hence not really declarative statements but open questions too. And what is perhaps still more remarkable, we will see that in the *Analytics*, which are ostensibly about mathematical science's necessary demonstration, Aristotle often reverts to ordinary, "original" reasoning about temporal, local, accidental things that just "happen to have happened," *ta sumbebêkota.*

Still, we cannot overlook the fact that Heidegger himself consistently directs his logical inquiry throughout to Aristotle's *De Interpretatione* and *Metaphysics* and that, by contrast, the *Analytics* and *Topics*—and the *Rhetoric,* to which he devoted part of his lectures of 1924—lose interest for him.[3] Thus, in focusing on these texts we will be putting different questions to Aristotle from those to which Heidegger eventually restricted himself. For Heidegger probes Aristotle for the *Seinsereignis* or event of being in which beings first took on the being they have for us now, an event in which all being came to be understood against the measure of *ständige Anwesenheit* or static presence. We, however, will leave the question of that event of being aside. Instead, we will ask about an original *Sein des Seienden,* a being of beings in which the being of the things that are is not yet "static presence" but still *genesis kai phthora,* concomitant generation *and* destruction, being *and* not being. And, more specifically, in turning to the *Posterior Analytics* and *Topics* we will ask about how one originally talked about this original being.

However, even if Heidegger does not ask it, this is still a Heideggerian question. For, if Gadamer is correct, the central theme even in the existential analyses of Heidegger's *Being and Time* is this orginal concomitance of being and not being of which we have been speaking. And this theme remains central throughout Heidegger's later works too, even after the "turn," when it became incontestably evident to him that this concomitant being and not being was not to be experienced by us as subjects creating it in acts or performances of our subjectivity but rather by us as dative objects, we might say, "to whom" it is disclosed and "from whom" it is simultaneously concealed.

In his "Martin Heidegger 75 Jahre" (GW 3, 186–96) Gadamer defends the thinking of the later Heidegger after the "turn"—though not Heidegger himself—against his critics. These critics, Gadamer recounts, allow that though Heidegger's *Being and Time* was surely a breakthrough, but "after the 'turn' (*Kehre*)," they say, "which also includes the perversity [*Verkehrtheit*] of his dreadful political aberrations into the lust for power and the machinations of the Third Reich, he no longer speaks of things with verifiable instantiations but speaks, instead, like one initiated in the mysteries of his god, Being" (190). In response to this criticism Gadamer would establish a continuity in the questions Heidegger asks by showing that from the beginning Heidegger always sought to start out not, as in German Idealism and its predecessors and followers, from consciousness and what is present to it, but instead from being (191). In keeping with this approach his initial question (in *Being and Time*) was "What is the being of human existence or being 'there' (*Dasein*)?" Certainly not consciousness, writes Gadamer:

> But what kind of a being is it that neither lasts nor obtains like eternal stars or mathematical truths, but, like all life suspended between birth and death, *is* always in [the process] of disappearing and yet, in its finitude

> and historicity, *is* a "there," a here, a now, presence at the moment, not an empty point, but the fullness of time and the collection of the whole? . . . Surely this "there" does not mean mere being present [*Anwesendsein*] but rather a happening [*Geschehen*]. (192; emphasis added)

Thus, Heidegger too, we see, asks about the being of *a* being, of *a* being, this is to say, whose being could not be adequately rendered in traditional "metaphysical" language.

Furthermore, Gadamer maintains, this remained his question, even after the "turn," when he asked about the being of the artwork, which, as yet another "there," instantiates a "happening of truth" (193). And contrary to Heidegger's critics, Gadamer contends, there are verifiable instances of what he is talking about here: if one looks at his own example, a Greek temple, one must agree, writes Gadamer, that "in the small, almost delicate measures of this temple—which appears to have been wrested, as it were, from an elemental world of overpowering size—stone and light *are* more authentically, [i.e.,] have come out into the 'there' of their true nature" (193; emphasis added). So it is, also, with the thing—"A thing, too," says Gadamer, "self-subsistent and pressed down to nothing, only *is* because there is a clearing (*Lichtung*) in the primeval forest of being that [at the same time] closes itself off and into itself" (193). And so too, finally, with the word:

> Here everybody sees that there are words that function like a mere signal (even if what is thus signaled is an out-and-out nonentity) and, again, other words—and not only in a poem—that themselves bear witness to what they impart, being, as it were, nearby to something that is, something irreplaceable, inexchangeable, a "there" that in the very enactment of speaking opens itself up. Everybody knows what "empty" of meaning and "full" of meaning refer to here. In following out what Heidegger's way of thought teaches us, we could come to see for ourselves that there, in the word, it is "being" that stays away or is present. (193)

Hence, even the discussion of authenticity and inauthenticity in *Being and Time* proves to be part of Heidegger's destruction of "metaphysics," for the point of it is that in our human being we are but one exemplification of that very concomitance of being and not being, "is" and "is not," which "metaphysics" had hoped to overcome. According to Heidegger, we never "are" purely, never "are" truly, authentic, rather we "are" authentic and "are not" authentic at the same time.[4] Hence, we self-contradictory human beings cannot be the pure being, the true self-identical being (*to ontôs on*) that Plato and subsequent "metaphysics" prefer, and in reference to which all other being was depreciated as mere *genesis kai phthora*, coming into being *and* concomitant passing away. And neither, Heidegger argues after the "turn," can the artwork be purely what it "is"—be just revelation and with no concealment—nor can a thing, a pitcher, for example, *nor can the meaning of the words we speak.*

Now, as Gadamer points out, it was precisely this last, the ambivalence of *onomata* or word names and of our *logoi* or utterances and arguments in these word names, that concerned Plato and compelled him to seek something over and beyond them that "really is," the *ontôs on*, and *ousia* or "beingness" itself (Heidegger: *Seiendheit*).[5] And this "beingness" Plato found in the ideas (see section 4.1.2 above). For in the hands of unscrupulous sophists a natural name's ambivalence becomes the means of passing off something for what it was not, for instance, a wrong, despicable, and bad action for what is right, decent, and good. It was to head off just this abuse that Plato postulated a different kind of being, an "is" that is not the "is" of what is concomitantly coming into being and ceasing to be, not the narrative historical "is" of what "is" and at the same time "is not" yet and "is not" anymore. The being he postulated could not be the "is," for instance, that someone's action or character "is" at some time, now or then, and at some place, here or there, but the timeless, placeless being of decency itself, *auto to kalon*, with no trace of the indecent attaching to it, of a decency, as the *Symposium* has it, that is precisely "not in one way decent (*kalon*) yet in another despicable (*aischron*), not at one time decent but at another time not, not in one regard decent but in another despicable, not decent here but despicable there . . . but being always in itself and by itself the one form that it is" (*Symposium* 211a–b).[6] Using Heidegger's language, we might say that Plato seeks a perfect self-identical authenticity wholly purified of any concomitant inauthenticity.

For as we have seen in the previous chapter, only if we look past the changing, contradictory physical thing to our unchanging idea of it, only in *apoblepein pros tên idean*, can we hope to find a firm purchase on which to take a stand against the sophistical wrestler's exploitation of the weakness of word names (*astheneia tôn onomatôn*) and keep from being thrown to the mat in the verbal wrestling in which he would engage us. This is the imagery Plato uses.[7] Even if his principal considerations, namely the just, decent, and good, provide precisely those subject matters proper to the three branches of rhetorical argument, his paradigm remains, as we know, the arithmetician or geometrician. For it is these mathematicians who have a static and precisely defined idea of "what it is" that they are talking about, of its *ti estin*, and who have a languange of unequivocal signs, "2" or "=," for instance, in which to do their talking and writing. Consequently, sophists, when they try to twist these mathematicians' meanings, get nowhere. Here there are no ambivalences and indeterminacies left for them to exploit, no "weaknesses" of mere names.

Thus, the "metaphysics" Heidegger would identify and "destroy" with his return to an earlier concomitant being and not being has its beginnings precisely in the matter of words and logic. And consequently, we might even say that though it seems that Heidegger's task in *Being and Time* is the *Destruktion* of Descartes's mathematical construction of the world as static *res extensae* whose only "change" is in location, Heidegger is also, and perhaps primarily, concerned even there to "take down" Plato's mathematical construction of ideal essences beyond the changing world and to "take down" the artificial sign language we use to talk about these ideal essences. And insofar as he returns us in *Being and Time* to a world of concomitant being and not being, even in this earlier work his concern is to return us from *speaking* in terminologically determinate signs to *speaking* in the ambivalent word names with which we tell how this narrative historical world happens. At the very least we can say that there is a logical turn implied, if not taken, even in *Being and Time.* And if this is so, just where Aristotle's *logical theory* fits into Heidegger's destruction and circumvention of "metaphysics" does indeed remain an open and important question. Is Aristotle's logic simply part of the "metaphysical" tradition and hence to be "taken down" too, or is Aristotle also a fund of pre-Platonic, premetaphysical ways of speaking and arguing about being?

To be sure, for the most part research into Heidegger's appropriation of Aristotle as an "earlier" thinker than Plato has turned not to Aristotle's logic but to his physics and its recovery of an an "inceptive" thinking that is "closer to the origin" (*ursprünglicher*), as Heidegger puts it.[8] For clearly, in even attempting a theory of *phusis* as *phuein,* of nature in process, and in returning Plato's separate (*chôristai*) and static ideas to physical process as the goal (*telos*) of a physical thing's growth and change from *not being* what it is into *being* what it is, Aristotle does get back of Plato's meta-physical thought. Thus, in part, at least, he restores the earlier concomitance of being and not being, and it would seem indeed that here Plato's looking away from the physical particular and looking toward the idea of what it is in essence had been reversed and an earlier way of seeing things recovered. For once again, as in pre-Socratic philosophy, we are to look *at* physical, changing being, not away from it to something else.

But this, of course, is only part of the story. For in Aristotle the changing world is, as we know, still to be founded in an *un*moved mover as the *archê,* the starting point and stopping point of all physiological explanation.[9] Thus, Plato's priority of changeless and timeless things over things in process is maintained after all, and in Aristotle, too, the more original concomitance of being and not being is once again displaced by the vision of a changeless pure being, a pure actuality with no not-being-yet and no not-being-any-longer attaching to it. Ultimately, it seems that in Aristotle's physics Plato, or at least Platonism, does prevail over Heraclitus.

We, however, want to define much more narrowly the question of whether or not in Aristotle's thinking Plato prevails over Heraclitus. Even so we want to raise it in a form in which Heidegger himself surely raises it, if only implicitly: namely, is there the same productive tension between Plato and continuing earlier ways of thinking in Aristotle's logical thinking, specifically, in the *Analytics* and *Topics*, that we find in the *Physics*? If we ourselves extend Heidegger's line of questioning to these books of the *Organon*, it turns out, as we will see, that there is. And are the traces of Heraclitus ultimately displaced there too in a Platonic turn to the mathematical? Not entirely. In fact, for all its reliance on Plato and the model of mathematical reasoning, Aristotle's logical theory may be said to preserve an "inceptive thinking of being," a thinking that maintains the concomitance of contradictory being *and* not being, even better than his physics does.

However, one other problem remains for our attempted application of Heidegger's thought to Aristotle's logical theory. Heidegger's own insistence on the *dis*junction, not *con*junction, of *alêtheuein ê pseudesthai* in Aristotle—or as Heidegger renders this, the capacity of a thing that is said *either* to "disclose" *or* to "conceal," but not both at the same time (see GBM 29–30, p. 453)—seems to run counter to the reading of Aristotle that we are proposing. For such a disjunction would eliminate the concomitance of being and not being that characterizes the original being prior to any metaphysical abstraction to pure being and "beingness." Still, the radical disjunction of "is" and "is not" in Aristotle's *Analytics*—in other words, the "law of noncontradiction"—would seem less a problem if we kept in mind that for Heidegger the *logos apophantikos*, namely the declarative statement treated in the *Analytics* and for which the "law of noncontradiction" holds, is not an original, but a derivative *logos*.

Strikingly, here in *The Basic Concepts of Metaphysics* (GBM), Heidegger prefaces his exposition of the *logos apophantikos* and of the idea of logic based upon it with allusions to the *Rhetoric* and to dialectic (the *Topics*?) as perhaps more "inceptive" ways of speaking:

> We said that the history of logic in the West was defined by the Greek theory of the *logos* in the sense of a declarative sentence [*Aussagesatz*], and that thereafter the science of languages was defined starting with this

theory as its basis. However, it must be mentioned at the same time that the very same Aristotle, who in taking up crucial initiatives from Plato penetrated to an insight into the structure of the declarative sentence, also recognized, and took on his *Rhetoric*, the grand task of submitting the forms and constructions of nonthetic speaking to interpretation. To be sure, for various reasons the power of logic was too strong to leave open the possibility that this attempt might be developed on its own. (GBM 439)

Presumably, the nonthetic or nonpropositional speaking referred to here is the exhortation-dehortation of consultative rhetoric, the accusation and defense of judicial rhetoric and the praise and censure of epideictic rhetoric (see the *Rhetoric*, book 1, chapter 3, 1358a36 ff.) For, as in *Being and Time* (SZ 32), Heidegger's example here (see 448) is the plea or *euchê*, which figures prominently in the first two of these kinds of rhetoric since they, as opposed to epideictic rhetoric, would elicit a decision from the audience. Accordingly, Heidegger, paraphrasing Aristotle's *De Interpretatione*, 17a5 ff., writes, "the investigation of this kind of speaking, which does not have the character of pointing something out, i.e., of establishing something and letting it be seen as what it is and how it is—the investigation of this kind of *logoi*—belongs in the *Rhetoric* and *Poetics*" (448).

As we know, however, there is yet another kind of sentence besides these subjunctive-imperative alternatives to the indicative declarative sentence (*Aussagesatz*), namely the interrogative sentence (*Fragesatz*), which is the proper province of the *Topics* and its exposition of dialectic. About this nonthetic sentence Heidegger gives us only tantalizing hints here. "Dialectic," he says,

> moves within a speaking [*logos*] and counter-speaking, within diction and contradiction. The possibility that a speaking, a *logos*, lies over against, and contrary to, another *logos*, the *antikeisthai* of *logos* and *logos* is understandable only if we know what the *logos* itself is. . . . We will pursue only one strand out of the complex of problems in the *logos* in order to explicate the problem of the "as" [*als*] and the "on the whole." (GBM 453)

As we will see here, dialectic can treat contradictory *logoi simultaneously* precisely because, unlike the declarative sentences of the *Analytics*, its premises are not thetical but antithetical, which is to say, precisely because they are not declarative but interrogative. In other words, they do not *state* or "establish" either that *x* is *y* or that *x* is not *y*, rather they *ask* whether *x* is *y* or *x* is not *y*. Thus, they leave in question both sides of a contradiction, both "it is" and "it is not," at the same time. And thus here in dialectic, at least, the "or" is not disjunctive at all, but conjunctive; here the "law of noncontradiction" does not hold. For instead of stating either/or, here we are asking whether/or, and, accordingly, we are to entertain not one of these contradictory possibilities to the exclusion of the other but both concomitantly.

5.2 Necessity and "Susceptibility of Being Otherwise" in Aristotle's Logical Theory

When Aristotle comes to Plato in his account of previous philosophies upon which he will build his own, he begins with the following well-known words:

> In the time of his youth, he [Plato] first became acquainted with Cratylus and the opinions of Heraclitus, namely that the entirety of things perceived is always in flux and that there is no scientific knowledge [*epistêmê*] about them, and even later he continued to accept these things as being so. (*Metaphy.* 987a33–35)

In light of this assertion we can readily grasp the point of the Heraclitian elaboration in Plato's *Theaetetus* of Protagoras's theory that "each human being is the measure," and the disclosure there of the "secret doctrine," namely that in perception there is in fact nothing static in either the perceiver or in the reality perceived but only evanescent confluences of fluxuations occurring on both sides. Consequently, in perception there exists neither a self to do the knowing nor any thing to be known. And with the dissolution of being (*to on, ousia*) into fluvian *genesis* or pure process, perception's claim to know scientifically (*epistasthai*) collapses (*Theaetetus* 151e–157c, 181c–183b). Still, as the dialogue goes on to show, we do know; so, we may infer, the object of our knowledge must be ontologically different from the fluxuating stimulus of sensation or perception (compare Aristotle, *Metaphy.* 987b5–6 on Plato and definitions that must be "about something else . . . and not things perceived" [περὶ ἑτέρων . . . καὶ οὐ τῶν αἰσθητῶν]).

Just how this argument would go is clearly indicated by two examples in the *Theaetetus,* neither of which can be pursued in the context of the discussion there: the first (154c) poses the problem of six dice which, if set next to four dice, are "more," but, if set next to twelve, are "less," all the while they themselves have not *become* more or less but *stayed* six. The point is that when we know six to be more than four and less than twelve, we are not looking with our body's eyes at six or four or twelve perceived fluxuating things like some particular dice we might have before us, but looking away from and beyond (*apoblepein*) these things with the mind's eye to (*pros*) static logical (mathematical) realities, in this case, to the numbers and to the numerically More and Less as such (see the similar problem of two *things* coming into being by being added to each other but also by the division of one *thing* in the *Phaedo*, 96e–97b).

The second example (163b–c)—a crucial one for us who are concerned to display hermeneutically the displacement of original argument in audible speech—distinguishes *aisthanesthai*, to perceive, from *epistasthai*, to know, by drawing an analogy with our merely perceiving, that is, merely hearing, a foreign language as opposed to knowing what is meant by its sounds. Implied here too is that the whole world of sensuous fluxuation is in some way just the showing up (*phainesthai*)—not only audible but visible—of a static, inaudible and invisible, purely logical reality separate and distinct from the sensuous fluxuation in which it appears. And this reality, which only *appears* physically but *is* in itself and not physically, is the reality of the ideas. In accord with this thought, we find Aristotle saying of Plato at *Metaphysics* 987b7–8 "among the kinds of being those of this kind he called ideas."

As a matter of fact, at the beginning of the *Theaetetus* (147d–148a)—and prior to the destruction of the thesis that knowledge is perception, which takes up the major portion of this essentially aporetic dialogue—we have an explicit statement of what *epistasthai* and *epistêmê, knowing* scientifically and scientific knowledge, would be, and of the ontological character of their objects. Socrates' interlocutors in the *Theaetetus* are mathematicians, it must be remembered, and they propose that any scientific definition should proceed according to the paradigm of defining the species of number by first gathering under one genus, "number," both the numbers formed by multiplying equal factors and the numbers formed by multiplying a greater by a lesser factor, and then, second, by dividing the genus again into two species to be called "equilateral" and "oblong," respectively. Now, the hope expressed here is that this same strategy of definition (*horismos*) could be used to secure a scientific definition of scientific knowledge. But this hope is noticeably unfulfilled in what follows. Hence, the patent irony of this passage, one which would not be lost on any of Plato's readers, is that this is not only a model for finding what the definition of scientific knowledge is, but, above all, an instance of scientific knowledge itself, namely pinning down what something really is, its *ti estin* and *ousia*, by locating it as one of a finite number of species, here "equilateral" and "oblong," of the appropriate one genus, here "number."

We should note as well that even the infinite number of cases of the thing so to be defined, that is, "oblong number" as 3, 5, up to 17 and beyond (147d), are no longer being looked at as materially instantiated, as three or five *things*, and so forth. Here there is from the start an *apoblepein pros tên idean*, a looking away from, *apo*, the physical thing and a looking toward, *pros*, the idea of what it is in essence. Hence, a pedagogically skillful ontological transition has been made from the previous example of a mere listing of a few of the numberless kinds of clay, for instance, potters' clay, brickmakers' clay, ovenmaker's clay, ad infinitum (147a–d), and for which only a physiological account or *logos* is provided and no definition: "Clay is earth mixed with water" (147c). This ontological transition has, as we have seen, already been prefigured in the *Phaedo* when Plato's "Socrates" turned away (*apo*) from physiological accounts and toward (*pros*) the *logoi* or verbal arguments (99d f.) and began his exploration of the "consonance" and "dissonance" of ideas with each other (see 101d), for example, of the idea of three with the ideas of odd and even, respectively (104e). (We remark, again, on the lingering traces of an original acoustical experience in the words "consonance" and "dissonance" that Plato draws upon to adumbrate the purely logical "sameness" and "difference.")[10]

Thus, even while the Platonic "Socrates" continues to argue in the orignal sense of *dialegesthai*, namely by talking a *question* through, and in responding to opposed arguments (say, that the soul *is not* immortal) and in proposing inconclusive counterarguments (say, that it *is*), Plato even in the *Phaedo* is subtly redirecting our attention away from the world of what *is* in process and, hence, concomitantly *is not*, and redirecting it toward a being that always and ever *is* what it is necessarily and cannot not be what it is. Nothing about this latter kind of being is in question, and consequently we no longer *ask*, as we do in dialectic, "Is it or isn't it?" rather, we *state*, in an affirmation (*kataphasis*), as in the *Phaedo*, for example, that "'Soul' is 'Life'" and infer from this another statement, a negation (*apophasis*), namely that "'Soul' cannot be 'Death'" (see *Phaedo* 105c ff.). Significantly, physiological, genetic not-being, some thing's or someone's passing away and not being any longer, has now been banished, and in its place remains only the dematerialized not-being of logical "dissonance" or difference: the immaterial *idea* of "Motion" does not blend, it is said in the *Sophist*, for example, with the *idea* of "Rest"; the idea of "Motion" *is not* the idea of "Rest" (compare the *Sophist* 255e ff.). With that, dialectic as *dialegesthai* or talking something through has been reduced to the dialectic of the ideas, namely the hypothesizing and testing of the compatibility and incompatibility of timeless, placeless classes of things with each other, which is to say, their noncontradiction or contradiction.

Indeed, "collection into a genus and division into species"—which is to say, argument by Aristotle's formal causality—and "noncontradiction" displace reasoning from the "topics" and become the sole legitimate means of argumentation, for these alone penetrate behind merely telling the tale of what comes to pass. With that, the foundations are laid for Aristotle's standard first and second figure demonstrative syllogisms, "All A are B; all C are A; therefore, all C are B," or "No A are B; all C are B; therefore, no C are A."

Here, then, is the thesis to be established: on the one hand, insofar as the Aristotelian theory of argument follows Plato in withdrawing to the paradigm of mathematical reasoning and science as a way to head off sophistical exploitation of a word name's equivocity, it perpetuates just this Platonic abstraction. To this extent, it perpetuates the very same conceptualization and dematerialization of negativity that we find in Plato, a conceptualization and dematerialization by virtue of which a material thing's *not* being yet or *not* being any longer is translated into a conceptual genus or species of things not being compatible with another genus or species. Indeed, the same desire for logical security and immunity to rhetorical sleights of hand manifested in the *Metaphysics*' postulation of the laws of noncontradiction and the excluded middle forces Aristotle to resume a Platonic ontological differentiation in his theory of argument that elsewhere he seemed ready to abandon.

On the other hand, where Aristotle's theory of argument still reflects an earlier, pre-Platonic understanding of argument—as does the *Topics* and even the *Posterior Analytics* in extended stretches—it actually reverses this abstraction and thus makes possible a restoration of dialectic in its original sense of simultaneously entertaining contradictories while talking something through.

5.2.1 Plato, Aristotle, and the privileging of demonstration: demonstrative reasoning in the *Meno* and the *Posterior Analytics*

To see how Aristotle has, in fact, recovered the dialectical background behind mathematical science's demonstration all the while he privileges the latter, let us look first at a paradigmatic instance of Plato's "metaphysical" theory of reasoning, the solution to the problem of how to double the area of a square in the *Meno* (82b ff.), and then let us look at the *Posterior Analytics* and at the *Topics* and ask to what extent Aristotle's paradigm stays the same as Plato's *but also*, and with Heidegger, to what extent it does not. In other words, we will be asking to what extent Aristotle's logical theory in these texts displays that Aristotle, despite himself, as it were, indeed remains a "more original" thinker than Plato, one closer to the "inception" of thought and to original argument.

To review briefly this well-known problem in the *Meno,* Socrates summons one of Meno's household servants in order to display to Meno that all apparently new understanding learned is really old understanding of which we are only reminded once the teacher has freed us of the erroneous opinions that have been blocking our rememberance of it. Hence, the student, here Meno's servant, must first be disabused of the opinions he has acquired from his previous experience of doubling things. Following the empirical method of trial and error, he tries to make a new square double the area of the first one by doubling the side of the first square and, when that fails, lengthening the side of the first square by one-half.

The trouble, of course, is that he is treating a mathematical problem as a problem of *technê* and *poiêsis,* namely how to make, by art, another physical square double the area of this particular square here in the sand, and not as a mathematical problem. As Aristotle tells us, unlike demonstration in science, "all art has to do with coming into being (*genesis*), and to practice an art is to consider how *one of those things that are susceptible of both being and not being* might come into being" (EN 1140a12–13; emphasis added). Art, in other words, has to do with making something and reasons about particular contingent realities at some place and time. The point here in the *Meno,* however, is precisely that Meno's servant has not yet made the abstraction from this material realm of art to mathematical, necessary being. Hence, he approaches the problem of doubling the area of *a square as such* by lengthening *this given square's* particular lines in order to see, empirically, what result he gets—a method that would not be misplaced at all if, for instance, he were a carpenter tying to double the area of a particular floor. Significantly, however, the problem requires doubling the area "exactly" (Aristotle: *akribôs*), which, as Socrates now proceeds to show, is to be accomplished only by "constructing" the new square on the diagonal of the first one. Hence, in the end, understanding the solution to the problem turns on understanding an unimaginable number, $\sqrt{2}$, that exists "exactly" only conceptually and in abstraction from all direct or remembered experience of perceptual, physical reality. For if the side of the first square is considered the unit, the side of the new square will, of course, be $\sqrt{2}$.

It is no accident that Plato chooses just this example involving an irrational number that forces the mathematical abstraction from experience, for if anything could be advanced—against any Aristotelian objections—as a *chôriston eidos,* a form separate from physical, material being and above it, surely it is $\sqrt{2}$. To be sure, to accomplish the necessary "reminding" (*anamnêsis*) here Socrates uses a particular drawing, but significantly no empirical measurements are taken nor could they be. By looking at the drawing and "seeing" that the new square contains four of the same triangular areas of which the original square had two, the servant now "sees" that in essence—not actually—the new square is double the area of the first, and, indeed, is "exactly" double. But what sort of square and diagonal, what sort of trianglular area and double area does he "see" here? Obviously in looking at the physical instantiations of these before him he is really looking over and beyond them and looking at the ideas of what they are. With Husserl we could say the intention has become eidetic: it is ideas that he "sees"—conceptually, not perceptually—in "looking away from" the physical examples and "toward the idea" of each.

Furthermore, we should note what has happened to speech here. To be sure, the original articulation of these ideal realities takes place in Greek: "He is a Greek, is he not, and does he speak Greek?" asks Socrates. "Indeed he does," responds Meno (82b). However, the meanings of the Greek words that he uses are now "exactly" defined, which is to say that the mere *onomata* or equivocal word names have now been converted into univocal *sêmeia* or signs in which any natural concomitance of contradictory meanings has been eliminated. In this way both his conceptual insights and the signs he now uses to designate them are secured against sophistical controversion by manipulation of a natural name's inherent ambiguity. That security did not exist as long as he was thinking merely empirically, which is to say literally, with no idea (*eidos, idea*) of what it was that he was talking about, and still using indefinite natural words to name particular physical things.[11]

Now, if we look at Aristotle's exposition, in the *Posterior Analytics*, of what he considers to be the paradigmatic form of *epistêmê* or scientific knowing, and its method of reasoning by syllogistic demonstration, we see presupposed just this transition from the variable being of empirical reality named in the words of natural language to the necessary being of eidetic reality designated by univocal signs. This becomes clear if we cast Plato's example in Aristotelian syllogistic form:

> The square B is a square constructed on the diagonal of another square A;
>
> A square constructed on the diagonal of another square is a square double the area of that other square;

So:

> The square B is a square double the area of another square A.

Actually, there are four things to be known here: (1) the individual or minor term, which would be "the square B"; (2) the universal or major term, here "a square double the area of another square"; (3) the particular or middle term, here "a square constructed on the diagonal of another square"; and (4) the conclusion that combines the first and third of these, the minor and major terms, through the mediation of the second or middle term. In the language of Aristotle's *Posterior Analytics*, Meno's servant is being asked to find the middle term, for this is the cause, ground, and reason (*aitia*) why the square B is double the area of the other square A, and, hence, the answer to his problem of how to construct a square double the area of another. We know scientifically, in other words, when we have found the middle term and can employ it in a syllogism to subsume the individual minor term under the universal major term: Square B belongs to the genus of "Squares double the area of another square" *because* it belongs to a species of that genus, "A square constructed on the diagonal of another square." (Compare the analysis in section 3.3 of *An. Post.* 79b9–13 on the middle term as the "cause" or *aitia*.)

Importantly, because the premises of the demonstrative scientific syllogism are necessary, the conclusion drawn from them follows necessarily: in fact, neither the premises nor the conclusion are "susceptible of being otherwise." It is precisely this necessity that distinguishes the demonstrative scientific syllogism from sophistical arguments, which are based on accidents or mere contingencies that just "happen to have happened" (*sumbebêkota*): "Thus, of corruptible things," says Aristotle,

> there is neither demonstration nor science in the strict sense, rather there is "science," as it were, only by accidents [κατὰ συμβεβηκός] since this is not science of what is itself universal but ["science"] only of what is so at some time or other and in some way or other [οὐ καθόλου αὐτοῦ ἐστιν ἀλλὰ ποτὲ καὶ πώς]. (75b24–27)

As opposed to scientific demonstration, sophistical arguments by accidents produce only the mere opinion that something is likely to happen or to have happened, with no real knowledge of why it has to be so necessarily and cannot not be so:

> Scientific knowledge and what is known scientifically are different from opinion and what is opined. For scientific knowledge is of the universal and is by necessities, and the necessary is not susceptible of being otherwise than it is [τὸ δ' ἀναγκαῖον οὐκ ἐνδέχεται ἄλλως ἔχειν]. There are some beings that are true, to be sure, but also are susceptible

of being otherwise. Now it is plain that scientific knowledge is not about these. (88b30–35)

Implied here, certainly, even if it is not stated expressly, is also that sophistical arguments employ words appropriate for beings of which nothing can be said necessarily, but words wholly inappropriate for demonstrative scientific reasoning. Sophistical arguments employ words, this is to say, whose meanings are as indeterminate as the beings or realities of which they speak. Scientific language, however, cannot allow this indeterminacy. If the arguments of science are in fact to follow necessarily, their language must "exactly" signify the fully determinate, metaphysical realities of which this language speaks, the placeless, timeless beings, that is, which always only "are" just what they are with no "are-not-here-now," "are-not-here-yet," or "are-not-here-anymore" attaching to them. Put another way, in Aristotle too, the naturally equivocal word names of ordinary speech must have been converted into univocal signs like $\sqrt{2}$ that designate static, self-identical eidetic being. They must, as Aristotle puts it, be *akribôs horismena* or precisely defined. So far, then, Aristotle seems to be every bit as Platonic as Plato and to provide no access at all to any "earlier," "more inceptive" kind of argumentation.

5.2.2 "Earlier," "more inceptive" argument "laid bare" in the *Posterior Analytics*

However, even in the *Posterior Analytics*' expostion of reasoning in the strict, demonstrative sense there are still traces of an earlier understanding of being and, correlatively, of a reasoning and onomatic language appropriate for this reasoning. We note especially that in the previous citation Aristotle writes, "there are some beings that are true, to be sure, but also *are* susceptible of being otherwise [ἔστι . . . ὄντα, ἐδεχόμενα δὲ καὶ ἄλλως ἔχειν]" (88b33–34; emphasis added). And surprisingly, the *Posterior Analytics* itself contains expositions of *this* kind of contingent being and truth even if this work's stated purpose is to clarify science and demonstration, in which such contingent being and truth is said to have no place.

Within our discussion in section 3.3 of the topic of *proteron/husteron* or prior/posterior we have already noted that in the *Posterior Analytics*' exposition of the *aitia*, the exposition of the cause, ground, and reason which the middle term provides (94a20 ff.), a good part of the discussion is devoted to nonmathematical, nonepistemic senses of *aitia*. To be sure, the particular *aitia* or "cause" which says "what it is to be the thing in essence" is thought of completely abstractly, as is, also, the *aitia* which provides the necessary *logical* preconditions for something to be what it is, and which is substituted here for the material cause, "the out of what" (τὸ ἐξ οὗ) (compare, for example, *Physics* 194b24–26). But the efficient and final "cause" are exemplified with reasoning that remains, as we have noted, very concrete and that has its place in the contingent and practical realm of "calculating" and "taking counsel" about things that just "happen to have happened." To illustrate the efficient "cause," or that by the agency of which something happens, we saw that Aristotle suggests the middle term, "those who had committed aggression," in a syllogism that we could reconstruct as "Those who had committed aggression are those who had war made upon them; the Athenians are those who committed aggression; therefore, the Athenians had war made upon them" (see 94a36–b9). And to illustrate the final "cause," or that "for the sake of which" something happens, we saw that he suggests the middle term "an act for the sake of normal digestion" in the syllogism, roughly, "Taking a walk after dinner is an act for the sake of normal digestion; an act for the sake of normal digestion is a thing conducive to good health; therefore, taking a walk after dinner is a thing conducive to good health" (see 94b8–26). Now, clearly, we are dealing here with temporal, contingent beings that *are* susceptible of being otherwise than we think, and clearly, too, we are conducting our reasoning in potentially equivocal word names, *onomata*, and not in univocal word signs, *sêmeia*, designating some sort of timeless, necessary, intelligible reality like "$\sqrt{2}$," wholly present and known with certainty.

Furthermore, we note now that this same deviation from the epistemic into the deliberative is evident, too, in Aristotle's account at 89b10 ff. of the special form of intelligence he calls *anchinoia* or acuity of intellect, namely our faculty for quickly and felicitously hitting upon the middle term and "reason" or "cause" for some thing's being the way it is. Aristotle poses three illustrative questions, none of them proper to the realm of necessary demonstration, for which precisely this faculty of *anchinoia* finds the answers: (1) Why does the moon always have its bright side facing the sun? (2) Why is that man there talking to a rich man? (3) Why are those men there friends? If we were to answer these questions syllogistically, we would have the following:

1. The moon is a body deriving its brightness from the sun;

   A body deriving its brightness from the sun is a body with its bright side always facing the sun,

   which is why the moon is a body with its bright side always facing the sun.

2. That man there is a man who needs to borrow money;
   a man who needs to borrow money is a man who talks to a rich man,
   which is why that man there is a man who talks to a rich man.
3. Those two men there are men with a common enemy;
   men with a common enemy are friends,
   which is why those two men there are friends.

In each case anyone who can find the middle terms, "a body deriving its brightness from the sun," "a man who needs to borrow money," "men with a common enemy," can answer the question posed, by drawing the conclusion of a syllogism mediated by that middle term.

It is striking that not one of these syllogisms actually displays the characteristics required for the strict scientific, demonstrative syllogism. As opposed to the mathematical problem of doubling the area of a square—for his part, Aristotle had been using examples from number theory as well as geometry—here there is precisely no looking away from particulars to the universal idea or form. Consequently, none of the terms states what "is" necessarily; instead the being of each thing spoken of is still in question: "Is it or is it not?" For far from being necessary, each being spoken of here *is* "susceptible of being otherwise" and must therefore be assumed not only to be, but "at the same time"—Aristotle: *hama*; Heidegger: *zugleich*—possibly not to be what it is. Nor, accordingly, are the words used to say these contingent beings anything like like "$\sqrt{2}$." Rather they are equivocal names for indeterminate beings.

It follows that, far from demonstrating scientifically in the strict sense, in both reasoning by efficient and final "causes" and reasoning from middle terms identified by "acuity of intellect" we are still reasoning about what we opine (*dokoumen*) to be the case, but might not be, and what seems (*dokei*) to be the case, but might not be. Here we have opinion (*doxa*) in relationship to seeming (*doxa*) and not yet science (*epistêmê*) in relationship to necessary metaphysical being that only is and cannot not be. We have not yet, this is to say, taken the step of mathematical abstraction from contingent physical particulars at some time (*pote*) and in some way (*pôs*), the step that, as we saw in our exposition of the *Meno*, is prerequisite for scientific reasoning. Rather, we remain "under way" within particular, temporal, spatial, self-contradictory being about which we continue to reason in ordinary, onomatic language.

Thus far, however, we have been considering only Aristotle's treatment of the middle or particular term, and of the "acuity of intellect" (*anchinoia*) or mental faculty that allows someone to grasp these middle terms. We find even more obvious traces of an earlier understanding of being and reasoning, however, if we examine Aristotle's account of intuitive intellection (*nous, noein*) of the major or universal terms in the *Posterior Analytics* at 2.19.99b15 ff. Significantly, Aristotle calls these major terms *archai* here, implying that the intuition of them is the intuition of the major *premise* as well: for example, the intuition of the term "animal," taken as the genus for the species "human being," is the intuition of the major premise, "All human beings are animals," which combines with "Callias is a human being" in mediating the conclusion, "Callias is an animal" (100a15–b4). It is this heir*archic*al ordering in "ranks," as it were, and precisely not the intuition of the quiddity of an isolated individual term, that Aristotle has in mind when, playing on the word *archê,* he speaks of individual soldiers in rout "having taken up their positions again under an *archê* or chain of command [ἐπὶ ἀρχὴν ἦλθεν]" (100a11–13): "Callias," this is to say, "takes his stand" in the battalion of "human being," which simultaneously "takes its stand" in the regiment of "animal." The intuitive act of *nous* or intellection in grasping the *archê* is thus an act that orders a delimited area of our experience hierarchically.

To be sure, the intuition of this *archê* implies perceiving things in a new way: "For," says Aristotle, "things, each taken as an individual [καθ' ἕκαστον], are perceived, but perception is of the thing taken on the whole [ἡ δ' αἴσθησις τοῦ καθόλου ἐστίν], for example, of human being [in general] and not of the human being, Callias" (100a17–b2). Here I have avoided the Latinate "universal" for *katholou* in order to leave the seminal ambiguity of this passage intact. For the issue is precisely at what sort of being this redirected perception or *aisthêsis* aims, which is to say with Husserl, what sort of being it "intends." *As a matter of fact, perception here is not aimed at all at a universal in the Platonic sense of a purely intelligible eidos or abstract form.*

To see why, let us go back to the passage preceding this one. At 100a4 f. we find the following:

> Now out of perception comes memory, as we say, but out of memory of the same thing often repeated comes experience, for in number many memories are one experience. But out of experience, or out of many things that have come to rest and are taken on the whole [ἠρεμήσαντος τοῦ χαθόλου] in the soul, as the one beside the many that, even so, is in them all and the same in each, [comes] the first principle of art and science [τέχνης ἀρχὴ καὶ ἐπιστήμης]—if in relation to process [περὶ γένεσιν], the first principle of art, and if in relation to being [περὶ τὸ ὄν], the first principle of science. (100a4–9)

Remarkably, we are told that we get not one *archê* out of this development but two, that is to say, not only the *archê* in regard to being that we were led to expect here at the conclusion of Aristotle's exposition of the epistemic apodictic syllogism (see 99b ff.), but also the *archê* "in regard to process."

For clarification of the difference between these two kinds of *archê* we can recur to the distinction Aristotle makes in the *Ethics* between the carpenter's and the geometrician's understanding of a right angle: "the one seeks it inasmuch as it is useful in regard to his work, the other, as a contemplator of truth, seeks it as a specific sort of thing" (EN 1098a29–32). In other words, as one who knows scientifically the geometrician has an *archê peri to on*, whereas the carpenter, as an artisan, has an *archê peri tên genesin.* But how did this distinction in the kinds of *archê* creep in here in the *Posterior Analytics*?

As a matter of fact, the entire chapter 19 of the *Posterior Analytics* reads like an appendix and very likely contains material that belongs in another context (compare *Metaphy.* 980b21 ff.). For though it was Aristotle's stated purpose here to have explained *nous* or intellection as one of the ways, like geometry, in which we stand in relationship to truths that are always true and are not, like the opinions of an artisan, susceptible to falsity (100b5–8), it can be asked if Aristotle has really accounted for the geometrician's intellection of the *archê* of science at all. For in starting from perception, memory, and experience of the changing world, he has accounted for the variable *archê* of the carpenter, to be sure, the *archê peri genesin* that takes experienced particular things "on the whole," but he has altogether omitted in his account the moment of *aphairesis,* or withdrawal and abstraction from sensory experience and perception, without which intuitive intellection of the timeless and invariable *archê* of science, the *archê peri to on,* is impossible. Indeed, we have just seen that in the *Meno* Socrates first has to get the servant to *suspend* the empirical and experimental, to set it aside, in order to get him to approach the problem mathematically. The whole point was to get him *not* to treat the problem any longer as a technical problem of how to make something. In Aristotle's account, however, this mathematical shift from looking at the world of physical things to looking away from it and toward the purely intelligible ideas is nowhere to be found.

Still, Aristotle's omission here makes this chapter all the more interesting to us, since we are looking for traces of a premathematical understanding of reality that allows, and does not exclude, the concomitance of being and not being, truth and falsity. For if we ask just which of these two *archai* Aristotle's own example, "All human beings are animals," exemplifies, we would have to answer, the *archê* in regard to *genesis* or what comes to pass, and not in regard to *to on,* what simply and always is. We would have to say, then, that in fact we are still in the realm of opinion and calculation and not yet in the realm of science.

For as Gadamer, for one, has shown, the redirection of perception in moving from each particular "this-Callias-here" to "Callias" as an instance of "human beings on the whole [*katholou*]" is still based on the similarity and analogy of one sensed perceived individual thing to another *and does not yet involve the transition to separate ideal realities apart from and beyond these individual realities* (see WM 333 and 407–9). Hence, seeing "this-Callias-here" as *like* other remembered "human beings" taken "on the whole" differs in a fundamental way from looking away from this square here to the mathematical idea of what it is to be a square in essence.

For "human beings on the whole" is still an *archê peri genesin,* an *archê* concerning what happens in time, and unlike a "square as such," it is not static at all but is itself genetic, changing. Ontologically, it is on the same level as the perceived particulars that come under its "command." In fact, its meaning, like that of a law in the tradition of common law, is defined anew each time it is brought to bear on a particular case (compare HHF 209 ff.). It is, to use another of Aristotle's examples in the *Ethics,* like the malleable leaden rule employed by the builders on the Isle of Lebos (EN 1137b30–31). Or, as we will see in the conclusion to this chapter, it is like like a principle concerning what is right and just (*to dikaion*), which must be applied with clemency and equity.

We see, then, that even in the *Posterior Analytics,* which is meant to provide the theory of strict demonstrative science, Aristotle has not yet completely abandoned another kind of reasoning in ambiguous names for indeterminate realities. While privileging strict demonstration about necessary beings, and in a language of determinate signs, he nonetheless preserves even here earlier premetaphysical forms of argument.

5.3 The Will to Truth, Apeirophobia, and the Law of Noncontradiction

In the previous section we discovered that beneath Aristotle's preferred form of argument by scientific demonstration, and evident in the very exposition of this form of argument in his *Posterior Analytics,* there are traces of an earlier kind of argument by dialectic. We saw, too, that while the premises and conclusions of scientific demonstration presuppose a static, necessary being that no longer can have been, or no longer can be, otherwise than it is, the premises and conclusions of the earlier dialectical argument still "say," and "tell of," the shifting, temporal, and questionable being that is "susceptible of being otherwise." It remains for us now to explore a correlate of this difference: *whereas argument by scientific demonstration presupposes the logical first principles of noncontradiction and the excluded middle, dialectical argument presupposes the suspension of these first principles, which, in fact, had never obtained for it.*

It is in Aristotle's *Metaphysics*, 4, that we find the classical formulations of the first principles of noncontradiction and the excluded middle: first,

> For it is impossible that the same thing both obtain and not obtain for the same thing and in the same respect [τὸ γὰρ αὐτὸ ἅμα ὑπάρχειν τε καὶ μὴ ὑπάρχειν ἀδύνατον τῷ αὐτῷ καὶ κατὰ τὸ αὐτό] (1005b19–20);

second,

> For it is impossible for the same person to assume that the same thing is and is not, as some believe Heraclitus to be saying [ἀδύνατον γάρ ὁντινοῦν ταὐτὸν ὑπολαμβάνειν εἶναι καὶ μὴ εἶναι, καθάπερ τινὲς οἴονται λέγειν Ἡράκλειτον] (1005b24–25);

and third,

> Since, moreover, it is impossible for the contradiction to be true at the same time in regard to the same thing, it is plain that neither, too, are contraries capable of obtaining at the same time for the same thing [ἐπεὶ δ' αδύνατον τὴν ἀντίφασιν ἀληθεύεσθαι ἅμα κατὰ τοῦ αὐτοῦ, φανερὸν ὅτι οὐδὲ τἀναντία ἅμα ὑπάρχειν ἐνδέχεται τῷ αὐτῷ]. (1011b16–18)

Upon these there follows the basic formulation of the correlative principle of the law of the excluded middle:

> Neither, however, is anything susceptible of being the middle between contradictories; rather, it is necessary either to assert or deny, whichever it be, one thing in regard to one thing ['Αλλὰ μὴν οὐδὲ μεταξὺ ἀντιφάσεως ἐνδέχεται εἶναι οὐθέν, ἀλλ' ἀνάγκη ἢ φάναι ἢ ἀποφάναι ἓν καθ' ἑνὸς ὁτιοῦν]. (1011b23–25)

In this section we will attempt to "destruct" or "take down" Aristotle's postulation of these principles; for only once we have taken them down and they no longer block our view of what is underneath them will we have "laid bare," and be able, then, to "lay out" hermeneutically, the earlier dialectical argument that precedes their postulation. To this end we will seek, first, to establish just what it was that led Aristotle to posit them to begin with and, thereby, to withdraw from original argument as *dialegesthai,* or talking things through in ordinary speech, and to withdraw to *apodeixis* or demonstration of what necessarily is the case and cannot be otherwise.

5.3.1 Contradiction and contraries in *Metaphysics*, book 4

A initial indication of the reason for this shift is given in the postulatory character of these presumably intuitive *archai,* these starting points, on which Aristotle would refound all argument. For a closer examination reveals that their real function is very much like that of Kant's postulates for practical reasoning: these principles are the "condition of the possibility," as Kant might have put it, of all demonstrative reasoning, without which it threatens to collapse.[12] That they work this way is shown by the very nature of the argument Aristotle provides for them. It is, we would underscore, *ex hupotheseôs.* In essence it runs: *If* these principles do not hold, *then* demonstration is impossible; but we want to engage in demonstration; therefore, they must (read: "had better") hold. From this *ex hupotheseôs* structure of his argument for the laws of noncontradiction and the excluded middle it becomes clear that Aristotle wants and needs these principles in order to head off some kind of danger to argument as a whole.

Now, just what this danger is, and who it is who poses it, becomes evident when we observe that, like all of his arguments *about* logic—logic, ethics, and physics, after all, are the three principal concerns of the *dialectical* argument treated in the *Topics* (see 105b19–26)—Aristotle's argument for these primary logical principles of argument is, in fact, still dialectical and not in the least the kind of induction or empirical *epagôgê* that leads to intuition of a necessary, noetic, self-evident truth, and which, given the stated purpose of the *Posterior Analytics,* 2.19, we would expect to be advanced in support of any *archai,* especially these most fundamental ones.[13] Obviously, then, neither those whose position he would refute nor the intended audience for his refutation are people who are already arguing in the preferred ways of scientific inference elaborated in the *Posterior Analytics,* namely demonstration and induction, and something else besides securing argument based on these forms of inference is at stake here.

As a matter of fact, instead of providing a demonstration of the principle of noncontradiction, Aristotle, in typical dialectical fashion, only counters the argument of someone who would dispute it (*ho amphisbêtôn*) (1006a13–14). For, far from being a demonstration in the strict, epistemic sense about things that are not "susceptible of being otherwise," Aristotle's actual argument here is by what he calls "refutational demonstration" (*apodeixai elenktikôs*), which is to say, for one thing, that, in responding to the contradictory position, it is dialogical and dialectical and, for another, that it at least entertains the possibility that that position might be true: against those who reject the principle of noncontradiction it can be shown, he maintains, that anyone who makes any argument at all, including an argument against the law of noncontradiction, in fact presupposes this law, since it is the prerequisite of any meaningful discourse.

His chain of reasoning here is complex and involves a sequence of several syllogisms. First comes a preliminary argument for the univocity of words: *If*—and we note again the *ex hupotheseôs* form—one is to say something significant both to oneself and to someone else, then what one says cannot be indeterminate in its signification, rather it must be definite (*horismenon*) (1006a25). *But* we do want to say significant things. And *therefore*, "let indeed . . . the word name signify something and signify one thing" (ἔστω δή . . . σημαῖνόν τι τὸ ὄνομα καὶ σημαῖνον ἕν) (1006b12–13). (We note, too, the third person imperative, *estô* here, "let it be that . . ." or "it shall be the case that . . . ," which, despite its common use in mathematical argument, undeniably has some of the original desiderative, subjunctive force, say, of the similar form "*elthatô*" in "Thy kingdom *come*.") And arguing dialectically by entertaining the contrary position, Aristotle continues,

> If, on the other hand, one were to say that the signification [of "human being"] is indefinite, it is clear that there would not be any argument possible [οὐκ ἂν εἴη λόγος]. For signification that does not signify one thing is signification of nothing, and if word names do not signify, our talking things through with one another [τὸ διαλέγεσθαι πρὸς ἀλλήλους], and in truth even with ourselves, has been destroyed. (1006b6–9)

Once granted, this prerequisite univocity of word names presupposes, in turn, that what the thing signified is, and what it is not, must be stabilized and established. If, for instance, the word name "human being" still signified what "human being" is and, at the same time, what "human being" is not, if, that is to say, it were still indeterminate in this way, it could in fact signify anything at all, unendingly and indefinitely—even "trireme" or "wall." For what is not "human being" is, among other things, "trireme," and if "human being" still signified "not human being" too, it would, among other things, signify "trireme" (see the argument at 1007b19 ff.). Here, finally, is where the law of noncontradiction comes in: *if* our word names are to signify one thing, *then* what they signify must be what it is and cannot, at the same time, not be.

With that, we have the answer to our question concerning the motive for Aristotle's postulation of the laws of noncontradiction and the excluded middle. From this argument it emerges clearly that Aristotle is in fact seeking to secure himself against the specific threat of the destruction of our talking things through (*anhairesis tou dialegesthai*), and we do not have to read much further before it becomes evident just where this threat comes from, namely from a sophism, Protagoras's and Cratylus's in particular, that would base itself on Heraclitus's "All things flow" and the dissolution of self-consistency implied thereby.

It is obvious, then, that with this dialectical argumentation *ex hupotheseôs* Aristotle is defending himself against those who, in exploiting the equivocity of ordinary speech—the *dunamis tôn onomatôn*, or power of word names, as Plato had called it, to mean opposite things simultaneously—seem able to controvert and destroy any reasoning and by turning its conclusion into its contrary. Thus, above all, it is to fend off being thrown by these sophists' wrestlers' tricks, their verbal sleights of hand, that Aristotle, too, argues for univocal significance and, consequently, for that "most secure" foothold, the *archê* of noncontradiction and the excluded middle, which univocity presupposes (see 1006a5–6: "we have shown that this itself is the most secure of all first principles [ἐδείξαμεν ὅτι βεβαιοτάτη αὕτη τῶν ἀρχῶν πασῶν]."[14]

We have seen, then, *against* whom Aristotle makes his argument here, but *for* whom does he make it? In regard to the audience intended we should note, in the first place, that, far from proving a scientific truth that we can see and know to be true, this looser, refutational form of demonstration only establishes belief and not knowledge. Moreover, Aristotle's argumentation is, in fact, not even so much dialectical—let alone scientific-demonstrative—as it is rhetorical: remarkably, he refers here to the law of noncontradiction as the "most unshakeable *belief* of all [βεβαιοτάτη δόξα πασῶν] [that] antithetical assertions are not both true at the same time" (1011b14–15; emphasis added), and at one point he even includes in his exposition the distinctly rhetorical element of *pistis* or conviction: at 1010a35 he says that "we must demonstrate to them [the Heraclitians] that there is a kind of unmoved nature [identical with itself] *and convince them* [δεικτέον αὐτοῖς καὶ πειστέον αὐτοῦς]" (emphasis added). This passage makes clear that Aristotle's postulation of the *archai* of the laws of noncontradiction and the excluded middle is in fact not addressed to those who would know epistemically and reason demonstratively in the strict sense (*apodeiknunai haplôs*), say, to mathematicians, but rather to those who wish to argue dialectically about matters of philosophy and who wish to secure their dialectical, and even their rhetorical, arguments against sophistical misappropriation of them.

Thus, though the *Metaphysics*, 4, is ostensibly about ontology and "being as being," its repeated references to Protagoras and the linking of him to Heraclitian doctrines on being show that its argument really has more to do with fending off sophistical tricks of confutation in the common forums of argument. The primary concern, this is to say, is not ontological but logical, dialectical, and even rhetorical. Indeed, the real question addressed is Plato's: namely, how to counter, on their own turf of dialectic and rhetoric, those sophists who, through manipulation of words and exploitation of their indeterminacy, can make a thing seem to be "just" and not to be, seem to be "decent" (*kalos*) and not to be, seem to be "beneficial" and not to be, both at the same time.

Indeed, on this point Aristotle is in complete accord with Plato, and in *Metaphysics*, 4, he is in fact only extending a line of thought elaborated in Plato's linking of Protagoras and Heraclitus in the *Theaetetus* (see the previous section). Furthermore, it is precisely because of the concern with sophistical refutation, which Aristotle *shares* with Plato, that he is constrained to reassert here the very two-tier "metaphysical" ontology of Plato's that elsewhere, in his physics and ethics, for example, he has called into question. For, of those who speak as Protagorean-Heraclitian sophists, he, like Plato, must say, "Those who talk this way altogether destroy essential being and the [essence of] what it was to be something [Ὅλως δ' ἀναιροῦσιν . . . οὐσιαν καὶ τὸ τί ἦν εἶναι], since for them it follows necessarily that all things must be said [merely] to have happened accidentally [συμβεβηκέναι] [and not to be]" (1007a21–23).

As Aristotle sees it, to reason with each other we must be able to say "fixedly" (*pagiôs* [1008a16]) whether something is or is not the case: we need, that is, to "pin down" what is so, and what is not, in order that these do not flow indiscriminately into each other: "The starting point in response to all these people [who hold such paradoxical beliefs] is from a definition" (1012a20). Accordingly, matters cannot be left on the level of those philosophers who believe, based on things perceived by their senses, "that contradictions and contraries hold at the same time"; for "they see that from the same thing opposites come into being" and mistakenly conclude that therefore "the same thing must be opposed to itself" (1009a23–26). Precisely in order to counter this way of thinking, contradictions in being itself must be eliminated and sense-perceived contraries thus reduced to contrary predicates of some static being underlying them, namely the *im*perceptible *hupokeimnon*, that itself is never the contrary of itself and hence never self-contradictory.

To this end a necessary and very Platonic metaphysical being is postulated that must always be what it is, and cannot not be, a noncontradictory being which alone would provide the premises for any argument. On the one hand, we have, to be sure, the indeterminate, infinite "all things," of Heraclitus's "all things flow," that fluvian, kinetic being which, suspended as it is in the self-contradiction of two contraries, of more and less, up and down, large and small, hot and cold, and so forth, can only be said to have happened accidentally and never be said to be. But from this we must distinguish, on the other hand, that static essential being which is always and ever (*aei*) what it is necessarily and cannot ever not be, and for which the law of noncontradiction obtains.

The ontological basis for this logical distinction is provided by a remarkably Platonic passage from *Metaphysics*, 7:

> Being [ἡ οὐσία] is of different kinds, namely the thing taken as a whole, on the one hand, and, on the other, the concept [ὁ λόγος]. That is to say, the one [kind of] being is such that the concept is to be taken along with the matter [σὺν τῇ ὕλῃ] while the other kind of being is entirely the concept [with no matter]. It follows that there is destruction of beings meant in the first sense, for there is also generation of these. The concept, on the other hand, is not the sort of thing that is destroyed, for neither is there generation of it. Rather, it is [what it is], and is not what it is not, both without generation and destruction. For it is not the being of "house" [τὸ οἰκίᾳ εἶναι] that comes to pass, rather the being of "this house here." (1039b20–27)

In returning to *Metaphysics*, 4, we find, correspondingly:

> Moreover, we will require them [the natural philosophers] to accept that there is another kind of essential being among the things that are [ὑπολαμβάνειν καὶ ἄλλην τινὰ οὐσίαν εἶναι τῶν ὄντων], for which neither motion obtains, nor destruction, nor coming to pass [οὔτε γένεσις] in any manner whatever. (1009a36–38)

In *Metaphysics*, 4, then, the ontological issue between Aristotle and Heraclitus is really the logical issue between Aristotle and Protagoras. It is the issue of apodictic logic versus the logic of dialectic in its original sense of *dialegesthai*, or talking something through by the patterns, the *topoi,* we usually do. And it is to fend off Protagoras that Aristotle insists on noncontradiction and thereby eliminates the natural presupposition of dialectic, namely that words which do not signify a static being but in some indefinite way name and tell a narrative coming to pass could in fact be said meaningfully.

In the last case we would have had the *logos* or speech of an earlier *dialegesthai,* the original *logos* of talking something through that is not what it is necessarily but instead is indeed "susceptible of being otherwise." Consequently, we would not have spoken about this being using univocal signs—say, "$\sqrt{2}$" or "=," for mathematics is the paradigm for all univocal signification—but in ordinary words whose sense remains richly equivocal. And consequently, about this indeterminate being and in this equivocal language we could not have made mutually exclusive affirmative or negative statements (*kataphaseis, apophaseis*), as premises from which to infer, in demonstrations, other statements.

But here, in *Metaphysics,* 4, at least, Aristotle decides for a demonstrative logic and against such discursive dialectic. For here the only alternative to logic's demonstration and its principle of noncontradiction seems to him to be logical anarchy: if "man" could also mean "not-man" it could mean, as we have seen, anything and everything, even "trireme" or "wall." And then, he maintains, the distinctions necessary for meaningful argument would collapse into Anaxagoras's total conflation, "all things were one and the same" (1007b19–28). The logical result of such a ontological doctrine that there are no static distinctions in things would, he argues here, be Cratylus's statement that we cannot state anything at all (1010a12–15).

5.3.2 Apeirophobia, *horror infiniti,* fear of the indefinite

All this might seem sufficient to make clear Aristotle's motives for postulating the principles of noncontradiction and the excluded middle, but in fact we have only scratched the surface of what is really going on here. Indeed, there is a more radical, much more revealing way to characterize what drives him, namely what Nietzsche would call the "will to truth" and Heidegger, following Nietzsche, the unwillingness to withstand the "thunderstorm" of the original concomitance of being and not-being and the drive to escape it. For if, in Aristotle, *thaumazein* or bewilderment is the origin of philosophy, relief from *thaumazein* in insight and knowledge is its goal; in Aristotle, having the answer is better than living in questionability. After all, Aristotle begins his *Metaphysics* by telling us, "By nature all human beings strive after insight" (Πάντες ἄνθρωποι τοῦ εἰδέναι ὀρέγονται φύσει) (*Metaphy.* 980a22). For our part, we could characterize the "striving" here, the "drive"—Nietzsche would translate *orexis* as *Trieb*—as a horror of the infinite, as a *horror infiniti*, so to speak, or, more appropriately, a *phobos tou apeirou* or apeirophobia.

The clearest evidence of Aristotle's apeirophobia is to be found in the *Posterior Analytics*, book 1, chapters 19–22. The problem Aristotle faces is that each of the supposedly definite terms of his demonstrative syllogism, major, minor, and middle, might spring a leak, as it were, into the infinite. In order to contain them, he asks about each—in characteristic dialectical fashion (see n.13 above)—"Is it, in fact, necessary that this come to a stop or is it susceptible of going on into the infinite?" (ἆρ' οὖν τοῦτο ἀνάγκη στῆναι, ἢ ἐνδέχεται εἰς ἄπειρον ἰέναι) (81b32–33). We have indeed an ancient Pythagorean strand showing in Aristotle here, one central to Plato's *Philebus*, in which doctrine of the delimited number (*arithmos*), that is, "just so many" of a thing and no "more" and no "less," is used precisely to head off those potential regressions into the infinite which sophists—*hoi deinoi anthropoi* or the frightfully clever people of the *Philebus* 16e—so adroitly exploit. "For, says Plato, "it is the application of number that distinguishes those who make arguments dialectically from those who make them merely contentiously (17a). In Aristotle's case we have a "sidewards," "upwards," and "downwards" threat of lapsing into innummerable infinity, a threat, that is to say, to the middle, major, and minor terms of the syllogism.

To illustrate this threat, as well as a seminal ambivalence in Aristotle concerning it, let us return to one of the three syllogisms from *Posterior Analytics* 89b10 ff. that Aristotle uses to clarify *anchinoia* or acuity of intellect in finding middle terms: "A man who needs to borrow money is a man talking to a rich man; that man there is a man who needs to borrow money; so (that is why), that man there is a man talking to a rich man." First, it is certainly possible that, just as "a man who needs to borrow money" provides the cause, reason, ground, and middle term linking the minor term, "that man there," to the major term, "a man talking to a rich man," it too has not been intuited immediately but has been mediated by a previous syllogism, and so on ad infinitum. For one could go on to ask for the cause, reason, and ground why "that man there is a man who needs to borrow money"—say, because "that man there is a man who lost his fortune." Now, to raise this sort of question, says Aristotle, is in effect to ask also "if demonstrations proceed into infinity" (εἰ αἱ ἀποδείξεις εἰς ἄπειρον ἔρχονται) (82a7–8).

We should note that in this case, even though it comes from the *Posterior Analytics*, the "demonstration," if it is a demonstration at all, surely would proceed to infinity. For as noted previously, we are actually dealing here with matters of *endoxa* or received opinion, seemingly more proper to the *Topics'* theory of dialectic than to the *Posterior Analytics'* theory of science and demonstration. Clearly, each of the terms here, "that man there," "a man talking to a rich man," and the middle which mediates these, "a man who needs to borrow money," derives from perception of genetic reality and not from any noetic intuition of static reality. Hence, the premises and conclusion combining these terms are questions of opinion; here the syllogism is derived "from the most widely received opinions possible" (ἐξ ὧν ἐνδέχεται ἐνδοξοτάτων) (81b20). And this, says Aristotle, is reasoning "merely dialectically" (19), not about "what is in truth" (ἔστι τι τῇ ἀλήθείᾳ) (21), but about only "what has happened to happen accidentally" (τὸ κατὰ συμβεβηκός) (25). Thus, as long as we are reasoning in this way from *endoxa,* we have precisely no *im*mediate certainty at all but are indeed still threatened by the "sidewards" infinite regress of a minor premise and its middle term, which are themselves mediated by a prior syllogism, which is itself mediated by a prior prior syllogism, ad infinitum. For *endoxa* is always mediated by *endoxa* mediated by *endoxa,* and so forth, from time out of mind. In short, to escape the *apeiron* we would, in fact, always already have to had redirected our attention away from the objects of perception and opinion, say, "that man there talking to a rich man because he wants to borrow money," and redirected it to the eidetic Platonic objects of *nous* or intellection (compare EN 1140b31 ff.). Our intellect would have to be aimed at the idea or *eidos* of what it is in essence to be "rich" or to be "a man who wants to borrow money," and our sole concern would have to be with which other ideas each of these ideas is "consonant" or "dissonant."

Similarly, we must ask in regard to the major premise and term, if it "goes upwards to infinity" (ἐπὶ τὸ ἄνω εἰς ἄπερον ἰέναι) (81b40), as Aristotle puts it: "Is it not necessary that this too come to a stop [ἵστασθαι ανάγκη] or will it too be susceptible of going on into infinity [ἐνδέξεται εἰς ἄπειρον ἰέναι]?" (81b36–37). To which he answers that, indeed, we must come to a stop at a highest genus, just as "downwards" (ἐπὶ τὸ κάτω) (82a2), in regard to the minor and premise term, we must come to a stop at the *infima species.* But for this *genos* to be reached "upwards" and this *eidos* to be reached "downwards," that is, for these potential infinitudes to be contained, our *syllogizesthai* or reasoning must once again have replaced its initially questionable and accidental content with what is necessary and eidetic.

In the end, this is simply another way of saying that the content of argument must be governed by the law of noncontradiction. Contrary to our assumptions in dialectical reasoning, in true demonstration we can no longer entertain the possibility that things might also happen not to be what they have happened to be accidentally; ultimately, whatever we speak of must necessarily be what it is self-identically and is not "susceptible of being otherwise" than it is. As *Metaphysics*, 4, makes clear, the first principle, the *archê*, of noncontradiction turns out to be a willful abrogation of the infinite regress into which any an-archic reasoning about what only "has happened to happen accidentally" inevitably issues:

> On the whole, those [Heraclitians] who speak this way destroy substantial being and what in essence it was to be something [ἀναιροῦσιν . . . οὐσίαν καὶ τὸ τί ἦν εἶναι]. . . . But what has happened to happen accidentally [το συμβεβηκός] always means predication in respect to some underlying thing [καθ' ὑποκειμένου τινός]. For if, on the other hand, everything is stated only in respect to what has happened to happen accidentally, there will be nothing primary of which it is said, and thus of necessity [the predication] *goes on into infinity* [εἰς ἄπειρον ἰέναι]. That, however, is impossible since not any more than even two [accidental happenings] can be stitched together in this way. For what happens accidentally does not happen accidentally to something else that happens accidentally save when both have happened accidentally to the same [third] thing. I mean, for example, [that we can say] that the white are cultured and the cultured are white only because both being and being cultured have happened accidentally to a particular human being [τῷ ἀνθρώπῳ συμβέβηκεν]. (1007a34–1007b6; emphasis added)[15]

Thus, Aristotle goes on to say, there is a crucial difference between saying, "The white are cultured" and saying, "Socrates is cultured." For in the latter case we have predicated an accidental happening not of another accidental happening but of an underlying substance, a *hupokeimenon*, that is what it is. Consequently, Aristotle concludes, "Not all things will [with Nietzsche, read: "shall"?] be stated as accidental happenings, for there will ["shall"?] be something too which signifies essential substance" (οὐ πάντα κατὰ συμβεβηκὸς λεθήσεται, ἔσται ἄρα τι καὶ ὧς οὐσίαν σημαῖνον) (1007b16–17).

To be sure, this argument displays a characteristic ambivalence in Aristotle, namely, on the one hand, the pre-Platonic physiologue's desire to have as the *hupokeimenon* and *ousia* a perceptible this-here-something or *tode ti*, and, on the other, the very post-Platonic, metaphysician's recognition that insofar as the *hupokeimenon* and *ousia* are in fact still perceptible being, they cannot yet be the fully determinate subject matter of an apodictical reasoning which, alone, would stop an infinite regress and, Aristotle believes, thus be immune to sophistical destruction. Having asserted in book 7 that one must distinguish between substantial being, *ousia,* meaning the concrete thing which is subject to generation and destruction, and, on the other hand, substantial being meaning the logical definition, which is not subject to generation and destruction (1039b20–27), he goes on to say that

> there is neither definition nor demonstration of substantial beings each perceived as particulars [τῶν οὐσιῶν τῶν αἰσθητῶν τῶν ἔω καθ' ἕκαστα οὔτε ὁρισμὸς οὔτε ἀπόδειξις ἔστιν], since these have matter of such nature as to be susceptible of either of being or not being. Hence, if each is taken as particular, all of them are perishable. Now, if demonstration is of necessary things and if a scientific definition too, like scientific knowledge, is not susceptible of being sometimes knowledge and sometimes ignorance—in contrast to belief, which is susceptible of sometimes being ignorance, and is about what is susceptible of being otherwise—it is plain that there is neither definition nor demonstration of these sense-perceived particular beings. . . . Consequently, in matters of definition we must not not ignore the fact that whenever one defines something taken as a particular, it is always possible to destroy that definition, for the sense-perceived particular thing is not susceptible of definition. (1039b2–1040a7)

This passage makes evident again just how much Aristotle reverts to Plato in regard to logic and reasoning if not in ethics and physics. To be sure, he attempts, on the one hand, to nullify Plato's postulation of the separate forms (*chôrista eidê*) and thereby to recover an earlier kind of philosophizing than Plato's in regard to the natural processes of generation and corruption. The forms, he even says, are just "twitterings" (*An. Post.* 83a34). But, on the other hand, when it comes to reasoning and argument itself, he in no way wants to abandon what he considers to be Plato's great accomplishment, namely, to have put an end to sophistical destructive argument precisely by separating definitions from the world of material, fluxuating, contingent things that have just happened to happen and thereby converting argument into demonstration. In other words, argument needs to be converted into demonstration *of* what must always be what it is necessarily and into demonstration *from* what must always be what it is necessarily and at which, accordingly, we can finally "take a stand" and avoid lapsing into infinite indeterminacy.

It follows not only that the subject matter of a demonstration cannot be the self-contradictory perceived being of the natural philosophers and physiologues, which *is* and *is not* in coming into being and passing away at the same time, but also that it cannot even be Aristotle's own *enhulon eidos,* the materialized idea, which is to say, "the logical definition taken together with the material" (σὺν τῇ ὕλῃ συνειλημμένος ὁ λόγος) (1039b23–24). Rather, if lapsing into the infinite and indeterminate is to be avoided, it can only be the *logos holos*, the immaterial concept in its entirety, and wholly separate from any matter (id.).

In *Metaphysics*, 4, where logical concerns drive the ontological, Aristotle, with an unnoticeable sleight of hand of his own, has already converted the *hupokeimenon* and *ousia* from perceptible beings, say, this particular Callias here, into eidetic beings, the imperceptible, universal beings that are what they are necessarily and forever and cannot not be. With Husserl, we can say that the "intentionality" has shifted, and Callias, as this perceived human being here (see *An. Post.* 101b1 ff.), has become the *eidos* "a human being," which always is what it is and cannot ever not be and which, in turn, is to be taken as the similarly static, ever present "biped animal" (see 1006a29 ff.). For the logical purposes of *Metaphysics*, 4, the *hupokeimenon* and *ousia* as the particular *tode ti* or "this something" have, from the start, become the *hupokeimenon* and *ousia*, both as the *to ti ên einai* or "what it was to be" the thing in essence.

5.4 Contradiction, Contraries, and Anarchic Argument

However, this is by no means the whole story. For elsewhere, specifically in the *Topics* and *Rhetoric*, Aristotle seems more than ready to meet sophistical argument on its own ground of accidental, self-contradictory occurrences, on the ground of what happens to happen, without taking refuge in static, eternally self-consistent being and, hence, seems more than ready to abandon not only Platonic metaphysical ontology for an earlier understanding of being but also Platonic metaphysically founded logic for an earlier understanding of argument.

Indeed, even the *Posterior Analytics*, insofar as it explains demonstrative logic precisely in contrast to dialectic, actually points to the limited domain of the law of noncontradiction and to the possibility of another kind of reasoning in which this law does not yet obtain. For instance, at 71b20 ff., when Aristotle enumerates the prerequisites for a demonstrative science that follow from the fact that "the thing of which we have scientific knowledge is, strictly speaking, incapable of being otherwise than it is" (72b15–16), he specifies that the premises of science's syllogisms are drawn from what is "true, primary, immediate, and prior" (71b20–23). But then he adds, "*A syllogism will indeed also be possible without these things*" (71b24–25; emphasis added). And at 72a8–15, in juxtaposition to the immediate truth of the premises of the demonstrative syllogism, we find a more specific statement regarding the nature of the premises of this other, nonscientific syllogism:

> To be sure, the starting point of demonstration is an immediate premise [ἀρχὴ δὲ ἐστὶν ἀποδείξεως πρότασις ἄμεσος], immediate in the sense that there is no other premise prior to it. Now, a premise is one or the other side of a declarative statement, namely one thing predicated of one [other] thing. If dialectical, the premise entertains equally that whichever side you want is true, but if demonstrative, it assumes that only one side is true. A declarative statement, however, is one or the other side of a contradiction. A contradiction is an antithesis that, as such, precludes there being anything in the middle between its parts. One part of a contradiction, an affirmation, affirms something about something else, but the other part of it, a denial, denies something of something else. (72a7–15)

If we read this carefully, we see that the *dialectical* premise, insofar as it "entertains" (*lambanousa*) both sides of a statement and contradiction, which is to say, both the affirmation and the denial, assumes *both* that something *is* true of something and, simultaneously, that it *is not*. Consequently, far from presupposing the law of noncontradiction, as does the demonstrative premise and *archê*, the dialectical premise in fact precedes the postulation of that law, namely, that it is *impossible* to "assume" (*hupolambanein*) at the same time that the same thing is and is not in the same respect (see *Metaphy.* 1005b25). And with that, it places the law of the excluded middle in abeyance as well, for the reality or being of which it speaks is left suspended in the middle between contingent being and not being.

How is this possible? It is possible because, as Heidegger has shown us, the dialectical premise or *protasis* is really not so much a declarative statement or *apophansis* that something is true or that something is not, as it is a questioning or *erôtêsis* about which of the two possibilities, whichever it might be, happens to be so. As we have already seen, in his *Basic Concepts of Aristotelian Philosophy* (GBAPh) Heidegger specifically elaborates on just this interrogative nature of the dialectical premise or *protasis*. To review: Heidegger relentlessly probes "*protasis*" for its background content, and in so doing he succeeds in hermeneutically exposing senses of it obscured by the usual logical-metaphysical translations of "premise" or, what is an even greater abstraction, "proposition." He displays that *pro-tasis* originally means something laid before us (Heidegger: *vorgelegt*), something pro-posed for our acceptance, but, also, something "conceded in advance" (Heidegger; *die Vorgabe*) and "not up for further discussion"

(GBAPh 19.6.24). Furthermore, this pro-posal and concession in advance is put forth, as we have noted in chapter 1, in the form of an *erôtêsis endoxos,* which Heidegger glosses as "an asking that stays within the circle of that about which there is an established opinion" (id.). We recall that in noting the *ara ge* construction, the "it is so, is it not," Heidegger points out that as an *erôtêsis* or asking, the dialectical premise is an *apokriseôs aitêsis,* "a plea for an answer, for concession, in advance, of the ground on which the discussion is to move" (id.).

Thus, in contrast to the premise of an apodictical scientific syllogism, which is a *logos apophantikos* or declarative statement of necessary fact, here indeterminacy and contingency show up in the intrinsic questionability of the premise even if, for the purpose of having any discussion at all, it must be "conceded in advance" that this premise will not be placed in question. In the dialectical syllogism, then, the premises are not at all statements about Platonic, "metaphysical" being that necessarily is what it is and cannot not be. Rather, each premise is a simultaneous, contradictory affirmation and negation of received opinion (*endoxa*) about a fluid, indeterminate being that "is" in being susceptible of being otherwise than it seems and is believed to be. Or, in Aristotle's own words,

> Dialectic, in contrast [to demonstration], is not about things so narrowly defined [as they are in science] nor about any one class of things. For otherwise it would not ask questions [οὐ γὰρ ἂν ἠρώτα]. On the other hand, it is not for the one demonstrating [something] to ask questions [οὐκ ἔστιν ἐρωτᾶν], because the same thing cannot be demonstrated from opposite things. (*An. Post.* 77a32–34)

Put another way, in being interrogative rather than declarative, dialectic leaves open, accepts, entertains that both of the contraries are likely (*eikos*) to some extent.

That it does is made particularly evident in the corresponding formulation of this distinction between the demonstrative and dialectical premise in the *Prior Analytics*: "The demonstrative and dialectical premise," we read there,

> differ since the demonstrative premise is an assumption of one or the other side of the contradiction. For one who demonstrates does not ask but assumes. But the dialectical premise, in contrast, is a contradiction in question [ἡ δὲ διαλεκτικὴ ἐρώτησις ἀντιφάσεώς ἐστιν]. To be sure, there will be no difference in regard to the development of the syllogistic line of reasoning for each, for both the one who demonstrates and the one who asks reason syllogistically, each by assuming that something holds or

> does not hold for something else. Thus, strictly speaking, the syllogistical premise will be assertion or denial of something about something else in the way we have said. However, it will be demonstrative if it is true and if it has been assumed on the basis of things postulated in starting from a principle [ἐξ ἀρχῆς]. In contrast, it will be dialectical if, on the one hand, in seeking to learn, it is a contradiction in question and, on the other, if, in reasoning syllogistically, it is an assumption of what seems to be so and is received opinion. (*An. Pr.* 24a22–24b3)

With the introduction of inquiry or "seeking to learn" (*punthanesthai*), this passage further underscores the continuing interrogative character, indeterminacy, and openness of any dialectical "assumption," "assuming," and "having assumed," i.e., of any *lepsis, lambeinein, eilephenai.* If for purposes of reasoning syllogistically the dialectical premise, like the demonstrative premise, affirms one side or the other of a contradiction, unlike the demonstrative premise, it continues to entertain, simultaneously, that the other side is also likely. Hence, it never completes the transition from *erôtêsis* to *lepsis,* from questioning to assumption, in the way the demonstrative premise does. And consequently, whereas the demonstrative syllogism starts with a principle (*archê*) that is true (*alêthes*), the dialectical syllogism starts from what only seems to be so (*to phainomenon*) and is generally believed to be so (*to endoxon*), but which nonetheless continues to oscillate indeterminately somewhere between either the definite assertion, "Yes, it is so," or denial, "No, it is not so." Hence, the underlying form of the dialectical premise remains the "contradiction in question," the *erôtêsis antiphaseôs* "Is it so or isn't it?" even if Aristotle's assimilation here of the dialectical syllogism and argument to the apodictical syllogism obscures this.

Put another way, the dialectical premise is not so much a statement *that* (*hoti*) something is so or *that* it is not, as it is a question *whether* something is so or not (*poteron ê ou*): "For its part," Aristotle writes in the *Topics,* "the dialectical premise is a generally believable questioning" (ἔστι δὲ πρότασις διαλεκτικὴ ἐρώτησις ἔνδοξος) (104a8–9). Hence, by nature—and as opposed to the nature of a contradiction—it leaves open and hanging in the balance both the two contradictory answers and declarative statements, namely that something is so and that it is not.

To be sure, the dialectical premise is a *kind* of answer insofar as it is proposed in response to a problem (*problêma*), for example, "whether pleasure is to be chosen or not" and "whether the universe is eternal or not," and problems exist, Aristotle continues, "when there are contrary arguments in support of the solutions to them, for since there are convincing arguments in support of both sides, they imply a perplexity whether a thing is so or not so" (104b7–14). Hence, it might seem that not the dialectical premise but the dialectical problem poses a question, and that the dialectical premise is an answer after all that does indeed foreclose on one side of the question or the other.

But Aristotle clearly does not want to make this sort of rigid distinction between the dialectical problem and premise. For instance, at 105b19–27 he writes that there are three principal kinds of dialectical premise, ethical, physical, and logical: "for example, *whether* one ought to obey one's parents or rather the laws" and "*whether* scientific knowledge of opposites is the same or not" and, as we have already heard, "*whether* the cosmos is eternal or not" (emphasis added), and for these *premises,* he goes on to add, we may construct corresponding problems.

If, then, the dialectical premise also poses a question, just what *is* the difference between a dialectical premise and a problem? The distinction is always blurred, but here is Aristotle's most specific answer:

> The problem and the [dialectical] premise differ, moreover, in the turn of speech. When something is said in the following way, "The definition of human being is, is it not [ἆρά γε], two-footed animal?" and "Animal is, is it not [ἆρά γε], the genus of human being?" a premise occurs. If, on the other hand, something is said in the following way, "Is two-footed animal the definition of human being or not [πότερον . . . ἢ οὔ]?" a problem occurs, and similarly in other cases. Hence, it is reasonable to conclude that problems and premises are equal in number, for from every premise you can make a problem by changing the turn of speech around. (101b29–37)

Significantly, the turn of speech or trope here is interrogative and not declarative in *both* the premise and the problem. Both are questions and neither answers in the strict sense. Hence, the difference is only in how the question is put. With its *poteron ê ou,* its "This or that—which is it?" the problem leaves the question completely in the balance and undecided. The dialectical premise, in contrast, with its *ara ge,* or "is it not," tilts the scales, so to speak, more in one direction than the other. Even so, it too by no means forecloses on the contrary answer. It proposes one answer but in such an interrogative form as to leave open the other and, hence, in full acceptance of the possibility that its proposal or *protasis,* unlike the *protasis* in a demonstration, is entirely "susceptible of being otherwise."

This inherent questionability and openness of the dialectical premise has a crucial consequence for our hermeneutical exposition of original argument: if in dialectic we are not yet reasoning about things properly formulated in definitive statements but still reasoning about things in question, if we are reasoning, this is to say, not yet about necessary, static, "beingness" or *ousia*, as we are in demonstration, but still about being that is susceptible both of being and not being, we are, in fact, still reasoning about *ta sumbebêkota*. We are in fact still reasoning about what happens to have happened, assuming that it has happened (or will have happened) at all. The significance of this point must now be clarified.

In the *Topics* we find "*sumbebêkos*," or "has happened accidentally," characterized in the following way:

> "What has happened accidentally" belongs to none of these [topics], neither to "definition" nor "property" nor "genus." Rather, though it is what obtains for a thing, it is also what is susceptible of obtaining and of not obtaining for any one and the same thing, as, for example, "being seated" is susceptible of obtaining and not obtaining for the same thing. And so it is, too, with "white," for nothing prevents the same thing from at one time being white and at another time not being white. (102b4–10)

Of course, we cannot overlook that, just as in the *Analytics*' exposition of demonstrative reasoning, so too in the *Topics*' exposition of dialectical reasoning an ontological distinction is maintained between a static *hupokeimenon* and *ousia*, an underlying and substantial being, on the one hand, that always is what it is and is not susceptible of being otherwise, and, on the other, the fluctuating contrary accidents that at *different* times hold for the *hupokeimenon* and *ousia* and can be predicated of it. Neither do the accidental happenings of "is white" and "is not white" hold at the *same* time nor is the underlying substance beneath these contradictory predicates ever not what it is. Hence, the law of noncontradiction seems to have been sustained in the *Topics*, not suspended. Indeed, the *Topics* itself begins as follows: "The purpose of this treatise is to find a method by which we shall, when starting from received opinions, be enabled to reason syllogistically about all problems put to us, and by which we ourselves, when taking over the argument, will make no contrary statements" (100a18–21).

Still, Aristotle is noticeably inconsistent in what he says about this. In the end it may well be that dialectical reasoning does allow contraries to hold at the same time for the same thing insofar as the reality or being, of which we predicate these contraries, is itself in question and hence suspended indeterminately in the "middle" between them. It may well be, this is to say, that not only are the contradictory predicates, "is white" and "is not white," accidental happenings, but also the very "being" to which they are said to happen accidentally. If so, the ontological difference between *sumbebêkota* and *ousia* collapses.

For in some fields of reasoning, at least, Aristotle might actually find himself joining those Protagoreans and Heraclitians who speak in such a way that they "altogether destroy substantial being and the 'what it was to be' a thing in essence [ἀναιροῦσιν . . . οὐσίαν καὶ τὸ τί ἦν εἶναι], since for them it is necessary to say that all things have happened accidentally [πάντα . . . συμβεβηκέναι]" (*Metaphy.* 1007a21–33). As a matter of fact, in his most daring and un-Platonic moments Aristotle lets it stand after all that accidental happenings happen to accidental happenings, that happen to accidental happenings, ad infinitum or *eis apeiron.* And with the acceptance of this fluvian, Heraclitian, substanceless, one-tier reality he in fact suspends Plato's ontological differentiation between *ousia* and *sumbebêkota* and lets stand as well the simultaneous being of contraries and contradictories.

Just where does he do this? Before turning to specific passages let us note, to begin with, that even the supposedly static *ousia* and *hupokeimenon* are themselves *verbal,* not nominative, constructs, and hence from the beginning they resist the reification that Aristotle, for his logical purposes, would impose on them. As Heidegger has made clear for us, like the German *Sein* and *Wesen,* which translate *ousia,* they themselves speak of a "thing" only as it happens to be going on, of a "thing" only as it is in be*ing* suspended in the middle of contradictory processes of coming into being and passing away.[16] Paradoxically, *to hupokeimenon* means, in fact, "the underly*ing,*" with no reference at all to what (*ti*) sustains this underlying, that is, with no reference at all to any static "thing."

With this in mind let us go back to the limitations placed on *sumbebêkota* in the *Posterior Analytics'* exposition of demonstrative reasoning in order to see then how many of these limitations are actually suspended in the *Topics'* exposition of dialectical reasoning. At 83a5 ff. of the *Posterior Analytics* we find the following:

> When I say "the white one is wood," I am saying then that what has happened accidentally to be white is wood but not that the white is the substance underlying the wood [τότε λέγω ὅτι ᾧ συμβέβηκε λευκῷ εἶναι ξύλον ἐστίν, ἀλλ' οὐχ ὡς τὸ ὑποκείμενον τῷ ξύλῳ τὸ λευκόν ἐστι]. . . . When, on the other hand, I say that the wood is white, I am not saying that there is something further that is white but which happens accidentally to be wood, . . . rather, the wood is the underlying substance. . . . If, then, a rule is to be made, let this last way of speaking be called predication, and the other way, in contrast, not predication at all, or at least not predication in the strict sense, but predication in regard to

> what has happened accidentally [κατὰ συμβεβηκὸς δὲ κατηγορεῖν]. "The white," then, exists as the thing predicated, while "the wood," on the other hand, exists as that of which it is predicated. Let it be established, accordingly, that what is predicated always be predicated of what it is predicated in the strict sense, and not predicated in regard to what has happened accidentally; for this is the way demonstrations demonstrate. (83a5–20)

Thus, at least for demonstrations, we must make the ontological differentiation or distinction in kinds of being if we are to ensure that any predication is predication in the strict sense: "such [predicates] that do not signify substantial being must be predicated of something underlying [them] [ὅσα δὲ μὴ οὐσίαν σημαίνει, δεῖ κατά τινος ὑποκεινέμου κατηγορεῖσθαι], and a thing cannot be white that is not first something else which then is white" (83a31–33); and therefore, as he has stated to begin with, it is necessary "that there be something first of which something is predicated, that anything else be predicated of this first thing, and that this regression come to a standstill [καὶ τοῦτο ἵστασθαι]" (83b28–30). To avoid predication by accidents this first being or *ousia*, at which we come to a standstill, must, as we have seen, have a different sort of "is" from the being of what happens accidentally to it: to be precise, it is always what it is and can never not be.

Hence, to return to Aristotle's example, however concrete and earthy it may seem to be, we must in fact abstract *from* "wood" in any shifting adjectival sense of "wooden" that might "be" otherwise, and abstract *to* "what it is to be" "wood" statically, always, and in essence. Or, stated more generally, if we are to avoid the loose *kategorein kata sumbebêkos*, we must distinguish the *ousia* from all the other nine adjectival and adverbial predications or categories that presuppose it and that can be predicated only of it and not of each other. We must distinguish saying the essential being of something, saying what it is, from saying how (*poion, pôs*) it is, where (*pou*) it is, when (*pote*) it is, how large (*poson*) it is, what it is in relation to (*pros ti*), and so forth (see 83b16 ff.).

So much for the requirements for demonstration. However, if we examine the special fields of dialectical reasoning, we see that these requirements for demonstration in fact do not always obtain. As we have just observed, dialectical problems and premises are of three kinds, ethical, logical, and physical (see *Top.* 105b19–27). In addition, we note now that the materials from which each of these three kinds of problem and premise will be constructed are the property, the definition, the genus (and species), and the accidental happening (*sumbebêkos*) (101b25), and since the principal concern of dialectical reasoning by topics is non-necessary being, it follows that of these four materials the accidental happening is the initial and principal one upon which dialectical reasoning will draw. Indeed, consideration of topics based upon the accidental happening precedes consideration of topics based upon the other three, property, definition, and genus and species; see the *Topics*, books 2 and 3, for the exposition of the topics to be derived from the accidental happening.

Thus, there is already a break with Plato here, who, in order to fend off sophist conflation and confutation, tries founding all dialectical reasoning (and even the art of rhetoric) on collection into a *genos* and division into delimited number of *eidê* (compare the *Phaedrus* 265a–266d). In Aristotle's *Topics*, in contrast, the discussion of the genus and its species comes second (in book 4) and is in no way foundational. And significantly, all of the topics appropriated from the *Topics* in the *Rhetoric*—that is, in the *Rhetoric* (1.7), on the more and the less, in (2.19), on the similar and different, on contraries, on the prior and posterior, and on the part and the whole, and those found among book 2, chapter 23's various topics—correlate with the *Topics*, books 2 and 3, on reasoning *kata sumbebêkos.*[17]

Now, in the *Topics*, and at the end of the preliminary description of the topics to be derived from the accidental happening (102b4 ff.), we find the following examples of *ethical* problems to be derived from the accidental happening:

> Also to be assigned to the "accidental happening" [τῷ συμβεβηκότι] are judgmental comparisons of things with each other, in whatever way these might be stated starting with the accidental happening. For instance, "Is the decent to be chosen over the beneficial?" [οἷον πότερον τὸ καλὸν ἢ τὸ συμφέρον αἱρετώτερον] and "Is the life of virtue or of delectation sweeter?" [πότερον ὁ κατ' ἀρετὴν ἢ ὁ κατ' απόλαυσιν ἡδίων βίον] . . . For in all such problems the search is for the alternative to which the predicate best happens to apply accidentally [ποτέρῳ μᾶλλον τὸ κατηγορούμενον συμβέβηκεν]. (102b15–21)

We have already seen that dialectical problems stated like these in the figure *poteron . . . ê* can readily be converted into dialectical premises by changing this trope to *ara ge*, in which case we would have, for example, "*Ara ge to kalon tou sumpherou hairetoteron*?" or "The decent is to be chosen over the beneficial, is it not?" We note further that the *erôtêsis endoxos* or "generally believed questioning" here, that is, the belief as to whether *to kalon* does indeed take priority over *to sumpheron*, is clearly one of the key questions for all ethical dialectic and *dialegesthai.* For instance, we read in the *Nicomachean Ethics* that there are three things to be considered in choosing to take up a course of action, the decent, the benefical, and the pleasant (*to kalon, to sumpheron,* and *to hedu*) and three contrary things in choosing to shun it, the despicable, the harmful, and the painful (*to aischron, to blaberon,* and *to luperon*; see EN 1104b30–34), and it is made clear that we go wrong in our taking counsel when we get the priorities here reversed and choose the pleasant over decent.

Now, significantly, in the *Topics* the predicated accidental happening, "to be chosen over the beneficial," is predicated of another accidental happening, "the decent." We note, furthermore, that the "underlying" subject, "the decent," is itself a qualitative predicate telling "what sort" (*poion*) of thing something is, and that it has precisely the *same* ontological status as the relational predicate (*pros ti*), "is to be chosen over the beneficial." In fact, then, neither of these "is" itself the substantial being, the *ousia* and *to ti ên einai,* that was said to be the only possible subject of predication in the strict sense. Thus, "the decent" has, in fact, the ontological status that "the white" has in the example "The white [one] is wood," which is to say, the forbidden or loose form of predication, where an accidental happening appears to be predicated of an accidental happening. Like "the white," "the decent," as the subject or *hupokeimenon* "underlying" the predication, is a qualitative adjective that says "how" without having first said "what." Hence, here there is no ontological difference at all between the subject and the predicate.[18] Put another way, there is no necessary, self-consistent *ousia* or *to ti ên einai* signified that always is what it is and cannot not be. Indeed, as historical narrative "tellings" of accidental happenings, *both* the subject and the predicate are susceptible of being otherwise and are left in the "middle" between being and not being. The law of noncontradiction is not yet in force.

Moreover, this destruction of essential being, which "lays bare" underneath it an infinite recurrence to self-contradictory accidental happening, not only places in abeyance the laws of the excluded middle and noncontradiction. The *archê,* as well, the self-grounding principle at which one could take a stand and stop (*stênai, histhasthai*) in one's search for grounds and on which one could found one's derivative conclusions necessarily and certainly, collapses into groundless infinity and is destroyed. *Argument here becomes anarchic once again.*

It is not difficult to see that this follows inevitably, for, as Aristotle has correctly observed, accidental happenings are precisely *sumbebêkota* and not *bebêkota*; by nature they happen to something else or, better, "with" (*sun*) something else as in the colloquial expression "What's happening with him?" Hence, if *ousia* is eliminated, we have the "tale" of accidents happening with accidents, happening with accidents, ad infinitum, *eis apeiron*. To take our example, the premise, "the decent is to be chosen over the beneficial, isn't it?" might be based on something like "For the moderate is the decent, isn't it?" or some other variation of "nothing in excess" (*mêden agan*). And beneath that might lie "For the wise is the moderate, isn't it?" and so forth, *eis apeiron*.

We note that none of these pro-posals or "premises" has the ontological reference of, for example, Euclid's "If equals are added to equals the sums are equal," where the words or names (*onomata*) are actually signs (*sêmeia*) that univocally signify static, necessary realities that always are what they are and cannot not be. Rather, in these pro-posals all the words name equivocally an accidental occurrence still suspended between being and not being. Put another way, precisely as an *erôtêsis endoxos*, each of these dialectical premises is a questioning of some of a received opinion that itself is still in question even if its pro-posal is, at the same time, a request that it be conceded.

Just this *anarchia* is implied when Aristotle says that, unlike logical demonstration, dialectic *does not* begin from an *archê*, "rather the dialectical [syllogism] is the one that reasons from received opinions" (100b18; see also *Metaphy.* 995b5–25 and note 17 above). For in dialectic the premise for any argument, as part of the infinite regression of an-archic reasoning, is always the conclusion of a previous argument, presupposing a previous argument, *eis apeiron*. As reasoning from received opinions, *endoxa*, it always picks up an argument from somewhere in the midst of its historical transmission and tradition from time out of mind and can never get back to some noetically intuited *archê* at which it could take a definitive stand (see HHF 209 ff. on "The Nature of Ethical Reasoning").

Indeed, *with Aristotle*, we might ask if we ever could. We might ask, that is to say, if there is any reasoning that is not ultimately dialectical and hence ultimately anarchic. In spelling out the specific applications of dialectical reasoning (*Top.* 101a26 ff.), Aristotle submits that it is useful, first, in exercizing the mind (*pros gumnasian*), useful, second, in conducting whatever anarchic discussions we "chance" to get involved in somewhere along the way (*pros de tas enteuxeis*), and, third and most important, useful in the philosophical *sciences* (*pros de tas kata philosophian epistêmas*).

In regard to the philosophical sciences, dialectical reasoning serves two purposes: first, precisely because it alone raises difficulties on both sides of a question (*pros amphotera diaporesai*) (101a36), it facilitates the perception of what is true and what is false. Here Aristotle makes clear in yet another way that anyone arguing dialectically entertains simultaneously that the premise proposed is true but also that it is not and, hence, entertains both the premise and the contradiction to it. For as Aristotle already implies here at the beginning of the *Topics*, dialectical argument will need to be not only construction of one side of a question but simultaneously destruction of the other, not only *kataskeuazein*, that is, but *anaskeuazein* and *anhairein*, expressions that will recur conjointly again and again in the subsequent elaboration of the specific topics in *Topics*, books 2–7. Indeed, it turns out that the subject matter of dialectical argument can only be stated in combining *two* arguments, one that constructs (*kataskeuazei*) the hypothesis that something "is" so, and another that destroys or deconstructs (*anaskeuazei*) this hypothesis in arguing that it "is not" so. For example, in regard to the argumentative strategy or topic called "definition of an accident," Aristotle writes, "One must, moreover, define the sort of things that are to be called what most people call them and the sort of things that are not to be; *for this is useful both in regard to construction and destruction* [of an argument]" (*Top.* 110a15–16; emphasis added). Thus, *hê technê dialektikê*, or the art of "talking something through," means entertaining two contradictory arguments simultaneously, and even when it is taking counsel with oneself, this process will take place between two "voices," each of which will contradict the other's position.

Beyond this, dialectic is also useful in the philosophical sciences, Aristotle says,

> in regard to what is primary in the first principles for each individual science [πρὸς τὰ πρῶτα τῶν περὶ ἑκάστην ἐπιστήμεν ἀρχῶν]. For it is impossible to say something about what is primary in the principles, based on the particular principles proper to any given science, since the first principles are prior to all the others. Consequently, then, it is necessary that we treat these primary first principles through the received opinions concerning each [διὰ δὲ τῶν περὶ ἕκαστα ἐνδόξων]. But this method is peculiar to, and most appropriate to, dialectic. (101a36–101b3)

One might ask, then, for just which forms of science there actually do exist intuited *archai* that are not founded on *endoxa*, founded on *endoxa*, founded on *endoxa*, *eis to apeiron*. Where, in fact, have we ever secured the foundations of our reasoning in the way proposed in the *Posterior Analytics* 2.19, namely by immediate intellectual intuition of a necessary immutable truth, an *archê peri to on*? Where, in fact, is argument not anarchic? Indeed, as we observed at the beginning of this section, in *Metaphysics*, 4, Aristotle himself, true to his statement in the *Topics* of the primacy of dialectic, argues not inductively but *dialectically* even in support of what he considers the most secure and primary *archê* and premise of all, the law of noncontradiction (see 1006a5, "this itself, the most firmly established of all first principles [βϵβαιοτάτη αὕτη τῶν ἀρχῶν πασῶν]").

5.5 In Defense of Anarchic Argument

There is, of course, another and even more likely possibility for anarchic argument besides the regress of grounds, for grounds, for grounds, and so forth, *eis to apeiron*, a possibility that Aristotle, at least in the *Posterior Analytics*, is equally at pains to resist, namely circularity (see *An. Post.* 72b26 ff.: "however, that it is impossible to demonstrate in the strict sense in a circle is obvious"). For example, in arguing for the conclusion that "The decent thing to do is the just thing," we could advance as premises "For the decent thing to do is the measured thing" and "The measured thing is the just thing"; and, in support of this last premise, we might continue to argue, "For the measured thing to do is the decent thing," and, *once again*, "The decent thing to do is the just thing." In this way we would have presupposed the conclusion as a ground for itself and thus violated the logical law prohibiting circularity or "begging the question."

We must ask, however, if legitimate argument, albeit argument *kata symbebêkos* and in a loose, nondemonstrative sense, might not proceed in just this circular way, as it often does, for instance, in ethical dialectic. This is to say that sometimes we do not go back infinitely (*apeirôs*), but round and round, without ever coming to a stop but getting clearer as we go along about what our words—say, "decent," "just," "measured"—actually say. If so, we would be involved in the "hermeneutical circle" of which Heidegger speaks, and Gadamer following him. Remarkably, in "laying bare" and interpretively "laying out" the original argument beneath Aristotle's metaphysical construction of argument founded in a supposedly self-evident *archê*, our hermeneutics of original argument would then have disclosed that originally argument is itself hermeneutical. And, indeed, precisely this turns out to be the case.

In *Being and Time* Heidegger puts it this way:

> A scientific demonstration ought not presuppose what it sets out to ground. But if our interpretive laying out of things is always moving already within what is understood and must sustain itself from this, how then is it supposed to display scientific results without moving in a circle? In particular, how is it to do this if, moreover, the understanding presupposed is still moving within ordinary knowledge of human beings and of the world [*in der gemeinen Menschen- und Weltkenntnis*]? (SZ 152)[19]

The point here is that in our reasoning we can attain no vantage point outside of, and above, the temporal, local process of reaching an understanding, a process in which we always already find ourselves under way. To attempt to avoid the circle is, Heidegger says, "to misunderstand understanding from the ground up, . . . for the decisive thing is not to get out of the circle but to get into it in the right way" (153). The circle, he says, "conceals within it a positive possibility of the most original form of knowing," and it is "the expression of the 'fore' structure of being-there itself" of "having in mind beforehand, foresight, forestalling" (id.). Being-there, *Dasein,* is, therefore, to be thought of precisely in contrast to the abstracted theoretical knower who looks on from above and charts what happens to happen below in terms of forms statically present to his or her consciousness: "Not too much, but *too little* is 'presupposed' for the ontology of being-there if one 'starts from' a worldless 'I' in order then to provide this 'I' with an object and an ontologically unfounded relationship to that object" (SZ 315–16).

We cannot, this is to say, reach insight into some sort of self-evident, timeless, placeless *archê* from which to derive our arguments about what is the decent or just thing to do. Rather, in deliberating about these things and taking counsel, we always find ourselves "there" in the midst of a tradition. We are already moving within a provisional understanding of what these words name, an understanding that is modified and amplified in the process of our application of it to the new circumstances confronting us.

If we were to take, for example, Jefferson's argument in justification of declaring the independence of the American colonies from the British crown, we would see that the "self-evident" truths with which he sustains his argument—that all human beings are created equal and endowed with unalienable rights to life, liberty, and the pursuit of happiness—are actually truths and premises of a very different sort from those "self-evident" principles supposedly displayed to us in moments of noetic insight into eternal verities. Rather, they are truths and premises, the truth of which becomes clearer only in the history of conclusions drawn from them in each particular circumstance. They are, to speak with Aristotle, *archai peri genesin,* starting points in relation to process, and in process themselves (see section 5.2.2 above and *An. Post.* 100a8–9). Indeed, Lincoln was getting clearer about them in his Gettysburg Address, and we today are in the infinite process of getting clearer still about what they can mean.

Gadamer's application of the "hermeneutical circle" to the understanding of a text provides us with another nice exemplification of the point here. He writes,

> He who wishes to understand a text carries out a projection. As soon as a first sense displays itself in the text, he projects for himself, in advance, a sense of the whole. And this first sense, in turn, displays itself only because one is already reading the text with certain expectations of a particular sense in mind. Understanding what is there in the text consists in working out a provisional projection which, to be sure, undergoes constant revisions as a result of one's further penetration into the sense of the text. (WM 251)

Here Gadamer not only tells us about the process of understanding texts but, in fact, provides a model for deliberation or taking counsel, which, after all, is the original form of reaching an understanding (*Sich-Verständigen*).

Let us return to Aristotle's example for dialectical deliberation, namely whether the decent is to be chosen over the pleasant and beneficial (see above and EN 1104b30 ff.). Clearly, our reasoning and argument about such things as this does not proceed from any noetic insight into a static reality that the words "decent," "pleasant," and "beneficial" could be said to signify. There are no self-evident truths here, no invariable *archai peri to on* or "principles in relation to being" (see *An. Post.* 100a9), at which one might stop in going back for some ultimate ground, and from which one might reason in going forward to a necessary conclusion. Rather, with indeterminate senses of these words pending, we proceed to reason to a provisional conclusion, which in turn requires revisions of our initial understanding of their sense.

Reasoning in common law, for example, is like this: there are no static essences or beings to which the law, as stated, refers. Rather, from within the history of precedent interpretations, interpreters render new decisions that, in turn, require modification of precedent interpretations. Far from being static, the law at any given time is no longer what it was and not yet what it will be. It "is" only in the history and process of its interpretations (see HHF 195 ff.). It follows that deliberation here is anarchic and circular, and properly so: each time, it begins from somewhere within a tradition from time out of mind, the origin of which is inaccessible to it, and comes back to where it started, but with new and increased understanding of the sense of its starting point, and this ad infinitum.

Now, if there is no underlying static essence here, no *ousia*, no *to ti ên einai*, no *hupokeimenon*, to be signified by the words with which we reason and take counsel, this must have important consequences for the nature of these words themselves. Accordingly, we must ask with precisely what sort of words these anarchic and circular deliberations will be argued, for it is obvious that here the univocal signs of a pure demonstrative science, which refer to stabilized, static, and noncontradictory being, would have nothing to refer to here and, hence, are inapplicable. "The just," this is to say, must be a different sort of word from "$\sqrt{2}$." But what, precisely, is the difference?

To answer this question let us begin with an intriguingly elliptical but suggestive passage in the *Posterior Analytics*: "For a demonstration," Aristotle says there,

> is not a matter for outward argument [οὐ γὰρ πρὸς τὸν ἔξω λόγον ἡ ἀπόδειξις]—since neither is the [demonstrative] syllogism—but a matter for the argument internal to the mind [πρὸς τὸν ἐν τῇ ψυχῇ]. For it is always possible to object to an outward argument [πρὸς τὸν ἔξω λόγον] but not always to an internal argument [πρὸς τὸν ἔξω λόγον]. (76b23–27)

What are we to make of this? For one thing, it clearly reaffirms what we have said about dialogical, dialectical argument, namely that in it, in contrast to demonstration, both sides of a contradiction are always in play; for as Aristole puts it here, an objection is always possible. For every assertion, "Yes, that is so," the negation, "No, that is not so," must always be entertained.

But let us focus on what this passage implies about the difference between the languages of dialectical and demonstrative argument: insofar as it is "internal to the mind," the language of a scientific, demonstrative argument does not depend on the ordinary language of exchanges with others, the language expressed aloud in speech. Indeed, since communication is entirely secondary, since, on the contrary, seeing and establishing for oneself the logical relationships that obtain among essential beings is the concern, in demonstrative argument the mind can proceed silently and without word names (Plato: *aneu tôn onomaton; Cratylus* 438d) from one unnamed idea or concept present in the mind, from one *eidos* or conceptual "look" to something, to another. Only when the need arises to present the argument to someone else, must we then have recourse to external signs for these internally envisioned ideas and concepts. External language here, sign language, is a secondary tool for communication, at our disposal if we should need it.[20]

In contrast, it is preexistent communal speech, in which we have "always already" been communicating from time *out* of mind (*exô têi psuchêi*), which alone makes dialectical argument possible. This spoken language does not consist of terminological, determinate signs that designate clear and distinct, static ideas, which we as individuals can have present in mind ahead of time. Rather, it is a language of still indeterminate, ambiguous, richly equivocal voiced names that have "always already" been existing outside (*exô*) you and me and between us—words we have heard from others, words within which we dwell "ecstatically" in our being outside ourselves and "in" the community of speakers. These words we "always already" find ourselves speaking, even when each of us speaks only to himself or herself in thought. Words here do not signify something already present to mind internally; rather, they are names that we call things and with which we call things into being by finding the just the right words to name them. In being heard from outside they first make acoustically present to us, even as they withhold from us, our fluctuating world, suspended as it "is" between the contradiction of being and not being.[21]

With that, our destruction of logic's demonstration would seem to be complete, for in original argument, it now emerges, we argue neither from static classes or forms of things nor with word signs that designate these. In original, predemonstrative argument the forms are indeed mere "twitterings," and words signs used to designate them would be objectless. But what are we left with then? Are there any positive consequences of this destruction of Aristotle's Platonic logical project and our disclosure of the original argument beneath it? Does not this suspension of the law of noncontradiction and return to anarchic reasoning in equivocal word names, whose sense is always in the process of becoming clear, only reopen the door to sophistical confutation? Does it not inevitably lead, as the Aristotle of *Metaphysics*, 4, seemed to fear, to the degeneration of reasoned discussion into war with words? Will not argument only devolve once again into the medium for a Thrasymachus or a Callicles to pursue ever more individual power and an ever larger, ever more unjust share of the available goods? And will not all of us then try to arm ourselves for this Hobbesian verbal "war of all against all" in the "pursuit of power after power that endeth only in death" with the sophist's verbal skill at making anything seem to be the contrary of itself? Given the contemporary deterioration of political discussion, that might seem to be the result, but it is doubtful that even Aristotle really believed that it was.

As a matter of fact, in his *Nichomachean Ethics* and *Rhetoric* he himself makes clear that in precisely those political and ethical questions where the just (*to dikaion*), the decent (*to kalon*), and the beneficial (*to sumpheron*) are at stake and the sophistical art of conflation seems most effective, there never is any fixed concept, any one thing and definition of these to which we might recur. Consequently, there exists here no necessary and static *archê* from which to start in our arguments, and at which we might come to a stop in our efforts to support our premises or argumentative proposals. Just this is the point of his critique of Plato's idea of the good at EN 1096a11 ff.: if there is no universal good, no good as a whole (*katholou*), but there are only particular goods, then arguments about what is good must be dialectical. It follows that these arguments cannot be transformed, as Platonists—the "friends" of 1096a13—seemed to have hoped, into scientific demonstrations. Neither can they be carried on in the interior language of word signs for envisioned *eidê* or conceptual "looks" to things; rather, they will take place in the exchanges of "outward argument" in word names.

In this regard we note again that for Aristotle there is no demonstration in the strict sense of something taken as a particular (*kath' hekaston*), but only of something taken as a universal (*katholou*). For instance, in *Posterior Analytics* 73a21 ff., it is argued that since the thing known by demonstration is "necessary" and "cannot be otherwise," it must be (1) true for all cases (*kata pantos*), (2) intrinsic (*kath' hauto*)—which is to say, not *kata sumbebêkos* or accidental—and (3) universal (*katholou*) and not particular. However, not a single one of these requirements for demonstration in the strict sense is met by the good, nor, consequently, by the beneficial, nor by the just, nor by the decent. And, as a matter of fact, Aristotle's own arguments about what is good in the *Ethics* remain consistently dialectical and never proceed from some noetically intuited *archê* but interrogatively from *endoxa*, from received opinions about what the good is, and, consequently, from how we hear it generally spoken of (*pôs legetai*).

This does not mean, however, that we are without defenses against sophistical corruption of our arguments, and clearly Aristotle himself does not think that it does. For there is indeed a valid way to talk things through with each other dialectically wherever demonstration is inapplicable, namely in conjoint *sumbouleuesthai*, in consultation or our taking counsel together. And, significantly, such taking counsel is always about what "is susceptible of being otherwise" and, consequently, about things that violate all three criteria for demonstration in the strict sense, namely that they be true for all cases, intrinsic, and universal. In this regard, compare, once more, EN 1112b9–12:

> Our taking counsel [τὸ βουλεύεσθαι] is thus about things that occur for the most part and when how these will turn out is unclear. It is about things in which there is something indefinite and that are of such magnitude that we do not trust ourselves sufficiently to wrestle with them alone and thus bring others to counsel us [συμβούλους δὲ παραλαμβάνομεν].

In other words, taking counsel is about an *erôtesis antiphaseôs* or contradiction in question. To review: "we take counsel," says Aristotle in his *Rhetoric*, "about what appears susceptible of being either way [περὶ τῶν φαινομένων ἐνδέχεσθαι ἀμφοτέρως ἔχειν], for no one deliberates about what is incapable of either having been otherwise or being otherwise in the future, or being otherwise now (*Rhet.* 1357a4–6). With these three tenses, "having been," "being in the future," "being now," Aristotle is, in effect, underscoring the role of deliberation or taking counsel in all three of the general forums of rhetoric, that is, in *dikanikê* or judicial rhetoric, which deliberates about whether an action *was* or *was not* just; in *sumbouleutikê* or consultative rhetoric, which deliberates about whether an action *will be* or *will not be* beneficial; and in *epideiktikê* or "showoff" rhetoric, which deliberates about whether someone *is* or *is not* decent (see *Rhet.* 1358a36 ff.).

But what defense has this deliberation against sophistical corruption, if, given the indeterminacy and contingency of these three subject matters, its argumentation can never be transformed into demonstration from an indestructible, incontestable *archê*? What defense can there be if there is no reduction possible of equivocal speech to univocal signs signifying invariable, static realities?

To answer this question we must take down the derivative and abstact, purely logical understanding of argument. Put in terms of the *Rhetoric*, we must get beneath the *logos* or logic of an argument to the *êthos* and *pathos* in which this *logos* was originally embedded. We must get back, this is to say, to the character of the speaker and the feeling that we undergo about the speaker and the subject matter he or she is presenting for our decision. For in the end, deliberation's defense against sophism, and hence the securing of any dialectical argumentation based in deliberation, cannot lie in securing first principles or *archai* from which to infer unassailable conclusions. Rather, *it lies in recovering for argument the ethical predisposition or* hexis *of the speakers who engage in it.* It lies, that is to say, in recourse to their *prohairesis tou biou*, the aim they have chosen for their life, be this aim their participation in the community of deliberators *or* be this aim the life of wanting ever more power and goods for themselves individually, the life of *pleonexia*. It lies in recourse to their consequent reasonableness, virtue, and goodwill or lack of these. (See *Rhet.* 1378a6 ff. and section 3.4.4 above on *phronêsis*, *aretê*, and *eunoia* as the principal constituents of *êthos* or character.)

Not only the *Rhetoric*, in distinguishing valid rhetoric from the sophistical corruption of rhetoric, adverts to the *prohairesis* [*tou biou*] (1355b18, 21); given our exposition in this chapter of *Metaphysics*, 4, and our disclosure of the deeper motives of Aristotle's argument, it should come as no surprise that we find a variation of this expression there as well, though on this occasion Aristotle uses it to contrast sophism not with valid rhetoric but with dialectic and philosophy (compare *Rhet.* 1355b17–21). "Sophistics and dialectic," he says,

> are concerned with the same kind of thing as philosophy, but philosophy differs from dialectic in the kind of thing it is able to do and from sophism, in the life it chooses [τοῦ βίου τῇ προαιρέσει]. Dialectic is an attempt at knowing the things philosophy knows; sophism appears to be philosophy, but it is not. (1004b24–26)

Although it is not said expressly, we may infer here that dialectic, though differing from philosophy in what it is able to do, does not differ from philosophy in the kind of life it chooses and, hence, that it does differ from sophism in just this regard. And we may also infer that dialectic and sophism are alike insofar as both remain on the level of what is "like the truth" or a likelihood, and that neither attains the truth that philosophy does, even if dialectic at least tries to attain it. This leads us, finally, to the conclusion that if one is arguing on the level of likelihood where the realities one treats are susceptible of being otherwise than they are and where, as we have seen, contradictories must be entertained simultaneously, the difference between a valid dialectical argument and a sophistical argument can only lie in the speaker's "choice of life." In other words, it can only lie in his or her character and the sincerity of the feeling he or she communicates. In short, our anarchic, dialectical deliberations about contradictions in question can indeed be secured against sophistical corruption, but not by purely logical means.

The distinction of valid from invalid dialectical deliberation requires, therefore, that the logic of the argument which the speakers advance not be divorced from their character, philosophical or sophistical, as this character manifests itself in what they say: *ultimately what speakers say is either sustained or nullified by whom they have chosen to be.* Consequently, in ethical and political issues, at least, dialectic, as detached theoretical consideration of general subject matters, must eventually be returned to its origin in rhetoric's exhortation concerning practical decisions. For given the ambiguity and indeterminacy inherent in any ethical question, there is no possibility securing the *logos* of the argument by *logos* alone, and rhetoric's two other "convincers," *êthos* and *pathos,* missing in dialectic, must inevitably come into play. For, as we have seen, there is no static, noncontradictory idea of the good to which we could recur in the hopes of refuting a bad man or woman who by exploiting the ambiguities of word names makes the unjust thing look just, the harmful thing look beneficial, and the disgraceful thing look decent.

Indeed, today, precisely our contemporary sophists' ability to make a dialectical and rhetorical argument seem to be purely logical and demonstrative is their most effective tactic in their self-aggrandizing pursuit of ever more power and wealth. For in giving the appearance of arguing from self-evident *archai* to necessary conclusions, they effectively divert us from their corrupt character and from their exploitation of the baser passions, from the bad *êthos* and false *pathos* on which their arguments actually rely, and on the basis of which these arguments are to be rejected.

It is not surprising, then, that Aristotle already requires for sound dialectical deliberation some very different intellectual abilities from the *nous,* or intuition of *archai,* and *anchinoia,* or quick grasp of middle terms, required for demonstration (see *An. Post.* 89b10 ff. and 100b5 ff.). As we saw in section 3.1, in addition to *phronêsis* or reasonableness, for deliberation, we must also have *sunesis* (EN 1142b34 ff.), *gnômê, sungômê* (1143a19 ff.), and *epieikeia* (1143a31 and 1137a31 ff.), that is to say, understanding, consideration, forbearance, and clemency. The point is that in our arguments for the just, the beneficial, and the decent we would move others to either a decision (*prohairesis*) concerning a course of action they might take themselves or to a judgment (*krisis*) concerning someone else's actions or character. And, in each of these, "I" must display for those "I" would exhort the ability to reason not from "my" own perspective but from theirs and, hence, "ours." Self-aggrandizement, *pleonexia,* must have given way to *philia* or kinship. (See *Rhet.* 1380b35 ff. on *philia* and 1385a16 ff. on *charis* or kindliness, and compare HHF 29–31 and 208 on *philia* as a prerequisite for genuine conversation.) Precisely this, and not recourse to self-evident *archai* and demonstration by the law of noncontradiction, is what prevents the destruction of our conversation (*anhairesis tou dialegesthai*) and is, therefore, the "condition of the possibility" of all reasonable consultation about the good, which is to say, of the just, the decent, and the beneficial.

6

Embodied Argument as Patho/logical: The Original Fusion of *Pathos* and *Logos*

In the last chapter we saw that the attempt to ward off sophism by recourse to self-evident *archai* and demonstration according to the laws of noncontradiction and the excluded middle ultimately fails: in those matters where sophism is most ruinous to community, in matters of the good, which is to say, rhetoric's three concerns of *to dikaion, to sumpheron,* and *to kalon,* argument is anarchic. For in these matters there is no static noncontradictory being, first conceived in intellection, then signified univocally, and then argued about demonstratively and conclusively in word signs. Rather, there is only shifting, temporal being, our understanding of which is transmitted acoustically in received opinions, and about which we do not demonstrate but rather take counsel and deliberate in talking things through together in the vocal word names of "outward argument" (Aristotle: *ho exô logos*). And if, having seen that in mathematical science demonstration effectively wards off sophism, one were then to seek to argue demonstratively about these ethical and political matters, one would, we have seen, in fact only open the door to sophistical deception. For sophists can argue for their own advantage most persuasively precisely by disguising their own arguments as objective demonstrations grounded in intuitively certain first principles and by thus concealing these arguments' real ground in the speaker's *êthos,* his or her life "choice" of self-aggrandizement, and in his or her disingenuous manipulation of the affects.

Sophism can be countered, therefore, only by returning to original argument, the validity of which depends not on its logic alone but on the character of the speaker and—and this becomes our concern here—on the affects or *pathê* this original argument would communicate. Sophism cannot be countered by merely laying bare dialectical argument beneath demonstration's abstraction from it, as we did in the last chapter, but only by also hermeneutically "laying bare," beneath dialectical argument, original rhetorical argument and thereby reestablishing rhetorical argument's original fusion of *pathos* and *logos*. Original argument, we contend, is to be found valid or invalid only as a patho/logical unity.

To say the same thing in a different way, original argument can be shielded against sophistical corruption only if, having been "laid bare," its communication is then "laid out" hermeneutically in its original, full *psychosomatic* nature and not left as the disembodied signals of one abstract "mind," "self," or "soul" transmitting its internal "information" to another. Argument, we maintain, can be shielded against sophism only if it is recognized as having been embodied all along.

Perhaps the easiest way to explain what is meant by embodied argument would be to contrast it with its opposite, disembodied argument, for example, a geometrical demonstration. We note in this regard that in part 3 of his *Rhetoric* Aristotle takes up declamation and delivery and, correspondingly, the appropriate variations of voice, *phônê,* in the speaker's communication of the desired *pathê* or affects, variations, namely in volume (*megathos*), pitch or tone (*harmonia*), and rhythm (*rhuthmos*) (1403b31 ff.). Here, in other words, Aristotle treats the variables in how an oration sounds physically to its hearers. However, he observes in conclusion, and in a typical depreciation of such considerations, that "all these are matters of the imagination and have to do with the listener, and for that reason no one teaches how to do geometry by means of them" (ἀλλ' ἅπαντα φαντασία ταῦτ' ἐστί, και πρὸς τὸν ἀκροατήν· διὸ οὐδεὶς οὕτω γεωμετρεῖν διδάσκει) (1404a11–12).

The point glossed over in this aside is that the aim of any *didaskalia* or instruction in how to do geometry is precisely not the aim of rhetoric: say, in Homer, that a physical person, Achilles, engaged in his practical existence should *hear* something (Odysseus's vivid narration of the Achaean's plight), imagine what has been heard, and then respond in action. Rather, in teaching geometry a disengaged mind or intellect should "see" something conceptually and theoretically, which means, if we may take the Greek *theôrein,* or "to look on," and *theôretês,* or "spectator," to be our guide, see it in the way a wholly unaffected, dispassionate observer sees it. "Seeing" in geometry is in no way imagination of physical perception and involves no physical interaction with either the speaker or what is spoken about; rather, it is "seeing" with the disembodied "mind's eye" (Plato, *Republic* 500b). It is for this reason that the kind of "speech" that induces geometrical insight never has an intrinsic physical dimension and that any "listener" who heard it never "underwent" (*epathen*) a physical affect (*pathos*).

Indeed, if a geometrical demonstration is to achieve what it is supposed to, the voiced sounds in which it is spoken must be utterly self-effacing and transparent, as are the sounds we make when we say, for instance, "The square of the hypotenuse of a right triangle equals the sum of the squares of the other two sides." For if we are being true theoretical geometricians, we do not hear and see, let alone taste, touch, or feel, anything physical when we are either speaking of such things or "listening" to someone else speak of them. Indeed, in the end we do not even imagine or picture anything physical. On the contrary, the whole point is that what we say, and what we hear someone else say, should shed and transcend every trace of physical experience. Consequently, in the best case we would neither voice it nor hear it at all. Rather, we would write it and read it in letters that for us had lost every vestige of pictograms, letters which only a printsetter would still see or notice, and which we, in looking away from them and looking to the intelligible reality which they signify, systematically overlook.

Then we would finally have eviscerated, *disembodied* argument, which is to say, the "communication" of one disembodied Platonic intellect to another.[1] Disembodied argument thus proceeds by abstraction from physical hearing of the voiced word and moves, first, to seeing a written word and silently imagining what it pictures, and ultimately to envisioning a purely intelligible reality with a pure, unaffected intellect.

Embodied argument, however, reverses this abstraction. Compare, for instance, "$7 + 5 = 12$," Plato's example in the *Theaetetus* (196a), with our parent's admonition, "Do you hear me!" In "seeing" the relationship of the numbers $7+5$ to 12 we arithmeticians are, like viewers or spectators, wholly detached and unaffected at any visceral level. Having no existential interaction with what we see, we are like Aristotle's divine intelligence or *nous*, which, in engaging in the pure activity of *theôria* or looking on, is an agent that moves other things in some unaccountable way while itself remaining unmoved and untouched by them (see *Metaphysics*, 12, 1072b14 ff.). But such was surely not the case when as children we heard our parent's "Do you hear me!" For hearing and understanding something like this is far more passion than action, far more a matter of what is done to us and happens to us than what we do. In this case we ourselves are not unmoved; rather, such a sound, if appropriately voiced—precisely with the right volume, pitch, tone, and rhythm—may even affect us physically with a wrenching of the "gut."

To make precisely this point concerning existential involvement Kierkegaard cites 2 Samuel 12: 1–14, where David, having disposed of

Batheseba's husband, Uriah, and having then taken Bathsheba to be one of his own wives, is confronted by the prophet Nathan.[2] Nathan tells David the parable of a rich man who had many sheep, but nevertheless stole the one sheep of his poor neighbor to fete an unexpected visitor. At first David *sees* what has happened, and, as a king looking on, he judges that "the man who has done this deserves to die" (6). To be sure, David is moved by righteous indignation, but he is not yet existentially engaged by the story himself; he is not yet willing to *hear* its message. That, however, is changed instantly with Nathan's "*You* are that man!" (7), and now David does not see theoretically, does not judge sovereignly "at a distance," but hears, viscerally, what is said to him and can respond to it in the first person: "*I* have sinned against the Lord," he says (13).

Thus, what someone undergoes in embodied argument and rhetoric is much more than a change of *mind* from dissent to assent, from "I don't see it that way" to "I do." On the contrary, it is a change of heart, a change in how one *feels* about something, which is to say, a "gut" change sometimes even from rebellious refusal to consent, from "Over my dead body!" to "Yes, I will."[3] This response is not just intellectual. On the contrary, such hearing is in a fundamental sense visceral.

Our task in this chapter is to elaborate this difference. In a *Destruktion* of book 3 of the *Rhetoric* on diction, delivery, and arrangement (*lexis, hupokrisis,* and *taxis*), we will see that in Aristotle a form of argument remains in the background that is, as Heidegger would have put it, "earlier" and "closer to the origin" than the purely logical argument of demonstration, even though for him demonstration is ultimately the paradigm against which other kinds of argument, namely dialectic and rhetoric, are to be measured. In this earlier, underlying form of argument nearly suppressed by Aristotle, the physical sound, voiced and heard bodily, is not ancillary, as it is in demonstration, but crucial; for it is the communication of *pathos* alone that transforms assent to consent, and it is the voicing, the volume, pitch, tone, and rhythm, that communicates *pathos.*

Following Heidegger's strategy, we will once again seek, hermeneutically, to get at this earlier form of spoken, audible, visceral argument by "taking down" the abstractions that have supervened upon it and thus "laying bare" and "laying out" its original nature. Precisely because of its seminal ambivalence in regard to embodied argument, we shall return now to Aristotle's *Rhetoric* as our starting point. For all the while this work affirms at a deeper level the unity of *pathos* and *logos,* it seeks strenuously to dissolve it and to create for human beings a purely rational discourse of the gods that would transcend the human being's "mixed" psychosomatic nature (compare EN 1117b27 ff.), and in which, consequently, *pathos* would be at best superfluous and at worst even detrimental. Thus, remarkably, in the end a mathematicized, Pythagorean "Plato" replaces Homer and Sophocles in the *Rhetoric* as the model for argument, even if it is this very same "Plato" that elsewhere comes in for Aristotle's most telling criticisms.

Here too, then, we will have occasion to explore a remarkable tension in Aristotle: in following a tendency in Plato, or at least a tendency in the mathematically oriented "friends" in the Academy, he turns to a metaphysical world of conceived *eidê,* essences, ideas, and, like the Socrates of Plato's *Phaedo,* thereby divorces the mind from the body, and to this extent he denies our original, auditory discursive experience. On the other hand, to the extent he acknowledges, after all, the impossibility of human beings ever attaining to such a divine life, and to the extent that he places us back in our human this-worldly ethical and political practice, he remains true to the physical, embodied, nature of our speaking to one another. Hence, though in Aristotle's *Rhetoric* the dualisms of mind and body, dualisms of the mental and physical, intellectual and visceral, visual and auditory, logical and pathetical, demonstrative and affective, are perpetuated and reinforced, he nevertheless continues to provide access for us to the earlier, more original form of argument for which these dualisms do not yet exist.

6.1 The Evisceration of Argument in Plato's *Cratylus* and *Phaedo*

Because the origins of this tension in the *Rhetoric* are to be found in Platic philosophy, before turning to the *Rhetoric* we need first to resume our investigation of key dialogues, to begin with, the *Cratylus.*[4] For of all the dialogues this one brings most sharply into focus a concern in Plato crucial to our own exposition, namely that words can spin free of "what it is" they name, the *ti estin,* and thereby obstruct rather than mediate our insight into it. Indeed, it is precisely this weakness of word names that makes sophistical misappropriation of them possible in the first place, for, as we have learned from the *Phaedrus,* it allows sophists to present something, not as what it is, but precisely for what it is not, love, for instance, as something disgraceful. Far worse than this, however, by manipulation of this weakness a wrong or unjust action can be passed off for right or just, a harmful action for beneficial, and an ugly and indecent action for decent. To counteract this sophistical sleight of hand, so the thought of the *Cratylus* goes, we must therefore find a vocabulary that cannot disguise and distort the reality of what a thing is, but instead always reveals it clearly and distinctly, and to do this we must find words names that correspond in some way or other to the essential nature of what they name.

What sort of words would represent the thing itself without getting in the way and obscuring it? What sort of words would remain one with the things they name rather than becoming divorced from them and going off on their own, as it were? How is the unity of *onoma* and *pragma* or, as a later rhetoric will term it, of *verbum* and *res* to be insured? These are the questions the *Cratylus* poses.

Significantly for us, in the *Cratylus*'s *elenchos* or refutation of mistaken attempts to explain this unity of right names with "what it is" they name, the first attempt treated tries to do this in terms of voice (*phônê*) (426c ff.). As the *Phaedrus*'s facetious definition of the four species of divine madness made clear to us, we must, of course, be careful not to take Plato's equally facetious exposition here in the *Cratylus* too seriously. Still, we may assume that what the dialogue says reflects, if only by caricaturing it, some commonly held opinion, some *endoxon*, that has a grain of truth in it. The thought is that certain phonemes or voiced sounds we can make imitate at least metaphorically the reality they represent. We say metaphorically, because, as we have seen in our study of the metonymic tropes, such imitation goes well beyond onomatopoetic rendering of perceived sounds and, by metophorics and metonymy, transference and renaming, correlates voiced sounds with similar but different perceived sights, tastes, touches, and smells, as well as inwardly perceived feelings and emotions. Thus the voiced rough sound of "rough," for example, comes, by metaphor and metonymy, to imitate a rough surface as opposed to the smooth sound of "smooth" that imitates a smooth surface. And from there we proceed, of course, to things like "a rough day" or "It went smoothly." In the theory treated in the *Cratylus,* liquids like "l" or "m" are said to imitate what is soft and fluid, whereas gutterals like "k" or "g" are said to be hard and to bring any fluidity up short. An "r," rolled on the tip of the tongue, on the other hand, as in *rhein,* to flow, renders motion and rapidity, whereas in bringing things to a stop, the dentals, "t" and "d," represent rest.

Leaving aside the lengths to which this playful dialogue takes this theory—Plato, it seems, is attempting a kind of refutation by a reduction to absurdity—we may establish at least this much in earnest: however this onomatapoetic imitation in sounds might succeed in correlating the voiced word name with the thing, *to onoma* with *to pragma,* the being it can imitate in sounds remains a fluctuating quasi reality that yields no real knowledge of a thing's real being or nature. If we are to know a thing and say what it is really (*ontôs*) and in truth (*têi alêtheiai*), and if we are to name its *ti estin*, sounds made over a length of time and that can only imitate its fluctuating appearance and disappearance in time are wholly inadequate and misleading.

The conclusion to be drawn, therefore, is that like the names of numbers and geometrical elements, our voiced word names or *onomata*, if they are to be accurate and precise, must be transformed into mere signs or *sêmeia*, namely, visual indicators that designate the thing in essence and in its essential relationships to other essential things. For instance, the sound "twelve" is to be converted into a purely conventional visual sign, "12," that indicates this number's being and place in the sequence of the other numbers, just as "line" is a purely conventional sound indicating that geometrical element's visual place in the generative sequence of point, line, plain figure, solid. As such, the sound "twelve" must be self-effacing and completely transparent, lest it assert itself in the place of the reality it was meant to designate. Indeed, it would be best if we made no physical or even mentally imagined sound at all when we think of "12" ourselves or get someone else to think of it. It would be best that it remain an unvoiced visible written mark. For only then would we know the real, *incorporeal* being of "12" without even a trace of our own *corporeality* in our knowing. What we would "say" to ourselves in this dialogue of the disembodied mind with itself would, as opposed to "the streaming out of the mouth in sounded utterance" (*Soph.* 263e), be without any voicing (*aneu phonês*) (*Epist.* 7.342a f.), and then we could think "12" *aneu tôn onamatôn*—without any names or words at all (*Soph.* id.; compare Gadamer, WM 384–85).

The spoken "twelve," and most of all the written "12," was never likely to block our comprehension of what it stands for. Such is not the case, however, with ordinary speech, tied as it is in some way or other to the sensuous, flowing world it renders in metaphoric, metonymic transferrence of original onomatopoeias to similar but different experiences. Indeed, it is all too easy to get caught up in the sounds we *hear* from speakers and be diverted, as the speakers themselves might be, from seeing and "reading" with the mind's eye "what it is," *ti estin*, that they are talking about.

As we have already noted, Aristotle himself sheds a good deal of light on Plato's line of thought here. We have read at *Metaphysics* 987a30 f. that in his youth Plato adhered in large part to the number theories of the Pythagoreans, that he learned, and precisely from Cratylus, the Heraclitian doctrine that knowledge of things perceived by the senses, *ta aisthêta*, was impossible because such things are constantly streaming (*aei rhêonta*). We can also learn from this passage that Plato accepted

Socrates' concern with definitions of ethical realities (*ta êthika*) but not Socrates' disregard of physics. And we learn, finally, that he concluded that such definitions must have as their concern not a being such as that we perceive but another kind of being, a being, this is to say, more like the mathematical being of the Pythagoreans' numbers. Thus, not just numbers but the ethical realities of the just or right thing, the beneficial thing, the decent or fine thing, which is to say, the three primary subject matters of rhetoric, are *mathêmata* to be taught and learned in instruction (*didaskalia, mathêsis*) according to the mathematical, arithmetical, geometrical model. In this way, much as the teaching of mathematics brings the student to see with the mind's eye what "twelve" or "line" are in essence and what in essence they are not, the teacher of these matters brings the student to see the *eidos* or *idea* which, in essence, each of these ethical realities is and which, in essence, each is not.

The task, accordingly, is to purify our speech so that the inevitable and unfortunate "stream out of the mouth in uttered sound" most reveals and least occludes what it was meant to designate. Like numbers or geometrical elements, our ethical words should be wholly severed from anything they might *sound* like in the physical world and thereby reduced to maximally transparent signs indicating static metaphysical essences. As we saw in chapter 4, the written mark or grapheme that one sees and reads gives the appearance of coming closest to this transparency to the *eidos*. (Derrida is right, of course, that even the written sign's transparency to the *eidos* is only an appearance, for there is no *eidos* to which the written sign points but only other signs.)

If we return from the *Cratylus* to the *Phaedo*, we can now see just what consequences this turn in Plato's thinking has for the disembodiment and evisceration of speech that we are considering. It will be recalled that having found no satisfactory knowledge in contemporary *physical* accounts of *physical* things, the "Socrates" of the *Phaedo*, quite in contrast to Aristotle's account of the actual Socrates in the *Metaphysics*, turns to the "mirroring" of physical events in *what we have to say* about them, turns, that is, to our *logoi* or arguments concerning them (99d ff.). To be sure, the initial task would be to give an account of these physical events in ethical terms, to account for them, in other words, as one might account for Socrates' being in prison and not having fled to escape execution. For he stayed, of course, because he reasoned it was "best," which is to say, because it was the just, good, and decent thing to do. The idea would be ultimately to explain the course of physical processes in the same way: whatever happens, happens by intelligence and because of, "for the sake of," its being best (98e f.; it is Aristotle's physics, to be sure, that will fulfill the promise here, not any of Plato's dialogues). Although this "Socrates," in contrast to Aristotle's "Plato," would presumably pursue physics, his concern here is, in accord with Aristotle's account, still with what we say about *to auto to kalon* and *to auto to agathon*, the decent itself and the good itself (*Phaedo* 100b). But not only with them. His concern is also with what we say about magnitude (*to mega*), and precisely here we do find foreshadowed that superimposition of Pythagorean mathematics and number theory on Socratic concerns which Aristotle attributes to Plato.

To review our previous investigation in section 4.1, the line of thought in the *Phaedo*, as in the *Cratylus*, is that to avoid being misled by sophistical controversialists (*antilogikoi*) who can make anything seem the opposite of itself, we need to get behind the words they use so loosely, to an idea that, unlike these words, cannot be made to "flow" from one meaning to its opposite. Just as we know that the spoken word "three" designates "3" and that this, in turn, belongs to the class of "odd," so too, the argument runs, we might know that the spoken word *kalon* designates *to kalon auto kath' hauto*, the decent itself by itself; and so it is too with the spoken words "good" and "just." But as long as we persist on the level of the spoken words with no clear and distinct idea of precisely what they designate, we leave ourselves open to sophistically induced confusions of what is decent, good, or just, with what is not. Furthermore, the argument continues, we get a clear and distinct idea about what something is in distinction from what it is not, *not by staying on the level of the sense-perceived particular and the physical voiced sound that in some way might imitate it*, but by abstracting and withdrawing from this and by first "setting down" (*hupotheuein*) what it is (*ti estin*) that the particular is a case of, and then *seeing* (*skepsein*) with which of each of the intelligible things that follow from it it is logically "consonant" and with which other consequences it is "dissonant" (101d). Hence, if one is perceiving two physical things, one cannot let oneself get involved in captious arguments about whether they "came into being" from doubling or halving another physical thing (101bf.). Instead, one must leave the physical things behind, and in looking away from them to the idea of what it is they are an instance of (*apoblepein pros tên idean*) set down and stabilize an idea of the number two. Then one needs to see that even is "consonant" with it, but that both three and the class to which three belongs, odd, are "dissonant" with it. And in some similar way, we may presume, in arguing a "case" of the right and just in a law court, we must first "look beyond" the case and "set down" and stabilize in our minds an idea of precisely what justice is. Mere speech on the level of the case itself would only confuse it with what it is not. The same would hold, too, if we were arguing about the beneficial in consultative rhetoric or the decent in a epideictic rhetoric (compare Aristotle's *Rhetoric*, book 1, chapter 3). Thus, the last vestiges of sound and voice, of the *phônê,* in *sumphonei* and *diaphonei,* being consonant and dissonant, are completely translated here, first, into the visual and then into the purely intelligible. After Pythagoras's music, it will be recalled, is to be thought of as *harmonia,* which is to say, not as something heard but as the envisioned dovetailing of the pieces of wood in a chariot or *harma* and, ultimately, as the purely logical compatibility of numbers in ratios, *logoi,* to each other (fourths, fifths, etc.). Plato's *sumphonei* and *diaphonei* here reflect this Pythagorean transition in thought from hearing acoustical voicings to reading the system of legible marks, the "score," as it were, of the symphony of sensuous reality.

Moreover—and this is the point for us now—this transition from one dimension of sense perception to another, and then finally from sense perception altogether to the purely intelligible object of *nous* or intellect, presupposes a correlative transition in the knower, *presupposes, this is to say, his or her evisceration.* For just as what is to be known has to have purified every physical aspect and is now neither heard nor seen (save with the mind's eye and not the body's), so too the knower must have been purified of the body's influences. Indeed, "to know" now means to have separated the mind from the body, for Plato has his "Socrates" say,

> Have we not been saying for a long time that the mind, whenever it makes use of the body for the sake of any examination, be it through seeing or through hearing or any other of the senses—for to examine something by the senses is precisely to examine it by the body—is then dragged by the body into the realm of what never stays the same? And it strays, bewildered and dizzy, as though drunk from taking hold of such things. (79d)

But, he continues,

> philosophy takes over the soul in this state, gently encourages it, and attempts to loosen and free it [from the hold of the senses], pointing out that examination by the eyes is full of deceit, by the ears, full of deceit, and by any of the other senses, and by persuading it to separate from these save where it is necessary to use them, and exhorting it to collect and gather itself in itself and to trust nothing else but itself and those existent things by themselves that the mind knows by itself. (83a–b)

Thus, not only is the thing known removed from its physical acoustical and even optical existence but also the soul or mind of the knower from its auditory and visual experience.

Most important for us is the separation here from the auditory and acoustical, from hearing and what is heard. For of all the senses, seeing is closest to purely intelligible examination, the *skopein* and *skepsis,* of which Plato speaks. As the perpetual oscillation of the meaning of *eideinai* between "seeing" and "knowing" evidences, the transformation and sublimation of sensuous seeing into "seeing" the purely intelligible is relatively easy. Hearing, on the other hand, cannot be transformed and sublimated in this way. Consequently it must be entirely abandoned and eliminated. For Plato the danger with hearing is precisely that when we hear we are not "by ourselves," *kath' hêmas autous,* and sovereign, but in and by an other, and at the disposal of this other. To use Heidegger's language in an interpersonal way that he does not employ but Gadamer does, in hearing (*Hören*) we belong to an other (*einem anderen gehören*) and obey this other (*diesem gehorschen*).

To be sure, on one level, certainly, Plato continues to acknowledge the validity of this passive-pathetical structure of auditory experience, for he speaks of the *pathos tôn logôn,* of our undergoing, and being affected by, what arguments do *with* us, and of what happens *to* us when we speak (*Philebus* 15d). And here it would seem that, as in Heidegger's *Basic Concepts of Aristotelian Philosophy* (GBAPh), hearing and not seeing would be the paradigmatic form of sense perception, and that the vocabulary of hearing would provide, if only metaphorically, the concepts with which to describe our mental experience. Nevertheless, the primary emphasis on self-possession (*enkratia*) and freedom (*eleutheria*) in Plato—and self-sufficiency (*autarkeia*) in Aristotle—thwarts this line of thought.

In the *Phaedo,* at any rate, Socrates remains supremely self-possesed (*enkratês, kath' hauton*) in facing the fear of death that might have overpowered a person of lesser courage. So too we, unlike the others there who go to pieces as Socrates takes the cup of hemlock, must remain self-possessed in the face of whatever feelings (*pathê*) we undergo, for in this way alone do we display that we are free and not slaves. Above all, then, the task is to remain sovereign in the same way that those who see remain sovereign over what they see arrayed before and below them.

Indeed, for Plato to know, *eidenai,* is to have an overview of things whose *eidos* and *idea* we have grasped in their relationship to the *eidê* and *ideai* of other things; then we have in*sight* into the essential a*spect* of a thing. Plato knows, as we have remarked, that this project can never be perfected by human beings, who inevitably are always at the mercy of forces beyond their control, and for whom any clarity and distinctness of things is simultaneously permeated with obscurity and confusion. Hence, the *eidos* and *idea,* the purely intelligible "look" of something, the grasp of which alone would bring stability and definition to what flows and fuses with its opposite, is something we look to (*apoblepein pros*) without ever actually being able to pin it down for good. In our pursuit of it, submission to the alteration of *euporiai* and *aporiai*, felicitous outcomes and unfortunate dead ends, is our lot (see the *Philebus* 15c). Still, the task is never to surrender but to struggle on for the unattainable. Such is the nature of *philosophia* or the love of wisdom, that it never attains to wisdom itself.

6.2 *Noêsis* and *phronêsis*: Aristotle's Adherence to, and Break with, the Platonic Theory of Argument

The question for us now is just how closely Aristotle adheres to this metaphysical and anti-somatic orientation of Plato's thinking. On the one hand, we have found good evidence already that in many ways Aristotle remains an "earlier" thinker than Plato and "closer to the origin." For, as we have seen, Aristotle, unlike Plato, is willing to allow for kinds of learning and truth that are not mathematical and can never be modeled on things like number theory or geometry. There is, in other words, a more obvious ambivalence and tension in Aristotle than in Plato insofar as Aristotle clearly states that mathematical thinking and its privileging of *apodeixis* or demonstration is inappropriate and even irrelevant in wide areas of our experience, among them, life science, the arts of making things, and, above all, the realm of rhetoric, namely politics and ethics with their concerns with the good or the just, the beneficial, and the decent. Hence, in breaking with mathematical Platonism, if not with Plato himself, Aristotle acknowledges that demonstration's most exact way of knowing a truth, this "best and most sovereign" (*kratiston*) way, cannot be made the paradigm of all knowing. In fact, in our taking counsel about the good, Aristotle points out, not *apodeiknusthai* but *endeiknusthai*, not exact demontration but rough indication, is to be sought:

> we must be satisfied, as regards such matters and reasoning from such premises, with indicating the truth roughly and in outline [παχυλῶς καὶ τύπῳ τἀληθες ἐνδείκνυσθαι]. . . . Indeed, it pertains to the educated to seek that measure of exactitude [τἀκριβὲς ἐπιζητεῖν] in each particular kind of thing that the nature of the thing allows, for accepting from a mathematician that he argue convincingly [μαθηματικοὺ τε πιθανολογοῦντος ἀποδέχεσθαι] is obviously as wrong as demanding demonstrations from a rhetor [ῥητορικόν ἀποδείξεις ἀπαιτεῖν]. (EN 1094b19–28)

At the same time, however, the much disputed "*deuterôs*" or "secondarily" used to contrast the practical with the contemplative or theoretical life in book 10 of the *Nicomachean Ethics*—"the life according to the other [ethical] excellence, however, is happy *secondarily*" (1178a9)—points up, at the very least, a continuing allegiance to the Platonic "mathematical" paradigm, an allegiance that persists, as we have already observed, in the *Rhetoric* too. For in the preceding characterization of the primary happiness found in divine contemplative activity (1177a13 ff.), Aristotle has revealed himself to be very much the Platonist. To attain *autarkeia* or self-sufficiency and to attain freedom from the pressures of time in *scholê* or leisure (see 1177b 22), Aristotle, too, would purify our minds of our physical involvement with the sense-perceived physical world, the world of contingent things that come to be and pass away in space in time and that impact on us and affect us. He would raise our thinking to a purely intelligible realm of "envisioned" realities that must be, eternally and aspatially, what they are by themselves. Such, then, is the life of wisdom or *sophia*, the life, that is, of *nous* and *noêsis*, or intelligence and intellection of intelligible first principles, and of scientific knowledge reasoned from them by necessary, demonstrative syllogisms (see EN 1141a9 f.). Here, then, just as in Plato's geometry or number theory, we set ourselves apart from our involvement with things and other people in the world and "see" (*theôroumen*) the static logic of things arrayed before us.

The *deuterôs*, then, is depreciatory and indicates Aristotle's clear preference for the divine (*theos*) life over the human (*anthrôpinos*) life even if for us humans the divine life is attainable only momentarily. In *Metaphysics*, 12, he even submits that "Such an uninvolved activity [*diagôgê*] is like the best activity possible for us for a short time" (1072b14–15), and he contrasts our human "moved" being with divine being, itself unmoved yet moving another (1072a25), and the latter is found superior and most sovereign (*kratistos*) precisely because it does what it does without suffering or undergoing any change at the hands of an other: a thing moved "is susceptible of being otherwise" (ἐδέχεται καὶ ἄλλως ἔχειν), he observes, but "if something moves while being unmoved itself and being in actuality, this is insusceptible of being otherwise in any way at all [οὐκ ἐδέχεται ἄλλως ἔχειν οὐδαμῶς]" (1072b4–8). Such is the pure activity of mind, namely intellection or *noêsis*, and such is the activity that we human beings are capable of in our most superior and sovereign moments. It is the "primary" best activity, as is its object, *to noêton*, the best possible object. "Intellection by itself [καθ' αὑτὴν] [is intellection] of the best thing by itself [καθ' αὑτὸ], and the more intellection is by itself, the more its object is by itself and best" (1072b17–18). Even the very choice of words here (*kath' hautên, kath' hauto*) is Platonic.

Even more important, however, given our task of hermeneutical destruction of abstractions from this original experience "there" "in the world," is that in this purified intellection privileged by Aristotle there is no longer involvement with any other person with whom we co-exist. We are no longer, to speak with Heidegger, *Mitdasein*, "being there with" others "in the world," but are by ourselves and unaffected by them. As Aristotle puts it in the *Ethics*,

> Also what is called self-sufficiency [ἥ τε λεγομένη αὐτάρκεια] will obtain most of all for the contemplative excellence. To be sure, the wise man needs the necessities of life as do the just man and the others, but these having been furnished, the just man needs other people towards whom, and with whom he can practice justice. The same holds for the temperate man, the brave, and each of the others. But the wise man can also contemplate while being by himself [καὶ καθ' αὐτὸν ὢν δύναται θεωρεῖν], and the more he does this, the wiser he is. (1177a20–35)

Hence, plainly, a sense of *loss* is expressed when Aristotle concedes at the conclusion of his *Nicomachean Ethics* that though this divine activity of contemplation is in accord with the highest excellence and affords the greatest happiness, we must nevertheless inhabit "secondarily" another world, since for "us" human beings, as opposed to gods, this pure envisioning of the objects of pure reason is ultimately only a projection. If we could achieve it we should, and only because we cannot, we must content ourselves with striving for it. We aim at it in our pursuit of it, but we never attain it. We continue under way in our mixed (*suntheton*) being (see 1177b29), which, insofar as it is *embodied* mind and soul and not just *nous*, must deal with what affects, moves, and changes us, namely, the perceived sensations we undergo and feelings, the *pathêmata* and *pathê*. But all the while we aim our lives at transcending this experience.

6.2.1 Aristotle's revocation of the theoretical and recovery of the practical

Despite his preference for the theoretical life, however, Aristotle is far from being focused exclusively on it. Rather, his attention is divided. For as superior, sovereign, and self-sufficient as such a life *would be*, it is not for us human beings after all, he says, but only for the part in us that is divine, namely *nous*: "such a life would surpass what is human," for "human beings are not pure but mixed" (1177b27–29; see also 1178a21). Thus, while Aristotle would reject those like Empedocles "enjoining a human being to think (*phronein*) human things" (1177b33), he allows that in the end we must do just that. Even if it provides only a secondary happiness, this worldly realm of both *agein* and *paschein,* of acting and undergoing, of deeds and experiences undergone, this place for the arts, or making things, and for political and ethical practice, or doing things, this original world of our "being there with others" (Heidegger: *Mitdasein*) *is* recognized as inescapable.

Now, as Aristotle himself acknowledges, there is reasoning and argument here too, and, as we already know, these cannot be the same as reasoning about pure intelligible being. For one thing, they are based, as we have seen in the previous chapter, on non-necessary, commonly held beliefs (*endoxa*), and not on certain truths. For another—and this will be our main concern in this chapter—the audience for an argument in this realm is not yet a spectator and is not unmoved and by itself (*kath' hauton*) but affected by what happens to it. Hence, not the demonstrative syllogism but the enthymeme will be the appropriate means of argument, which is to say, not the demonstration *to* detached, dispassionate onlookers, not instructing (*didaskein*) them about something else besides themselves, but the convicing (*peithein*) *of* them themselves, as co-participants in a situation, who together the with speaker are undergoing what has "happened to happen" (*ta sumbebêkota*) to them and are affected by it. Here, obviously, not just the disembodied *psuchê* or *nous,* soul or intellect, of the listener is to be led to conviction by the en-*thym*-eme, but, as we have learned from Heidegger, the bodily *thumos* (see section 2.2 above).

We see, then, that despite his express preference for the theoretical over the practical, in the end Aristotle's own turning back from *nous* and *noêsis* to *phronein* and *phronêsis,* his turning back, that is, from pure intellection of eternal truth to discernment in practical human matters, and to our existence "there" in the world, runs parallel to our hermeneutics of original argument. For this turn has important consequences for him not only in regard to what argument is about but in regard to how it works.

In regard to what practical argument is about, we note that, according to Aristotle, the wise, for example, Anaxagoras and Thales, are said to have neglected the human goods (*ta anthrôpina agatha*) and were therefore called (*sophos*) but precisely not discerning (*phronimos*) (EN 1141b4–8); they were divine, perhaps, but impractical. *Phronêsis* or discernment, however, *is* practical (1141b23), and this means that it concerns the particular being or realities "in the world" that are "susceptible of being otherwise." To review what we have learned so far, discernment is not only knowledge of things taken on the whole (*tôn katholou*); rather, it must also know each thing individually (*kath' hekasta*). For it is practical and "practice concerns each thing individually" (1141b14–17). This means, as we have seen, that it cannot reason by demonstration. For rather than reasoning syllogistically from universal to particular, or inductively from particular to universal, for the most part it will reason *analogically* from particular example to particular example (see *Rhet.* 1357b26 ff. and chapter 3 above). Hence, rather than arguing that "As a whole, white meat is good for you, and this chicken is white meat, so it will be good for you," it argues, without recourse to any static universals and entirely from within the temporal flux of its experience, "that chicken then was good for you, so this one now will very likely be too" (compare 1141b17–22).

Our concern now, however, is with how practical argument achieves its effect. In this regard it is to be noted, first, that in practices and actions guided by discernment, such as behaving justly or bravely or according to any of the other practical excellences, we do what we do in reciprocal relationship with others, *pros allêlous* (1178a10), and precisely not each by himself or *kath' hauton* (1178a13). Thus, argument here will always involve two *voices* and will have the form of oral-aural taking counsel (*sumbouleuesthai*) in talking things through (*dialegesthai*) with another person out loud, and this, even when this other person's voice is internalized in someone's taking counsel with himself or herself.

Second, discernment governs practices and actions that are never detached from but always involved "in the feelings" (*en tois pathesi*) we have about things and which we undergo in dealing with them (1178a13). For discernment guides us in reaching decisions and making choices in matters of justice, bravery, temperance, and the various ethical excellences (*êthikai aretai*), and these ethical excellences are right habitudes (*hexeis*) toward the feelings (*pathê*) and thus concern our entire, "mixed" (*suntheton*) nature (1178a20–21); they all involve our habituated predisposition to the mean between the extremes in regard to a feeling (compare EN 1106b36–1107a8), say, reacting to a fearsome situation with too much fear or too little. It is for precisely this reason that the gods, in contrast to human beings, can carry on an activity but never ethical practices. Gods could not practice courage, for instance, for courage involves a rational and measured predispostion toward the feeling of fear, but what feelings of fear could the gods be said to undergo? Nor temperance, for to what "bad desires" are they susceptible (see 1178b10–17)? But such, we may infer, is not the case for us human beings, whose rationality has an irrational dimension of our existence with which to contend. Compare, for instance, EN 1102b13 ff.: "For we praise the reasoning alike of those who are master of themselves and those who are not, and of the part of their soul having the faculty of reasoning, . . . but there seems to be something else in them that by nature goes counter to reasoning and fights and resists it." Any human reasoning in practical matters must come to grips with this "something else," namely feelings. For if we are not "right" (*orthos*) in relation to this nonrational dimension of ourselves, we will be powerless to decide for, and choose, the things that in our deliberations we reason to be just, beneficial, and decent:

> What affirmation and negation are to our thinking something through [ἐν διανοίᾳ], pursuing a course of action and fleeing it are to our striving for something [ἐν ὀρέξει]. Therefore, since ethical excellence is a predisposition to choose a certain way, but choice is a deliberate striving for something, both the reasoning must be true and the striving must be in the right direction [δεῖ διὰ ταῦτα τόν τε λόγον ἀληθῆ εἶναι καὶ τὴν ὄρεξιν ὀρθήν]. (EN 1139a21–25; see above, section 3.1)

In contrast to the gods, then, we do live in a practical world, and we reason and argue in it too, but obviously not in the godly way of "geometricians." For the arguments we use have not so much the form of instruction of an individual to the point where he or she "sees" the truth of the matter by himself or herself (*kath' hauton, kath hautên*), as they have the audible form of voiced condemnation, exhortation, reassurance, prohibition, exonoration, chastisement, praise, or plea, which would change how someone is predisposed to feel about something *viscerally*, and which moves him or her to decide on, and take up, a course of action, to a *krisis* and *prohairesis*. For viscera, Homer, as the next section will make clear, would say *kardie, thumos*, but also *phrenes*, that is to say, "guts," and this *phrenes* surely puts the cognate word *phronêsis* in a new light; *phronêsis*, discernment, quite appart from Aristotle's frequent, and Plato's even more frequent, intellectualization of it, is not in the least a function of the disembodied mind.

The tension and even contradiction in Aristotle's thinking here is constitutive of the entire *Organon*, but of the *Rhetoric* most manifestly. On the one hand, throughout the *Rhetoric* the ideal for argument remains what it was in the *Analytics*, namely the argumentation and reasoning of a mathematically logical, deductive science based on intellection of eternal, self-evident first principles, and conclusive demonstrations of what follows from them necessarily. Here disembodied, dispassionate intelligence and discursive thinking, *nous, dianoia, are* the requisite mental faculties. On the other hand, in the actual practice of the enthymemic and topological reasoning described in the *Rhetoric*, Aristotle finds himself constrained to deviate from his ideal of demonstration.

For, first of all, as we have already seen, in these kinds of reasoning we proceed *from* shared provisionally accepted likelihoods of which we are convinced, and not from intuited insights into first principles, from *endoxa*, this is to say, and not from established, incontestable *archai*. Consequently, we proceed *to* inconclusive and reversible decisions and choices, and not to incontestable assertions. But second, and most important for us now, in rhetoric's acoustical argument for listeners we reason, not as detached and disembodied intellects, and not as self-sufficient, sovereign agents "above it all," but as patients "there" "in the world" simultaneously *undergoing* what happens to us and moves us to decide one way or the other, namely the *pathêmata* and *pathê* as these are communicated by the voice. As we know from the *Ethics*, choice or *prohairesis*, and correspondingly, we may assume, the decision or *krisis* that precedes it and is induced by the rhetorical *pistis* or convincing argument, are much more than unmoved belief (*doxa*) that something is so (see llllb31 f.). Hence, in arguing for a specific choice or decision we must bring about specific changes, in ourselves and each other, by logical means indissociable from their affective, pathetical content.

The tension here, which informs the whole of the *Rhetoric*, is displayed right at the start in book 1, chapter 1. At 1354a12 ff. the very Platonic argument is made that in matters of what is just and right a speaker's efforts to move the judge (*kritês*) and stir the *pathê* are wholly extrinsic to a clear statement of the facts and deeds and wholly incidental to a syllogistic argument for their justice or injustice. *Yet*, at the same time, Aristotle, insofar as he distinguishes rhetorical conviction from dialectical argument, acknowledges at least implicitly that judging or deciding a case involves more than dialectic's coming to the belief that something is or is not so. For a dialectical syllogism can produce a belief, but beyond this the judge must have been convinced to decide the case, convinced to judge, in other words, that an act was right or wrong, and accordingly, to exonorate or condemn the one who did it. And since it is not enough for the judge to have merely seen what the case is a case of, syllogistic inference gives way here to a *pistis* or convincing (*pithonos*) argument that moves and convinces (*peithei*) the judge and, counter to what Aristotle might have at first suggested, gives way properly and necessarily, not regrettably. The *logos* and *sullogismos* by themselves do not suffice for a *pistis*, and the other or means of conviction, it turns out, are thus not extrinsic at all but essential and intrinsic, namely the *êthos* or character of the speaker communicated by the argument and, what is our concern here, the *pathos* or feeling it communicates to the audience. And, accordingly, already in chapter 2, 1355b26 ff., Aristotle himself says expressly that the means of conviction are three in number, and, hence, not the *logos* of an argument alone but its *êthos* and *pathos* must be treated.

6.2.2 Instruction and conviction, *didaskalia* and *peithô*, in Aristotle's *Rhetoric*

To understand the discrepancy here, let us go back, for a moment, to the origins in Plato of Aristotle's attack here on traditional rhetoric. Early in the *Gorgias* we find Socrates in the process of exposing Gorgias's art of rhetoric as a mere experiential knack without insight into what (*ti*) the things really are that it treats, namely the just and unjust (*Gorgias* 454b; see above, chapter 4, note 23). Socrates has convinced Gorgias of a distinction in the ways of convincing someone of something, a distinction between *peithô* or conviction by *didaskalia* or instruction, and merely rhetorical *peithô.* Would you distinguish, he says to Gorgias, between having learned something in the mathematical way (*memathêkenai*), in the way, for instance, we learn about numbers, from merely having been convinced of something (*pepisteukenai*) (454c–d)? Of course. And is there not a corresponding distinction between the results of these two processes of conviction, namely a *mathêsis* or a mathematical sort of insight on the one hand, and *pistis* or a conviction on the other? For it is clear, he says, that *pistis* can be true or false, but *epistêmê*, or the scientific knowledge based on *mathêsis*, cannot (454d). And, given that there is a difference between *memathêkenai* and *pepisteukenai* and between *mathêsis* and *pistis*, which kind of *peithô* or persuasiveness, Gorgias, must your rhetorical art be concerning the just and unjust? Of the merely convincing sort (*pisteutikes*) or of the instructive sort (*didaskalikes*)? Surely, only the first, for the rhetor is merely convincing (*peistikos*) (455a).

In sum, Plato sorts things out here according to two groups of words: on the one hand, we have *pistis* (conviction or belief), *pisteuein* (to believe), *peithein* (to convince someone of something), and *peithô* (the process of conviction and persuasiveness), and, on the other hand, *didaskein* (instruction), *didaskalia* (a course of instruction), *didaskalikês* (instructive), *mathanein* (learning), *mathêsis* (insight or the learning of an insight), *mathêma* (an insight taught), and *epistêmê* or the scientific knowing that results from *didaskein* and *mathanein.* For Plato, in contrast to Gorgias, Tisias, and all the famed teachers of rhetoric, who would merely persuade by working on the passions (see *Phaedrus* 266c f.), the first set concerns things wholly incidental and ancillary to argument, whereas the second set concerns only the things that are essential to it.

Now, for Plato's student Aristotle the same thing would *sometimes* seem to be the case. For at the opening of his *Rhetoric* Aristotle, we can see, has resumed this very argument of Plato's. To be sure, unlike private argument by means of a logically strict syllogism, rhetoric, because it is public, will resort to a *pistis,* which is to say, to an argument that convinces, persuades, brings about belief, and that will be trusted (*pisteuthesetai*) by the audience. Still, it is the speakers' real business, the business, for instance, of advocates before a judge, to enable their audience to "*theoretically envision* the truth of the matter adequately" (θεωρεῖν ἱκανῶς τὸ ἀληθές) (1354b7; my emphasis). It is precisely not their business, on the other hand, to stir "objection and pity and rage and the like feelings in the soul" (τὰ τοιαῦτα πάθη τῆς ψυχῆς), for these "are extrinsic to the subject matter and are in regard to the judge" (1354a16–17). Hence, the *pistis*, it says here, is to be divorced from such things: indeed, "The *pistis* is a kind of demonstration [*apodeixis tis*], insofar as we in fact are most persuaded of something [*pisteuomen*] that we consider have been demonstrated [*apodedeichthai*] (1355a4–6). So, concludes Aristotle, the teachers of rhetoric would have done much better to concentrate, not as they have, on ways of moving the passions, but on the speaker's demonstration, namely, the enthymeme or the correlate in rhetoric to the logical syllogism: "the rhetorical demonstration," says Aristotle, "is the enthymeme" (ἔστι δ' ἀπόδειξις ῥητορικὴ ἐνθύμημα) (1355a6). To be sure, the logical syllogism has to do with *to alêthes*, or what is true, whereas the enthymeme has to do with verisimilitude or what is like the truth (*to homoion tôi alêthei*), but the way to know the latter is to know the former: "The ability to hit upon things commonly believed [τὰ ἔνδοξα] is like the ability to hit upon the truth" (1355a17; compare the *Phaedrus* 262a f.).

So why an art of rhetoric at all? Because, as we have heard, of the cognitive incapacity, the stupidity, of most audiences: "Moreover, in regard to some," Aristotle states, "even if we possessed the most exact science, it is not easy for us as speakers to convince them of something. For the argument appropriate to science is a kind of instruction [διδασκαλίας γάρ ἐστιν ὁ κατὰ τὴν ἐπιστήμεν λόγος], but [for these people] instruction is impossible" (1355a24–27). In sharp contrast with the *Nicomachean Ethics* and even subsequent passages in the *Rhetoric*, there is no indication here that the truths argued about in rhethorical deliberation are of a different sort from scientific truth and therefore do not lend themselves to a high degree of exactitude no matter who the audience is. There is no acknowledgment yet that they accord with a kind of truth-knowing (*alêtheuein*) altogether different from science. (See section 3.1 above and EN 1139b15–15: "Let us say, then, that the ways in which the soul knows the truth [ἀληθεύει ἡ ψυχή] are five in number.") At this point in the *Rhetoric* Aristotle argues only that because of the audience, not because of the subject matter, "it is necessary to make convincing arguments and speeches by means of things held in common, as we said in the *Topics* concerning chance conversation with the masses [περὶ τῆς πρὸς τοὺς πολλοὺς ἐντεύξεως]" (1355a27–29), that is, as in discussion with those simpleminded people "who are incapable of seeing multiple connections and of reasoning for any length of time from one thing to another" (1357a3–4). *However,* Aristotle, even in this opening chapter of the *Rhetoric,* already descends a bit from this epistemological snobbery. At 1355a29 ff., for instance, he tells us that rhetoric is necessary not only to accommodate inferior minds but also as a theory of refutation or counterargument: "It is necessary," he says, "to be able to convince people of the opposite point as is also the case in the syllogisms [of dialectic]. . . . None of the other arts argues syllogistically to the opposite point; only the art of dialectic and the art of rhetoric do this."

But why, then, does Aristotle say that we should study rhetorical refution *in addition* to the dialectical refutation elaborated in the *Sophistical Refutions* and *Topics*? What does rhetoric per se add to the theory of refutation? In the first place, we should study rhetorical refution specifically, he says, because dialectic teaches destruction (*lusis*) only of invalid syllogisms, but rhetoric, destruction of valid enthymemes as well as invalid ones: "As has been said previously, signs that something is so as well as the enthymemes argued from them, even if these enthymemes be valid, are destroyed" (1403a2–3; see 1357b13–14). For example, the argument that, since Socrates was both wise and just, the wise are just, is based on a fallible "sign" or indication—a *sêmeion,* as opposed to the *tekmêrion* or infallible indication—and it is destructible (*luton*) even if it be true (1357b13–14). This would also hold for the argument "Dionysius is a thief, for he is bad" (1401b10). The point is that in rhetoric there are *degrees* of validity, hence a valid but weak argument can be refuted with a stronger one. That it can is plainly *not* because of the inferiority of rhetoric's audience but because of the difference in rhetoric's subject matter, the different kind of being or reality that it treats. As Aristotle himself acknowledges, "there is little of what is necessary from which rhetorical syllogisms are [derived], since in fact for the most part that about which decisions and inquiries are made is susceptible also of being otherwise [ἐνδέχεται καὶ ἄλλως ἔχειν]" (1357a22–24). Because the subject matter is uncertain, arguments about it can only be *more or less* probable, and a probable argument can be countered by a more probable one.

Furthermore, the likelihoods argued about in rhetoric are in fact known in a different way even from the truths of dialectic. For they are not theoretical but practical truths, and they are known from within the temporal and local situation in which they appear and not to the individual by himself or herself (*kath' hauton, kath' hautên*) but, originally, *to us collectively who are there in the midst of them, in medias res,* so to speak, or, as Heidegger puts it, "there" "with others" "in the world."

Rhetorical truth, in other words, is not *seen* by the detatched individual theoretical observer, but *believed* in common with other participants in a practice. That is why in the very passage where Aristotle disparages those incapable of epistemic instruction, he adds that in rhetoric "it is necessary to make convincing arguments and speeches by means of things held in common [διὰ τῶν κοινῶν]" (1355a27). To be sure, the depreciatory reference to the *polloi* or "masses" that Aristotle then attaches to this assertion (29) manifests his continuing preference for scientific instruction, and he makes it seem that the *enteuxis* or chance conversation characteristic of rhetorical argumentation is something that someone with the most exact science would condescend to engage in only for the sake of an uncomprehending audience. Indeed, in the passage in the *Topics* to which Aristotle adverts here we find, in a similar vein, that "having counted up the beliefs of the masses, we shall converse with them [ὁμιλήσομεν πρὸς αὐτούς] not on the basis of beliefs foreign to them but on the basis of beliefs with which they are at home, simply redirecting whatever they appear to us to say improperly" (*Top.* 101a30–34).

However, if we look past the obvious condescension in these passages, we can observe that, as opposed to demonstrative logic, both dialectical and rhetorical argument are to be grasped as association (*homilia*) among participants. Hence, argument here is actually not inferior to demonstration but essentially different in kind. As opposed to demonstration and even dialectic's theoretical argument, rhetoric's nontheoretical, practical argument happens within a temporal situation and happens to a speaker and an audience, both of whom are "always already" "underway" within shared beliefs or *endoxa.* These *endoxa* are not certain epistemic truths (see *Top.* 101b21 and *Rhet.* 1355a17), and despite insinuations here that they are to be deployed rhetorically only by someone who sees through them to a higher truth, it turns out that any *enteuxis,* any conversation in which we chance to find ourselves involved, cannot be converted into science. That it cannot is not at all, it turns out, because of the inferiority of its audience but because of the wholly different nature of its truth and, in rhetorical argument, because of the finite situation, "there," "in the world," of each of those engaged in coming cooperatively to an understanding of this truth and undergoing existentially the process of taking counsel with each other, their *sumbouleuesthai.* In this regard we note the "middle" or reflexive form of this Greek verb: lying between the active and passive, our "taking counsel with" others involves not only what we do as agents but also what we undergo as patients as a result of our action. It involves, this is to say, the *pathos tôn logôn,* our undergoing, feeling, experiencing what our arguments do to us and with us.

This brings us back to the central question of this chapter: if in Aristotle the *pistis* and *logos*, the conviction and reasoning, of rhetoric differ from demonstrative argument essentially, and not just incidentally in accommodating an inferior audience, what, then, is their relationship to *pathos* as another *pithanon* or means of arguing rhetorically and convincing, besides the *logos* or argument itself? Is the *pathos* just to be added on to the *logos* as ornamentation, ornamentation that is useful, to be sure, in propitiating and manipulating the audience, but wholly "extrinsic to the subject matter" (ἔξω τοῦ πράγματος) even so (see 1354a17–18)? Certainly, if rhetorical argument were not different from demonstration, *pathos* would be extrinsic ornamentation, and often Aristotle seems to reason in just this way. But we have already seen that the rhetorical argument or *logos*, precisely insofar as it is a *pistis* or means of convincing of someone and not mathematical instruction, is different and, it turns out, different in such a way that *pathos* is not extrinsic to the rhetorical *logos* at all, but is intrinsically unified with it. In a striking contradiction, Aristotle both denies and implies this unity.

To be sure, Aristotle is considerably less clear in acknowledging that *pathos* is intrinsic to a rhetorical *logos* than he is in acknowledging that *êthos* is, which, as we know, he considers the "most powerful" means of conviction (1356a13). In book 1, chapter 2, at 1356a16, for instance, a critical reference is made, not to those who exclude *pathos* in their account, but, once again, to those who instead give it the central place, and this only reiterates the contention in chapter 1 at 1354a13 ff. that previous authors on the art of rhetoric are to be criticized for having stressed but a small and inessential part of rhetoric, namely engendering of the *pathê*. For only the *pisteis* or ways of convincing are essential. Everything else, says Aristotle, is merely an accessory, an add-on (*prosthêkê*). The core of the *pisteis*, as we have just heard, is the enthymeme whereas the engendering of the *pathê*, for example, pity and anger, is "irrelevant to the subject matter" and "extrinsic" to it (1354a14–18).

In book 1, chapter 2, however, the engendering of the right *pathê* is at least said to be one of the three *pithana* or means of conviction, albeit the least important. Accordingly, we may assume that even if it does not deserve the exclusive attention given it by previous authors, as one of the three *pithana* it deserves some attention nonetheless. Indeed, we find here the following account of the *indispensable* importance of *pathos*:

> Moreover [conviction occurs] through the listeners whenever they are brought to a feeling by the argument [ὅταν εἰς πάθος ὑπὸ τοῦ λόγου προαχθῶσιν]. For we do not render decisions in the same way when we

> are pained as when we are happy or in the same way when we are feeling friendly and when we are feeling hostile. (1356a14–17)

There are several striking things in this passage. The first is the emphasis given to listeners (*akroates*). In demonstrative logic we can make our argument whether or not there is anyone to hear it, or better said, anyone to see its point, for, as we noted at the end of the previous chapter, a demonstrative *logos* or argument is at first internal (*eisô*) to the reasoner; he or she must have thought it through to its conclusion before presenting it to others. In contrast, a rhetorical argument, a *logos* which is a *pistis,* is, as we have seen, transactional. Paraphrasing Berkeley, if someone makes a rhetorical argument in a forest and there is no one there to hear it, there is no argument—*esse est audi.* In order for a *pistis* to be a *pistis* there must be interaction because neither the speaker nor the audience are removed, impartial spectators "up there"; rather, both are participants "down here" in the process of reaching an understanding that takes place not in them but between them. The second point worthy of note is the passive *proachthôsin,* "are brought to . . . "; for clearly, unlike learning to see a mathematical kind of truth, reaching an understanding here is not so much something we do as something we undergo. Not so much *agein,* doing, as *paschein,* suffering, is constitutive of it. We *are made* to feel a certain way; we *are put* into (*eis*) a certain *pathos* or frame of mind. Finally, the verb itself *prosagein eis,* literally "to impel or lead forward into something," negates any lingering pretension to intellectual detachment. In coming to understand a rhetorical argument or *pistis* we are precisely not detached and unmoved but engaged in, and changed by, what is happening to us and with us.

With all this Aristotle is clearly acknowledging that making practical decisions and passing judgments—again, unlike reaching theoretical insights—does not occur in an affective vacuum, but rather always takes place within an pathetical setting from which it and the argument leading up to it are indissociable. (Compare section 2.2 above and Heidegger on the *Stimmungen* or affective voicings in which we always already find ourselves hearing what we hear [SZ 134 ff.].) It follows, then, that the engendering of the right *pathos* is, in fact, not a mere "add-on" to the *pistis* at all but is, instead, intrinsic to it.

That the *logos* or argument, if it is to be a rhetorical *pistis,* is indissociably linked to *pathos* is further substantiated in book 2, chapter 1, at 1377b16 ff. After having concluded book 1 with the discussion of arguments by recourse to the *topoi* or "places" to find premises for rhetoric's enthymemes, Aristotle proceeds here to a consideration of what else a rhetorical argument, as opposed to a purely logical argument and even to a dialectical one, would require. For, as we have seen, the province of rhetoric coincides neither with the province of epistemic demonstration covered in the *Analytics* nor with the province of dialectic covered in the *Topics*. Even in regard to its own topics, the rhetorical art is the *antistrophê* or counterpart to the dialectical art, and not only because the topics in rhetoric generate enthymenes and examples rather than dialectic's full syllogisms and inductions, but because rhetoric has topics that concern *pathos* as well as *logos*. Indeed, because of their intrinsic affective dimension, most of the exemplary topics in book 2, chapter 23's random list are obviously inappropriate for dialectical argumentation. Almost without exception, they are made by existing individuals in a particular situation with its intrinsic pathetical "feel" to it, and many, in fact, are taken from tragic theater.

Hence, the exposition of the rhetorical art must necessarily, and not coincidentally, proceed to material peculiar to rhetoric, and we find Aristotle saying,

> Since rhetoric, on the other hand, aims at decisions [ἕνεκα κρίσεως ἐστίν]—for decisions decide between the courses of action advised and a verdict is also a decision—it is necessary not only to see to it that the argument will demonstrate what it should and be convincing, but also to predispose and ready the one judging and deciding [καὶ τὸν κριτὴν κατασκευάζειν]. For in regard to convincing it makes a great difference, most of all in courses of action advised, but in verdicts too, how the one speaking appears and what sort of disposition those themselves to whom he speaks assume he has towards them, and how too they themselves happen to be disposed. The sort of appearance the speaker gives is more useful in advising courses of action, whereas disposing the hearer in a certain way [τὸ δὲ διακεῖσθαί πως τὸν ἀκρατὴν] is more useful when verdicts are to be rendered. For things do not appear the same to those feeling friendly as to those feeling hostile. (1377b22–33)

We note, first, that in this passage the distinguishing characteristic of a rhetorical argument, as opposed even to a dialectical one, is its purpose. As opposed to demonstrative and dialectical arguments, both of which bring about theoretical insight, the task of rhetorical argument in either its consultative or judicial capacity, if not its epideictic one, is to bring about a practical decision (*krisis*). And the fact is that decisions, unlike insights, are not detached and impartial but partisan insofar as those deciding are part of the evolving situation that will be further defined by their decision. They too, this is to say, are affected by what will happen. This holds even for a judicial decision insofar as any interpretive application of right and wrong in deciding a particular case continues to define what is right and wrong both for the judge as well as for the accused. Hence, the kind of unmoved objectivity that characterizes a *theoretês* who sees something or even a *poietês* who makes something is not possible for a *kritês* who decides and renders judgments. As participants "there," the judges themselves are moved and changed by what occurs.

Put another way, in legal matters, and even more so in political and ethical ones, we do not have the subject matters of rhetoric "in view" before us; rather, *precisely as hearers* we always find ourselves already in the midst of them and inextricably caught up in them. What occurs here is thus not unaffected, unmoved intellect knowing static ideal truth; rather, it is also physical and sensuous experience. We decide in accord with what we are made to feel about the world, the world, this is to say, with which we are involved in undergoing the *pathêmata* and *pathê* that we feel (*paschomen*). Of necessity, then, an argument or *logos* that would influence our decision must "bring" us to share in the appropriate "gut" experience, and not just demonstrate something for us. It does not suffice for a rhetorical argument to merely show, point out, and demonstrate to us the "look" or *eidos* of something in relationship to the "look" of other things.

We should note, too, that Aristotle again recurs to *passive* constructions here, *pôs diakeisthai, pôs diakeimenoi.* The speaker and the hearer both have to *be* disposed, both have to have *been* put in a certain frame of mind, for the one to get the other to decide (*krinein*). For within this realm of wavering appearances, of things showing up first one way and and then another, how things appear to us depends on what disposition or "voicing" we find ourselves in when they appear, depends, this is to say, on how we "have been made ready" (*kateskeuasmetha*) to hear them. For Aristotle, then, there is in rhetoric, unlike the Platonic paradigm of demonstration and even unlike dialectic, no such thing as affective neutrality after all.

6.3 The Original (Homeric-Tragic) Pathetical Understanding of Argument and Its Reflection in Aristotle's *Rhetoric*

In this passage from the *Rhetoric* (1377b22–33), then, we begin to recover traces of an earlier conception of argument, *logos,* nearly obliterated by Platonic metaphysics. In Aristotle, as we will now see, there remain traces of the older, Homeric tradition that Platonism had sought so strenuously to displace with mathematical instruction leading to an incontrovertible insight. Let us first consult Homer and Sophocles, and then correlate what we have found with specific expositions in Aristotle's *Rhetoric.*

6.3.1 The *thumos, kardie,* and *phrenes* as the seat of visceral reasoning in Homer

For his part, Homer, in unreflectively maintaining the original psychosomatic unity in reasoning and argument, works with a cluster of nearly interchangeable words, *thumos, kradie,* and *phrenes,* all of which have to do with the chest or "guts," or *stêthê* as the seat of both feelings and thoughts, and which thereby annul any dissociation of the two that post-Platonic philosophers might want to make. Thus, we find in the *Iliad,* for instance, at 14.156, "she rejoiced in her heart [*thumos*]" or at 14.158, "he became hateful to her in her heart [*thumos*]," *but also,* at 1.193, "so long as he mulled this over in his mind [*phrenes*] and in his heart [*thumos*]," which indicates that the thought process of mulling over something is identically a matter of wits (*phrenes*) and heart (*thumos*). And, indeed, the Greek *hormaine* (mulled over), as a variation of *horman,* has a uniquely passionate urgency about it and is anything but cooly cerebral.

So it is too with *kradie*; for example, at 9.646 we find "But my heart [*kradie*] swells with rage," and at 2.171, "as suffering reached his heart [*kradie*] and spirit [*thumos*]," but also at 21.441, "How mindless [*anoon* (*nous*-less)] is the heart [*kradie*] you have." And in regard to *phrenes* we find "Thus anguished in his breast [*stêthê*] Agamemnon often did groan from the depths of his heart [*kradie*], his wits [*phrenes*] set quaking within," and at 13.487, "all of single heart [*thumos*] and mind [*phrenes*]." *Phrenes,* then, is just as much the place of intellection (compare Aristotle's understanding of *nous*) as it is the place of turbulent feeling: "Hector knew at once in his heart [*phrenes*]" (22.296), it is said, or "But you be not of such a mind [*me . . . noei*] towards me in your heart [*phrenes*]" (9.600).

Now just what is this visceral knowing in one's heart, this "gut" knowledge? And how is it communicated in spoken exchanges? Perhaps the best way to get at this original form of knowing is through the verbal cognate of *phrenes, phronein,* or to be of a certain mind as in *ison emoi phroneousa*: "he being of the same mind as I" (*Iliad* 15.50). Significantly, the place of *phronein* is in the *phrenes* and *thumos,* in the viscera and heart, as we see, for example, in "in their heart [*phrenes*] neither being mindful [*phroneontes*] of divine vengence nor having pity" (*Odyssey* 14.4), and also in "thinking [*phroneosa*] this in her heart [*thumos*]" (*Odyssey* 2.116). We also see that, accordingly, there is a fusion of mind and feeling in any *phronein,* as this fusion is displayed, for instance, in "Cheiron, being in a friendly frame of mind [*phila phroneon*]," or, in contrast, in "and (as) wolves and lambs are not like-minded in spirit [*homophrona thumon*], but forever are ill-intentioned [*kaka phroneousi*] towards each other, so it is not for me to love you nor you to love me" (*Iliad* 22.263–65).

However, the "gut" feeling in any *phronein* is perhaps best evidenced in Sophocles' *Ajax* at 942 where we find Tekmessa saying, "It is for you to believe [*dokein*] this misery, but for me, to know [*phronein*] it all too much." Even more succinct and poignant is Antigone's very physical response in *Oedepus at Colonus* (1741) to the chorus's "You both have just escaped an evil fate": *phroneô,* she says, "I know."

To see how traces of this earlier psychosomatic understanding of argument persist in Aristotle, let us take an example from Homer to which Aristotle explicitly alludes in his exposition of those *pathê* crucial to any *pistis* or convincing argument, namely the failure of Odysseus, Phoenix, and Ajax, Agamemnon's embassy to Achilles, to overcome his wrath (*mênis*) for Agamemnon's having taken his prize, Briseis, and dishonering him, and to move him to a decision to rejoin the war with the Trojans. In book 9 of the *Iliad,* line 309, and in response to the first of three empassioned but unsuccessful *logoi* and *pisteis,* namely Odysseus's, Achilles begins, "I must tell it as it is straightforwardly and *as I feel* [*phroneô*]." And in what follows Achilles makes clear precisely that how he feels has not been changed one bit by what Odysseus has just said.

Just this is the point: Odysseus's *logos* fails as a *pistis,* fails to convince, *but precisely not because its enthymemes lack logical validity.* On the contrary, they are, here in summary form, cogent enough: "If you do not rejoin the war, our ships and we ourselves will be destroyed" (9.230–31), so "Up with you" (247); or "You cannot undo what will have happened if you do not rejoin the war," so "Take heed long beforehand" (250–51); or "Your father, Peleus, urged kindheartedness [*philophrosunê*] instead of anger" (255), so "Desist and let go the anger that pains the heart [*thumalgeia*]" (259); or "You will have great wealth, you will have your love, Briseis, back unviolated, you will have great honor, you will have occasion to best your rival, Hector," so "Rejoin the war" (261–307).

No, Achilles' response, even if it does provide a refutation (*lusis*) of the last of these enthymemes in countering, by the topic of "the more and less," that a long and peaceful life back home is a greater good than any of the rewards from Agamemnon that Odysseus can promise, shows nevertheless that Odysseus's speech has failed precisely because it does not get Achilles to think and feel (*phronein*) differently in his *thumos, kradie, and phrenes.* Its failure, then, is patho/logical: it is not on the level of any pure *logos,* in itself, but of *pathos* and *logos.*

Indeed, Odysseus knew all along that it was on the "gut" level that his speech must work: "These things he [Agamemnon] would carry out for you *if you would but change from your anger,*" he says at 299. Achilles' enmity, his mistrust and hatred of Agamemnon, and above all his rage at Agamemnon's slighting of him remain, despite the "multi-inventive" (*polumechanos*) Odysseus's best efforts, unchanged—or perhaps in part because of them, for the epithet *polumechanos,* by which Achilles, too, names Odysseus (308), scarcely establishes that either he or his argument is trustworthy (*pistos*). Achilles is unmoved in his heart and, hence, still totally untrusting and unconvinced: he remains *apistos.*[5]

Odysseus, of course, had first sought to displace the feelings of enmity and anger that Achilles has for Agamemnon by communicating the feeling of kinship (*philophrosunê*) (256): *Chair', Axhileu;* "To your health, Achilles," he begins (225). But in the end, and above all, he tries to evoke in the place of enmity and anger the feeling of pity (*eleos*): "But if Atreus's son is too much hated [*apêchtheto*] in your heart [*kêr*], he and his gifts," says Odysseus, "at least take pity on [*eleaire*] all the Achaeans beset along the front" (300–303).

Now, pity, *as Aristotle points out,* is sharing in the fear (*phobos*) felt by someone else: "Such things as people fear for themselves are what they take pity for, if they happen to another" (1386b27–28). And fear, in turn, is "a pain or disturbance stemming from our picturing a destructive or painful evil just about to happen" (21–23). Hence, to evoke pity, Odysseus is concerned throughout his speech to communicate as vividly as he can the magnitude of the calamity staring the Achaeans in the face and the fear he, as one of them, feels: "we look upon an all too great grief, favorite of Zeus, and are afraid," he begins (229–30). *By Aristotle's own account,* we remark, this is just what he should do: it follows, Aristotle maintains, "that those who enhance their effect by gesture, voicings [*phonai*], and dress, and, in general, by their dramatic delivery [*hupokrisis*] necessarily evoke pity more. For by putting the bad thing before our eyes, they make it seem near, as either just about to happen, as it were, or even having happened already" (1386a28-b6). Consequently, Odysseus's "narration" (232–46) must be anything but the dispassionate statement of the facts that Aristotle had once said should suffice for inducing a favorable decision (*krisis*) (1354a16–17). On the contrary, things are appropriately portrayed as unsurpassingly frightful. Fires and lightning are said to accompany a now indomitable Hector's truculent raging about in anticipation of the dawn, when he and the Trojans might descend upon the ships, set them ablaze, and slaughter the Achaeans driven from them by the smoke. This impending catastrophe is set off all the more starkly by Odysseus's evocation, at the end of his recounting, of "horse-pasturing Argos," the safe and peaceful homeland. Precisely as Aristotle tells us, "For the most part it is fearful [*phoberon*] to be at the disposal of another" (1382b5), in particular one (like Hector) whose "virtue is outraged" (1382b1) and who is capable of doing something out of enmity and anger (1382a33–34). So, concludes Odysseus, "In terror I dread these things in my heart [*phrenes*]" (244).

Achilles, however, is deaf to all this, as Odysseus knew deep down that he would be: "if you would but hear me," he interjects at 263, as if he senses that Achilles isn't listening. Thus, there is no change of heart in this listener who will not listen and will not be convinced to let his anger go (see 260). As a consequence—and precisely not because of any "logical" incoherence—the *pistis* must fail. To be sure, Odysseus may have succeeded in partially ingratiating the rest of the Achaeans and even himself with Achilles, for Achilles can counsel and exhort "the others" to sail away for home (416–17), and his doing so presupposes some element of *philia* or friendship that he feels for them. But with Agamemnon, he says, no taking counsel is possible any more: "I will contrive with him no counsel [*boulê*]" (374). For to Achilles, Agamemnon, and quite possibly Odysseus too, is still a hated enemy and no friend: "For hateful [*echthros*] to me like the gates of Hades is he who conceals in his heart [*phrenes*] one thing and says another" (312–13), a remark pointed to Odysseus even if ostensibly referring to Agamemnon. Agamemnon, in any event, is not to be trusted: "He deceived me . . . and he will not convince [*peisei*] me" (344–45). And, indeed, no convincing (*peithein*) is possible where the one who would convince the other is hated and not trusted (*pistos*). No *logos* here can be a *pistis* that convinces the heart, for it cannot communicate the prerequisite *pathos*: "Not even in this way would Agamemnon convince [*peise*] my heart [*thumon*] until he has made good all this outrage that pains the heart [*thumalgeia*]" (386–87).

6.3.2 Aristotle's reception of the Homeric understanding of argument

Ultimately, since Odysseus has to speak for Agamemnon and not only for himself, the task assigned him is impossible, and this, we remark again, *by Aristotle's own standards regarding the prerequisites for an effective pistis, namely, together with good enthymemes, communication of the right pathos.* If we follow Aristotle, it is clear that in regard to *pathos*, Odysseus's strategy had to be to displace enmity with friendship and anger with pity, but given the circumstances, he lacks all means to accomplish this. For as concerns the prerequisite feeling of the audience for the speaker, friendship as opposed to enmity and hatred, there are, Aristotle tells us (1378a6 ff.), three constituent traits of those for whom we feel friendship and because of which we have faith (*pisteuomen*) in what the speaker says and find the speaker worthy of belief (*pistos*), and this "*quite apart from his demonstrations*" (ἔξω τῶν ἀπδείξεων) (8; emphasis added). These traits are his or her *phronêsis* or discernment, *aretê* or ethical excellence, and *eunoia* or good intentions. All of these are required, but try as he might, Odysseus, for obvious reasons, cannot establish even one of them on behalf of Agamemnon, who in Achilles' eyes has behaved deceitfully (344) and outrageously (369). Compare, also 345: "I know him well . . ."

As concerns the other *pathê*, in particular, calmness (*praotês*), and ultimately pity, as opposed to anger (*orgê*), Odysseus is equally disadvantaged, and again, remarkably, disadvantaged by Aristotle's own standards. For how one decides, we know, depends on how one feels (1378a20) because, as Aristotle says, "the same things do not appear the same to one who feels friendly and to one who hates, nor to those who are angered and to those peaceably disposed" (1377b31–32). We have just seen that for Achilles there is no possibility of feeling friendship toward Agamemnon, and that he decides, accordingly, against Agamemnon's offer and Odysseus's argument. But perhaps we have not yet considered the most significant obstacle for Odysseus here, namely, the anger that Achilles will not "let go."

Aristotle tells us—and here the reference is specifically to Achilles (see 1378b31 ff.) and is not just coincidentally applicable to him—that anger is in response to a slight or belittling which can take three forms, contempt, insult, or outrage (*kataphronêsis, empêreasmos, hubris*) (1378a15 ff.). Achilles has suffered all three, though in his case it is outrage that Aristotle singles out, quoting the *Iliad*, 1.356: "He has dishonered me and seized my rightful prize and keeps it," and the last line of 9.646–48, "Yet still my heart [*kradie*] swells up in anger, when I remember / The disgrace that he wrought upon me before the Argives / The son of Atrius, as if I were some dishonored vagabond" (Lattimore trans.). And, Aristotle explains, "Dishonoring is a kind of outrage, and the one dishonoring does indeed slight. For what is valued not at all, neither as good or as bad, has no honor at all" (1378b29–31). (See Agamemnon to Achilles, 1.180: "I have no regard for you" [σέθεν δ' οὐκ ἀλεγίζω].)

As long, namely, as Achilles' *pathos* of anger is not to be calmed (*praunesthai*; compare Aristotle, 1380a5), there is no chance that Odysseus's exhortatives to decide—"up," "take thought," "desist," "let go," and so forth—will result in the decision or *krisis* he seeks, no chance, that is, that the mere *logos* divorced from *pathos*, the reasoning by enthymemes and examples, will carry. For, as is characteristic of rhetoric in distinction from demonstration and even dialectic, the conclusion drawn is not in the indicative but in the imperative; not a change of mind but a change of heart is sought, not intellectual assent to a proposition but voluntary consent to an exhortation. Hence, clearly, *and by Aristotle's own standards*, any *logos* in rhetoric, any *pistis*, must be not only *apodeiktikos* or demonstrative, but also *pistos* (1377b23) if it is to serve the purpose of rhetoric, which is not to lead to an insight by instruction but to lead to a *krisis* or decision by convincing. That means that it must simultaneously predispose (*kataskeuazein*) the listeners in such a way as to make them receptive (1377b24). For, save for the requisite *rhaistônê* and *diagôgê*, noetic insights in response to a demonstration do not depend on the *pathê* prevailing in the listeners, but phronetic decisions in response to an imperative do depend on the *pathê* and, consequently, so do the *logoi* or arguments that would induce them.

Thus, we see, precisely when we apply Aristotle's own exposition, that Odysseus has only hopelessly inadequate means to calm Achilles' anger and, hence, to convince him to decide to return to the battle. To be sure, in regard to externals, Aristotle writes, "it is plain that those disposed in the opposite way to being angered are calm, as when at play, when laughing, when at a feast, when in prosperity, when enjoying success, when full and satisfied, and when, on the whole, feeling no pain" (1380b2–4). For pain is an extrinsic physical precondition of anger (1378a32), and "hence the suffering, the poor, those in love, those who thirst, and, in general, those not succeeding in getting what they desire are given to anger (1379a13–15). Viewed in the light of this Aristotelian analysis, Odysseus can be said to have chosen the opitimum time—the end of a lavish meal, of which he reminds Achilles in his introductory toast: "We have good things in abundance to feast on" (9.223–24). He chooses a time, this is to say, when Achilles should have been momentarily relieved of the desire for Briseis, a desire in which he feels himself thwarted and which, because of the pain attending his inability to satisfy it, predisposed him to anger in the first place.

But in regard to the possible means listed by Aristotle by which the speech itself might change Achilles' anger, Odysseus has virtually nothing to work with. For he can portray Agamemnon neither as not having slighted Achilles (1380a10), nor as not having intended to do what he did (11–12), nor as sorry for what he has done (13), nor as humbling himself and not gainsaying Achilles (21), nor as someone to be feared or someone to make him feel ashamed (33). Indeed, as Achilles's response to Odysseus makes all too evident, Agamemnon stands opposed to every one of these. At best, to predispose Achilles to calmness Odysseus might try to show that Agamemnon is now inclined to grant Achilles favors (see Aristotle, 1380b33). But given the history of his deceit, that would surely not be convincing either.

In short, by Aristotle's own criteria, Odysseus's argument fails not because of the invalidity of its enthymemes nor any inappropriateness of its examples, but precisely because Odysseus cannot predispose Achilles to feel differently. Thus, Achilles may be said to *see* the plight of his comrades clearly enough, but not to *hear* the exhortation addressed to him. He has not changed his mind, for he has not been convinced in his heart.

Plainly, then, as the remarkable applicability of Aristotle's *Rhetoric* to Homer displays, Aristotle himself still knows and acknowledges an *intrinsic* role of *pathos* in the success or failure of any *pistis* or rhetorical *logos* even if he seems at the start to dismiss *pathos* as a merely extrinsic (*exô*) add-on and accessory (*prosthêkê*).[6] Thus, Plato's attempt to purify argument of adulteration by the affects and to eliminate Homeric influences from our understanding of argument has both been resumed and simultaneously destroyed by Aristotle, who in part, at least, perpetuates the Homeric tradition in his *Rhetoric.* If nothing else, Aristotle's ten chapters of brilliant phenomenological exposition of the *pathê* (2.2–11), chapters which Heidegger found so compelling (see SZ 138–39), make clear the ineradicabilty of Homer from his thought.

6.4 Embodied and Disembodied Argument in Aristotle's *Rhetoric*: Patho/logical Imitation in Voice versus Eidetic Signification

Now, what does this perpetuation in Aristotle of Homer's original understanding of argument say concerning the embodiment of rhetorical argument? To what extent does the original patho/logical fusion in rhetoric imply a fusion of the intellectual and physical? The answer is already partially given, insofar as the element of the self that receives rhetorical argument has been shown to be the heart, viscera, or even "guts" that hear, not a detached intellect that sees. Using a destructive reading of Aristotle's *Rhetoric* as a basis, we need now to "lay bare" and "lay out" hermeneutically just how communication takes place on this heart-to-heart, visceral, or "gut" level, to "lay out," this is to say, how one psychosomatic unity engages another in original, patho/logical argument.

To begin with, we should note that any *logos* demonstrating how things stand only shows us *what* the case is a case of. Here we could say, with Plato, that in having left particulars behind and in speaking of universal essences of things, their quiddities or "whatnesses," the speech used signifies static *eidê,* the conceptual "looks" of things, and establishes their relationships of sameness as, or difference from, other *eidê* (see *The Sophist* 249e f. on *tauton* and *thateron*); speech here establishes which classes of things are included in, or excluded from, which other classes, as in "all x are y" or "no p are q."

Put another way, in this kind of speaking, which really only translates writing or the graphic significations of the *eidê* "written in the soul" (*Phaedrus* 278a), there is no imitation, but only designation or signification. Hence when we say that "This is two, and two is an even number, so this is an even number," or "This square is a straight-sided figure and no straight-sided figures are circles, so this square is not a circle," none of the sounds we make have any imitative value. Accordingly, the voicing and speaking of the words "two," "even number," "straight-sided figure," and "circle" is—as long as we are doing mathematics and not some odd sort of poetry—wholly irrelevant, and our argument might better have been written on a surface, and seen and read rather than spoken aloud and heard. (See the exposition of the *Phaedrus* in section 4.3 above.)

If, on the other hand, we wish to say something not about static *eidê* but about the changing world of particular perceived physical things, for example, "The leaves are rustling in the wind," using, not coincidentally, the more "gutsy" Anglo Saxon and not the more "intellectual" Latinate English, what we say has a double valence to it. To be sure, by abstracting from the voiced words, we could still "read" them as a statement of some "objective" state of affairs. In this case we would continue to treat each word as a sign or index of some essence for which, in order to be more precise and scientific, we might better substitute a technical term, usually from a "dead" language like Latin or Greek, for which we have lost all ear, and that literally terminates any indeterminacy and ambivalence in our language. (The doctor who treated me for a pinched nerve was surprised to learn that his technical term *stenosis* actually meant such an inexact thing as a "narrowing.") Ultimately, however, we would want to replace all imprecise qualitative descriptions, which, after all, even the Latin and Greek terms still are, with spatial coordinates and quantitative measurements.

But if the ambivalence of our original words is left alone, they might lead us in another direction. They might be taken as sound that imitates some experienced perception, either directly and onomapoetically, as does "rustling," or indirectly by sometimes extended and no longer traceable metaphorical metonymies from one field of sense perception and feeling to another (see section 6.1 above on the *Cratylus*). Either way, here the sound counts, and to some extent we have entered the realm of the poetic.

Now, we should note that such imitation in sound is never of some "pure" thing detached from its pathetical setting; the sound, in other words, does not imitate the thing as we see it and classify it intellectually; rather, it imitates what we feel of the experienced particular thing and, at the same time, how we feel about it in our *phrenes, kardia, thumos,* or "guts." Indeed, if we were to approach the sound only as an imitation of the thing as we know it cognitively, we would be on our way to abstracting from it and already moving in the reverse direction, namely toward objectification and terminological signification, and this is precisely what happens in the *Cratylus* dialogue. On the contrary, it must be stressed that, in contrast to the static *eidos,* the named thing as it sounds to us audibly is never "purely" cognitive but always has intrinsic affective quality about it. Hence, as Heidegger has shown us, it is mistaken from the start to see the affective quality as our own subjective, "emotive" imposition on an objective reality in itself, for this is a derivative understanding arrived at only *after* terminological abstraction has taken hold, an abstraction made possible only by a "dimming down" of the *pathê* to an affective neutrality (see SZ 138).

Experienced from our original standpoint within our physical perception of physical appearances, any such dualism as cognitive/emotive collapses. For not only do the perceptual qualities of red, wet, cool, rough, hot, and so forth, all of which have an inevitable affective dimension, belong to the thing in itself as it shows itself in our speaking of it, but also the more obviously affective qualities like frightful or calm. Every named thing has a certain "feel" to it, and contrary to modern objectivism, the *sea* is calm and not the people who perceive it. Indeed, the affective and perceptual in anything we feel are indissociable, and the imitation in the voiced name is of both together as a unity. As Odysseus's vivid narration of the catastrophe threatening the Achaeans shows, no word communicating how things sound to us, and, by metaphor and metonymy, look, taste, smell, and feel to the touch, is without its positive, neutral, or negative affective charge. Today's quantititative and "unfeeling" neutral affective charge, as in *cold, dry, hard* casualty statistics, would be, were we not inured to it, the most shockingly affective charge of all.

Now, since, as Aristotle agrees (see 1403b20 ff., 1404a20 ff.), it is voiced sound that by imitation conveys this perceptual affective reality to another person, voiced sound that communicates how it feels and how we feel about it, what Odysseus's narration sounds like is intrinsic to his communication to Achilles. This means that not only what (*quid*) he says is crucial to the conviction he seeks to communicate, but also at which time in the sequence of his speech he says it (*quo quidque loco*) and how (*quo modo*) (see Cicero, *Orator* 14.43).

With these last two we have come to a consideration of what Aristotle calls *taxis*, *lexis*, and *hupokrisis*, of arrangement, on the one hand, and diction and delivery, on the other. Aristotle treats these in book 3, all the while, to be sure, he characteristically renounces them as concerns forced on us only by the intellectual inferiority of our audience:

> Besides, diction has the reputation of being a vulgar matter, as well it ought to have. Nevertheless, the whole concern of rhetoric being with appearances, we must deal with it, and not because it is correct to do so, since by rights we should seek in regard to our speech nothing more than to avoid either inflicting pain or causing delight, but because we are constrained to do so. By rights, namely, the case ought to be fought out by means of the facts themselves, and, hence, other things extrinsic to demonstration [τἆλλα ἔξω τοῦ ἀποδεῖξαι] are beside the point. But even so, diction can accomplish a lot, as we have said, given the bad state of the listener. To be sure, in any instruction [ἐν πάσῃ διδασκαλίᾳ] matters of diction do play a necessary albeit small role; for it makes some difference in regard to making things plain if they are put one way or another, but not such a great difference. (1403b36–1404a10)

The conclusion of this passage is already familiar to us: "All these things," says Aristotle, "are matters of the imagination and concern the listener, and for that reason no one teaches geometry by means of them [διὸ οὐδεὶς οὕτω γεωμετρεῖν διδάσκει]" (1404a11–12). We note the continued predominance here of the mathematical paradigm in Aristotle's thinking on rhetoric: "by rights" any *logos*, and even if it is a rhetorical *pistis*, should be a demonstration or *apodeixis*. It should be instruction or *didaskalia*, and instruction in the way that geometry is instructed. Anything more is only a concession to our listeners.

However, this is only part of the story, for as in book 2 so also in book 3 is an earlier understanding of rhetoric in fact preserved even in Aristotle's very rejection of it, namely the understanding of rhetoric in Homer and Sophocles, from whom Aristotle ends up taking his examples. Thus, book 3 on arrangement, diction, and delivery is very much like book 2 on the *pathê*. For in starting with an apparently obligatory dismissal of the subject matter that he will treat, Aristotle goes on to treat it with extraordinary care and incisiveness. In other words, we find in book 3 the same seminal ambivalence that we find throughout the *Rhetoric*: sometimes the rhetorical *pistis* or means of conviction is reduced to a demonstration, and other times, in what almost seems to be a retraction of this reduction, the ways in which a *pistis* must in fact go beyond any *demonstration* are carefully and subtly elaborated. So it is here, too, in regard to arrangement, diction, and delivery.

As we have seen, insofar as conviction or *pistis* involves three *pithana* or elements of conviction, *logos, êthos,* and *pathos,* and not just *logos,* conviction inevitably goes beyond logical demonstration. Furthermore, in matters of *pathos* the concern is with a visceral "guts" to "guts" or heart-to-heart communication to the listeners or hearers and, consequently, with the phrasing and physical voicing (*phonê*) of what they hear. Seen this way, delivery or *hupokrisis* is thus crucial. But when conviction is reduced to *apodeiksis, pathos* becomes incidental and the phonic and hypocritic are dismissed as adventitious and superfluous. For in this case the concern ceases to be with what the speech sounds like physically and becomes entirely a matter of its intellectual clarity or *sapheia* to one who must *see* the result of a demonstration, not *hear* an appeal to the "gut."

The point for us is that though Aristotle leans heavily toward the reduction of conviction to demonstration, with the consequent diminishment and neglect of both the affective as well as the correlative phonic-acoustical and hypocritic, he nevertheless preserves strands of a concern for these that lies "closer to the origin," as Heidegger would say; and as his extensive exemplification with epic and tragic poets displays, he never dismisses them entirely. Thus, we will see once again that with Aristotle we are able, despite his continuing allegiance to Platonism, to get back to the original form of argument and to lay this out hermeneutically. For in Aristotle conviction remains more than demonstration, after all, and traces persist of argument in the way as it had been originally in Homer, Aeschylus, and Sophocles. In the end, in Aristotle all rhetoric must still be embodied in a physical voicing. Even "written diction" (*lexis graphikê* [1413b3]) is to be composed with an ear for what it will sound like when spoken out loud, as well as an eye for its logical symmetry and clarity. (Otherwise, we note, it would be as much a contradiction in terms as is the expression "literary rhetoric.")

6.4.1 The *Rhetoric* on delivery and diction (*hupokrisis* and *lexis*)

Let us proceed, then, to a close examination of the text in question, book 3 of the *Rhetoric.* In the opening chapter (1403b6 f.) Aristotle rephrases his earlier characterization of the three *pithana* or aspects of convincing someone of something. He now speaks of attaining conviction in regard to *pathos* "by making the judges themselves feel a certain way" (τῷ αὐτοί τι πεπονθέναι οἱ κρίνοντες) (1403b11), in regard to *êthos*, "by the speakers' being received in a certain way" (τῷ ποιούς τινας ὑπολαμβάνειν τοὺς λέγοντας) (12), and, in regard to the *logos*, "by a thing's having been demonstrated" (τῷ ἀποδεδεῖχθαι) (13). However, to this list of the means of convicing he now adds *lexis* and *taxis*, diction and arrangement, with no indication that these additional items are any less intrinsic than the others. For, he says, it is not sufficient to have merely grasped "*what* things one should say [ἃ δεῖ λέγειν]; rather, one must also necessarily have grasped *how* to say them [ταῦτα ὡς δεῖ εἰπεῖν]" (15–16; emphasis added; compare above on Cicero's *quid, quo quidque loco,* and *quo modo*). He then submits that first to be considered is "how the facts by themselves [αὐτὰ τὰ πράγματα] contribute to conviction" (19), but, second, how "the setting out of these in appropriate diction" (τὸ ταῦτα τῇ λέξει διαθέσθαι) (20) contributes to conviction and, third, "the matter of delivery [τὰ περὶ τὴν ὑπόκρισιν], which, though *it has the greatest power [of conviction] of all,* has not yet been taken up" (21–22; emphasis added). Consideration of declamation had come late even to the tragedians and rhapsodists, he says, because the poets had recited their own poetry, but now "it is clear that *such things are as much a concern of rhetoric as they are of poetry*" (24–25; emphasis added).

Accordingly, he then provides a specific account of delivery:

> It itself lies in the voice [ἐν τῇ φωνῇ], how it ought to be used in regard to [communicating] each feeling [πρὸς ἕκαστον πάθος], for instance, when to use a loud voice or when to use a soft voice or when to use a voice in between these, or how to make use of tone and pitch, for instance, when to use a high shrill voice or a deep voice or a voice in between these, and what rhythms to use for each of the feelings to be communicated. For three things are under consideration here; these are volume, intonation, rhythm [ταῦτα δ' ἐστὶ μέγαθος ἁρμονία ῥυθμός]. (25–30)

Having said this much, however, Aristotle now inserts the charactistic concession and qualification: all these things, he says, have become important only because of the sad state of the citizenry, a state displayed in the very fact that those who have mastered delivery are the ones who currently prevail in political debate (31–35). To be sure, it is the poets, he says, who, "naturally," initiated the concern with voice, "for word names are imitations [τὰ γὰρ ὀνόματα μιμήματα ἐστίν], and of all the parts of the body available, voice is the most able to imitate" (1404a20–22). But here, instead of elaborating this seminal assertion and arguing the importance of voice for rhetoric, Aristotle turns it into an *a fortiori* argument *against* the contemporary concern with voice: if even the poets, who initiated it and whose concern it properly is, have now abandoned it, should not rhetoricians abandon it too (24–36)? Indeed, if one could pursue rhetoric in the way it ought to be pursued, voice would be beside the point, he says, "for the diction of argument is different from the diction of poetry" (28–29).

Implied here is his central contention that, like mathematical words and unlike poetical words, rhetorical words are *not* imitations for our imagination, not onomatopoetic, metaphoric, metonymic, word names at all, but signs and indices (*sêmeia*). For the task of rhetorical words, he maintains, is precisely not to communicate the *pathê* embedded in the sound of a word and to engage and move hearers, but to signify the facts clearly (*saphôs*) and transmit them in such a way that detached onlookers may see how things stand. Paradigmatic would be a statement like the one taken as an example in Plato's *Theaetetus*, "7 + 5 = 12," any voicing of which, as we have observed, is at best wholly irrelevant and at worst an impediment to the transmission sought. By this argument, we note, the content of Lincoln's sonorous "four score and seven" with its assonances and alliterations would best be transmitted with the written sign "87."[7] Indeed, we find in the *Rhetoric* at 1404b1 f. "let the excellence of diction be defined as being clear [ὡρίσθω λέξεως ἀρετὴ σαφῆ εἶναι]—an indication of this desideratum being that an argument, if it does not make things plain [ἐὰν μὴ δηλοῖ], does not perform its task."

There is, to be sure, another consideration besides the clarity of one's diction: without sacrificing clarity, diction must, Aristotle tells us, hit the mean between a lowly, humble style, which is too commonplace to gain attention, and an over-elevated style, which, aside from putting people off, only obscures what one is saying (1404b6 f.). Diction should be slightly unusual or "strange" but not excessively so. Even so, even these considerations of the level of diction have to do only with achieving so much aesthetic pleasantness (*to hedu*) as is possible without diminishing one's clarity. They do not, in other words, have to do with anything intrinsically affective. When, for instance, Aristotle says that the level of one's style must accord with one's station and not be out of character (1404b16 f.), he himself becomes a veritable sophist in arguing that all this is a matter of appearances, the contrivance of which, unfortunately, is forced on us by the audience's inferiority and should be cleverly concealed. There is even a tangential reference to voice here, but the hypocritic slips into the hypocritical when it is said, approvingly it seems, that like other actors (*hupokrites*) Theodorus can make his voice "seem to be" that of the character he is portraying (23 f.). Aristotle's point is that, analogously, our diction should *seem* to be that of the character we wish to be perceived as having.

Perhaps most exemplary, however, of Aristotle's tendency to reduce the "gut-to-gut," "heart-to-heart" comunication of felt reality from speaker to hearer, to the eviscerated transfer of insight from one disembodied mind to another, is his treatment of rhythm. It will be recalled that rhythm along with intonation and volume were the three principal elements of delivery and the communication of the *pathê* by imitation in voice (1403b26–31). But at 1408b21 ff. where the discussion of rhythm is resumed, the only indication that it has any affective function at all is found in the systematic exclusion of rhythms like the trochaic tetrameter, which, with its Dionysiac "rolling pulse" (*trocheros rhuthmos*), is too close to the indecent cordax dance and might move us all too much (1408b36–1409a1). Once again something that ought to be considered primarily in regard to its affective consequences, here rhythm, is treated, instead, only in regard to the aesthetic pleasure and mnemonic assistance that it provides.

Also striking in this passage, given Aristotle's general rejection of Pythagorean mathematical thinking in his physics and ethics, is his recourse to the Platonist-Pythagorean language of *to peras, to apeiron,* and *ho arithmos,* the limit, the unlimited or indeterminate, and the number, which sets a limit to what otherwise might run on into indeterminacy (compare the *Philebus* 23b ff.). If, on the whole, Aristotle's concern with the nonmathematical subject matters of life science, ethics, and politics leads him away from thinking in these terms, surprisingly in matters of rhetorical diction, where they would seem most misplaced of all, he returns to them. In maintaining that diction must be rhythmic without being metric, he says, "What is lacking in rhythm is unlimited; it is necessary, however, that limits be set, but not by meter. For what is unlimited is displeasing and incomprehensible. But by number everything is limited [ἀηδὲς γὰρ καὶ ἄγνωστον τὸ ἄπειρον. περαίνεται δὲ ἀριθμῷ πάντα]" (1408b26–28). On this account rhythm has, to be sure, an aesthetic function to insure that the listeners are not displeased by what they hear, but above all it has a cognitive function: only what is limited by number can be *seen* as a whole and comprehended, hence if our diction or manner of speaking is to be understood, it must be delimited in this way, albeit never exactly (32). Quite in keeping with the separation of the mental and physical we have seen, for example, in Plato's *Phaedo,* here any bodily affects that rhythm might communicate in order to get us to *hear and do* what is being urged are left out of consideration, and attention is paid solely to the instructional uses rhythm might have in getting us to *see and comprehend* what something is.

The same thing can be said when Aristotle gives preference to periodic diction, which turns back on itself, *lexis katastrammenê,* as opposed to the diction of ordinary speaking, *lexis eiromenê* (1409a22–1409b6).

For the diction of ordinary speaking is *aêdes dia to apeiron* (displeasing because of its unendingness)—we get tired as long as we do not see the end or *peras* ahead—whereas periodic diction has a beginning and end and, consequently, an overseeable size. Thus, it is both pleasurable (*hêdeia*) and nicely instructive (*eumathês*), pleasurable, because it is limited (*peperanthai*), and nicely instructive because, having a definite numerical measure, it is easy to remember. Within periods, we should note, too, antithetical phrasing is to be preferred over parallel phrasing for precisely the same reasons, preferred, that is, precisely *not* because of the acoustical effect of this diachronic trope, *not* because of its antiphonal tensions and cadences voiced over time in rhythm, tone, and volume, but because of its 1:1 ratios and envisionable symmetry (see 1409b33–1410a23).

This "numerical" effect of antithesis can be heightened by superimposing on it the scheme of *parisosis* (isocolon), which is to say, by making the two *kôla* or sections equal (*isa*) in length, and heightened even more, by further superimposition of the scheme of *paromoiosis*, that is, by making either the beginnings of both *kôla* alike, as in anaphora, or the ends, as in epistrophe; this is accomplished either by repeating the same word, as in Aristophanes' *agron . . . agron* (a field . . . a field) or giving different words similar endings as in Homer's *dôrêtoi* (presentings) . . . *pararrêtoi* (pleadings) (see 1410a24–1410b5). That the similarity here is a repetition of *voicing* which might communicate acoustically a particular *pathos* to the hearers of it is passed over, again typically, without mention. For, once again, Aristotle's concern is solely with envisionable numerical proportion. It is as if we were not to hear poetry and speech but to envision the patterns behind it, much as Pythagorean students of harmony were not to hear musical chords but envision the ratios obtaining between their components.

So far, then, Aristotle has consistently adhered to Plato's attack on the sophist perversion of rhetoric and even Plato's turn from the temporal/acoustical to the spatial/visual. He has consistently sought, this is to say, to reduce rhetorical conviction to instructional demonstration by mathematizing it and stripping it of the thing with which the sophists had primarily concerned themselves, specifically, *pathos* and the communication of *pathos* in voice with the appropriate audible diction, and declamation. But in the ensuing discussion of *asteia*, a kind of sophistication and urbane cleverness, and *eudokima*, or that which earns one fame and approval (1410b6 ff.), notable inconsistencies in Aristotle's heretofore very Platonic project begin to appear.

At first, the criteria for assessing *asteia* and *eudokima* seem to be the familiar ones, namely that they are pleasurable (*hêdu*) and that they contribute nicely to instruction (*to manthanein*). In that they bring flashes of insight seemingly effortlessly, they are pleasant, "For instruction that is accomplished easily is naturally pleasant to everyone. Words, however, are what signify something; hence those words that produce insight in us are the most pleasant [τὰ δὲ ὀνόματα σημαίνει τι, ὥστε ὅσα τῶν ὀνομάτωον ποιεῖ ἡμῖν μάθησιν, ἥδιστα]"(1410b10–12), and "It follows necessarily then that diction and enthymemes such as produce quick insight in us [ὅσα ποιεῖ ἡμῖν μάθησιν ταχεῖαν] are urbane and clever" (20–21). Here, too, we note the obvious shift in attention from rhetoric that convinces someone to decide on something, to instruction that gets someone to see something and, correlatively, from speech as word names and naming, to speech as signs and signification. The use of *manthanein* and *mathêsis* and, moreover, the linking of these words with *gnôsis* (cognition) and *dianoia* (discursive thought) at 25–26 make clear that, just as *dianoia* displaces *melos* or melody in the considerations of the *Poetics* (see section 6.5 below), concern with the cognitive and logical displaces concern with the tonal and vocal here.

For our part, we have seen that word names call the things of the world into acoustical presence by naming them in the way, for instance, that recitation of Homer's poetry calls up the world of the Greeks. Beyond this, we have seen along with this naming of things there also takes place, in indissociable conjunction with it, the communication of the tonal affective setting, the "voicing" in which alone these named things can first assume their being, that is to say, be "what they sound like." Word names, as even Aristotle allows, imitate and communicate the *pathê* acoustically, by voice, to those who hear these names spoken (1403b26–28). See, for example, *Iliad* 1.34, and the oft-cited "with the sea crashing" (πολυφλοίσβοιο θαλάσσης), which communicates acoustically the turbulent setting of the priest Chryses' prayer to Apollo. Thus far in the discussion of the *asteion* and *eudokimon*, however, neither what words imitate nor what they sound like is the concern, rather only what they signify and put before our eyes (*pro ommatôn*; 1411a26 ff., 1411b4 ff.). The sole pathetical consideration is the reduced and wholly ancillary one of pleasurableness: only because the *asteion* and *eudokimon* provide quick insight are they pleasurable or, more to the point, not unpleasant (*aêdes*) and disruptive, for as we read at the beginning of book 3, in regard to the stimulation of *pathê*, "we should seek nothing more for an argument than that it neither pains nor delights" its audience (1404a4–5). Thus far, then, there is nothing new here.

However, the *asteion* and the *eudokimon*, Aristotle goes on to point out, are best evidenced in antithetical diction, to be sure, but, also, he says, "in word names when these are metaphorical" (τοῖς δ' ὀνόμασιν, ἐὰν ἔχῃ μεταφοράν) (1410b31–32). He then proceeds to qualify this assertion by saying that this last applies only when the metaphors "are neither too far afield, in which case the sense of them is hard to see, nor commonplace, *in which case they would leave us unmoved* [οὐδὲν γὰρ ποιεῖ πάσχειν]" (33–34; emphasis added). Let us first consider the point that good metaphors which are not far-fetched provide insight. Like all the vocabulary of approval-winning diction, metaphorical words, says Aristotle, should put things "before our eyes, for we must see action as if it were being done now rather than as if it were about to happen" (1410b34–35). This occurs, for instance, in the sayings of Aision that "they [the Atheneans] had emptied their city into Sicily" "so that Greece cried out," both of which metaphors, "emptying" and "crying out," says Aristotle, put the event "before our eyes" (1411a25–28). Metaphors of this type make things present and contribute thereby to *energeia* or "actuality" of diction (see 1410b36).

But surely this is not all they do. Indeed, as was the case when we examined the first chapters of book 2 on the *pathê*, the examples Aristotle chooses—there from Homer, here from contemporary rhetoric—take him further than he had said he intended to go in acknowledging the centrality of the affective. The announced point is that metaphors signify quickly and clearly how things stand, and not that by imitation they communicate vividly how things feel to the speaker. But in fact this last thing is precisely what these metaphors do. Their *energeia* or actuality consists not in their clarity (*sapheia*) but in their very moving images (*phantasiai*) that make us feel (*poiei [hemin] paschein*) (see 1410b33) that the speaker and we ourselves are on the scene, in the middle of things and experiencing them physically, viscerally. *Energeia*, then, is really what Quintilian will call *enargeia* or "vividness." Indeed, some of the manuscripts of the *Rhetoric* even have *enargeia* instead of *energeia* here, which is certainly how Quintilian must have read this passage (see Inst. Or. 6.2.32).

For how is this "*energeia*" to be acheieved? "By [a metaphor's] 'putting things before our eyes' I mean," says Aristotle, "that it signifies them as in action [ὅσα ἐνεργοῦντα σημαίνει]" (1411b24–25). This is to be accomplished by "making the inanimate animate by use of metaphor," a device of which *Homer* is said to be a past master (32). To be sure, on the surface of it we are still concerned here with the clear signification of how things stand, and not the onomatopoetic communication of how they feel. The remarkable thing about the examples Aristotle takes, however, is that, in fact, they all are personifications which intrinsically involve and communicate strong human *pathê* or affects. When, as in Homer, a rock is said to be "shameless" (1411b35, *Odyssey*

11.598), or an arrow to fly "eagerly" (1412a1, *Iliad* 4.126), or spears to be "longing to taste flesh" (1412a2, *Iliad* 9.574) or to "drive in frenzy through the breast" (1412a2–3, *Iliad* 15.542), then, says Aristotle, we have *energeia*. The argument seems to be that such prosopoeia and vivification makes things actual, that it presents them as they are, and that this, in turn, "wins approval" (*eudokimei*) (1411b33). But surely, as Aristotle must have accepted when he drew upon these examples, Homer is not just contributing to approval with such vivifying metaphors, nor even just putting things before our eyes (*poiein pro ommatôn*) (see 1411b4) merely to "create in us a flash of insight" (*poiein hemin mathêsin tacheian*) (see 1410b20). On the contrary, primarily and in the first place, Homer is charging things with *pathos*; he is making them affective, *poiein paschein*, as Aristotle himself had put it (1410b33), and this, so that we will *feel* a certain way about them.

For the transference or *metapherein* of the prosopoeia here is a transference of how the thing *feels* to us, back into the thing portrayed. Thus, as in Odysseus's narration to Achilles, the transference, in naming the way it does, first communicates the original affective setting of any facts, deeds, and actions (*pragamata*), which only subsequently we might proceed to objectify and signify. Since, in following the Platonic mathematical abstraction, Aristotle's concern is with *sapheia* and *mathêsis*, clarity and cognition, he is inattentive to the concrete affective background of our experience to which Homer as an earlier poet always responds. But unlike the "Socrates" of the *Republic* who would eliminate the element of imitation in any narration in Homer (see book 3, 396d ff.), Aristotle, in leaving his Homer quotations unaltered, makes no attempt here to uproot Homer's historical narrative speech from its original embeddedness in the *pathê*. He thereby neglects the affective dimension of what we say, perhaps, but by no means does he deny it or even suppress it.

As a matter of fact, this has been the case all along. If, for instance, we go back to the initial discussion of metaphor in book 3 (1405a5 ff.), we find that it is metaphor most of all that has about it clarity (*to saphes*), pleasurableness (*to hedu*), and unusualness (*to zenikon*), in other words, precisely the traits we have come to expect in good prose diction, none of which have anything to do with *mimêsis* or imitation. However, at 1405a31 we find a striking qualification regarding the appropriateness of metaphors that does have to do with *mimêsis*: a metaphorical word "goes wrong in its syllables," says Aristotle, "if these are not signs *in a pleasant voice*" (ἐὰν μὴ ἡδείας ᾖ σημεῖα φωνῆς), as for instance, when "Dionysius the Brazen" names poetry "Calliope's scream" (*kraugê*) (31–33). The ensuing line (34) is corrupt and not easily pieced together, but certainly Aristotle is warning us here that how a metaphor *sounds* when voiced is intrinsic to its aptness (*to prepon*), or, in the case of *kraugê*, lack thereof. The problem is not just a matter of pleasurableness but of the discrepancy between the ugly, crowlike *kraugê*, with the gutterals k and g at the start of its two syllables, and the sweetness of poetry. As a metaphor "*kraugê*" may *signify* what poetry *is* but it fails to *imitate* how poetry *feels*.

The thought here is further elaborated in a striking passage at 1405b6 ff.:

> As does their ugliness, so too the beauty of words lies *either in their sounds or in the thing signified by them* [ἐν τοῖς ψόφοις ἢ τῷ σημαινομένῳ]. . . . For it is not as Byson says, namely that no one ever speaks in an ugly way since speaking either in the one way or the other both signify the same thing [τὸ αὐτὸ σημαίνει]. That assertion is false, for the one way is the more prevalent usage *and is more like the thing than the other and more suitable in putting it before our eyes* [καὶ ὡμοιωμένον μᾶλλον καὶ οἰκειότερον, τῷ ποιεῖν τὸ πρᾶγμα πρὸ ὀμμάτων]. Consequently we must posit that one way is either finer or uglier than the other. For both signify the fine or the ugly but not by both being fine or ugly themselves. Or if they both do, one does it more and the other less. Therefore metaphors are to be produced from what is fine and beautiful either in the voicing, or in the power of expression, or in the imagery for sight, or in some other sense perception [τῇ φωνῇ ἢ τῇ δυνάμει τῇ ὄψει ἢ ἄλλῃ τινὶ αἰσθήσει]. (1405b6–18; emphasis added)

There follow several remarkable illustrations: had Homer substituted *phoinikodaktulos* or, worse, *eruthrodaktulos* for *rhododaktulos* in his famous *rhododaktulos êos* or "rose-fingered dawn," the primary mistake would not consist in the signification of the wrong color, that is, in the signification of "crimson" or "red," respectively, instead of "rose" (19–20). In fact, these standard variations in the English translations of the color words in this passage may be over-differentiated since Aristotle seems to be saying here that all three in fact signify the same color and that the error is not at all in *what* is signified. Rather, the error lies in *how* each of these alternative words communicate the thing they name. Thus they go wrong, we may assume, in either their "voicing, or in the power of expression, or in the imagery for sight or in some other sense perception" (17–18). Or, again, it is one thing to call Orestes a "mother-slayer" and quite another to call him a "father-avenger" (23–24).

Surely the point here is not just Frege's about "morning star" and "evening star" having the same reference but different meanings. For to say "mother-slayer" instead of "father-avenger" is not only to construe things, *ta pragma*, differently *but to give them a different affective feel.* At its peripheries any signification here thus recurs to an onomatopoetic voiced imitation of a feeling that conjures up in the soul of the listener felt images (*phantasiai, pathêmata tês psuchês*), images not just for hearing but, by no longer traceable associations and metaphorical metonymies, for sight, smell, touch, taste, and the affects as well. Here, then, Aristotle retreats considerably from his initial attempt to reduce the *pistis* to demonstration and, hence, to purify *logos* or argument of its original visceral *pathos*, and in so doing, he still allows us to see the shape of the rhetorical *logos* beneath the abstractions to dialectic and demonstration that have nearly covered it up.

Sometimes, in fact, Aristotle ends up reaffirming the original unity of *logos* and *pathos* in rhetoric precisely by his very own tactical and quite sophistical recommendations that we deliberately create a discrepancy between these two lest we seem too poetic or transparently disingenuous. For instance, at 1407b29 f. he suggests, "When speaking of something ugly or unseemly, use the name if the circumlocution is ugly and the description if the name is ugly." Or, at 1408b6 ff., he suggests that "if the names are harsh, don't be harsh in your voicing [τῇ φωνῇ] and facial expression." On the whole, however, such discrepancies are to be avoided, and this recommendation, too, discloses traces of original argument. In particular, overblown words that exceed the proper *pathos* for what they communicate should be shunned, for they lead to "frostiness," which is to say, to a style and diction that leaves the audience "cold" and unresponsive (1405b35 ff.). Here Aristotle's concern is with *to prepon* and *aprepeia* or appropriateness and inappropriatness: "One's diction displays appropriateness" he says, "when it expresses *pathos* and *êthos* and is in keeping with the subject matter before us" (1408a10–11). And pathetical or affective appropriateness, he says,

> consists in the diction of someone angered if the subject be an outrage, or of someone disgusted yet supremely reserved if the subject be impious or disgraceful things, or in speaking with respect if the subject be praiseworthy things, with humility, if piteous things, and similarly in regard to the rest. For both the facts and appropriate diction are convincing, . . . and the listener always feels the same way as the one speaking affectively even if the latter has nothing to say [καὶ συνομοπαθεῖ ὁ ἀκούων ἀεὶ τῷ παθητικῶς λέγοντι, κἂν μηθὲν λέγῃ]. (1408a16–24)

If we look beneath the concluding depreciatory aside here, we can see that despite Aristotle's oft-stated aversion to "unscientific" affective rhetoric and his contempt for those inferior audiences that require this sort of persuasion, he acknowledges in this passage, after all, that any argument that is a rhetorical *pistis* and convinces someone to decide in a certain way inevitably has an affective dimension that must at least harmonize with its "pure" logic. Remarkably, we can say in support of this point that in the realm of rhetoric even affectively neutral words can be affectively inappropriate precisely because of their neutrality. For speech is inappropriate not only when its *pathos* is so overblown and thus so "frosty" as to leave us cold but, conversely, when it tells of tragedy with the toned-down, "cold" objectivity appropriate for the transmission of statistics.

6.4.2 *Taxis* (arrangement) and the communication of *pathos*

Now, significantly, in turning to Aristotle's discussion of *taxis* or arrangement, which concludes the *Rhetoric*, we find the very same pattern we have observed in his discussion of the relationship of the *pathê* to *lexis* or diction. The initial position he takes in regard to arrangement, too, is that a *pistis* should be reduced to an *apodeixis*, that convincing someone should be reduced to demonstration. Consequently, he rejects as "ludicrous" the traditional understanding of arrangement according to which a speech is divided into a *prooimion* or introduction, a *diêgesis* or narration, a *pistis* or proof, *ta pros ton antidikon* or refutations of the opponent, and an *epilogos* or peroration. (Compare the similar condemnation of traditional rhetoric in the *Phaedrus* 266c ff.) He argues, instead, that there are really only two parts, a *prothêsis* that sets forth the facts of the case and a *pistis* or proof that makes the case (1414a30–1414b13). "For it is necessary," he says, "to state the case at issue and then to demonstrate it [τὸ πρᾶγμα εἰπεῖν περὶ οὗ, και τοῦτ' ἀποδεῖξαι], since it is impossible to have stated your case and not demonstrate it or to demonstrate it without stating it beforehand" (1414a31–33). But having said this, Aristotle once again proceeds to elaborate on the earlier tradition he has just dismissed and to take up each of the traditional parts of a speech, not only with regard to the contribution they make to statement and demonstration of the case but, also, to conviction by *pathos*.

When considering the *prooimion*, for instance, he compares it to the prologue in poetry and the prelude in flute playing, "for all these things are beginnings, and beginnings of the sort which prepare the way for what follows" (1414b19–21). "Now, the flautist's prelude," he continues,

> is like the *prooimion* of the epideictic speaker, for flautists too, in playing as a prelude whatever they are prepared to play well, tie it into the opening

key of the piece [συνῆψαν τῷ ἐνδοσίμῳ]. And in epideictic speeches one is also supposed to write in this way, saying right away whatever one wishes while setting the tone and tying it in [ὅ τι ἂν βούληται εὐθὺ εἰπόντα ἐνδοῦναι καὶ συνάψαι]. (21–26)

Like so many others in the *Rhetoric,* this passage is strikingly ambivalent. On the one hand, in treating introductions as pat flourishes or cadenzas Aristotle reduces them to mere ornamentation. They are, he says, appropriate for "epideictic" speeches, where, as the name indicates, the point is not so much to convince someone of something as to "show off" one's skills. But at the same time the references to the *endosimon* and to *endounai* reveal a deeper and earlier understanding of what is at stake here. For the *endosimon* is the opening phrase of a piece of music that sets the key and tone of it. It establishes, in other words, the ineliminable affective "voicing" and mood (Heidegger: *Stimmung*), establishes just *how* the communication will be heard. The foreground point of this passage is, to be sure, that these matters are entirely incidental, and at 1415b6 we find the usual disclaimer that they are of interest only "in regard to a bad listener who listens to things extrinsic to the case." But the contradictory background point remains that they are in fact intrinsic. Once again, and despite Aristotle's avowed Platonism in regard to matters of rhetoric, an earlier pre-Platonic tradition is still perpetuated in him.

That it is is made evident as well in his exposition of the narration, the proof, and the epilogue. The narration would seem to correspond to the *prothêsis* or setting forth of the case in preparation for the proof that follows it. Because Aristotle would like the *pistis,* here in the special sense of the part of arrangement called the "proof," to approximate logic's demonstration, one would expect him to assign the same kind of affective neutrality to the narration leading up to the *pistis* as would be appropriate for a *prothêsis* leading up to a demonstration. But, significantly, he makes no attempt at all to do this. On the contrary, when speaking of narration in a defense, he suggests that "we should should speak of deeds as having been done in the past *unless speaking of them as being done now conveys either compassion or indignation*" (1417a12–13; emphasis added). The clear implication is that when the present tense does convey compassion or indignation, we should by all means use it instead of the perfect. (For the affective use of the historical present see the discussion above on Odysseus's narration to Achilles.) And at 35–39 we find Aristotle saying, "Furthermore choose from among the affective expressions [ἔτι ἐκ τῶν παθητικῶν λέγε] that also tell what similar behavior follows from the affect that both you and your opponent display, as well tell what behavior is peculiar to you or to him." For an explanation of this we are once again referred to Homer, namely his "For thus did she speak, hiding her face with her hands" (1417b5, *Odyssey* 19.361). As Homer relates it, her gesture, Aristotle says, indicates that she was anguished enough to burst into tears.

It is important, too, that in regard to the ethical dimension of the narration Aristotle makes a quite remarkable distinction between Socratic and mathematical arguments. The narration *must* have *êthos*, he says; it must display the character of the speaker (1417a16–17), and one way it does this is precisely by displaying the *prohairesis* or choice of a goal and purpose (*telos*) for his or her life that the speaker has made (17–19) (see section 3.4.4 on the *prohairesis* of the speaker). Now, *in contrast to mathematical arguments (mathematikoi logoi)*, which, he says, have no *êthos* because they display no choice of a goal for the sake of which the speaker acts, Socratic arguments, he maintains, do display such a goal and, consequently, do have *êthos* (19–21). Accordingly they, and *not mathematical argument*, are the model we should take for the rhetorical narration. This point is crucial since mathematical argument *is* the model for a demonstration. For Aristotle is acknowledging here that, insofar as the proof is preceded by a narration, not only as the preliminary *prothêsis* or "setting forth" of the relevant facts suitable for a demonstration *but also* as the communication of the character of the speaker, the proof that follows this narration must be something else besides a demonstration after all.

Of course, he is not saying explicitly that Socratic arguments should be the model also because they have *pathos*. Nevertheless, Socratic and mathematical speech are surely to be contrasted with regard to *pathos* as well as *êthos*, and this by Aristotle's own account. We should keep in mind that *êthos* and *pathos* blend in Aristotle, too, and not only in the earlier pre-Platonic tradition and in the later reception of it in Cicero and Quintilian. For instance, *philia* or friendliness toward the audience is a crucial part of the *êthos* a speaker must display as well as one of the *pathê* to be communicated to the audience, and hence *philia* is a bridge from *êthos* to the *pathê* (see 1378a18 on the conjunction of *eunoia* or meaning well, *philia*, and the *pathê*). It follows that any point made in Aristotle about *êthos* plainly has implications for *pathos* as well.

But even more remarkable than Aristotle's linking of *pathos* and *logos* in the narration is his concession that the *pistis* itself has an affective dimension, for this most clearly of all would make it irreducible to a demonstration. Although the opening statement in the discussion of the *pistis* says that "Proofs ought to be demonstrative" (Τὰς δὲ πίστεις δεῖ ἀποδείκτικας εἶναι) (1417b21), this, it turns out, does not mean that being demonstrative is all they ought to be.

To be sure, enthymemes are to be the centerpiece of the *pistis*, and on the dubious principle that one cannot "think and chew sweets" at the same time, Aristotle submits that *pathos* must not be mixed with enthymemes, for like two simultaneous opposed motions they would nullify each other (1418a12–14). Similarly, the mixture of *êthos* with enthymemes is to be avoided. Actually, he says, such a mixture is impossible anyway since enthymemes are a form of demonstration and "demonstration contains neither *êthos* nor choice" (16–17).

However, along with enthymemes, Aristotle asserts, "maxims are to be used—as in the narration, so too in the proof";

> for they serve the ethical [ἠθικὸν γάρ], as in "I have given it to him knowing that 'One ought to trust no one' "—or, on the other hand, they serve affectively [δὲ παθητικῶς] as in "I am not sorry, though injustice was done to me, for 'If he has the profit on his side, I have justice on mine.' " (1418a17–21)

Here it emerges that the proof is in fact more than an enthymeme and, consequently, more than a demonstration too. For by Aristotle's own admission proofs need maxims precisely because enthymemes and demonstrations could not provide the *êthos* and *pathos* that a proof needs to be convincing.

Finally, the original unity of *pathos* and *logos*, and the consequent impossibility of Aristotle's attempt to reduce rhetorical argument as a whole to demonstration, is made undeniably clear in his discussion of the epilogue with which he concludes the *Rhetoric*. For an epilogue, he says, has four functions (1419b10 f.): first, "to make the listeners favorably disposed toward the speaker himself and ill-disposed toward the speaker's opponent" (πρὸς ἑαυτὸν κατασκευάσαι εὖ τόν ἀκροατὴν καὶ τὸν ἐναντίον φαύλως) (10–12); second, to amplify what is favorable to the case and to depreciate what is not (12); third, "to put the listeners in the right *pathê*" (εἰς τὰ πάθη τὸν ἀκροατὴν καταστῆσαι) (13); and fourth, to refresh their memory by recapitulation (13). Significantly, only the last of these has a predominantly logical and demonstrative function.

The first, predisposing the audience to feel a certain way about the speaker, concerns the conjunction of *pathos* and *êthos*; "For it is natural," says Aristotle, "that after the demonstration [μετὰ τὸ ἀποδεῖξαι] that what you say is true and what your opponent says false, you then proceed to praising yourself and censuring the opponent and to shaping an appropriate image of yourself and of him" (14–15). The second, amplification and depreciation, is not explicitly concerned with either *êthos* or *pathos*, to be sure, but, it obviously comes after, and goes beyond, any demonstration: "*after having already demonstrated* your point" (μετὰ τοῦτο δεδειγμένων ἤδη), says Aristotle "amplification or depreciation is the natural thing" (20; emphasis added). It is at least implied here that, though amplification and depreciation attach themselves logically to argument by the dialectical topic of the "more and the less," they originate in rhetorical tropes that give things a certain feel, for example, hyperbole and litotes (exaggeration and understatement). They are, this is to say, more concerned with *diatithenai* and *kataskeuazein*, or predisposing and readying the audience to feel a certain way about the things under discussion and about the speaker, than with *apodeiknusthai* or "showing" dispassionate spectators how things stand. This, after all, is why they are not taken up as part of the reasoning by topics, part of the *logos* itself.

Thus, upon the amplification or depreciation there follows, third, and again as if by the intrinsic nature of the subject matter, the concern of putting the listener into the right *pathê*. Pity, horror, anger, hate, jealousy, and contentiousness are mentioned specifically here (25–26). What is striking about the exposition of the *pathê* this time is that the usual qualification is missing completely, namely that all such concerns for the listeners result only from their incapacity to follow an extended argument (compare, for instance, the first of this sort of comment at 1355a24 f.). On the contrary, the invocation of the *pathê* is now said to be only "natural." Thus, here; at least, the audience or listeners (*akouontes*) are not dismissed as inferior intellects but recognized as those who hear the sound of what is said to them, and who must thereby be convinced viscerally to decide a certain way—this now in plain distinction from unmoved onlookers or spectators (*theôretes*) who by instruction are made to see clearly the point of a demonstration.

The treatment of the diction of the epilogue at the conclusion of this chapter and, in fact, of the *Rhetoric* itself, only reinforces this point and hence effectively nullifies Aristotle's attempted reduction of the rhetorical *logos* to the dialectical and, ultimately, the demonstrative *logos*. In a passing reference to *lexis asundêtos* or the fitting use of asydeton or the omission of conjunctions—and on one of the few occasions where he acknowledges the affective dimension of rhythm and tempo—Aristotle cites Lysias's "*eireka, akekoate, echete, krinate*" as appropriate diction for the epilogue (1420a6–7). Any English translation is hopelessly inadequate here, say, "I have spoken, you have heard, now you have it, you decide." For like Caesar's "Veni vidi vici," the Greek is much quicker, more direct, and more emphatic than the English. Aristotle's point is that if, in contrast, Lysias had used polysydeton, "*And* I have spoken, *and* you have heard, *and* you now have it, *and* you decide," not the clarity (*sapheia*) of *what* is said would be destroyed, but, because of the change in the sound of *how* it is said, the appropriate affective and convincing effect. Lysias, this is to say, would have achieved a measured solemn feel to his speech, but for precisely that reason it would have died on the vine.

6.4.3 The *Rhetoric*'s neglect of *hupokrisis* (delivery)

In conclusion to this section we must ask why, if Aristotle does acknowledge the importance of sound and voice and the significance of the fact that rhetoric is something heard by listeners, he pays so little attention to rhetoric's fundamentally acoustical nature. For in the end he *has* paid a great deal of attention to the communication of *pathos* despite his oft-repeated disparaging of it, but for some reason he has paid almost no attention to the acoustical dimension of speech, which alone communicates *pathos.* Indeed, in the *Rhetoric* and, as we will see in the next section, in the *Poetics, hupokrisis* or delivery very nearly vanishes. Typically, for instance, such references as we find to tropes like anaphora, antithesis, isocolon, and epanalepsis (see, for example, 1410a23 ff.), and even the concluding remark at 1420b2 on asydeton in the epilogue, treat these not in reference to how they affect listeners when spoken out loud, but only in reference to the contribution they make to *sapheia* and *asteia,* to clarity of presentation and "urbane" facilitating of comprehension. Moreover, the comprehension meant, we discover, is not so much by listeners who are supposed to hear what is urged as by readers who are supposed to see what is meant.

The passage at 1413b8 f., in which Aristotle distinguishes between the *lexis graphikê* or written diction and *lexis agônistikê,* the diction of speeches that "contest" something out loud, is exceptional in this regard and, hence, of special importance to us. *Lexis graphikê,* in which the proper use of the (Greek) language (*hellenizein*) is the primary concern, we are told, "is the most exact" (ἔστι . . . ἡ ἀκριβεστάτη), whereas *lexis agônistikê,* in contrast, is "the one that lends itself most to delivery [ἡ ὑποκριτικωτάτη]" (8–9). For *lexis agônistikê* has one of two forms, either ethical (*êthikê*) or affective (*pathêtikê*) (10), and needs, for just this reason, we may presume, to be enacted vocally or declaimed (*hupokrinesthai*) (30). Indeed, its preferred figures of speech, in particular anaphora, or repetition of the beginning, but also asydeton, would, like "the man carrying a beam" (28–29), labor clumsily to no effect were they to remain written words without declamation. Put in more modern terms, they would be like notes in one of Bach's musical scores, whose exact logical relationships best become evident to one who reads them but whose affective communication can be accomplished only when they are converted into audible sound.

For instance, says Aristotle, such an anaphora as the actor (*hupokritês*) Philemon's, "He is the one who robbed, he is the one who deceived, he is the one who finally undertook to betray you" (23–25), would, if just written and read silently, seem like simple-minded reiteration of the same thing (19–20). To avoid this appearance, says Aristotle, "it is necessary that the speaker modulate what is the same, which, as it were, opens the path to delivery [ὥσπερ ὁδοποιεῖ τῷ ὑποκρίνεσθαι]" (22–23). It is the same with asyndeton too, for example, "I came, I met, I entreated" (29): "for it is necessary to enact [such things] vocally [ἀνάγκη γὰρ ὑποκρίνεσθαι] and not say them in the same character and tone, as if one were saying just one thing" (30–31).[8]

We should note that here neither of these two dictions, neither the written nor the agonistic and declamatory, is said to be inferior, neither said to be superior. On the contrary, each has an appropriate place where the other would be inappropriate, and hence we need to know both (1413b5). Indeed, "if put alongside of each other the written speeches seem too cramped in an agonistic setting while those of an orator, which sound good spoken, seem idiosyncratic when we take them in hand to read" (14–16). In correlating the three kinds of rhetoric with these two styles (see 1414a8–17) Aristotle contends that most of all, epideictic or "showoff" rhetoric requires the precision of written diction, whereas political rhetoric, most of all, the declamatory inflection of agonistic, spoken diction: "This, however, is where voice is needed and, most of all, where a strong voice is needed" (τοῦτο δὲ ὅπου φωνῆς καί μάλιστα ὅπου μεγάλης) (16–17). Although somewhere in the middle, judicial diction, as we might expect, given the attack on sophistical distortions of it in book 1, chapter 1, should be closer to the precise than the hypocritic and more logical than affective (19).

But once again, and characteristically, Aristotle does not pursue the ethical and affective functions of voiced, enacted diction. For, significantly, its diachronic tropes are of importance to him, it turns out, only in regard to their usefulness for amplification and not in regard to their specifically affective communication. His point is the purely logical one that whereas the use of multiple conjunctions, or polysyndeton, reduces many things to one, anaphora and asyndeton allow us to give added weight to one thing by letting us split it up into many (1413b32–1414a7). The use of these diachronic tropes in spoken language is thus said here only to provide reinforcement of the point one seeks to demonstrate. Hence here, voiced speech, instead of doing what is proper to it, namely communicating *pathos*, merely comes to the aid, as it were, of the more precise written language in performing what are essentially the latter's tasks. It seems here that if Aristotle had his way, spoken language would be a useful trick to resort to, but on the whole, the nearer it stays to the precision of writing, the better: "Of the agonistic speakers those such as Charemon are praised, for, *like a writer of speeches, he is precise* [ἀκριβὴς γὰρ ὥσπερ λογογράφος]" (1413b12–13; emphasis added).

Indeed, the insistence here on precision or *akribeia* signals Aristotle's ultimate retreat into Platonism. To be sure, in even undertaking an exposition of rhetorical argument he has penetrated behind the abstractions of Platonism, but in the end he has uncritically perpetuated in the *Rhetoric* these very same abstractions.

This was not always the case. As we know, elsewhere, in the *Nicomachean Ethics,* for example, instead of insisting on *akribeia* he was ready to relinquish it. We are already familiar with the reference to *akribeia* in the *Nicomachean Ethics* at 1094b13: "For the precise is not to be sought to the same extent in every form of argument" (τὸ γὰρ ἀκριβὲς οὐχ ὁμοίως ἐν ἅπασι τοῖς λόγοις ἐπιζητητέον), and, he continues, "It pertains to the educated that they seek only as much precision [ϵπὶ τοσοῦτον τἀκριβὲς ἐπιζητεῖν] as the nature of each kind of subject matter allows" (23–25). And what are the subject matters in which precision is not to be sought? About this Aristotle is quite specific; they are, we note, the very subject matters of epideictic and judicial rhetoric, namely, "the decent and the just" (τὰ δὲ καλὰ καὶ τὰ δίκαια) (14).

It is remarkable that in these assertions, coming as they do, just prior to Aristotle's criticism of his Platonist "friends" who seek a precise idea of the Good, Aristotle is speaking against precision, not for it. Contrary to what the Pythagorean followers of Plato at the Academy might think, argument about the matters for decision and choice, Aristotle wants to say, is not the kind of thing that can be put on a precise basis.

The analogy he draws to make this point is also familiar to us and ties the discussion into rhetorical argument explicitly: "for accepting from a mathematician that he argue convincingly" (μαθηματικοῦ τε πιθανολογοῦντος ἀποδέχεσθαι), says Aristotle, "plainly is just as wrong as demanding demonstrations from a rhetor [ῥητορικόν ἀποδείξεις ἀπαιτεῖν]" (26–27). In other words, precision and demonstration are *not* to be demanded of a rhetor, rather something quite different from these, namely *to pithanon* or what is convincing. *Here,* in pointing out that ethics and politics are not fields for precise argument, Aristotle acknowledges that rhetoric, the way we argue about these matters, is not precise either; in this regard a rhetorical *pistis,* he says *here,* is to be distinguished from a demonstration, not reduced to it. The precision or stringency characteristic of the *logos apodeiktikos,* or demonstrative argument, cannot be sought in ethical, political, rhetorical arguments. *Here* Aristotle gets beyond Platonism or, to speak with Heidegger, behind it to an "earlier" way of thinking "closer to the origin."

In the *Rhetoric,* however, he seems to shy away from the abyss of rhetoric's proper imprecision (see section 5.3.2 above on Aristotle's apeirophobia). Indeed, even as he returns us in the *Rhetoric* to the original experience within a world of indeterminate, imprecise contingent things that we sense and feel and about which we take counsel and deliberate with each other, he is, we now see, simultaneously retreating after all to the security of the mathematically precise. Platonism and the "metaphysical" have prevailed. We will see next that the same thing happens in the *Poetics,* albeit in a somewhat different way: there, too, the turn away from the voiced and heard and the turn to the envisionable and logical suppresses original acoustical experience.

6.5 The Rise of the Visual and Demise of the Acoustical in Aristotle's *Poetics*

To comprehend fully the ultimate suppression of acoustical experience in Aristotle's *Rhetoric* and, at the same time, to uncover the special nature of rhetoric's original voiced *logos* or argument, we need now to go even further outside the "Organon" than the *Rhetoric* does, outside, that is, the Aristotelian technical studies specifically directed to the various forms of *logos* but which, significantly, and unlike the *Rhetoric,* neither concern themselves with the communication of *pathos* nor give any indication that argument is for listeners, *akouontes,* namely, *On Interpretation,* the *Categories,* the *Prior* and *Posterior Analytics,* the *Topics,* and *Sophistical Refutations.* Indeed, the *Rhetoric*'s own retreat to the "purely" logical concerns of the "Organon" compels us beyond even the *Rhetoric* itself to the *Poetics.* For, as we have just seen, the *Rhetoric* treats diction, arrangement, and delivery or dramatic performance (*hupokrisis*)—concerns central to the *Poetics*—as ancillary, extra-logical considerations forced on us by the inferiority of popular audiences, and that we might best dispense with, had we to reason only with properly cultivated individuals (see, for example, 1355a27). Even so, much of the *Rhetoric*'s exposition of the "extra-logical" is, as we have noted, so painstaking that it cannot be considered in the least dismissive, for example, the treatment of *êthos* and *pathos* in book 2. And if such matters are at first presented as "extra-logical" concerns, the very detail and incisiveness of their treatment alerts us to their intrinsic pertinence to argument after all, at least to argument as it was originally carried on. Thus, it emerges that Aristotle's equally painstaking exploration of the dramatic in the *Poetics*, which in many ways takes up again those very "extra-logical" considerations of the *Rhetoric* but without the latter's depreciation, could have intrinsic importance for speech and argument, intrinsic importance, that is, for our hermeneutical "laying bare" and "laying out" of *logos* in its original sense.

As it was to the *Rhetoric*, so, too, will our approach to the *Poetics* be a *Destruktion*. For rather than treating the *Poetics* as a consistent theory of tragedy, we will treat this work, too, as the productively *in*consistent and tense intertwining of earlier, pre-Platonic ritual understandings, and later, post-Platonic intellectualist understandings, and we will take down the *Poetics*' own later superimpositions in order to "lay bare" and "lay out" the hidden foundations and ground beneath them. In this way, we will be able to penetrate behind Aristotle's exposition of tragedy as representation for spectators (*theôretes*) looking on from a distance and surveying a logical "whole," to an earlier understanding, still present in the *Poetics*, of tragedy as ritual reenactment for an audience (*akouontes*), themselves caught up in the rhythms and cadences of the voices that they hear, and with that, we will have in fact "laid bare" simultaneously the circumstances of original, oral-acoustical argument.

This, of course, is to reverse the actual tendency of the *Poetics*, namely away from the acoustical and toward the visual. We will see that this superimposition of visual on acoustical thinking in the *Poetics*, and of post-Platonic understandings of tragedy superimposed on pre-Platonic ones, is discernible even in the basic vocabulary with which Aristotle works. Consequently, though Aristotle himself does not distinguish, for instance, between *mimêsis* as ritual reenactment, which is its earlier sense, and *mimêsis* as educational portrayal or re-presentation of a thing's typical features, which is a later overlay, we, for our part, must make such a distinction if we are to get beneath the surface of the *Poetics*. In like fashion, we must distinguish, though Aristotle never does, between *katharsis* as cognitive lustration or clarification of potentially destabilizing passions and the deeper level of *katharsis* as ritual expiation for our misdeeds. In other words, where Aristotle in his exposition of tragedy has suppressed lingering traces of ritual experience undergone acoustically, and where he displaces such acoustical experience with theoretical insight, it is our task to restore what has been suppressed and displaced to its place alongside what it contradicts.

Specifically, we will see that in the *Poetics* Aristotle's thought is predominately visual, to be sure, but, remarkably, in part still acoustical. Hence, in going back to this text we reach a decisive moment in the development of Western metaphysical thought when the visual paradigm has come to prevail but not without leaving traces of the "earlier" acoustical experience that it would displace. For if in the *Poetics* the withdrawal to a "divine" *apathes theôria*, an unaffected looking on, has always already been made, our original existence "in the world" is nonetheless not entirely suppressed, our existence, that is to say, "there" with and among other people, in oral-aural interaction with whom we undergo and communicate the things that happen to us and are felt by us, the *pathêmata* and *pathê*. In the *Poetics*, then, we are not quite yet the "unmoved movers" that we aspire to be in the pursuit of pure *theôria* and in reasoning by strict, scientific demonstration; we are not quite yet the pure, dispassionate agents who undergo nothing more as patients (compare *EN* 10.1177a12f., *Metaphy.* 12.1072b15ff., and section 6.4.3 above).[9] Or, put in terms of the *Poetics*, we are not quite yet onlookers who see from a distance and no longer hear the voicings (*phônai*) of the play that would draw us into their melodic cadences and rhythms. Only with these acoustical and melodic foundations more clearly laid out before us will we be able, second, to *re*construct Aristotle's visual and metaphysical understanding of tragedy as precisely what it is, namely a self-contradictory turn away from tragedy's acoustical and melodic underpinnings, a turn that for all its self-contradictoriness has defined the subsequent course of Western thought and, most importantly, the West's understanding of *logos*, of speech and argument.

6.5.1 The musical, acoustical ground of speech

"Tragedy," says Aristotle, compactly summarizing the exposition to come,

> is the imitation of an action serious and complete [Ἔστιν οὖν τραγῳδία μίμησις πράξεως σπουδαίας και τελείας]. It is of limited size with each of the forms of pleasing speech used separately in its various parts. It is imitation not by reporting but imitation of people doing things, which, by compassion and fear, achieves the purification of such passions undergone as these [τὴν τῶν τοιοῦτων παθημάτων κάθαρσιν]. I call speech pleasant that has rhythm, pitch and melody, whereas I mean by "in forms used separately" that some [tragic effects] are achieved with only meter but others, in turn, with melody. (*Poetics* 1449b24–32)

In regard to the continuing earlier pre-Platonic and pre-metaphysical dimension of the *Poetics* it is most striking here that Aristotle bases his exposition of tragic poetry on a rehabilitation of *mimêsis praxeôs*, imitation of an action, by dramatic reenactment in voice and dance (see also 1447a13f.), and this despite Plato's previous withering critique of just such *mimêsis* in the *Republic.* A review of just a few key passages in the *Republic* suffices to make clear just how sharply Aristotle breaks with Plato on this point and how conservative and retrospective his own reappropriation of traditional *mimêsis* really is. For thematic in the *Republic* was the thesis restated at the beginning of book 10 that the *mimêsis* of tragic performance, far from having any psychological benefits, brings about the "ruination . . . of the thinking of those hearing it if they do not have the remedy against this ruination, namely insight into how such things [imitated] really happen to be" (595b). And whereas at least here in Aristotle's *Poetics* melody, meter, rhythm, pitch are said to be crucial for the cathartic effect, in the *Republic,* these acoustical, musical elements of poetic imitation, once stripped away, turn out to have been only the cover for the imitator's own lack of insight (601a). Indeed, the acoustical musical elements of tragic *mimêsis* are, to take Plato's deliberately absurd analogy, comparable to the colors when someone paints a picture of a bit and reins and then tries to pass the painting off as a real bit and reins and, worse, to pass the painting off as proof of his or her insight into what a bit and reins are really like. In fact, the colors are mere pleasing ornamentation with nothing real behind them, and so too, by analogy, are the "meters, rhythms, and intonations" in voice, with which the acoustical artist works.

But even this provocative analogical argument is not enough for Plato, for by itself it would divert us from the real danger at hand, to which he would direct us. The actual point he wants to make is that the acoustical imitations in meter, rhythm, and pitch that we *hear* are much more disastrously misleading than any colors that we *see* could ever be: the auditory and not the visual is, after all, the primary means of communicating and sharing the *pathos* or the feeling that someone is undergoing, and hence the auditory can influence our "thinking something through," our *dianoia,* in a way that nothing visual ever could. For whenever we set about thinking something through, whenever we deliberate or take counsel about something (see 604c), a fierce struggle, an *agôn,* is joined between what is best and worst in us, between what is rational and irrational, between the reasoning (*logos*) that we do actively and the feelings (*pathê*) that we undergo passively. (We note a disjunction of *logos* and *pathos* here corresponding to the *Phaedo*'s disjunction of mind and body.) The reasonable side of us, Plato's "Socrates" says here, displays a constant disposition of character "always at one with itself." But the unreasonable side, namely the complex of our feelings, is of multiple and various character. Hence, this *agôn* between the active and passive is ultimately between what would hold us together as one integrated personality and what, in driving us to distraction, would cause us to dissolve and go to pieces (604e). In a stable person "law and reason" prevail over feeling and prevent this disintegration (604b). But precisely this predominance of *logos* over *pathos* is undermined by the acoustical nature of vocal poetic imitation in meter, rhythm, and pitch (see 603b). For unlike the visual, the melodic-acoustical goes directly to the feelings and only reinforces their domination of us: "It is plain," says Socrates here, "that by nature the imitative poet does not aim at such a [rational] part of the soul . . . rather, he concerns himself with the part given to agitation, the unstable part, for this is the part easily imitated (605a). And it is by just this imitation or *mimêsis* that he introduces "ruination" to the soul.

Seen against the background of this radical critique, Aristotle's talk of a *katharsis* or purification of the things that we experience passively, of the *pathêmata*, his talk of a *katharsis* achieved by allowing ourselves to undergo such *pathê* or feelings as compassion and fear, is strikingly traditional. As a matter of fact, Aristotle responds to Plato's unrelenting attack on performative *mimêsis* not only by taking *mimêsis* as the single basis for his positive analysis of epic, tragic, and comic poetry but even by praising it as an essential and distinctively human component of the learning process (1448b6–19). How, we must ask, is this possible?

One key to Aristotle's rehabilitation of performative *mimêsis* is his perpetuation of the earlier, tragic understanding of *manthanein* or learning expressed in Aeschylus's *pathei mathos* or "learned by having undergone."[10] The point is that in learning by *mimêsis* we have learned precisely not as in the Platonic paradigm of mathematics, that is, by looking on as something is demonstrated, but rather by feeling something directly with our own body, as it were. We have learned by undergoing something that happens to us and with us experientially. Learning here is not theoretical; it is not the learning of someone unmoved who beholds what is displayed before him or her, rather it is an intensely involved learning by doing, learning, namely, by what Aristotle has called *mimêsis praxeôs* or imitation of an action. "Imitating is innate in human beings," says Aristotle, "and exists from childhood on, and they differ from other animals in that they are the most imitative and do their first learning by imitation [τὰς μαθήσεις ποιεῖται διὰ μιμήσεως τὰς πρώτας]" (1448b5–9). In poetry and tragedy this imitative learning is accomplished by dramatic reenactment, which is to say, by *hupokrisis.*

It is not to be overlooked, of course, that Aristotle has already begun shifting the sense of imitation and learning here from something acoustical and involved to something visual and detached; the very next lines (1448b10 ff.) turn to learning the general characteristics of something by seeing (*horan, theôroun*) a painted re-presentation of it, thus confronting us with a marked ambivalance on Aristotle's part to which we must return later. But that he has not abandoned the earlier understanding of learning by *mimêsis* as physical reenactment, and that he has never completely lost Aeschylus's tragic sense of learning, the sense of becoming "learned by having undergone," is made clear by the perpetuation in his definition of tragedy of an ancient idea of *katharsis* by ritual reenactment (see the citation of 1449b24 f. above, p. 273). In the back of Aristotle's mind there is, in other words, still an idea of learning, not just as a matter of cognition but of recognition (*anagnôrisis*), and such learning as this means undergoing a change in how one feels. Learning remains for Aristotle the *katharsis* of, and expiatiation for, our wrongdoing. It is just this release in *katharsis* and expiation to which the *manthanein* or Aeschylus's *pathei mathos* alludes, the learning of his "learned by having undergone." Here the *katharsis* has to do with *sôtêria,* with deliverance and salvation, as in the *sôtêria dia tês katharseôs* or "salvation through *katharsis*" of which Aristotle himself speaks, at 1454b15, in regard to Orestes in Euripides' *Iphigenia in Tauris,* 1168.

We are indebted to Aryeh Kosman's extraordinarily illuminating piece "Acting: *Drama* as the *Mimêsis* of *Praxis*" for calling attention to this crucial phrase in Aristotle.[11] Kosman argues convincingly that the *Poetics* is to be taken as an extension of the *Ethics* into the realm of our unforeseeable and unpreventable wrongdoing. Whereas in the *Ethics,* he points out, we learn of cognizant, reasoned restraint of our passions and cognizant, reasoned guidance of our deliberations to a choice of what is right, decent, and good, in the *Poetics* we learn of the limits to our cognition and reasoning, and, beyond this, we also learn of the unknowing and inevitable transgression of what is right, decent, and good that results from these limits. With Oedipus at Colonus or Orestes we, the audience of the tragedy, "learn," by what happens with our own body, what it is like to undergo the penalty for our transgression, but also what it is like to experience release from that penalty, to experience *katharsis.* In what he or she undergoes, in his or her *pathêmata,* the tragic hero atones for our own misdeeds, and we, in reenacting these *pathêmata* and this atonement ourselves, are set free.

Citing Cyril of Jerusalem, Kosman suggests that some traces of this same Dionysian ritual, *katharsis* by reenactment, are still to be found in early Christian understandings of the celebration of baptism and the Eucharist:

> O strange and inconceivable thing! We did not truly die, we were not truly buried, we were not truly crucified and raised again, but if our imitation was in a likeness, our salvation is in truth [ἀλλ' ἐν εἰκόνι ἡ

μίμησις, ἐ ν ἀληθείᾳ δέ ἡ σωτηρία]. Christ was really crucified, and really buried, and truly rose again; and all these things have been freely granted us, that by communion in his sufferings in imitation, we might gain salvation in truth [ἵνα τῇ μιμήσει τῶν παθημάτων αὐτοῦ κοινωνήσαντες ἀληθείᾳ τὴν σωτηρίαν κερδήσωμεν].[12]

Now, it is crucial for our recovery of the acoustical ground of speech in Aristotle that any such *mimêsis* as reenactment leading to *katharsis* and *sôtêria* is precisely *not* to be effected in the medium of paintings that we see but in voice (*phônê*) that we hear, and voice, to be sure, that is not in the single meter and monotone of Plato's preferred sober narration (see *Rep.* 397b–c) but, on the contrary, is richly rhythmical and tonally inflected. This, the *Politics,* if not the *Poetics,* makes unequivocally clear in the locus classicus for Aristotle's understanding of the *katharsis* of the *pathê*:

> For we see some held under the sway of such emotions [as pity and fear] and who, as a result of sacred melodies, when they make use of them and plunge their soul into an orgiastic state, are set right as if they happened to have undergone healing and *katharsis.* And those must indeed undergo this same thing who feel pity and who fear, and who generally feel the other passions in the measure that falls to each of these, and there must come to pass for all some kind of *katharsis* and pleasant alleviation. (1342a7–15)

Indeed, the whole argument here turns on the fact that music is not just pleasant adornment after all; rather, we also *learn* character from it, that is, we experience the passions and acquire thereby an appropriate disposition toward them:

> Furthermore, those hearing imitations all come to share in the same felt experience [ἔτι δὲ ἀκροώμενοι τῶν μιμήσεων γίγνονται πάντες συμπαθεῖς] apart [from the speech and through] the rhythms and melodies themselves. . . . For contained in rhythms and melodies are likenesses of anger and gentleness, further, of courage and temperance, and all the opposites of these, as well as all the other dispositions of character, likenesses that most closely correspond to the true nature of these. And this is made plain by what [these rhythms and melodies] do, for we change in our soul when hearing them (1340a13–23),

and "From these things it is plain that music is able to produce a kind of character in the soul" (1340b11–12).

Importantly, Aristotle points out here, even if, as we will see, he soon retracts it, that visual depictions are at best only signs (*sêmeia*) of character and hence are *not* imitations of it (1340a 33), whereas melodies themselves *are* imitations of character (1340a39–40). Furthermore, he adds that one cannot acquire the character merely by looking on as others reenact it, rather one must participate in being "oneself a communicant in the deeds" (αὐτὸς κοινωνῇ τῶν ἔργων) (1340b24). This makes clear why the instructional *mimêsis* is primarily acoustical: like sound, indeed, *as sound*, it must be undergone and experienced and responded to with one's whole psychosomatic being, even in gestures and dance. Put another way, learning character is a function of listening to, hearing, and rehearsing physically, what we hear someone telling us.

These obvious challenges to Plato are the most dramatic evidence of Aristotle's perpetuation of an earlier priority of hearing over seeing, but there are subtler traces of this priority that we should not neglect. For instance, we find that in the *Poetics* Aristotle establishes a quite un-Platonic continuum between the "voices" of the flute and the lyre and the human voice of poetry insofar as all of these imitate precisely in meter, rhythm, and pitch, which are the components of melody (1447a19 ff.). To be sure, the human voice does differ from the "voice" of an instrument in that it develops significant speech (*logos*) out of these components of melody, but we should note that even so this significant speech still remains embedded in its acoustical medium and is not yet severed from the latter in the way that it would be, for instance, when we use words to signify Platonic forms, and when the voiced sound that we make no longer bears any intrinsic relation to the thing we would communicate (see section 6.1 above on the *Cratylus*).

Moreover, even if Aristotle does, on occasion, speak of plain speech or prose in distinction from verse (1447a29), as if to say that voicing in *rhythm and meter* might be divorced from speech after all, this, in fact, does not in the least imply that voiced *pitch*—acute (high), grave (low), and middle (see 1456b32)—would be extrinsic. For even in prose the pitch determines whether an utterance (*logos*) is, for instance, indicative, as in *dídomen* ("we give") or imperative, as in *didômen* ("let us give"). We note in this regard the passage at 1456b9 ff. on, the forms or "gestures of diction" (*schêmata tês lexeôs*), namely "the command, the plea, the narration, the threat, the question, the answer," which are specifically said to be the special subject matter of the art of dramatic, verbal reenactment (*hupokrisis*), and the passage at 1461a25 ff. on *prosodia* or intonation. Obviously what something *sounds* like in the voicing of it is intrinsic even to plain speech, too, and not just poetry.

Moreover, even with regard to voicing in rhythm and meter, and quite apart from pitch, Aristotle often speaks as if these, too, far from belonging only to poetry, had *a natural and intrinsic correlation with the logical content of what we say,* or what is more, as if in tragedy, at least, that logical content, even had musical origins. For instance, Aristotle sees an intimate connection of tragedy with the dithyramb as well as flute playing (1447a14–15) and with Dionysian phallic songs and processions (1449a10–11), and he acknowledges that tragedy has its beginnings in the satyr plays (1449a23).[13] To be sure, he adds that in starting from these origins Aeschylus then began the shift from tragedy based in the chorus, which Aeschylus had reduced in size, to tragedy based on *logos* or the protagonists' argument and speech. Accordingly, Aeschylus raised the number of protagonists from one (a single epiphany of Dionysius) to two. Then, as a further step in this development of the dialogical out of the musical, Sophocles, Aristotle continues, added yet a third protagonist (1449a16–18). We should note, however, that this development per se does not yet imply any separation of the logical from its natural embeddedness in the musical, that is, in the tonal, metric, and rhythmic. On the contrary, the shift in emphasis in Aeschylus and Sophocles to the logical is said to require *an appropriate change from one meter to another.* As tragedy and its diction became less satyric and comic and more solemn, says Aristotle,

> the meter changed from [trochaic] tetrameter to iambic. For at first one used tetrameter on account of the poetry's being satyric and more dancelike. But once the diction [of the protagonists] came to prevail, nature itself found the appropriate meter. (1449a19–20)

Later on we find, similarly,

> the heroic is the most stable and profuse of meters . . . while iambic and tetrameter are the most moved, tetrameter for dance and iambic for action. . . . Nature itself teaches how to choose what is fitting in this matter. (1459b37–60a5)

Thus, in the *Poetics,* if not in the *Rhetoric,* even a primarily "logical" diction still remains grounded in the musical, acoustical setting natural for it, namely, iambic verse. What is more, the iambic, as Aristotle himself notes, is far from being purely logical and acoustically, affectively neutral. On the contrary, it has a definite acoustical "feel" or *pathos* to it as the very origin of the word makes clear, for, says Aristotle, it was, in fact, the natural meter in which people "derided each other" (ἰάμβιζον ἀλλήλους) (1448b33).

We remark, finally, in regard to this continuing embeddedness of the logical in the musical, that Aristotle speaks not just of the diction of the protagonists but also of the *diction of the chorus*: "The parode," he says, "is the entire first diction of the chorus [ἡ πρώτη λέξις ὅλη χοροῦ]" (1452b23). Plainly, the logical content in the diction of a chorus cannot be separated from its acoustical setting and ground, and insofar as the diction of the protagonists arises out of the midst of the surrounding chorus, a continuum is established in Aristotle, reaching from the diction of the protagonists, itself inflected, as we have seen, back to the lexical intonations of the chorus. Indeed, precisely in seeking to maintain this continuity Aristotle objects to Agathon's and others' misuses of the chorus as an arbitrary *embolima* or something just "tossed in" here and there. In this, he says, Aeschylus and Sophocles were better than Euripides, for the chorus "is to be taken as one of the players and must be a part of the whole and must take part in the action" (1456a25–33). What is more, in keeping with this observation, at 1452b19–23 Aristotle had listed all the parts of a tragedy in reference to the melodies of the chorus: the prologue is what comes before the entrance of the chorus; the episodes are what occur between the melodies of the chorus; and the exodos is what comes after the last melody of the chorus has been sung. Thus, an earlier understanding of our original acoustical experience is, indeed, perpetuated in Aristotle's *Poetics* by the continuing embeddedness there of what is said, of *logos* and *lexis*, speech and diction, in the voiced song.

Before proceeding to Aristotle's revocation of the acoustical ground of speech we have "laid bare" here, let us note, finally, that this acoustical ground has important implications not just for the tragic art itself but for those listening to tragedy. For only as listeners, *akouontes*, do they remain taken up and involved as communicants in an experience they feel and undergo. This fact bears directly on the *Rhetoric*, for there, too, in sharp contrast with the books of the logical *Organon*, what is said in any *logos* is stated expressly to be for listeners. Only as listeners, only as an *audience* as opposed to spectators, do those for whom something is said remain under way in the midst of what occurs without yet having construed it in some sort of *optical* mapping of it from above. Thus, it follows from the very nature of the *pathêmata*, of the experiences felt and undergone by the tragic hero and participated in by the audience, that voice is the only medium in which to communicate them. For unlike a sight, voice—music, *to melos*—is always undergone and never susceptible to distanced observation. Unlike a sight, which leaves the viewers safely at a distance, a voiced sound draws the listeners out of isolated self-possession (*autarkeia*) and into physical communication in gesture and dance. Last in the chain of physical communicants taking part in the poetic event as it is told—we might now best say, sung—by the poet and retold and reenacted by the chorus and actors is, of course, the audience, who "learn by having undergone" which is to say, by hearing, and not by seeing at a distance. (See the *Ion*, 533d–535a and 535b ff., for Plato's critique of precisely this Dionysian involvement.) Thus, to the extent the *Poetics* remains acoustically based, the very thing that Plato sought to banish, the submission of the audience to the passions that come over it in acoustical experience, is uncovered there. It is uncovered, however, only ultimately, as it was in the *Rhetoric*, to be buried and lost again, as we will now see.

6.5.2 The *Poetics*' turn from acoustics to optics

In the end Aristotle is far too much a Platonist to stay with this earlier understanding of learning by undergoing and the priority it gives to acoustical experience, and this is clear even when he treats musical *katharsis* positively, as he does in the *Politics*. For *katharsis* is effected best, he points out there, by a kind of music which, insofar as it is *just* voice, the voice of the flute, and *not at all* speech, is purely acoustical and precludes communication of "envisionable" thought and logic altogether; after all, he points out, as opposed even to the lyre, with the flute it is impossible to play and speak simultaneously (1341a24–25). Indeed, the flute, we read now, "is *not* for character building, for, on the contrary, it is orgiastic," and, hence, to be used "on those occasions when looking on is able *to effect katharsis rather than learning* [ἡ θεωρία κάθαρσιν μᾶλλον δῦναται ἢ μάθησιν]" (1341a21–23; emphases added). This means, first, that the flute, though supremely cathartic, is not instructional; in other words, we do not *learn* character or anything else from it. Second, though the flute can provide beneficial *katharsis*, we read here that it cannot even do this for the one playing it or for someone caught up in the sound of it, rather, only for someone who is just "looking on."

The divorce of *katharsis* from learning that emerges here is then even more sharply drawn in regard to the appropriate use of harmonies and meters; some of these *are* considered "ethical" and of use in character building, and these we are to engage in ourselves. These, we might say, are "manthanic" or instructional. But others are held to be *only* cathartic and are to be "heard" by spectators, if such a thing is possible, but not performed personally, for their effect on the soul would then be too strong (1342a1 ff.). And it now turns out that the *katharsis* by "sacred melodies," of which we heard previously (see above and *Pol.* 1342a7 ff.), belongs to precisely this category of the dangerously excessive effects on the soul and, by implication, that we should find *katharsis* never as performers of the sacred melodies and as dancing communicants in the rites for which they are employed, but only in "looking on," in *theôria.* All at once, *katharsis,* as well as *sôteria* or salvation, has ceased to be something undergone bodily by dancers and has become a matter of getting clear about something intellectually. (It is as if African American Baptists had suddenly become European American Unitarians. Indeed, if white America is ever to recover from the evisceration of its experience in hyperliteracy, from the devolution of its "communication" to the transmission of information, and from the consequent disintegration of community into monadic individuals at computer terminals, it will be black America that makes this recovery, this reversal of what takes place in Aristotle, possible.)

Moreover, with the divorce of melodic *katharsis* from *mathêsis,* and with the concomitant ban on direct participation in melody making, it is clear that Aristotle has already begun to eliminate the idea of *manthanein* or learning as participatory *mimêsis,* or at least to severely restrict it. In regard to the *melos* of the flute and Phrygian modes and meters, the choral dithyramb in particular, we are no longer to learn by partaking in an acoustically transmitted event that we feel and undergo in imitative reenactment of it ourselves. That would only make us vulgar and cost us our status as free men (see 1340b7ff. and 1341a9f.). No wonder, then, says Aristotle, that Athene, as the tale goes, found a flute and threw it away, "For education by the flute contributes nothing to thinking something through [*dianoia*], whereas we attribute to Athene science and art" (1341b6–8). Surely, with this privileging of *dianoia* over an acoustical experience undergone, Aristotle is no longer confronting Plato but siding with him.

Now, as a matter of fact, along with the tendency to rehabilitate the earlier dramatic *mimêsis* that Plato had condemned, there had always been in the *Poetics,* too, this contradictory and very Platonic tendency away from learning by mimetic physical participation and toward learning by detached mental envisioning. As we have seen, it is said early on there that we learn by the engaged imitation exemplified in tragedy; for, to repeat, "Imitating is innate in human beings and exists from childhood on. And they differ from other animals in that they are the most imitative and do their first learning by imitation" (1148b5–9). But, as already noted, there is a striking ambivalence in this passage, for if Aristotle initially had in mind learning by the *mimêsis* of reenacting someone's actions, by *mimêsis praxeôs,* plainly he has also already turned here to learning by a very different *mimêsis* of representation, that is, by visual portrayal of a thing's essential features. This learning comes not at all by our own temporal, heard, voiced, embodied reenactment of an action but by viewing at a distance imitations in space such as painted images. For in explaining his point he now continues:

> We delight in viewing [χαίρομεν θεωροῦντες] the most exact liknesses of even those things that we find most painful to look at themselves, such as grotesque wild animals and corpses. . . . For people delight in seeing likeness because it happens that in viewing them they learn and reason syllogistically [συμβαίνει θεωροῦντας μανθάνειν καὶ συλλογίζεσθαι] what each is, what sort of thing it is. (1448b10–17)

If Plato, with his deliberately absurd analogy of the painting of a bit and reins, did not take the visual imitation seriously, Aristotle certainly does. Indeed, *mimêsis* now means representation in space, and it has forfeited its original sense of dramatic reenactment over time.

Crucial here is the shift to a new kind of *manthanein* and *mathêsis* from which the affective, pathetical dimension of Aeschylus's *pathei mathos*, "learned by having undergone," is eliminated. Learning is no longer learning from within experience while things happen to us "there" *in* the passage of time. Rather, learning now is learning from *above* time and place, learning, namely, that has as its "object" rational comprehension of the *eidos* of things or "what" (*ti*) they "look" like. Learning is "getting the picture" of things. And in this new learning the seat of cognizance and apprehension, the *psuchê*, is no longer down "there" in the body, no longer caught up in undergoing the body's sensations of the physical world, and no longer itself enacting the imitation from within the event.[14] Rather, from a distance, *psuchê* looks on and sees what is arrayed before it. In effect, it is no longer an embodied audience that hears at all but a disembodied spectator that sees. In other words, the acoustical has been displaced by the visual.

We should note, too, that a de-acoustification of language itself follows necessarily from this removal of the *psuchê* from experience undergone bodily, and relocation of it at the vantage point of a detached onlooker. As we have seen, originally, words, as names or *onomata*, were metaphoric-metonymic transformations of voiced imitations of acoustical experience, and to be sure there are still obvious traces of this phonetically based language in Aristotle's discussion of speech and diction in the *Poetics*. But these traces are, we now observe, largely covered over.

For with the removal of the *psuchê* from acoustical experience, words must become significations of the new reality and being that this *psuchê* now "sees" before it; the poet's word names, this is to say, become the logician's word signs signifying the "look" or *eidos* of things beheld theoretically. Audible *onomata,* onomatopoetic namings, that originate initially in voiced imitations of the sound of something, must now be seen as *sêmeia* like "$\sqrt{2}$" or "=," that is, voice*less* visible signs of what, in essence, an unimaginable conceptual thing "looks like," visible signs signifying its purely intelligible "*eidos*" or form. Today, after Derrida, we would say that, consequently, *graphein,* marking in visual space, must no longer be based in *legein* or speaking in acoustical time but given its own priority, and in his *Poetics* even Aristotle himself seems to be torn between thinking of language primarily as spoken and primarily as written.

This tension is most obvious in Aristotle's account of the verbal component of tragedy, *lexis* or diction (1456b9 f.), an account that runs parallel to the treatment of diction in the *Rhetoric,* book 3, with the latter's express preference for the exactitude of *lexis graphikê* or written diction (see above, section 6.4.2). Indeed, we note that from the beginning the exposition here in the *Poetics* is oriented away from voiced speech even if, as the derivation of *lexis* from *legein,* to talk, suggests, Aristotle still takes voiced speech as his point of departure. To begin with, at 1456b3–8 he has already relegated considerations of diction's role in engendering the *pathê* to the *Rhetoric*—though he conveniently dodges the question there too—since in the tragedy, which is the concern of the *Poetics,* the *pathê* will also be engendered by something else besides speech, namely the *sustasis* or composition of the play. This in itself makes clear that in the *Poetics* the *voiced sound* of what is said will now be of only marginal interest. For it is by voiced sound that diction communicates the *pathê,* but for the *Poetics,* at least, this function of *lexis* is now incidental and to be reassigned to *sustasis.* Indeed, in the *Poetics* how a *logos* or speech is to be voiced is deemed wholly irrelevant to diction and relegated to a separate discipline of delivery or performance (*hupokrisis*) of which Aristotle is just dismissive here as he is in the *Rhetoric.* (See 1456b9–19, for example: "For neither knowledge nor ignorance of such things brings any reproach against the art of poetry worthy of being taken seriously" [13–15]. The standard translation of *lexis* as "style" instead of "diction" is a literary strategy that only covers up Aristotle's remarkable deletion here of voice from "speaking" [*legein*], that is, from the way a speech [*logos*] is spoken [*legetai*].) Hence, it is all the more striking that Aristotle still proceeds to base his account of diction on words as they are voiced. The basic elements or *stoicheia* of diction are, he says, *voiced* sounds, namely the vowel, half-vowel, and mute, the *phônêen, hêmiphônon,* and *aphônon* (see 1456b22–31, and section 3.4 above).

With words compounded of these vocal elements, however, the shift from audible mimetic sound to envisionable eidetic signification becomes obvious. For the indivisible syllables are said to be a voicing precisely without significance, a *phônê asêmos* (1456b35), but the words and the utterance (*logos*) made up of these are said to be a "compound significant voice" (*phônê sunthetê sêmantikê*) (1457a12, 24). And with that the acoustical tone yields in importance to the meaning signified and, we might add, what we hear and undergo, to what we see and comprehend.

In fact, it turns out that from the start Aristotle has always subordinated diction to *dianoia,* subordinated how something sounds to what the speaker, having "reasoned something through," has in view. By itself this would not necessarily imply that acoustical communication in voice had been displaced by pure conceptualization and an eidetic logic best communicated voicelessly in writing. For *dianoia,* says Aristotle, is concerned with "whatever it pertains to speech (*logos*) to provide, part of which is demonstration and refutation, *and part of which is providing for the feelings undergone such as pity or fear or rage and the like*" (1456a36–b1; emphasis added). Still, he goes on to say that "the excellence of diction lies in its clarity and not being lowly" (1458a18), which means, of course, that the sound of the poet's words should have a certain distinction about it in order to raise the words above the merely pedestrian, but significantly, that this elevation is now our *only* concern with how they sound. What *pathos* might be communicated by the way they are voiced is precisely not a concern, for the first task is to communicate clearly (*saphôs*) the "thought" behind the words, the *dianoia.* The first task, that is, is to demonstrate clearly through what the characters say "how a thing is, or is not, what it is [in essence]" (τι ὡς ἔστιν ἢ ὡς οὐκ ἔστιν) (1450b12). Indeed, "diction," says Aristotle, "is expatiation by means of putting things into words" (λέξιν εἶναι τὴν διὰ τῆς ὀνομασίας ἑρμηνείαν) (1450b13–14).

With this reduction of tragic diction to clear expatiation Aristotle has effectively contradicted his initial definition of tragedy as the "imitiation of actions" rather than the "reporting" of them (1449b24–27). From the start, he has, in fact, already returned to Plato's privileging of narration over *mimêsis* (see *Rep.* 392d ff.), all the while he would have rehabilitated *mimêsis* against Plato's attack.

That he has is as obvious at the end of his *Poetics* as it is at the beginning: when evaluating the relative merits of tragedy and epic, Aristotle, in his typical dialectical fashion, starts with a concession to his opponents who favor epic over tragedy. Often, he allows, "vulgar" reenactment does count against tragedy, and the epic precludes this vulgarity precisely because it is reporting and not imitation by actors on stage (1449b12). But, he responds, "the tragedy must be able to do what is proper to it without [bodily] motion, just as the epic can; for in the reading of tragedy it is made plain what sort it is" (1462a17–18). Hence, he concludes, if some restrained motions and forms of dance are permissible accoutrements for tragedy (1462a9), the gyrations of indiscrete flute players—and even those of the poet Pindar (!)—prove to be not merely unnecessary but objectionable (see 1461b30 ff.). Indeed, an unmoved, uninvolved *reading* of tragedy would be fully sufficient: "The power of tragedy [to achieve its cathartic effect] also exists without a protagonist and performers," says Aristotle (1450b18–19), and "what is fearful and pitiful can, to be sure, be generated from the visual staging [*opsis*], but also solely from the [the playwright's] composition [*sustasis*] of the actions" (1453b1–3).

Not surprisingly, when Aristotle makes this point that a reading without reenactment can still achieve the tragic effect, he completely neglects the fact that such a "reading," even if no longer a performance, would still be out loud and heard by the reader and audience, and that this hearing is something felt and undergone bodily and hence not a matter at all of just "getting the picture" intellectually. For his entire emphasis now is on the logical composition or *sustasis.* To be sure, he adds that "it is necessary that the story be so composed that, without seeing the actions that came to pass, the one hearing of them trembles and pities at what happened, *as someone hearing the story of Oedipus would undergo this* [ἅπερ ἃ πάθοι τις ἀκούων τὸ τοῦ Οἰδίπου μῦθον]" (1453b4–7; emphasis added). But remarkably, Aristotle overlooks the acoustical-pathetical dimension of what he has just said. His point is only that one can dispense with *hupokrisis* and *opsis,* performance and visual staging, and still *see* the logic of the composition.

By this account even the tragic *katharsis* of fear and pity, which in the *Politics* was said to result from something like becoming entranced by sacred melodies, and which surely was a physical acoustical experience felt and undergone in the imitative motions of one's body, now becomes a matter of intellectual insight. For far from being the result of one's own ritual reenactment of the redemptive sufferings of another, *katharsis* of fear and pity now comes from *detached observation of what these are in essence when someone else undergoes them. Katharsis* becomes, that is to say, a seeing and knowing these *pathê* for what they are, a seeing and knowing precisely by onlookers who, if affected vicariously on one level, ultimately sense that on another level they are really removed and unaffected and, hence, free. Whereas in the soteriological experience of *katharsis* one reenacts the passions of another in order to be redeemed from the debt of one's inevitable transgressions, *katharsis* now results from sensing in cognition one's own transcendence of the *pathê.* Not mimetic participation but contemplative detachment and impassivity is the principle here.

The characteristic substitution of spatial size (*megathos*) for temporal duration (*mêkos*) in Aristotle's conception of tragedy follows naturally from this shift away from the passion of acoustical experience and to the sovereign *autarkeia* of envisioning. For time, with its measures by beats in meter, rhythm, and tempo, is the dimensional form of the acoustical, the material content of the acoustical being tone, timbre, and pitch; but space, with its measures of height, width, and depth, is the proper dimensionality of the visual, its content being color and shape. Of course, Aristotle does not deny that the tragedy does have a temporal duration, and he compares it with epic in precisely this regard, for the epic can go on for an unlimited time (1451a15 ff.), whereas the tragedy's duration cannot exceed the retention of the audience.

Still, Aristotle, we learn now, conceives of the tragedy predominantly in spatial, visual terms. As is well known, he likens a good tragedy to a living thing, the beauty and unity of which consist not only in the right spatial relationship of its parts to each other—here is where the composition or *sustasis* comes in—but also in its having not just any size but the size that is right for it:

> For the beautiful consists in the size and the arrangement [τὸ γὰρ καλὸν ἐν μεγέθει καὶ τάξει ἐστίν], on account of which neither the smallest living thing of all would be beautiful nor the largest. For in the first case our envisioning of it would be confused [συνγχεῖται γὰρ ἡ θεωρία], the time for its occurrence being nearly imperceptible. And in the second case our envisioning does not happen all at once, rather the unity and wholeness of the envisioning eludes the the ones who envision [ἀλλ' οἴχεται τοῖς θεωροῦσι τὸ ἓν καὶ τὸ ὅλον ἐκ τῆς θεωρίας]. (1450b37–1451a5)

Despite the reference to time here it would be wrong to say that Aristotle means what he says about envisioning the spatial size of the tragedy only metaphorically and that his primary focus really remains on its acoustical temporal duration. For, in the first place, the recurring references to *theôria* or envisioning in this passage are not abandoned at all when he continues his analysis of the tragic; rather, they become definitive. In the second place, his emphasis here is, and henceforth continues to be, on the *taxis* and *sustasis* of the parts, their placement and co-placement. Even if taken metaphorically, place, location at a place, is the paradigm, not the temporal sequence. For the concern now is with how a thing that we "see," albeit intellectually, is put together: internally its parts must be fitted together *logically*, and externally it should have a limit or *horos*, and this, as the origin of the word in *horan* or "seeing" suggests, is "in view," which is to say, comprehensible as a whole (1451a6). In retrospect from the *Poetics* it now becomes clear that when Aristotle spoke in the *Rhetoric*, book 3, of the *taxis* or arrangement of a *logos* or speech, he, no less than Plato in the *Phaedrus*, was thinking visually and spatially, not acoustically and temporally—and this despite the obvious fact that the parts of any speech are originally spoken and heard over time and not read across a surface. Indeed, the very word *taxis*, from *thattein*, meaning "to place," presupposes the shift from what is heard to what is seen, a shift, that is to say, from orality to literacy.

Although there is some ambiguity at first (see 1450b26–30), ultimately in the *Poetics*, too, the beginning, middle, and end of a well-composed *muthos* or story are, like the parts of a well-composed *logos* or speech, not to be experienced and undergone acoustically in time. Rather, they are to be understood as parts of a unified "living being" of which we have an overview (1459a19–20). Thus, it is precisely *not* as if the tragedy, or, for that matter, the speech, were like a melody that began out of silence at some time past, came over us and, at its climax, enthralled us in the symphonic interweaving (*symplokê, desis*) of its voices, only then for these, having transformed us, to fade away into dissolution (*lusis*) and inaudibility. Rather, says Aristotle, like the "living thing," the tragedy is to be envisioned all at once (*hama*), present, in view, in its entirety. In short, we are not to hear the poet's tragedy any more than we are to hear the orator's *logos*. Rather, much as Plato would have taught us not to *hear* melodies and undergo them in time but to *look* over and beyond them to the idea of them and to envision the ever present, static logic of the harmonic laws governing them (see *Rep.* 531a–b), in Aristotle our task is to get the logical "picture" of whatever we might hear.

That is why for Aristotle the primary task of the poet is not at all to compose in "pleasant and appropriate meters," though he or she should do this too, but to tell "what is possible either according to likelihood or necessity" (1451a39). In other words, the poet's story must have a *logical* line to it or plot, for as it is treated by the historian, what is past and particular is credible even if we cannot see the logic of it, but, Aristotle adds, what is possible and universal, as it treated by the poet, is credible only if we can see its logic (1451a39–b8).

Crucial here are the logical terms "according to likelihood" and "according to necessity." For these are expressions found in the *Organon*: as we know from the *Prior* and *Posterior Analytics* and the *Topics*, the first is said of dialectical arguments about what is "susceptible of being otherwise" and the second is said of scientific arguments that demonstrate what has to be so and cannot be otherwise. We see, in other words, that the organic unity of the tragedy is now modeled on reasoning and the logical relationship of antecedent and consequence: the end, says Aristotle, must follow from the beginning and middle "out of necessity," or as what happens "for the most part" (1450b30), where "for the most part" substitutes here for "according to likelihood." Even Homer is praised because he omits events that are not in a logical sequence, events, this is to say, that are neither likely (*eikos*) nor necessary (*anakaios*) to the extent that the one event follows logically from the other and not just temporally after it (1451a24–29). Thus, ultimately the tragedy and even the epic are to be intellectually viewed as written arguments, and not heard, felt, and undergone as musical occurrences. Just as in the *Rhetoric*, in the end, meter and, we may presume, pitch and melody, too, turn out to be wholly ancillary.

What is more, even fear and pity, the *katharsis* of which the tragedy should provide, will arise from the logical *sustasis*, the composition or "placing together" of the parts of the story and precisely not from any experience the audience undergoes (1453b1–3). For this reason the "complicated" story line involving reversal and recognition are preferable in Aristotle's view to the "simple" story line, where the "binding" and "unraveling" lack the logical coherence that a properly constructed reversal and recognition display.

This assertion is striking, for the reversal and recognition, he tells us, are, for the one undergoing them, the conversion of an intended result into precisely the opposite of what was expected and foreseen. For instance, Oedipus had expected to be made happy by the news of who he was, and he had expected the fear for his mother to be relieved, but just the reverse happened (1452a23–27). For Oedipus, then, what happens violates and disrupts the logic of his thinking. What he undergoes is *for him* entirely illogical and intrudes from beyond the horizons of his finite comprehension. But exactly this is not be the case *for us*, who are no longer communicants in the reenactment of the *pathê* and *pathêmata* he experiences, but who look on from above and see the logical "likelihood" or even "necessity" of what for him is a bolt out of the blue.[15] Whereas before, in commiseration with his fear, we might have experienced compassion for him and felt saved from our own fear by experiencing this very compassion, now we are removed from feeling any passion at all. Our constitutive passion, this is to say, has become the requisite dispassion for *theôria*. Once again, the soteriological *katharsis* of expiation by reenactment has become Plato's *katharsis* of purification by metaphysical abstraction.

No wonder, then, that in the end music and melody have become for Aristotle mere incidental adornments which produce only a secondary "pleasure," and that the "power of tragedy" to effect *katharsis* is said to exist even "without protagonists and performers" (1450b18). For in contradiction to Kosman's contention that the *Poetics* carries the *Ethics* over onto the new ground of human finitude and error, the *Poetics* could also be said only to repeat what happens in the *Ethics*: in the end our engaged action and the inevitable involvement in wrongdoing that comes with it give way to the highest good of metaphysical *theôria,* of dispassionate, unmoved looking on (see EN 1177a11 ff.). In the end Aristotle, *like* Plato, flees the possibility of having something happen to him. *Like* Plato he too shies away from the stream of time that, like a melody, comes over us, in order that he might find safety in a distanced beholding, which alone would ensure *autarkeia*—full self-possession and independence. Thus, despite its many important traces of an earlier oral-aural experience, the *Poetics* may be said to repeat the *Rhetoric*'s abstraction from the acoustical to the optical.

7

Conclusion: Nietzsche's Recovery of Original Acoustical Experience: The Birth of Argument Out of the Spirit of Music

τοῦ δὲ λόγου τοῦδ' ἐόντος ἀεὶ ἀξύνετοι γίνονται ἄνθρωποι καί πρόσθεν ἢ ακοῦσαι καὶ ἀκούσαντες τὸ πρῶτον. [Of the Logos, this being what it is, human beings are always uncomprehending both before having *heard* it and once they have *heard* it.]

(Heraclitus, Fr. 1)

οὐκ ἐμοῦ ἀλλὰ τοῦ λόγου ἀκούσαντας ὁμολογεῖν σοφόν ἐστιν ἕν πάντα εἶναι. [Having *heard* not me but the Logos, it is wise to agree that all things are one.]

(Heraclitus, Fr. 50)

Um dies zu begreifen, müssen wir jenes kunstvolle Gebäude der apollinischen Kultur gleichsam Stein um Stein abtragen, bis wir die Fundamente erblicken, auf die es begründet ist. [To grasp this we must take away the artful structure of Apollonian culture stone by stone, as it were, until we catch sight of the foundations on which it is grounded.]

(GT §3; KSA 1, 34)

As we saw in the beginning of our study, in the Marburg lectures of the summer of 1924, *Basic Concepts of Aristotelian Philosophy* (GBAPh), Heidegger begins to work out his project of the *Destruktion* of the metaphysical tradition in an appropriation of Aristotle's

Rhetoric. As it was three years later in *Being and Time*'s (SZ) exposition both of our being "there," "in the world," and "with others," and of our employment of tools, ready at hand, to take care of things in going about the practical tasks of day-to-day life, Heidegger's stategy in these earlier lectures, too, is, first, to "lay bare" our original way of existing by taking away the layers of abstractions superimposed upon it, and then, second, to "lay out" hermeneutically or interpretively our original way of existing as this is now uncovered and disclosed beneath the abstractions that have been removed. In this way, the derivative "metaphysical" world of statically present beings given to a theoretical onlooker, say, Descartes's quantifiable extended things just lying about on hand, is shown to be "founded" in another, original world of temporal being, from which theoretical "metaphysics" had abstracted and which it had obscured. In the *Basic Concepts* lectures, however, this strategy of *Destruktion* and "grounding" is applied specifically to speech and argument (*Sprache, logos*): using Aristotle's *Rhetoric,* Heidegger sets out to display, first, that science's demonstration, the *apodeixis,* is an abstraction founded in *dialegesthai* or "talking things through" by "topics" or the natural lines of reasoning given in natural speech, and, second, that even this dialectic's disengaged, theoretical *sun-logismos* or combination of utterances, *logoi,* is, in turn, an abstraction to be founded in rhetoric's engaged, practical *en-thumêmê* or the convincing combination of spoken phrases, *logoi,* that would move a hearer in his or her *thumos* to decide on a course of action. Rhetoric, as well as Aristotle's treatise on it, Heidegger's 1924 lectures show, is thus not of marginal philosophical interest; rather, it is the original way we speak to each other when taking care of practical tasks in the temporal world. Hence, rhetoric is at the crux of our own *Destruktion* of argument as traditionally conceived.

In returning now to Nietzsche, the radical destroyer of traditional conceptions who for us will prove to be the unacknowledged father of much of Heidegger's fundamental ontological project, we will pursue, in conclusion to our own hermeneutical exposition of original argument, a thought broached by Heidegger in 1924, to be sure, but quickly abandoned by him in the course of his own *Destruktion* of "metaphysical" abstractions. Having called *akouein,* hearing, the primary sense perception, Heidegger, as we learned, turns nevertheless to a vision-based *theôria,* a looking on. In this way he repeats the very same movement of thought we have displayed in Aristotle's *Rhetoric* and, in fact, even in the *Poetics,* in which, remarkably, the audience's bodily involvement in the dance, *orchê,* of the chorus disappears and the previously fundamental role of *to melos,* the musical strain, is systematically diminished to an ancillary *hêdusma* or pleasant adornment. Recurring to Nietzsche, we will attempt to reverse this turn to the optical and thereby to "lay bare" and "lay out" hermeneutically the *acoustical* ground, or better said, ground*less* origins of speech.[1] Indeed, Nietzsche, in ultimately rejecting the idea of founding and *fundamenta* altogether, will call this "ground" the *Hintergrund, Unterground,* and even *Abgrund,* that is, the background, underground, and nonground or abyss. With Nietzsche, we will find that there is no *Destruktion* of metaphysics' timeless, tenseless, static presence as long as one has not penetrated behind envisioned, written, and read word signs, and penetrated, first, to spoken and heard word names that tell narratively what happens over time, and penetrated, then, beyond even this, to the melodic *Hintergrund, Untergrund,* and *Abground* in which the spoken word originates.

7.1 A Nietzschean *Destruktion* of the *logos*

Indeed, it is not difficult to show that the history of metaphysics begins with an abstraction and withdrawal from acoustical experience of temporal being and with a turn to an optical supervision, an overview, of static spatialized being, a turn coincident with the turn from *phônê* and *phasis,* voice and saying something out loud, to *graphê,* the written mark, or in the terminology of Eric Havelock and Walter Ong, the turn from orality to literacy. As we have seen, this withdrawal and turn begins at least with Plato's rejection of epic and tragic *mimêsis,* the *mimêsis* of the rhapsode and the dramatic actor (*hupokritês*) (see the *Ion* 533c–536d; *Rep.* 392d–398b, 595a–608b), with Plato's consequent rejection of the continuing concern with these forms of *mimêsis* in rhetoric's treatment of diction (*lexis*) and delivery (*hupokrisis*), and with Plato's turn to the envisioning (*thea*) and contemplation (*theôria*) of the ideas (*eidê*), which is to say, of the conceptual "looks" that things have about them.

Exemplary here is Plato's conversion of the acoustical musical experience of hearing the *melos* into the theoretical science of harmony (see *Republic* 530c–531c): *harmonia,* after all, comes from *harma,* the chariot, and has to do originally with joining and pegging parts into a visual, spatial whole. In the hands of Pythagorians, from whom Plato takes it over, the science of harmony becomes the science of the *logos, logos,* of course, not as a voiced utterance but as an enumerable mathematical proportion, the ratio, of what "fits" together spatially. This *logos* is not heard but seen and "read"; for the one who has been taught the science of harmony no longer hears the melody but, much like someone who takes the score along to read during a performance, envisions, instead, a graphic distribution of different components in the spatial *sustasis* or com-position placing them in relation to each other. So, too, rhetoric becomes for Plato the theoretical science of dialectical com-position: in an act of intellectual *aphairesis*, of withdrawal and abstraction, what we hear in time, as it comes over us and transforms us who undergo its effect, is left behind. To be sure, the word "*sumphonein*," or "to be con*sonant* with," that Plato uses in the *Phaedo* to characterize the combinative logic of each of the visible *eidê* or intelligible "looks" of things, with the others, say, of "Three" with "Odd" but not with "Even," still perpetuates, as we have noted, an earlier phonic, vocal background understanding of speech (see 100a, 104c). However, in the end the envisionable, spatialized latticework of *genos* and *eidê*, say, of the *Phaedrus*'s genus "Madness" in its sinister/left forms of "Gluttony," "Dipsomania," and "*skaios erôs*" or "Left Love," *placed* over against its rectitudinous/right forms of "Prophecy," "Lyric Musicality," "Cathartic Healing," and "Divine Love," a latticework that we *see* arrayed before us, becomes the new focus of our redirected attention, and the phonetic and acoustical origins of speech fall into oblivion (see *Phaedrus* 264c–266c). As in the Pythagorean conversion of *logos* from "speech" back into its original sense of "ratio," here too the *logos* of *dialegesthai* or talking something through vocally in time is converted into the *logos* of a "dialectical" spatial organization that we see and read.[2] And, analogously, even tragedy, we learn, would no longer consist in the communication of affects by its sound but in its envisionable "spatial" com-position: "as if," writes Plato, "one were to think that the tragedy is anything other than the proper composition [*sustasis*] of these [parts] placed [*sunistamenen*] in relation to one another and the whole" (*Phaedrus* 268d).

In contrast, Aristotle, as we have attemped to display here, would seem in many respects to have recovered an "earlier" understanding of a *logos* "closer to the origin," an understanding nearly buried in Plato. After all, he writes a *Rhetoric* whose third part, as we have seen, is devoted to spoken diction, and a *Poetics* which at least partially rehabilitates a kind of *mimêsis* or imitation that involves the audience's bodily participation in musical, and even "orchestral," or dancing reenactment of an action. Despite this recovery, we have found, however, that in the end Aristotle only perpetuates and solidifies the Platonic "metaphysical," "theoretical," "scientific" withdrawal and turn from the acoustical to the optical.

For even if his *Rhetoric* devotes ten quite extraordinary chapters to a phenomenological exposition of the affects intrinsic to rhetorical conviction (book 2, chapters 2–11), affects that can be communicated only acoustically, which is to say, musically by intonation, phrasing, candence, tempo, rhythm, and the like, it still treats rhetoric primarily as the "counterpart" to dialectic, in which the affects play no role at all, save that they must be neutralized. Thus, Aristotle says right from the start that, like dialectic, rhetoric should be concerned not with the affects—and, we infer, not with the *lexis* and *hupokrisis,* the audible diction and delivery that communicate the affects to hearers—but only with the *logos,* now meant in the reduced sense of dialectic's syllogistic argument. *Logos* is thus severed from *pathos* after all; speech, and argument in speech, is severed from affect, and, consequently, the logically envisionable is severed from the acoustical. This split, in the dichotomy of the cognitive and emotive, will go unchallenged until, and, given even Heidegger's ultimate neglect of it, go unchallenged except for, Nietzsche's radical *Destruktion* of the "theoretical" and "scientific" and his reduction of these to acoustical art and of acoustical art, in turn, to bodily life.

Similarly, in Aristotle's *Poetics* we found that in the end the tragedy will achieve its *katharsis,* not bodily by the acoustical experience of the *melos* undergone by the audience (*hoi akouontes*), who are drawn into the dance and gesture of the imitative reenactment, but cognitively by detached spectators (*theôretes*), who, in grasping the intelligible logic of the organically composed overseeable whole with its beginning, middle, and end fitted together harmoniously, are purified of the influence of any affects exceeding the mean that would keep them subordinate to rational limitation. The making of melodies, *melopoia,* is, it turns out, a matter of mere pleasant adornments, *hedusmata,* and not intrinsic to the art of tragedy at all (see 1450b16). On the contrary, the intrinsic essence of tragedy is said to lie in its *overseeable,* logical unity. In the end, then, Aristotle only repeats Plato's conversion of tragedy from the acoustical to the optical: the *sustasis* or composition, says Aristotle, too, "is the primary and most important element of the tragedy" (1450b22), and, he continues,

> It has now been established for us, then, that the tragedy is the imitation of a complete and whole action having a certain size [ἐχούσης τι μέγεθος]. . . . A whole is what has a beginning, middle, and end. A beginning is what does not necessarily have to be after something else [μὴ ἐξ ἀνάγκης μετ' ἄλλο ἐστίν], but after which something else either is naturally or comes to pass [πέφυκεν εἶναι ἢ γίγνεσθαι]. The end, in contrast, is what itself is naturally [πέφυκεν εἶναι] after something else, either of necessity or for the most part, but after which nothing else is. A middle is what itself both is after something else and also after which something else is. Accordingly, it is necessary that well-composed stories neither just happen to begin nor just happen to end somewhere or other; rather that they have made use of the ideas we have mentioned. (1450b24–34)

We note in this passage Aristotle's pronounced tendency to abstract *from* the temporal sequence of historical-narrative story or *muthos* as it is told and heard—"Once upon a time this came to pass, and then this, and then this . . . ," and so forth—and his tendency to abstract *to* what Nietzsche will call a "logical schematism." The finite forms of the temporal *gigignesthai,* or "to come to pass," already start to give way here to finite forms of the timeless logical *einai,* or "to be." "Comes to pass," this is to say, gives way to "is." With that, the timeless logical connections of one thing not following *upon* another *temporally* but "following" *from* another *logically,* that is, "for the most part" (*epi to polu*) and even "of necessity" (*ex anagkês*), have insinuated themselves into the account of tragedy. What matters now is that the composition of the components, beginning, middle, and end, be overseeable and comprehensible, that one event be *seen* to follow logically from another and not merely be *heard* to follow it temporally as in music. Once again, it is only Nietzsche who will call this canon of envisionable organic unity and logical consequentiality into question. "The requirement of unity," he writes in the fall of 1869, "unjustified, as we saw, is the source of all perversions in the opera and in the song" (1 [49]; KSA 7, 24); "The piece of music: it is a mistake to talk here about the architechtonics of the whole and similarly with drama. Where are the laws of sequentiality?" (1 [53]; KSA 7, 26).

It falls to Nietzsche, in other words, to overthrow the two-millennia-long Platonic-Aristotlelian "historical effect," to reverse, this is to say, the metaphysical withdrawal and turn away from the acoustical to the visual. As we will now see, this overthrow and reversal finds its clearest execution in his *Birth of Tragedy Out of the Spirit of Music,* all the inadequacies of this inchoate study notwithstanding. For Nietzsche's project of *Destruktion* in that work is to display the tragedy of Aeschylus and Sophocles as the repenetration and suffusion of the visual, three-dimensional spatial Apollonian world of the epicist Homer by the Dionysian sonic temporal world of the folk poet Archilochus and, thereby, to return the Apollonian as such to the Dionysian musical and acoustical *Hintergrund, Untergrund,* and *Abgrund* out of which it originates and by which it is sustained. To be sure, there was musical accompaniment to the rhapsodist's singing of Homer, the accompaniment, namely, of the lyre or cithara. But tragedy, as Nietzsche's radical reflections display, reveals the influence of another, primal music of Archilochean heritage, namely, the music of the flute and Pindar's dithyrambic hymns, the very music which, as we have seen, Aristotle takes great pains to discredit. "Indeed," says Nietzsche,

> it becomes tangibly clear thereby [in the contrast of Homer and Pindar] that between Homer and Pindar those orgiastic Olympian ways of flute

> playing must have rung out, that even in the age of Aristotle, in the midst of an infinitely more developed music, still carried people away into drunken enthusiasm and most assuredly, in its original effect, stirred all the poetic means of expression of contempory human beings to imitate it. (GT §6; KSA 1, 49)

Nietzsche's destructive task accordingly is to ground the beautiful Apollonian dream pictures, conjured up in all vividness before our eyes by Homer's tales, in another, primary experience, an experience from the very pain and contradiction of which these dream pictures only momentarily release us. The Apollonian, namely, is to be grounded in its background, underground, and groundless nonground of the Dionysian ecstatic "rush" (*Rausch*) that dissolves individuality and fuses each of us with each other and with all things, but that, in shattering acoustically the spatial and logical distinctions of "this here" as opposed to "that there," reveals to us the underlying insignificance of all significance we had assigned to things. Thus, the Apollonian dream images that we see before us are to be resolved into an undifferentiated flow of time, not observed, but undergone physically, somatically, acoustically, as it comes over us, and the experience of which can be communicated only in the music we hear and to which we dance.

It is the chant and dance of the chorus, therefore, which, in contrast to Aristotle's ultimate dismissal of it, must be seen as the core of the tragedy, and not, as Aristotle would tell us, the logical composition, not the thought, the action, the story, or least of all the dialogue: "The Greek chorus," writes Nietzsche in the fall of 1869, "is, first, the live soundingboard and second the megaphone through which the actor cries out colossally his feeling to the spectators, and, third, it is the passionate, singing spectator, become lyrical, who has found in it his voice" (1 [4]; KSA 7, 11).

In support of this line of thought we might add that perhaps even more than the chorus of the Argive Elders, it is Aeschylus's Cassandra whose antiphonal speech, embedded as it is in the aboriginal cry, lets us hear this indefinite and indeterminate Dionysian acoustical underground from which the vision of the actions on the *skênê* or stage arises and back into which it is resolved. "Otototototoi popoi da," she cries out, "oh oh oh oh, ouch ouch, ah"; "ê ê, papai papai," "aye, aye, ouch, ouch"; "iou, iou, o, o kaka," "ohoh, ohoh, oh oh, shit" (*Agamemnon* 1072, 1114, 1215), all of which provide the tonal-pathetical setting for her own version of the wisdom of Silenus that it would be best never to have been born at all, and if born, to die early: "Alas, poor men, their destiny. When all goes well a shadow will overthrow it. If it be unkind one stroke of a wet sponge wipes all the picture out; and that is far the most unhappy thing of all" (1326–30 [Lattimore trans.]). And so, too, Creon's speech at the end of Sophocles' *Antigone* collapses back into its underground of the repeated primal cries of "iô" (1261, 1283), "oimoi" (1271, 1317), and "aiai aiai" (1290, 1306), which invoke the ineliminable tonal setting for his final utterances. "Speech," Nietzsche observes in the spring of 1870, "arose out of the cry with its accompanying gesture; here by the intonation, the volume, the rhythm, the essence of the thing is expressed and, by the gesture of the mouth, the accompanying image of the essence, the appearance" (3 [15]; KSA 7, 63).

On Nietzsche's understanding there are, accordingly, four stages to be elaborated in the birth and the death of tragedy. First comes the "iron age" with its battle of the titans and its "bitter folk philosophy," and second, the stage of the so-called naive artist Homer, whose "naïveté," contrary to what a Rousseau or Schiller might think, can only be understood against the prior experience of the titanic realm, on whose chaos it superimposes an ordering, to be sure, but by suppressing, with "forceful manic mirror images" and "pleasurable illusions," a "terrible depth in the way one sees the world" and "a hypersensitive capacity for suffering" (see GT §4; KSA 1, 41–42). Homeric naïveté is thus only to be grasped as "the perfect victory of the Apollonian illusion" (GdT §3; KSA 1, 37). But this "naively beautiful" Homeric world must, in turn, yield to the third stage, in which the "stream of the Dionysian" "breaks in upon it" and "swallows it up" (GT §4; KSA 1, 41). With that tragedy is born, but only to decay and die in stage four, the "stiff majesty" of Doric art (GT §4; KSA 1, 41) and the Euripidean post-tragedy based on "Socratic" cognizance and logic and, now in complete disjunction from this cognizance and logic, extraneous stimulation of the affects (see GT §§11–15).

Thus, Nietzsche's radical question is this: What if "for us the period reached last, that of Doric art, ought not to count as the culmination and aim of those art-drives [the Apollonian and Dionysian]" but rather the "sublime and exalted artwork of Attic tragedy" (GT §4; KSA 1, 42)? In other words, what if the verdict of Platonic and Aristotelian metaphysics were to be undone and the supposed "culmination" in conscious knowledge of what is statically present in view were shown to be a degenerate abstraction from the original experience of hearing and responding in dance to the tones of the *melos*?

Let us review Nietzsche's distinction between the Apollonian and the Dionysian "drives," as he calls them. The Apollonian drive produces the realm of *Schein,* the sheen of appearance shining forth (GT §1; KSA 1, 26), for Apollo is the "shining one," "the light divinity," the god of all "picture-making powers and plasticity [*bildnerische Kräfte*]" (GT §1; KSA 1,

27). Hence, the Apollonian artist "likes to *look* at these things closely (*sieht gern und genau zu*), for out of these pictures he interprets life for himself" (GT §1; KSA 1, 26; my emphasis); and in this way, in "freedom from the wilder stimulations," he makes life "possible and worth living" (GT §1; KSA 1, 27). But this is the "reality" of dream and appearance, and as such it is subject to disruptions. To the horror (*Grausen*) of the dreamer, these disruptions, these intrusions of the real "reality" beneath the dream, arrive as suspensions of the *Satz vom Grund* (GT §1; KSA 1, 28): *nihil est sine ratione* or "nothing exists without a rational account." Implied here is that the logical basis of our conscious, envisioned "chart" of differences and relations is suddenly kicked out from beneath it: logic's "laws" of noncontradiction, ~(A•~A), and self-identity, A = A, which alone preserve its unified logical composition and make rational accounts possible, lose their validity, and we are plunged into the very groundlessness of anarchic reasoning that Aristotle, in his own *Grausen* or *apeirophobia*, had sought so strenuously to head off (see section 5.3 above).

This very horror, however, is at the same time its contrary, *Rausch*, the "rush" of intoxication that overcomes us when individuation dissolves and we, "singing and dancing," experience a "festival of reconciliation" (GT §1; KSA 1, 29). Now we experience the underlying realm of Dionysius, the primary acoustical realm of rhythm and tone, the realm of music. The visual world of shining pictures and three-dimensional images has been absorbed back into the acoustical experience from which they arose to begin with. By "Dionysian," writes Nietzsche in early 1871,

> I understand, first, all art that is not the appearance of an appearance but the appearance of being, the mirroring of the eternal aboriginal one [*des ewigen Ur-Einen*], and hence, second, our entire empirical world, which, from the vantage point of the aboriginal one is a Dionysian artwork, *or from our standpoint, music.* (7 [126]; KSA 7, 184; emphasis added)

Music here is not the Doric "architectonics in tones, but in tones only hinted at, like those of the cithara" (GT §2; KSA 7, 33), for this latter "tone" is far removed from the "shattering force of the tone, the unitary stream of the *melos,*" that characterizes Dionysian music, far removed from the dithyramb, "a bodily symbolics not just of the mouth, the face, the word, but of *full blown dance gestures that set all limbs in rhythmical motion*" (id.; emphasis added). Hence, while in the Apollonian realm we looked on tranquilly as visions loomed up before us, we now find ourselves undergoing and feeling physically what the primal sounds we hear do with us. In this way only Nietzsche, we see, is able to lay bare the original acoustical experience that Plato would banish and that even Aristotle deletes from his accounts of speech and tragedy.

But how did this nonground of tragedy get covered up in the first place? This, it turns out is the work of a philosopher, namely, Socrates: in Euripides' tragedy by consciousness, cognizance (*Erkenntnis*), and thought, tragedy is torn up from its ground. Euripides, whom, significantly, Aristotle finds the consummate tragedian, and who could be said to be driven just as much as Aristotle by what we have called apeirophobia or the fear of indeterminacy, had sought to correct the unclarity and impenetrability attaching itself to the works of Aeschylus and Sophocles: "With all the brightness and facility of his critical thinking," writes Nietzsche in the *Birth of Tragedy*,

> Euripides had sat in the theater and strained to recognize in the masterpieces of his predecessors, as if these were paintings darkened over, each and every trait, each and every line. And here there now confronted him something that ought not to be unexpected for anyone initiated into the deeper secrets of Aeschylean tragedy: he perceived something incommensurable in every trait and every line, a certain deceptive determinacy, but at the same time, a puzzling depth, yes, even infinity of the background. The clearest figure still had something of a comet's tail about it that seemed to point into an uncertainty upon which no light could be shed. (GT §11; KSA 1, 80–81)

We note the turn here from the acoustical/temporal to the optical/spatial: in order to make sense of tragedy, to bring all of it within thought's purview and comprehension, in order to get the visual picture of it, Euripides was thus constrained to wage war on its incomprehensible Dionysian underground. That which is incommensurable with the principles of logic and which by nature keeps to itself and withholds itself *from view* was to be eliminated. But in thereby eradicating the Dionysian acoustical root of the Apollonian visual dream, he cut the latter off from its source and found himself left with only a desiccated, empty form: tragedy now as a "game of chess," mere "cool thoughts" into which he then imported "fiery affects," say, in Medea's gruesome violence. (We note, for example, that unlike Aeschylus's Dionysian chorus of furies, Euripides' Medea comes not from the underground chaos preceding Greek Olympian order; rather, she is an alien brought in from the exotic East.)

Hence, just as in Socrates and the subsequent tradition, conscious cognizance and thought is severed from its ground in affect and feeling, and these, in turn, degenerate into ancillary means of rhetorical persuasion, which is to say, conning people into something, and pleasant ornamentation, so too in tragedy the musical and acoustical, which communicate affect and feeling, become a mere secondary stimulant—the greatest of the *hedusmata*, or decorative pleasantries, as Aristotle puts it. And having been displaced by an abstract theoretical optics, the primary acoustical experience thus falls into oblivion.

When Nietzsche argues that Euripides brought the *spectator* onto the stage, the *theoretês, der theoretischer Mensch*, namely, Socrates and Euripides himself, as a self-conscious commentator on his own "tragedy by consciousness," we should make no mistake about what this means for what had been the *audience* of tragedy. In *hearing* the *melos* that audience had itself been drawn into the choral dithyrambic chants and dance and, like early Christians in their mimetic reenactment of the Eucharist, had only then seen the reincarnate deity arise on the scene before them out of the midst of their original acoustical communion.[3] In Euripides, however, this audience that hears and then sings and dances with the chorus has now become a mere onlooker with an overview of the whole. As Nietzsche had put it earlier in 1869:

> Long before Socrates was alive Socrates was the element in the tragedy that dissolved it. The lack of music and, on the other hand, the exaggerated monological development of feeling, necessitated that dialectic come to the fore. The musical *pathos* is missing in dialogue. (1 [15]; KSA 7, 14)
>
> In Socrates the principle of science moves in; and with that [comes] the battle with the unconscious and its annihilation. (1 [27]; KSA 7, 17)
>
> Euripides introduced dialectic, the tone of the courtroom, into the dialogue. We see the vexing consequence here: if one separates feeling and understanding, music and deed, intellect and will, unaturally from each other, each separted part shrivels up. (1 [49]; KSA 7, 25)

With Euripides, says Nietzsche, "dialectic penetrates the heros of the stage, and they die of a superfetation of the logical" (1 [7]; KSA 7, 12–13); "Music is the mother of tragedy" (1 [7]; KSA 7, 13); "The music drama is the high point; it is dissolved by expanded reflection" (1 [28]; KSA 7, 18).

The truly radical and revolutionary dimension of Nietzsche's exposition here lies in its complete inversion of Platonic-Aristotelian "metaphysical" priorities: on Nietzsche's account the ordered world of sights is not higher than, and prior to, the nonordered experience of sounds, and the experience of sounds is thus not, as in Pythagorean doctrines of harmony, a fallen version of the world of envisionable ratios, rather the reverse. In support of this thesis Nietzsche takes, as an example, Schiller's account of the poetic experience: "He [Schiller] allows, namely, that as the condition preparatory to the poetic act, he did not have before him and in his possession some sequence of images ordered causally in his thoughts but, on the contrary, [found himself undergoing] a musical mood or voicing [*eine musikalische Stimmung*]" (GT §5; KSA 1, 43). Or, as Nietzsche restates this, "The 'I' of the lyricist thus resounds [*tönt*] out of the groundlessness of being [*Abgrund des Seins*]" (id.). Put another way, "The plastic artist, just as the epicist who is related to him, has sunk into the pure viewing of pictures. The Dionysian musician, without any picture, is himself only aboriginal pain and the aboriginal resonance [*Urwiderklang*] of this pain" (GT §5; KSA 7, 44).

What is to be learned from this radical rethinking of Western priorities? Let us say, to begin with, that here in the original poetic experience *logos* is still embedded in *pathos,* speech still embedded in a "feel" or affective tone to things as this is undergone, *epathen,* in the primary experience of voice and melody beneath any overseeable system of differences and relations among significations; *logos,* namely reasoning argument in speech, originates, this is to say, in a primary acoustical experience where the principle of sufficient reason, *nihil est sine ratione,* and the logical "laws" of noncontradiction and self-identity propping it up have yet to obtain. Thus, in Nietzsche, as opposed to Derrida, the *pharmakon* that subverts and shatters the ordered realm, the *Hexentrank* or witches' brew (GT §2.3; KSA 1, 32) and *Zaubertrank* or magic potion (GT §§3, 13; KSA 1, 35, 90), as Nietzsche calls it, is not "writing" or *graphê*; it is not visual, readable markings in space signifying another differentiated visual order of significations located some *place* else, ad infinitum, but rather the temporal rising and falling tone of *phônê* and *melos* that we hear, feel, and undergo bodily (*paschomen somatikôs*) for the *time* it reverberates and resonates in us and with us. Voice is the an-archic, unfathomable, bottomless underground, not on which the logical rests, but in which it floats precariously. When the logical foundation drops out, as it does in the primary Dionysian experience of music, *graphê* collapses into *phônê,* writing into voice, not vice versa.

"Music," writes Nietzsche in the winter of 1870,

> is a language that is capable of an unending clarification of meaning. Language makes its meaning clear only by concepts; hence feeling what someone else feels occurs in language through the medium of thought, and this sets limits to language. But this holds only for objective, written language. The spoken, intoned word rings, and the intervals, the rhythms, the tempi, the volume and emphasis, are all symbolic for the content of feeling that is to be represented. All this belongs to music too. The great mass of feeling, however, does not express itself by words. And the word,

> too, merely points in its direction. The word is the surface of an agitated sea storming in its depths. Here we have the limits of the word-drama, its incapacity to represent things alongside each other. (2 [10]; KSA 7, 48)
>
> Music, however, says out loud the soul of the dramatic action. Words, after all, are the most deficient indices. (2 [11]; id.)

Nietzsche the musician thus alerts us to an earlier, premetaphysical dimension of *logos* of speech and argument that remains inaccessible both to Derrida and Heidegger. For Derrida, unlike Nietzsche, cannot get behind visible, readable signification to its origins in vocal naming, cannot, this is to say, get behind Plato's and Aristotle's literary *sêmainein* to the poet's oral *onomazein*; and Heidegger, unlike Nietzsche, and despite his own early advertences to the ineliminable *Stimmung* or voicing underlying every *logos*, cannot get behind the poet's *onomazein*, to the primal reverberations of acoustical, musical experience in which this *onomazein* or naming is inextricably embedded and from which it originates.

With Nietzsche, then, we can resume our own *Destruktion* layer by layer. Having taken down and removed the abstraction of the word sign designating the conceptual look of something envisioned intellectually, and having "laid bare" beneath it the spoken onomatopoetic word name, we can "lay out," as we have, the original lyrical-poetic event of vocal *onomatopoiein*, naming according to the sound of a thing that we hear, say, "smooth" and, by metaphor or "carryover" and metonymy or "renaming," naming other sensuous-somatic "feels" to something as in a "smooth" surface or taste. This metaphorical, metonymic proliferation is enhanced, as we have shown, by synechdoche, or carrying over the name for a part to the whole or vice versa, and polyptoton, or carrying over the name into other parts of speech as in the transformation, by "multiple inflection," of the adjective "smooth" to the participle "smoothing" from the verb "to smooth out."

What we have exposed so far, then, are the origins of logical argument in metonymic tropes. For as Nietzsche puts it, "every concept is a metonymy and cognition proceeds in concepts"; and, he continues,

> Logical thought, little practiced by the Ionians, develops very slowly. Logically invalid conclusions we might better comprehend as metonymies, comprehend, that is, rhetorically, poetically. All rhetorical figures, i.e., the essence of speech and language, are logically invalid conclusions. It is with these that reason begins! (19 [215]; KSA 7, 486)

Moreover, Nietzsche, in shedding more light on what Gadamer has called the "prior accomplishments" of speech, explains how such metonymics and metaphorics actually work in generating original argument by similarity and difference, argument, this is to say, which only later rigidifies into an abstract logic of classes, and "causal" explanation: "It is tropes," Nietzsche tells us, "and not unconscious syllogisms, on which our sense perceptions rest. Identifying similar things with similar things—finding out which similarity exists of one thing with another—is the original process" (19 [217]; KSA 7, 487), and, he continues, "The only way that we get a multiplicity to submit is by making up genera, for example, by *naming* a whole lot of different kinds of action 'bold' " (19 [215]; KSA 7, 486; emphasis added).

> All explanation and cognition is actually only finding a rubric for something. The multiplicity of things is put under one heading when we consider it as innumerable actions, so to speak, of *one* quality, for example, as actions of *water* as in Thales. Here we have a metaphorical transference: an abstraction grasps together innumerable actions as one and then counts as a cause. What is the abstraction (property) which comprehends the multiplicity of things? The quality "watery," "wet." The world is wet, therefore "being wet" is the entire world. (id.)

Changing Nietzsche's thought here only slightly, we could say, for our part, that Thales' causal "explanation" of all things as "water" is not so much a generalization of an immediately perceived, *unnamed* quality, as Nietzsche seems to be saying when he moves from *Wasser* to *wässerig* but then to the very different stem *feucht*, as it is a renaming or metonymy, by the trope of polyptoton, of the *onoma* or word name "water" in "watery" and "wet." Thales' thinking, this is to say, follows a sequence of vocal modulations or inflections of a word name (compare Riedel, *Hören auf die Sprache*, 347, on the "transformation of names" (*Umwandlung von Namen*). As a matter of fact, Nietzsche comes close to putting things this way himself in summing up the point of this passage: "Metonomy: a logically invalid conclusion." He notes, "A sum of predicates is mistaken for one predicate (definition)" (id.). Or, as he puts it in an essay from this same year (1873), "On Truth and Lying in the Extra-moral Sense,"

> What is truth? A mobile army of metaphors, metonymies, anthropomorphisms, in short a sum of human relations which, having been heightened poetically and rhetorically, are carried over and embellished, and which, after being long in use, seem to a people to be firmly established, canonical and obligatory. (KSA 1, 880)

If we redirect Nietzsche's critical intentions—*he*, after all, is concerned to show that all reasoning is a falsification of a prenominative, immediate sensuous experience—we can easily apply what he says in maintaining, for our part, that all demonstration by classes and all explanation by causes is a petrification and falsification of original argument based in the ground of speech and naming. Nietzsche, this is to say, considers even speech that names a "lie" concealing what "is" really, whereas we, following Heidegger, can consider speech to be the "house of being," or that which lets anything be what it is in the first place. As we have heard, *Es sei kein Ding, wo das Wort gebricht,* "There be no thing where the word breaks down." Nothing exists for us human beings as what it "is" until we have found the word and name to call it into being.

However, with Nietzsche and not against him, we have in fact gone beyond Heidegger and "laid bare" beneath this layer of metonymic-metaphorical nominative speech the ultimate origins of argument in the ground and soil of voice or, as Nietzsche would put it, in "the spirit of music" (*dem Geiste der Musik*). For if we push our *Destruktion* radically enough, Thales' metonymic reasoning, it turns out, is still a "founded phenomenon"; it is ultimately grounded in the primary experience of tone. "The philosopher," Nietzsche tells us in speaking of Thales in *Philosophy in the Tragic Age of the Greeks,* "tries to let the collective *ring* of the universe re*sonate* in himself and to reproduce it out of himself in concepts (*Der Philosoph sucht den Gesamt*klang *der Welt in sich nach*tönen *zu lassen und ihn aus sich herausstellen in Begriffen*) (PhTZAG §3; KSA 1, 817; emphasis added; see Riedel, *Hören auf die Sprache,* 352). He continues,

> What the verse is for the poet, dialectical thinking is for the philosopher. He reaches for it in order to maintain his enchantment, in order to petrify it. And just as for the dramatist word and verse are only stammering in a foreign language in order to say in it what he has lived and seen and what he could make known directly only through gesture and music, so too expression of every deep philosophical intuition by dialectic and scientific reflection is, to be sure, the only means to communicate what was seen, but a pitiful means, in fact, at its base, a metaphorical and completely unfaithful translation into a different sphere and language. Thus, Thales saw the unity of what is, and when he wanted to communicate this, he spoke of water. (id.)

To be sure, with Nietzsche's recurrence here to the visual vocabulary of "seen" and "saw," the intrinsic relationship of *logos,* of speech and argument, to audible music is announced only then to be obscured. *The Birth of Tragedy Out of the Spirit of Music,* however, has already shed light for us on this relationship, for it has made clear that all word names and metonymic transformations of them, though eventually in*scribing* an envisionable system of differences and relations, continue even then to in*voke* their origins in the experience of a primal voicing of things. It is this primary acoustical experience that Nietzsche alone, not Heidegger, not Derrida, and not even Gadamer, recovers for us.

7.2 Aboriginal Sonority

The consequences of this recovery of original acoustical experience for our hermeneutics of original speech and argument are far-reaching. Theologically, for example, it would mean the recovery, too, of an earlier, rhetorical understanding of Scriptural translation. Translations of biblical speech, for instance, which try only to render accurately the cognitive content of the original Hebrew and Greek texts would be seen to have deleted the acoustical basis of their communication. For, as is in fact the case with most contemporary translations, they provide texts that are impossible to make resonate and ring, texts with no voice, no tone, no *melos* audible in them any longer. Consequently the communication can no longer be the communication of the pathetical ground of what is said, from viscera and will to viscera and will, but only communication of information, data, facts, from one eviscerated, disembodied mind to another, and even for someone with ears—"Let him who has ears, hear" (Luke 8:8)—there is no longer any message to be heard. Not only the Psalms, then, are melodies to be sung, not "texts" to be read, but the entire Hebrew Bible and New Testament.[4]

And what, after Nietzsche, should we say, for instance, about Lincoln's great political addresses? If Nietzsche is right, these too, like tragic drama and music, have their real being, not at all as written texts to be read silently, but only in their vocal reenactment and declamation. For surely not cognitive information signifiable by written signs is meant to be communicated by these addresses but rather that original unity of *logos, êthos* and *pathos* expressed in phrasing and tonality, in the voicing or *Stimmung* of the *melos*, from which the *logos*, the speech and argument, arises and back into which it continues to resonate.

With that we are brought back to our starting point, the concluding passages of the Second Inaugural Address:

> Fondly do we hope, fervently do we pray that this mighty scourge of war may speedily pass away. Yet, if God wills that it continue until all the wealth piled by the bondsman's two hundred and fifty years of unrequited toil shall be sunk, and until every drop of blood drawn with the lash shall be

> paid by another drawn with the sword, as was said three thousand years ago, so still it must be said, "The judgments of the Lord are true and righteous altogether."
>
> With malice toward none, with charity for all, with firmness in the right as God gives us to see the right, let us strive on to finish the work we are in, to bind up the nation's wounds, to care for him who shall have borne the battle and for his widow and his orphan, to do all which may achieve and cherish a just and lasting peace among ourselves and with all nations.[5]

If we give primary attention to how this speech—which is precisely not a "text"—sounds, we hear at once that Lincoln begins this cadenced conclusion to his address with the diachronic trope of symphony, each of the two members of which are introduced with alliteration of the aspirated and softened labial "f" and the epistrophic "ly" of "Fondly . . . , fervently." The assonance of the long but soft ringing vowel "ay" in "pray" with "away" in which this phrase resolves itself only heightens, by contrast, the abrasive, hard "k" gutteral sound in "s*c*ourge."

The metonymic, metaphorical "*scourge* of war," is of course, tied by the logical topic of similarity to the "blood drawn with the *lash,*" and the following symphonic linking of the "drop of blood drawn with the lash" and "another drawn with the sword," each synechdoches for slavery and war, respectively, "furnishes" (Aristotle: *porizetai*; Gadamer: *leistet*) the enthymeme from the topic of similarity, namely, that the cost of slavery, the "lash," is like the cost of war, the "sword," and therefore it is "true and righteous altogether" that the first should be paid for with the second.

Suppose, however, that Lincoln had argued *only* "logically" here, say, with the enthymeme "Slavery is like war (similar things are to be predicated of similar things); therefore, the cost of war is only equal to the cost of slavery." Obviously, there would then have been no *peithô,* no conviction, achieved. For, though a *reader* of this enthymeme, were it just written and not spoken, might end up seeing the point and believing that the conclusion is valid, the *audience,* for whom it is actually intended, would remain unchanged in regard to how they feel about the matter and, hence, unmoved to decide to act in certain way. The audience would remain unmoved, that is, to show mercy to the hitherto hated, and soon to be defeated, enemy. Hence, the voicing of what Lincoln has said, and the *êthos* and *pathos* by that voicing, are, as Lincoln clearly knew, intrinsic to his communication.

For he now moves to the real "conclusion" of his argument, which is not a statement of static states of affairs to be pointed out or demonstrated, and to which a spectator might respond, "Yes, I see that that is the way things stand." Instead, it is an exhortation to decide on a future course of action to which an audience must respond, "Yes, we will"—namely, "*let us strive on* . . . to finish, to bind up, to care, to do." With this urgent pulse of symphonies asyndetically linked, Lincoln impels this phrase to its dramatic climax in the "just and lasting peace," which, not by chance, responds to the "scourge of war," which we heard near the beginning, in an antiphony heightened by the contrast of the frictionless fluidity of "peace" with the harsh scraping of "scourge." Certainly, far more is intended here than that this antiphony might "furnish" an enthymeme by the topic of contraries, say, "War is harmful (contrary things can be predicated of contrary things); therefore peace is beneficial." Indeed, that the *thumos* of the audience is to be changed by the en*thym*eme, and not just the view of the matter held by uninvolved, disengaged spectators, becomes audible in the phrasing with its modulations in rhythm, pitch, timbre, and volume, modulations that must be assigned to Lincoln's enactment and delivery (*hupokrisis*) of this speech, even if we, superliterate and elocutionarily deprived as we are, can now scarely recover and reenact them.

For, in fact, the fulcrum on which everything turns here is the explicit evocation of *pathos* and *êthos* in the symphonic-antiphonic "With malice toward none, with charity for all." In this we *hear* communicated, first, Lincoln's own *êthos,* which is to say, his own *phronêsis* or discernment of what is just and right, his own *eunoia* or benevolence and good intentions, and his own *aretê.* This last is now cast as the virtue of *chesed, agapê, charitas,* which is to say, not in Greek terms of ethical excellence, but in biblical terms of the humility of the wrongdoer who, in knowledge of his having been forgiven, forgives infinitely the wrongs of others. Thus, in this "With malice toward none, with charity for all" there is also named the basic shift Lincoln seeks in the audience's *Befindlichkeit* and *diathesis,* in the way the audience "finds itself feeling" about the matter and in its predisposition toward it; there is communicated in this speech, this is to say, the shift in *pathos* without which this *logos* could never carry conviction, a shift from emnity and hatred to kinship and affection. For none in Lincoln's audience could have resolved to "finish the work we are in, to bind up the nation's wounds, to care for him who shall have borne the battle and for his widow and his orphan" were they not moved by the resolute rhythm and tenor of these phrases to feel compassion for those whom they once wished to destroy, and if they were not drawn away from enmity and into community with them. With hearing these words of Lincoln, each "I" standing over against each other "I" antagonistically in the battle for victory is, like the early Christians hearing eucharistic hymns (John 1:1–5, 9–14, Philippians 2:6–11), drawn, somatically and acoustically, back into the communion of the choral dance, each one reconciled with each other one.

Thus, it is Nietzsche alone, with his radical probing of the Dionysian *Hintergrund, Untergrund,* and *Abgrund* beneath the *logos* of the spoken word, who displays for us what actually transpires here. "Under the magic spell of the Dionysian," he tells us,

> not only the bond between human being and human being is closed together again; estranged, inimical, or subjugated nature celebrates again its festival of reconciliation with its prodigal lost son, the human being. . . . [N]ow all the rigid, inimical lines established between human beings by need, caprice, or "smart-aleck" fashions break to pieces. Now, with this gospel of world harmony, each feels not just reconciled, fused, with his neighbor but one with him, as if the veil of Maja were ripped to shreds and now only ragged remnants of it were left fluttering about the aboriginal One. Singing and dancing, the human being expresses himself as a member of a higher communion; he has forgotten how to walk and speak and, dancing, he finds himself on his way to soaring into the ethers. (GT §1; KSA 1, 29–30)

Not that the early Nietzsche of *The Birth of Tragedy Out of the Spirit of Music* (1871) was entirely clear or consistent about these things, as the later Nietzsche of the "An Attempt at Self-criticism" (VSK; KSA 1, 12–22) (1886) acknowledges. In this piece Nietzsche credits his early work with recognizing that "the problem of science [*Wissenschaft*] cannot be recognized on the ground and basis [*Boden*] of science" and that science in fact has its ground and basis in art (VSK §2; KSA 1, 13), but it was crippled in its efforts to elaborate this thesis, and having established that science must be viewed within the optics of art, it could not reach the insight that art, in turn, must be viewed within the optics of life and living (*Leben*) (VSK §2; KSA 1, 14), which life and living is indissociable from body (*Leib*) (VSK §4; KSA 1, 16). It was, of course, held back by its inablility to affirm life and body, by its romanticism of 1830 under the mask of the pessimism of 1850 (VSK §6), and by its "artist-metaphysics" (VSK §2) and entanglement in German music. Hence, it could not learn the art of this-worldly consolation "on this side" instead of the art of the consolation of the "beyond"; it could not say "to the devil with all metaphysical consolations and, first off, with metaphysics" (VSK §7, quoting from *Also sprach Zarathustra*).

But it suffered from another constraint that is of more interest to us here: it was still in the form of a scientific treatise and thus unable to break cleanly, Nietzsche says, with science's "logic and logicizing of the world," with the tendency, born of "physiological fatigue," to go on being ever "more scientific" (*wissenschaftlicher*). It could not, that is to say, find the form of speech in which to render its discoveries. To have really penetrated to the ground and basis of science "It should have sung, this 'new soul,'" says Nietzsche, "and not have talked" (VSK §3, KSA 1, 15), for "it is one who knows [*ein Wissender*] who is [still] talking there" (VSK §4; KSA 1, 15). In the end Nietzsche realized that his own *Destruktion* of metaphysics required a language that was more than signs to be read silently, a language that was instead onomatopoetics to be heard spoken out loud. Perhaps the same should be said in self-criticism of our own attempt here at a hermeneutics of original argument.

Notes

Chapter 1

1. Martin Heidegger, *Ontologie* (*Hermeneutik der Faktizität*) (GA 63) (Frankfurt, 1988).

2. In "Der eine Weg Martin Heideggers" (Martin Heidegger's One Path), GW 3, pp. 417–30, Gadamer unfolds the meaning of Heidegger's locution "hermeneutics of facticity." Beginning with "facticity," he points out the origins of this word in German theology: the belief in the resurrection of Christ is for Christians the "fact" "behind which one cannot go" in the search for foundations of the faith and, hence, the "fact" with which one must start. For Dilthey, and then Bergson, Nietzsche, and Natorp, such a "fact" becomes life itself (see pp. 421–22). Accordingly, in a "hermeneutics of facticity" Heidegger would interpretively lay out "life" as it is lived, and, taking it as uncircumventable, he would make no attempt to "found" this "life" in anything assumed to be beneath it and further back. We will take the same approach to original argument in our attempt here to "lay it bare" and "lay it out" interpretively.

But perhaps even more important than the word "facticity," Gadamer points out, is the genetive "of" in "hermeneutics of facticity." For this looks like an objective genitive and might make it seem that "facticity" is the kind of subject matter or object to which an interpretion might be applied from outside by a detached theoretical observer. In actuality, however, this "of" is possessive: the interpretation will be facticity's own interpretation of itself out of, and from within, its own "factual" situation. Though we will attempt to maintain this hermeneutical principle, too, in our hermeneutics of original argument, our success is bound to be limited. For what follows is, after all, a book to be read, not a speech to be voiced. It necessarily takes the stance, therefore, of a theoretical onlooker.

3. It is symptomatic that perhaps the most important advances in the contemporary understanding of argument, namely Steven Toulmin's, would penetrate behind logical syllogistic inference, to be sure, but, in the end, penetrate only to judicial, adversarial rhetoric and not to the "con-sultation" of *sumbouleutikê* rhetoric, which presupposes a community of those who feel kinship and friendship (*philia*) for each other. See Toulmin, *The Uses of Argument* (Cambridge, 1958), Toulmin et al., *An Introduction to Reasoning* (New York, 1984), my own *Hermeneutics and Human Finitude* (HHF), pp. 19–31, and, in

particular, Gadamer, WM 306: "The one who asks for counsel [*Rat*] presupposes, just as much as does the one who gives it, that the other person is bound to him in friendship. Only friends can give each other counsel, or, seen another way, only counsel that is meant in a friendly way makes any sense to the one receiving it."

4. The expression "possessive individualism" is, of course, C. B. Macphearson's. See his still unsurpassed *The Political Theory of Possessive Individualism* (New York, 1962). As a correlate of Macphearson's disclosure of the roots of English liberal economics and politics in the possessive individualism of Hobbes and Locke, I propose that the roots of modern Anglo-American theory of argumentation, which parades as the only rational, unprejudiced "logic," lie in that same possessive indivudalism. My point is that in this tradition of British empiricism and analytic philosophy even discussion is hereby reduced to an "exchange" between self-interested, private parties for whom no sense of community with, or loyalty to, the other "discussant" exists any longer. "Discussion" thus develoves to its etymological origin of "smashing to bits" (v. the Latin *discutio*) and becomes a bad translation of Plato's "*dialegesthai*" and Gadamer's "*Gespräch.*"

5. In essence we will be using Heidegger here against Heidegger, for Heidegger himself did not pursue for long the project we will pursue, namely a hermeneutical exposition of speech and argument as this occurs in the everyday world of getting things done. In my view the principal reason for his not doing so lies in his tendency from early on to portray the public world of everyday practical speech negatively as "everydayness," "mediocrity," "ruination," and "fallenness" (*Alltäglichkeit, Durchschnittlichkeit, Ruinanz, Verfallenheit*). Viewed this way, practical speech itself has to look like "mere talk" and even "empty babble," to which existing individuals have abandoned themselves and in which they dissipate themselves and "go up" (*aufgehen*) like smoke. As the theory and practice of practical speech, rhetoric then becomes indistinguishable from sophistical manipulation of the emotions. No wonder, then, that having said that Aristotle's *Rhetoric* is to be taken as "the first hermeneutics of the everydayness of [our] being together with one another," Heidegger says next that "Publicness, as the kind of being belonging to the 'everybody,' not only has its way of feeling [*Gestimmtheit*] but uses feeling [*Stimmung*] and 'peps things up' by creating it for itself. The rhetor speaks into a feeling and speaks out of, and from a feeling. He needs an understanding of the possibilities of feeling in order to awaken it and steer it in the right way" (SZ 138–39).

As a consequence of this critical bias Heidegger does not stop at the "facticity" of life in the world after all. Rather, in his own way he too, like Plato and gnostic Neoplatonists, would push behind it to the real thing—authenticity—of which it is only a degenerate manifestation, namely to the private self that, once the talk of the world and others in it has gone dead, hears, alone and by itself, its ownmost anxiety's empty and voiceless call of nothingness. See, in this regard, Jacques Taminiaux's superb *Heidegger and the Project of Fundamental Ontology* (Albany, 1991), in particular, chapter 3, "The Reappropriation of the

Nicomachean Ethics: *Poiesis* and *Praxis* in the Articulation of Fundamental Ontology," pp. 111 ff., for a devastating and accurate criticism of Heidegger's contempt for the inevitable untidiness of reasoning in the realm of "everyday" public *praxis* and his consequent retreat to an elitist monological *theôria*, or *Denken an das Sein.*

6. See Gadamer, *The Idea of the Good in Platonic-Aristotelian Philosophy* (IGPAPh), pp. 18–19, on Socrates' steadfast and unerring insight into the good as a paradigm for Plato's doctrine of the forms.

Chapter 2

1. *Grundbegriffe der Aristotelischen Philosophie* (henceforth GBAPh). What I will say here is based on the typescript of these lectures in the Marcuse Archiv in the Stadtsbibliotek in Frankfurt a.M. References will be to the dates of each lecture. It was Theodore Kisiel who alerted me to the existence and importance of this remarkable text. For an excellent analysis of its place in the development of Heidegger's thought see Kisiel's *The Genesis of Heidegger's Being and Time,* (Berkeley, 1993), pp. 286–301 and 558 n.19.

2. See, for example, SZ §34 and also §13, pp. 59 ff., "The Exemplification of Being-in by a Founded Mode. Knowing the World," where Heidegger displays that "Knowing [*Erkennen*] is a mode of being-there founded in being-in-the-world" (SZ 62). In other words, he "destructs" *Erkennen* in order to lay bare its origin and basis in being-in-the-world. Similarly his GBAPh would "destruct" the theoretical *logos apophantikos* and found it in rhetorical speech.

3. To be sure, in Heidegger there is a conflicting tendency to condemn rhetoric as the "mediocre" and "everyday" form of speech of the "everybody," *das Man,* much as Plato, and sometimes even Aristotle, had condemned it as the speech of hoi polloi or the ignorant multitude of people. This tendency in Heidegger eventually proves to be strong enough to block investigation along the lines we are pursuing here. Already in GBAPh we have an important indication of Heidegger's ambivalence regarding the relationship of dialectic and rhetoric when he expresses admiration for Aristotle's accomplishment in reversing, *through dialectical definition,* the fallenness of rhetorical speech in the everyday world: "As the Greeks themselves realized," says Heidegger, "this process of living, of losing oneself in the world, in what is usual, and of falling into the world in which one lives, became, precisely through language, the basic danger for their being. The proof of this circumstance is the existence of sophism." And hence, he continues, "We need to take the measure of just what it means that Aristotle gets [language] back out of this exteriorization of Greek existence, out of conversation [*Gespräch*] and idle talk [*Gerede*] and brings speaking to the point where he can say that *logos* is *logos ousias,* or speaking about the subject matter and what it is" (30.5.24). Seen this way, the speech of rhetoric emerges, not as the original speaking to which our *Destruktion* must get back, but as decadent talk; and dialectical definition emerges not as an abstraction from our concrete being in the world but as the means by which we might recover ourselves from

that world to which we have lost ourselves. "In Plato's and Aristotle's time," adds Heidegger, "existence was so loaded down with babble [*Geschwätz*] that it took all the efforts of both men to make science a serious concern" (id.).

The fact that Gadamer does not view conversation—*das Gespräch*—as idle talk and babble but as the paradigm for reaching and understanding, allows him, in contrast to Heidegger, to recover speech as the center of human community and ultimately brings him much closer than Heidegger to the hermeneutics of original argument undertaken here. Only Gadamer, not Heidegger, can speak of "the original nature of the conversation as the relation of question and answer" that underlies even the abstraction of Hegel's "monologue of thought" (WM 351).

4. The "our" that I have inserted here is, in fact, quite uncharacteristic of Heidegger, who despite his efforts to speak "hermeneutically" from within the situation he is speaking of, and to speak "out" of it, stays aloof here and does not see himself as a participant in the "everydayness" he is describing. The word "everydayness" already has a critical and pejorative connotation here. The theme in the background is Kierkegaard's, namely the self's evasion of itself and failure to "relate itself to itself." As a consequence, Heidegger quickly loses Gadamer's insight that originally any "I am" is also "we are" and that originally what "I say" is what "we say." (See, e.g., WM 361: "Speech is the in-between [*die Sprache ist die Mitte*] in which the partners [in a conversation] reach an understanding, and agreement about the subject matter takes place.") Consequently, he tends to "leap over" the fact that I cannot invent my own private self any more than I can invent my own private language. Seen Gadamer's way, not all "publicness" is "mediocrity." Indeed, even the apparently private "taking counsel" with myself that leads up to any decision and choice is, as we will see in our elaboration of Aristotle's *bouleuesthai* in the *Ethics*, always to be "grounded" in the original "taking counsel with" others, that is, in *sumbouleuesthai*.

5. We must ask, however, if in the end phenomenology does not divert Heidegger from his initial project of "factual" hermeneneutics. For he ultimately abandons his exposition of practical speech from within our live experience as hearers of it—"the situation at a given time" "there" "in the world"—and begins himself to describe phenomenologically, in apophantic, declarative statements, how things look to an onlooker. Instead of rhetoric's exhortation and dehortation (*protropê, apotropê*), accusation and defense (*katêgoria, apologia*), and praise and condemnation (*epainos, psogos*), the speech, the *logos* or *Rede*, to which he devotes himself eventually becomes Aristotle's *dêloun* or "making plain what one is 'talking about' in the speech" (SZ 32): "Aristotle explicated this function of speech more precisely as *apophainesthai*. The *logos* lets something be seen (*phainesthai*) . . . *apo*—starting from the thing itself being spoken of" (SZ 32).

Of course, any philosophical thinking requires this theoretical abstraction to reflection *about* things and will be couched in the language of this reflection, but increasingly Heidegger's speech seems to sever its ties with practical speaking and hence seems less and less to be "facticity's hermeneutics," less and less facticity's own interpretation of itself from out of its original experience. We can certainly say, for example, that the turn to phenomenological exposition diverts Heidegger from the original oral-aural nature of speech.

In his *Basic Concepts of Metaphysics* Heidegger writes,

> this very Aristotle, who in taking up crucial initiatives from Plato penetrated to an insight into the structure of the [declarative] sentence, also recognized, and took on in his *Rhetoric*, the grand task of submitting the forms and constructions of nonthetical speaking to interpretation. Of course, for various reasons the power of logic was too strong to leave open the possibility that this attempt might be developed on its own. (GBM 439)

We might ask, however, if the same thing might be said of Heidegger himself. Having acknowledged other kinds of speech besides the *logos apophantikos*, did he too not succumb to the power of this *logos* and phenomenology's thetical, propositional speaking? What ever happened, for instance, to the rhetorical *logos* as the *euchê*, or bidding, that Heidegger, in following Aristotle's lead (*de Interpr.* 17a4), juxtaposes to the *logos apophantikos* (see SZ 32 and GBM 448)? (See note 10 below.)

6. M. F. Burnyeat's extroadinarily careful and scholarly discussion of the enthymeme (see "Enthymeme: Aristotle on the Logic of Persuasion" in *Aristotle's Rhetoric*, ed. D. J. Furley and A. Nehamas [Princeton, 1994], pp. 3–55) is ultimately disappointing. His argument is convincing enough that enthymemes are not in principle truncated syllogisms, as the tradition has often contended, but rather "demonstrations of a kind" in which *enthumêmata* are advanced, namely "considerations one is swayed by when reflecting on an issue where conclusive argument is not to be had" (p. 12); however, it lacks the depth and perspicuity of Heidegger's radical, if reckless, "laying bare" of the traces of the earlier and original *thumos* in *enthumeisthai*, traces, to be sure, no longer perceptible even to Aristotle himself, for whom "to take under consideration" would be a quite appropriate translation of *enthumeisthai*, but which continue to resonate, nonetheless, beneath the surface of what he says.

7. Inevitably one thinks in this regard of Augustine's distinction between merely assenting to something intellectually and consenting to do it, which implies an act of the will. See, for instance, *Confessions* 8.5, where he relates that although he had become intellectually certain—"*certum habebam*"—that he should decide for the life of charity over concupiscence, and on one level was even willed to do so, on another more fundamental, carnal level he was not willed to do so and, hence, could not decide for the life of charity.

It is precisely here, I think, that E. Garver's account of the role of the *pathê* in rhetorical reasoning, despite its notable advances beyond all previous discussions of the *Rhetoric*, falls short. See his *Aristotle's Rhetoric* (Chicago, 1994), pp. 104–38, "Deliberative Rationality and the Emotions." The issue turns on the word *krisis* and whether it is to be taken as judgment or decision. Garver recognizes that the *pathê* are crucial to the shaping of judgments, and he, too, cites Lincoln's Second

Inaugural Address, to make his point: only by transforming the "triumphal feelings of vindication" in his audience into "feelings of humility," says Garver, does Lincoln get them "*to regard* the losing side differently" (135; emphasis added). But surely Lincoln is not trying merely to get us to regard the enemy differently, but above all to get us to decide to treat them differently from the way we had previously been willed to treat them. As in rhetoric generally, the *krisis* he seeks is not a judgment that something is so, but a decision to do something, and it is in inducing the latter that a change in how the audience *feels*, in their *diathesis* and *Befindlichkeit*, becomes crucial. Heidegger alone brings this to light.

8. Garver also gives special emphisis to this phrase (p. 115 ff.) though he quickly shifts back from momentarily translating *krisis* as "decisions" (p. 116) to translating it as "judgments," as he had to begin with.

9. The unstated reference here is to Aristotle's *Nicomachean Ethics*, 1102b29–1103a1:

> For while the vegetative part of the soul has no conversance at all with reasoning [οὐδαμῶς κοινωνεῖ λόγου], the visceral [ἐπιθυμητικὸν] and generally desiderative part does somehow take part in it, in listening to reason and being obedient to the rule of reason [ᾗ κατήκοόν ἐστιν αὐτοῦ καὶ πειθαρχικόν], as when we say of our father and our friends that they have "reason" on their side [ἔχειν λόγον]—but not "reason" in the mathematical sense. That, in fact, this unreasonable part is somehow convinced by reasoning is indicated by warning as well as every kind of reproach and encouragement [ὅτι δὲ πείθεταί πως ὑπὸ λόγου τὸ ἄλογον, μηνύει καί ἡ νουθέτησις καὶ πᾶσα ἐπιτίμησίς τε καὶ παράκλησις].

It is obvious why this passage, invoking, as it does, specific types of oral-acoustical conviction in specific contrast to the reasoning of mathematics, and linking, as it does, the rational to the affective and "visceral" (*epithumêtikon*), would attract Heidegger's attention.

10. Even as early as GBAPh Heidegger begins to pass over this oral-acoustical nature of original language as speech. Indeed, his single-minded interests actually lead him away from our original experience of hearing someone's rhetorical call and lead him back to the very *logos apophantikos*, the declarative statement, that was supposed to be displayed as derivative. In *Being and Time*, for instance, we find appended to the claim that *logos* as speech is to be taken as *dêloun* or "making plain" (SZ 32) a quite remarkable assertion: "The *logos*, he says, "is *phonê* [voice] and, to be sure, *phonê meta phantasias* [voice along with imagination] or vocalization out loud in which each time something is *sighted* (*etwas* gesichtet *ist*)" (SZ 32–33; emphasis added). We note that the weight shifts here from voice, which is intrinsically acoustical, to *phantasia*, which is related to *phainesthai* and is primarily visual.

This shift is attributable in part, at least, to Heidegger's dismissal of the "public" world, and to the consequent interiorization of hearing, evidence of which we find as early as GBAPh. For instance, in the very same lecture where we learn that *akouein* or hearing is *aisthesis* proper, or perception as such, because it is "the possibility of our being together with each other," we find:

> A human being is not only a being who speaks and hears, rather for himself he is the sort of being that listens to himself. Speaking, as speaking out loud about something, is at the same time speaking to oneself. Hence the definition, *logon echôn* [having speech], implies, beyond this, that he listens to his own speaking. (30.5.24)

The way is paved here from hearing exterior speech to the interior experience of the call of conscience, which is precisely not the "voice of conscience" (SZ 268) and in which precisely "nothing" is heard any longer (SZ 280).

Building upon Derrida's *La voix et le phénomène* (Paris, 1972), Jacques Taminiaux argues convincingly that the voiceless call of conscience in Heidegger is an extension of Husserl's phenomenological voice, a "silent and solitary voice, which has nothing to do with signs, indications and expression and even monologue" and "is the pure appearing of ideality in the indivisibility of the *Augenblick*, the blink of an eye, the instant" (Taminiaux, *Heidegger*, p. 66). And he adds that similarly in Heidegger's call of conscience, "we find the most intimate connection between phenomenon and *logos*, because what this voice gives for hearing, *it also presents to a seeing*. The call does nothing but open and disclose; it is through and through *Erschliessung*, disclosing" (p. 67; emphasis added). It is clear that with its interiorization acoustical experience has in fact been completely sacrificed to the optical. Put another way, the word that Abraham, in Kierkegaard's *Fear and Trembling*, *hears* spoken to him by another in the instant of anxiety has in Heidegger become the empty antithesis to the sudden full *sight* of the *eidos* of the Beautiful, into which Diotima initiates Socrates (*Symposium* 210e: "suddenly he will *see* a beauty marvelous in nature" [ἐξαίφνης κατόψεταί τι θαυμαστὸν τὴν φύσιν καλόν]; emphasis added).

Chapter 3

1. Again, this is not the direction in which Heidegger himself moves. See chapter 2 above, notes 4 and 5. Indeed, support for this approach must ultimately be sought elsewhere, for instance, in Kevin Robb's very fine book, *Literacy and Paideia in Ancient Greece* (New York, 1994). Robb points out that the earliest ancient Greek inscriptions we have, the Dipylon Oinochoe (wine jug), the Nestor Cup from Pithekoussai, the Xenos Oinochoe from Ithaca, the bronze statuette from Thebes dedicated to Apollo, all appear on ordinary-use items for oral practices, namely "symposia," the guest-friendship (*xenia*), funearary dedications, and so forth, each of which were "conducted in epical speech, [and that] must have been the very stuff of Hellenic life, happening 10,000 times a day in every part of oral Greece" (p. 61).

2. In regard to the *Wirkungsgeschichte* or "effected-effective history" (see Gadamer, WM 283 ff.) leading up to, and following from, Peter Ramus (1515–72), the most useful analysis for us is Walter Ong's *Ramus, Method, and the Decay of Dialogue* (Cambridge, Mass., 1958). This work argues convincingly that Ramus's reduction of rhetoric's "invention" to the use of ten standardized topics and of rhetoric's "arrangement" to syllogistic *structures* or "trees" ranging from the most general propositions down to the most particular, is, we could say with Gadamer, "effected" historically by a visualization and spatialization of argument made possible only by the conversion of speech to writing. Ramus's reassignment of this newly conceived "invention" and "arrangement" to dialectic and philosophy and his consequent diminishment of rhetoric to considerations of "style," taken as mere secondary ornamentation, and "delivery" also reflects a prior turn from the spoken to the written word as the primary concern, a turn that, as we will see in the next chapter, begins at least as far back as Plato. To Ong's thesis we can add that the characteristic separation of the "cognitive" from the "emotive," which is the historically "effective" result of Ramus's juxtaposition of rhetoric with philosophy and of his depleting rhetoric of its cognitive functions, was reinforced by Antoine Arnauld's *Port-Royal Logic* (1662), which argues that valid reasoning proceeds by induction based on experience and is only corrupted by the sound of words, a theme taken up by the Royal Society in England in its rejection of rhetoric altogether: "Who can behold, without indignation, how many mists and uncertainties, these specious Tropes and Figures have brought on our knowledge" (see Thomas Sprat, *The History of the Royal Society of London*, ed. J. I. Cope and H. W. Jones [St. Louis, 1958], p. 112). As we will see, Plato's postulation that spoken words are only signs for cognitive truths that we can know quite apart from words has, with the Royal Society in England, come to predominate, even if in the context of a quite un-Platonic empiricism. The point is that rhetoric, at one time the theory of the spoken words or *rhêmata*, has been definitively overridden by written science and banished to belles lettres. Thereafter we are left with a *contradictio in adjecto*: "literary rhetoric," or "literary speaking."

3. There are two very distinguished precedents for the hermeneutical exposition undertaken here of the five kinds of *alêtheuein* or ways of knowing the truth distinguished by Aristotle in book 6 of the *Nicomachean Ethics*, Heidegger's (see PS, 21–64, "A Preparatory Overview of the Ways of *alêtheuein* [*epistêmê, technê, pronêsis, sophia, nous*] [EN 6.2–6]") and Gadamer's (see WM 295–307, "The Hermeneutical Relevence of Aristotle"). Obviously, it cannot be our purpose here to outdo either of these remarkable expositions, but rather, with different concerns, only to apply them both in a new way and extend them in a different direction.

Heidegger interprets this text within the project of fundamental ontology leading up to *Being and Time*'s attempt to found what "is" in the constitutive accomplishments of *Dasein* or "being-there": the five kinds of *alêtheuein* are laid out hermeneutically as five ways that an existing individual "being-there" "in the world" originally makes open and available to itself the various beings of that world, makes open, this is to say, what is, *das Seiende. Technê* is rendered, accordingly, as *Sich-Auskennen* or being versed in something, knowing how to go about something, being familiar with the tricks of the trade; *epistêmê,* as *Wissenschaft* or science; *phronêsis* as *Umsicht* and *Einsicht* or circumspection and perspicacity; *sophia* as *das eigentliche Verstehen* or "understanding in the proper sense"; and *nous* as *Vermeinen,* "having in mind" or "an intending something which perceives that thing" (GA 19 22). As in *Being and Time* Heidegger is concerned with how each of these figures not only in *Entdecken,* in *Dasein's* discovering and uncovering what is in truth, but also in *Verdecken,* that is, in *Dasein's* covering up the truth of what is and concealing it from itself. The concern, in other words, is with overcoming *Unkenntnis, herrschende Meinung, Irrtum,* ignorance, prevailing opinion, error (23), and penetrating *Vorurteile* and *Selbstverständlichkeiten,* prejudices and things taken for granted (24), a theme that will be taken up again in *Being and Time*'s acerbic critique of *das Man* or the "everybody" of "But everybody says this!" Indeed, we find passages here that prefigure *Being and Time* almost perfectly (and Wittgenstein's linguistic-critical approach as well): "I can just spout off statements and understand them," says Heidegger, "without having an original relationship to the being about which I am speaking. . . . In this way *legein* [speaking] takes on a peculiar independence from *pragmata* [things]. One resides in idle talk" (25).

We, however, will have something quite different in mind from Heidegger, for it is not our task to call received opinion into question critically and to privilege, instead, some supposedly undistorted scientific *Sachlichkeit* or factual truth, but rather to justify dialectic's and rhetoric's reasoning from received opinions (*endoxa*) precisely as we find it. In this regard, Gadamer, in building upon the later Heidegger's own "turn" away from the strategies of *Being and Time,* comes much closer to our own concerns. For in his analysis Gadamer wants to set off *phronêsis* or discernment from the other four ways of *alêthuein* in order to derive a paradigm for a different but no less valid kind of understanding, a hermeneutical or interpretive understanding, namely, that would be distinct from science's methodical objectification of its subject matters. "For the ethical knowing that Aristotle describes," Gadamer writes,

> is obviously not knowing objects [*kein gegenständliches Wissen*]; the knower, this is to say, does not stand opposite some state of affairs that he establishes to be the case, rather he is directly affected by what he recognizes: what he knows is something he has to do. (WM 297)

Furthermore, Gadamer's Hegelian emphasis on the original social context of every individual, the rootedness of every "I" in the communal "We," allows him to incorporate phenomena in his explication to which Heidegger had to remain largely indifferent, specifically *epieikeia,* which we will call "clemency" instead of the standard "equity," but which Gadamer renders most accurately of all as the requisite "letting up [*nachlassen*] from the strict letter of the law" (301) in one person's application of the law to another, *sunesis* or the understanding

(*Verständnis*) shown by someone for someone else (but see SZ 123–24 for Heidegger's own treatment of understanding in this sense), and *gnômê* and *sungnômê*, which we translate as consideration and forbearance and Gadamer, as *Einsicht* and *Nachsicht* (306; but see SZ 123 for *Nachsicht* as a form of *Fürsorge* or "caring for" someone else).

However, Gadamer is aiming here at a theory of *Verstehen* or understanding of written texts. Thus, even if he builds this theory on the *Sich-Verständigen* that takes place between two people, on their reaching and understanding in conversation (*Gespräch*) with each other, the focus for him cannot be, as it will be for us, on the rhetorical process of conviction taking place among two or more people "taking counsel" with each other; and to a certain extent, at least, Gadamer will therefore perpetuate the priority that we find in Heidegger of the visual over the auditory. (*Nachsicht* in Heidegger is obviously a variation on *Umsicht* or circum*spection.*) In the end, Gadamer's concern is not so much with understanding taken as hearing and obeying what someone is advising someone else to do, as it is with understanding taken as seeing (reading) what a text means; hence, the acoustical communication of *êthos* and *pathos* and the shift this communication induces in the *Befindlichkeit* of the listeners, in the way they feel about the speaker and the subject matter, cannot be the concern for Gadamer that it will be for us. This is not to deny, however, that Gadamer has important things to say about *bouleuesthai* or taking counsel as the fundamental *communal* interaction. Quite in contrast to Heidegger, who roundly condemns the rhetorical realm of public discourse (*Öffentlichkeit*), he does. See, for example, WM 306 and my HHF 56–58.

4. Heidegger orders his interpretation of these five ways of *alêtheuein* around two questions: "how the being looks that these ways of *alêtheuein* uncover," and "whether the *alêtheuein* in question also discloses the *archê* of this being," *archê* taken here in the wide sense as starting point or orgin (PS 31; see also 37–38). As a consequence his organization of the five differs noticeably from ours: in his reading *sophia* and *epistêmê* are grouped together, with *sophia,* which includes *nous* within itself, receiving priority because it discloses the *archê.* Similarly, *phronêsis* and *technê* are grouped together, with *phronêsis* receiving priority for the same reason, namely that it uncovers the *archê* of what the action chosen is for. Again, Heidegger's concern is quite distinct from ours: he treats all of these as ways of uncovering and disclosing what is and opening it up for us to *see.*

5. Because of the judicial context in which Aristotle introduces the word, the usual translation of *epieikeia* is "equity" (see EN 1137b31 ff.), but as I have indicated above (see note 3), this translation is too narrow and obscures the original sense of the word as "easing off" or "letting up" from rigid adhearance to one's own point of view (see also HHF 78–85). We will pursue this word later on, too, in the context of Gadamer's contributions to the rehabilation of dialectical argument, but for now, clemency—to be taken in the sense of kindness and even mercy—will serve as the translation.

6. Elsewhere, Heidegger alerts us to the abstraction in an *epistêmê* conceived of in this way as the theoretical "science" of what is ever "one and the same." "What does *epistêmê* mean?" he asks:

> The verb which belongs together with it is called *epistasthai*, i.e., to place oneself in front of something, to linger with it and to stand before it. *Epistasis* means, among other things, lingering in front of something, taking notice of it. This standing in front of something that takes notice, that lingers for a while with it, this "*epistêmê*," implies, and has as its result, that we become versed in a thing and are knowledgeable about it. Once knowledgeable in this way, we can look after the thing in question, in front of which we stand, while taking notice and lingering for a while with it, and we are able to to look after something, since we are "in the know" about it. Hence, we translate *epistêmê* with "to be in the know about something" [*Sich-auf-etwas-verstehen*]. (*Heraklit* [GA 55], Frankfurt a. M., 1979, pp. 191–92).

Striking about this passage, and quite in contrast to the exposition of *epistêmê* in his earlier *Platon: Sophistes* (PS 19), is not only Heidegger's recovery of the primacy of particularity over abstract universality, but also his subtle way of undoing the reversal of agent and patient that occurs in later, derivative understandings of *epistêmê*. For originally, he points out, *epistêmê* did not mean one's own putting something in front of oneself, as in "to get the picture of something" or *sich etwas vorstellen*, but the reverse, *sich vor etwas stellen*, namely "to put oneself in front of something," "in front of something" that makes itself clearer *to* us when we linger with it long enough and attentively enough to take notice of it. Our knowing, it now becomes clear, is originally not, as Heidegger had seemed to be saying previously, the result of some performance or accomplishment of consciousness in constituting a thing for itself but rather the result of the thing's own disclosing something of itself all the while it keeps to itself. In line with this thought, and in playing upon the *stê* and *sta* Greek stems in *epi-stê-mê* and *epi-sta-sthai*, Heidegger avails himself here of the German *vor-stehen* or "to look after something" and *ver-stehen auf* or "to be in the know about something." Importantly, both of these expressions leave the thing "looked after" and "known about" in the primary place and make the human knower secondary to it. Precisely this priority is reversed when science starts to objectify things, to constitute, construct, and construe them, by putting them in front of consciousness. When such *Vor-sich-stellen* or "putting something in front of oneself" becomes total the world is reduced to *das Gestell*, the sum of all things that can be "put" in front of the knower.

A central concern in this book is with the consequences for argument and reasoning of just this reversal. The point for us is precisely that once science's *apodeixis* or demonstration becomes the paradigm, as to some extent it already does in Plato and Aristotle, and once dialectic and rhetoric are to be grounded in demonstration rather than vice versa, the human subject that puts things in view before itself and surveys them has displaced the listener to the spoken word in which the subject matter discloses itself to us. Like the later Heidegger, we too are seeking here to recover what has been displaced, and to undo this inversion.

7. Of all of the consultative soliloquies in the *Iliad*, Odysseus's at 11.404 ff., Menelaus's at 17.91 ff., Agenor's at 21.553 ff., and Hector's at 22.99 ff. (see Mark Edwards, *Homer: Poet of the "Iliad"* [Baltimore, 1987], pp. 94–95), Hector's consultation with himself on whether or not to flee before Achilles' onslaught illustrates perhaps best the origins of anyone's taking counsel with himself or herself in taking counsel with others; for it follows seamlessly upon Priam's and Hecuba's pleas to him to withdraw within the gates of Troy. Indeed, however much isolated and on his own he may be, the Homeric hero always deliberates as a member of a community and according to its standards, and not as a private person. In this regard, Michael Naas's *Turning: From Persuasion to Philosophy* (Atlantic Highlands, N.J., 1995) is right on the mark in arguing that Achilles' self-excommunication from the Greek councils—viz., his throwing down the scepter traditionally passed from one speaker to the next (*Iliad* 1.245) determines the entire later course of the *Iliad*. Compare, for instance, Achilles' outright and stunning rejection of Odysseus's proposal to reconcile with Agamemnon and rejoin the Greeks: "I will consult with him neither on any counsel nor action" (οὐδϵ τί οἱ βουλὰς συμφράσσομαι, οὐδὲ μὲν ἔργον) (9.374) (See Naas, *Turning*, pp. 143–44).

8. Because of the early Heidegger's concentration on what he interprets as the "everyday," "mediocre" "idle talk" of the "everybody," there is no framework available to him within which to "lay out" hermeneutically the communality of original argument. Hence, he too perpetuates the monologism of derivative demonstration all the while he would penetrate to an "earlier," "more inceptive" *logos* or speech "closer to the origin." The origins of *bouleuesthai* in *sumbouleuesthai*, of taking counsel with oneself in taking counsel with others thus escapes him.

9. Of course, as Heidegger has shown, *all* argument, including science's, takes place in the affective setting that is the "condition of its possibility" (see chapter 2 above). The *pathos* that preconditions science is only less obvious, for it parades as the *pathos* of *apatheia*, of affective neutrality, as the feeling of not feeling anything. It is what we might call a "deficient mode" of feeling, which like the "deficient mode" of anything, is a positive instance of its being or existence. A broken or misplaced hammer, for example, *is* still very much a hammer, in fact, is more obviously a hammer than one that works and is ready at hand (see SZ §16, 72–76). A dialectical analysis of this affective neutrality, for example, Kierkegaard's, reveals, moreover, that it is not really neutrality at all but a "gut" feeling of despair and defiance, even if it hides this from itself. We will have more to say about this point later on when we consider *splanchna* or *viscera* and the New Testament's revisceration of rhetoric (see below, chapter 6, note 1).

10. Elsewhere, of course, Aristotle seems to suggest that epideictic rhetoric does *not* really seek a decision from the audience and that it differs from consultative and judicial rhetoric for just this reason. As we have heard, "It is

necessary that the hearer be either one who looks on or one who decides [ἢ θεωρὸν εἶναι ἢ κριτήν]. . . . The hearer who looks on decides, to be sure, but only about the capability of the speaker" (1358b 2–8). The introduction of the *theôros* or onlooker here, precisely in distinction from the *kritês* or someone who must make a decision, presages the abstraction in dialectical argument from rhetorical deliberation's *prohairesis* and *krisis*, choice and decision, presages, this is to say, dialectic's turn away from involvement in the practical to the detached and purely theoretical observation. We note that even when dialectic takes up ethical matters, it asks, not from within a particular situation what to do "there," but things like whether *in general* pleasure is to be chosen or avoided (see, e.g., *Top.* 104b5–6).

11. Induction in the strict sense leads to intuition of self-evident starting points or *archai* for syllogistic demonstrations (see *An. Post.* 2.19), but there is no equivalent to such self-evident starting points in either rhetoric or dialectic. For all argument in rhetoric and dialectic begins from *endoxa* or received opinions, which are taken for granted, to be sure, but are by no means self-evidently true. Rather, they are only "likely" to be true (*eikos*).

12. As noted previously, for a very thorough textual analysis of what Aristotle has to say about the enthymeme one could not do better than M. F. Burnyeat's "Enthymeme: Aristotle on the Logic of Persuasion," in *Aristotle's Rhetoric*, pp. 3–55. However, in the end Burnyeat remains very much within the tradition of English philosophy of language, remains, this is to say, a captive of the Royal Society's understanding of argument, according to which all argument, the enthymeme included, is to be viewed against the standard of logic's demonstration, and for which the communication of *pathos* is not just extrinsic but distortive. The enthymeme, he tells us "is a *sullogismos* of a kind and a demonstration of a kind, a deduction from which you cannot expect everything you would normally expect from a valid deductive argument" (p. 30).

13. Burnyeat even dismisses, as a subsequent insertion in the Aristotelian text, the standard definition of the enthymeme as having one less premise than the dialectical syllogism, that is, as an "*ateles sullogismos*" or incomplete syllogism (ibid.; see p. 46 f.). His painstaking textual history is entirely convincing, but in the process of constructing it he has entirely overlooked the real significance of the enthymeme's omission of premises that are common knowledge, namely that rhetorical argument can only proceed if some things are "always already" (Heidegger: *immer schon*) taken for granted and held to be true by the speaker and audience in common (compare Burnyeat, p. 22).

14. The expression "interminable debate" is, of course, A. MacIntyre's: "The most striking feature of contemporary moral utterance is that so much of it is used to express disagreements; and the most striking feature of the debates in which these disagreements are expressed is their interminable character. I do not mean by this just that such debates go on and on and on—although they do—but that they apparently can find no terminus" (*After Virtue* [Notre Dame, Ind., 1984], p. 6). Compare in this regard "The Insufficiency of MacIntyre's Alternative to Analytical Theory" in my HHF 38–67.

15. Kevin Robb, in a remarkable exposition of the argumentative differences between Socrates and Euthyphro in Plato's *Euthyphro* dialogue ("Euthyphro's *Exemplum* from Epic in 399 B.C.: A Bizarre Legal Case," in Robb, *Literacy and Paideia*, pp. 169–74), points out that it is a principal characteristic of oral culture to argue by the similarity or analogy of precedent examples to the present case as Euthyphro does, namely that since Zeus put his own father (Kronos) in bonds for swallowing his children, and since that father had in turn castrated his father (Ouranos), there is nothing wrong with Euthyphro's prosecuting his own father for murder. Robb observes that "[t]he suppressed premise, never articulated, seems to be that the acts of castration, fettering and legal indictment all belong loosely to the class of actions that involve sons 'moving against' fathers" (p. 171). What Robb does not see is that he, too, like Plato, is measuring original, oral argument in a retrojection of literary standards wholly inapplicable to it: analogical argument, which, he says, is

> so fundamental to persuasive or "rational" thinking in all oralist societies—always falls short of strict demonstration. In argument from analogy that required the narrating of specific (but paradigmatic) actions, neither language nor thought ever attains the true universal, and so such argument never deploys a middle term. (p. 173)

Following Heidegger's lead we, in contrast to Robb, will ask, not in what ways original oral argument by similarity and difference "falls short" of demonstration by a logic of inclusion in or exclusion from classes of things, but rather in what ways demonstration is an abstraction and withdrawal from original oral argument, for which there is no need to establish a middle term in the first place. In general I would note that Robb, like Havelock, whom he is following here, seems still to be so much in the shadow of Anglo-American analytical philosophy that he does not see the loss which occurs in the transition from orality to literacy. Though this transition per se was never a concern for Heidegger, he does make possible radically new ways to approach it, which we are elaborating here.

16. There is, of course, an obvious overall plan for the *Topics*: book 1 is a general introduction to the nature of dialectical reasoning and spells out four basic considerations on which it turns, definition (*horos*), property (*idion*), genus/species (*genos/eidos*), and accident (*sumbebêkos*) or what has just "happened to happen" (see 1.5). Roughly speaking, books 2 and 3 then consider arguments about accidents, book 4 considers arguments about genus/species, book 5 arguments about properties, and books 6 and 7 consider arguments about definitions. Book 8, finally, considers general stategies of argumentation. The problem with this way of arranging things is that considerations of the basic topics, namely arguments by similarity and difference, by the more and the less, by part and whole, by prior and posterior, as well as by inflection, are strewn throughout, and one finds no unified account of any one of them. We will attempt to remedy this deficiency by giving priority to the *Rhetoric*'s exposition

of the topics, which is considerably more coherent, and by imposing even on the *Rhetoric* an order of our own. Still, we must never forget that precisely because we are always "underway" within our *rhêsis* or speech even when speaking about it, a systematic overview or charting or rhetoric is possible neither for us nor for Aristotle.

17. We note that this original thinking by similarity or the likeness of different things is characteristic of Homer, who never abstracts to conceptual classification but always reasons by the similarity of one imaginable thing to another. As an illustration, here is just one of Homer's splendid similes, the image of the armies drawing up before Troy:

> These, as the multitudinous nations of birds winged, of geese, and of cranes, and of swans long-throated in the Asian meadow beside the Kaijstrian waters this way and that way make their flights in the pride of their wings, then, settle in clashing swarms and the whole meadow echoes with them, so of these the multitudinous tribes from the ships and shelters poured to the plain of Skamandros, and the earth beneath their feet and under the feet of their horses thundered horribly. They took position in the blossoming meadow Skamandros, thousands of them, as leaves and flowers appear in their season. (*Iliad* 2.459–68 [Lattimore trans.])

18. The origins of some of the key words of Aristotle's physics and metaphysics in judicial rhetoric—most notably, *kategorein*, meaning "to accuse," as the origin of "category," but also *aitiasthai*, meaning "to put the blame on" someone, as the origin of *aitia* or cause—substantiate nicely the thesis here that the origins even of the most theoretical argument are to be found in rhetoric's practical argument. Compare, for instance, *Rhet.* 1358b10–11: "But [the concern] of justice [is], on the one hand, accusation [δίκης δὲ τὸ μὲν κατηγορία] and, on the other, defense."

19. The original, Homeric power to see similarity even in the most disparate and different things is often evidenced in the ultimate aptness of Homer's seemingly incongruous similes; for example, the serene quietness of the snowflakes, simile for the rocks hurled in battle, only highlights the ferocious din of the latter's crashing against their targets (compare Edwards, *Homer*, p. 106):

> And they, as storms of snow descend to the ground incessant on a winter day, when Zeus of the counsels, showing before men what shafts he possesses, brings on a snowstorm and stills the winds asleep in the solid drift, enshrouding the peaks that tower among the mountains and the shoulders out-jutting, and the low lands with their grasses, and the prospering work of men's hands and the drift falls along the grey sea, the harbours and beaches, and the surf that breaks against it is stilled, and all things elsewhere it shrouds from above with the burden of Zeus' rain heavy upon it: so numerous and incessant were the stones volleyed from both sides. (*Iliad* 12.277–87 [Lattimore trans.])

20. For *genesthai* (ingressive aorist), or "to happen," Heidegger (and Luther) would say *geschehen* (see SZ 20), for which "to historize" is a perfectly dreadful

translation. The point is that with this word, *gignesthai, geschehen,* we are telling the narrative-historical (*geschichtliche*) story of what "comes to pass," "there," in the world, at a place and time.

21. In *An Inquiry Concerning Human Understanding,* §7, part 2, we find, for instance, "The appearance of a cause always conveys the mind, by a customary transition, to the idea of the effect. Of this also we have experience. We may, therefore, suitably to this experience, form another definition of cause and call it an object followed by another, and whose appearance always conveys the thought to that other" (Library of Liberal Arts [New York, 1955], p. 87).

22. "Die Sprache ist das Haus des Seins" (Heidegger, "Über den Humanismus," in *Platon's Lehre von der Wahrheit* [Bern, 1954], p. 53).

23. "Kein Ding sei wo das Wort gebricht." This is the last line of Stephan George's poem "Das Wort," which Heidegger elaborates in his "Das Wesen der Sprache" in *Unterwegs zur Sprache* (Tübingen, 1959), pp. 157–216. Salient in this essay, in which "Die Sprache ist das Haus des Seins" occurs again (p. 166), is its attempt to recover, behind the conception of the word as a sign convened upon to designate a thing that already is, the original understanding of the word as a name that gives a thing its being in the first place, that "brings it into the clear" by naming it (see 163–66). It would appear, Heidegger concedes, that first we have things for which we then invent words as labels or signs (p. 164); however, this appearance only blocks our access to our original experience, not of what we do with words, but of what words do *for* us when we find the words to say something, to name it, to call it into being. Heidegger, just as he did with the tool in *Being and Time* (SZ 72–76), makes his point here negatively with what is "obtrusive," namely, with what word names, like a broken, out-of-place, or missing hammer, fail to do for us when we cannot find the name for something, when the word name withholds itself and won't come to mind, and our thought collapses into inarticulateness. This original experience of a word's coming to mind or withholding itself makes plain that words as significations are secondary. In our own distinction here between the original understanding of the word as a name or *onoma* and the derivative understanding of the word as a sign or *sêmeion,* we will be concerned to exemplify and substantiate just this Heideggerian point.

24. See Havelock, *Preface to Plato* (Cambridge, Mass., 1963), pp. 167–70. In discussing how to "put things before the eyes" of one's audience Aristotle himself recurs to speech that personifies, as in Homer's "Then, shameless, the boulder rolled down into the valley" (*Odyssey* 11.598) (see *Rhet.* 1411b23–34).

25. I have taken examples from Lausberg (HLR) but also from Arthur Quinn's *Figures of Speech* (Salt Lake City, 1982) and E. A. Corbett's *Classical Rhetoric for the Modern Student* (New York, 1990).

26. It is not surprising that Heidegger challenged this academic paradigm, too, and that Gadamer was struck by the singular and unreproducible intensity of Heidegger's *voice* in the early lecture courses: "Again, it is something extrinsic in Heidegger's appearance," he writes,

> by which something intrinsic was made known—his voice. This voice, in the lower registers very powerful and nice sounding at that time, gave the impression in the higher registers, and in the excitement of the lecture, of being peculiarly strained and, without being loud, overexerted. A cause for anxiety and itself anxious, it always seemed on the verge of cracking and losing its balance. For, plainly, it was not a lack of breath and voice control in speaking that pushed him forward in this way to the outermost margins and ultimate limits of speaking. No, it appeared that what took away his voice and breath here was that he was driven to the outermost margins and ultimate limits of thinking. (GW 3, 189)

Heidegger, we should recall, was concerned, even in reading, to speak out of the factual situation and, hence, to communicate the "voicing" or *Stimmung* that was the condition of its possibility, to communicate the *diathesis*, the *Befindlichkeit*, the feeling in which he found himself. See section 2.2 above on his rendering of Aristotle's *diathesis* as *Befindlichkeit.*

27. In his *Poetics of Music* (New York, 1947), Igor Stravinski expatiates on time as a correlate in music of space in the visual arts; and the timbre and volume of tone, we may assume, thus become the musical correlate of the quality and brightness of color (see pp. 28–46).

28. For a quite useful but largely unphilosophical account of the rhetoric of the Gettysburg address, see Gary Wills, *Lincoln at Gettysburg* (New York, 1992).

English is rich in consonnants, particularly, dentals and gutterals. Hence, it is highly expressive in its profanity. But it is muted in its vowel colorations and thus can scarcely achieve the melodiousness, say, of Luther's play with the vowel shifts (*Umlaute*) of the subjunctive in "Was h*ü*lfe es dem Menschen, wenn er die ganze Welt gew*ö*nne und Schaden n*ä*hme an seiner Seele" or the vowel modulations in Mozart's (Da Ponte's) "Dove sono i bei momenti di dolcezza, e di piacer." It is no accident that these languages, German and Italian, have sustained great musical traditions, for they have not only the consonants necessary to mark off segments of time but also the vowels to achieve modulations in tone.

Perhaps this is the place to note, however, that German is a language "closer to the origin" of speech than the Romance languages, and, in fact, the large part of English based in French and Latin, insofar as German words are compounded of other words still in use in the language and therefore resist the tendency to abstract terminological signification and classification. For instance, where we say "porcupine" and no longer hear the Latin *porcus* and *spinus*, pig and spine, of which it is composed, the German says *Stachelschwein*, or "prickly pig"—something "ready at hand" that you would certainly not want to put your hands on.

29. In his "Is There an Ethical Dimension to Aristotelian Rhetoric?" (in *Essays on Aristotle's Rhetoric*, ed. Amélie Oksenberg Rorty [Berkeley, 1996], pp. 116–41) Troels Engberg-Pedersen comes close to recognizing the intrinsic role of *êthos* in any rhetorical argument, and on the way to this recognition he offers a useful defense of my translation of *peithô* and *peithein* as "conviction"

rather than "persuasion." In reviewing the traditional condemnation of rhetoric implicit in "persuasion," he finds, as I do, that

> we take it that if rhetoric is concerned with generating *peithô*,it is *not* concerned with *truth.* We therefore translate *peithô* as "persuasion" and focus exclusively on the element of causing the audience to have some belief or other. Moreover, the modern distrust of rhetoric will more or less automatically make us interpret this aim *in malam partem.* If rhetoric is concerned with persuasion, not only is it not concerned with truth, but also, quite likely, with deflecting the audience from the truth. (p. 124)

He then proposes, as I have, the translation "conviction" in the place of "persuasion," but for some very different reasons.

For him, in addition to overcoming some of the negative connotations of "persuasion," "conviction" is preferable because it indicates that the orator "is trying to generate . . . *a belief about certain facts*" (id.; his emphasis). I, however, want to go much further than this: in my view "conviction" best reflects the special nature of original rhetorical argument as an attempt to win, not assent to a belief, but consent to a decision. Conviction, in other words, is the process of *convincing* someone to decide on a course of action, and it is here where the *êthos* of the speaker, his or her trustworthiness, becomes crucial.

I have two criticisms of Engberg-Pedersen's appropriation of M. H. Wörner's conception of rhetoric as *Wahrheitsfindung* or "finding out the truth" (see Wörner, *Das Ethische in der Rhetorik des Aristoteles* [Freiburg, 1990]. First, there is no recognition evidenced that there are different forms of *alêtheuein*, ways of standing in relation to the truth, and different kinds of "truth" in regard to different kinds of beings, about some of which, namely those that "are susceptible of being otherwise" than they are, there is no possibility of knowledge beyond ever questionable *endoxa* or received opinions. Second, there is no distinction made here between getting listeners to hear and decide to do something and getting theoretical onlookers, albeit inferior ones, to see and believe how things stand. Even if Aristotle *sometimes* seems to say so, rhetorical speeches are not, I contend, popularized versions of scientific demonstrations for scientific societies, not science "made easy" for laypeople. On the contrary, precisely as exhortation and dehortation, defense and prosecution, praise and condemnation, they are a quite different matter, and one with a very different purpose from scientific instruction, as *sometimes* Aristotle also makes clear.

Chapter 4

1. Heidegger's remarkable 1924/25 lectures, *Platon: Sophistes* (PS), make clear the shift in his interest away from the rhetorical and practical to the phenomenological and theoretical: the objection to sophism that Heidegger finds in Plato, one very much in accord with his own thinking at that time, is

that sophism is not *sachlich,* not based in disclosing the subject matter or *Sache* itself phenomenologically, but concerns itself instead with manipulating the "everyday" "mediocre" opinions about things bandied about by "everybody." Seen this way, Plato becomes an ally in Heidegger's own efforts to break through traditional ways of seeing things. As a consequence, however, any protreptical or exhortative dimension of the dialogues becomes inaudible for him.

2. In regard to recovery of the rhetorical, protreptical dimension of Plato's dialogues we owe the most, of course, to Konrad Gaiser. See his *Protreptik und Paranese bei Platon* (Kohlhammer, Stuttgart, 1959), especially pp. 150–55 and 192–94 on *parainesis* or "wooing" (*Werben*) in the *Phaedo.* However, rather than Gaiser's *Formgeschichte,* which traces the rhetorical elements in Plato back to their precedents, the approach taken here will be the opposite, *Wirkungsgeschichte*: Plato will be interpreted retrospectively starting from his "historical effects" in Aristotle. And for this Gadamer, of course, is the principal influence; see WM 284–90, "The Principle of a History of Effects." For the *Wirkungseinheit* or "unitary effect" fusing Aristotle with Plato, see Gadamer, *The Idea of the Good in Platonic-Aristotelian Philosophy* (IGPAPh).

For our general understanding of Plato we will rely throughout this chapter on WM 368–75, "The Model of Plato's Dialectic," and the exposition of the *Cratylus,* WM 409–22. (Compare my "Plato as Impulse and Obstacle in Gadamer's Development of a Hermeneutical Theory," in *Continental Philosophy IV: Gadamer and Hermeneutics,* ed. Hugh Silverman [New York, 1991], pp. 23–41.) For our specific discussion of the *Phaedo,* however, we will take many of our leads from Gadamer's "The Proofs of Immortality in Plato's *Phaedrus*" (DD 21–38). The issue for Gadamer is, to be sure, not the one we will be addressing here, namely the tension between argument as *dialegesthai* or "talking something through" and argument as *apodeixis* or demonstration, but Gadamer's "hermeneutical" reading, which stresses the particular "occasion" for the dialogue, namely who is speaking to whom when and where, and in response to what question, and which emphasizes, accordingly, that the dying Socrates is raising an existential question for an audience of Pythagorean mathematicians, will be of considerable usefulness to us.

3. See the *Rhetoric,* 1355b16–19, where Aristotle, in comparing rhetoric with dialectic, maintains that, as in dialectic the task is to distinguish between genuine and apparent reasoning, so too in rhetoric it is to distinguish between what is really trustworthy and convincing (*to pithanon*) and what only appears to be so. He then adds that the difference between *dialecticians* and sophists lies not in their respective arts but in the way of life to which each is committed, or, we might say, what they are "out after" from the start: "For sophism does not consist in a capability," he says, "but in a choice" (ἡ γὰρ σοφιστικὴ οὐκ ἐν τῇ δυνάμει ἀλλ' ἐν τῇ προαιρέσει) (17–18). However, in contrast to "dialectician," "rhetor" or "orator" can refer to either the science and art employed, in which case the speaker is good, or to the "choice," in which case the speaker is bad. In Aristotle "sophist" is thus reserved for the corruption of dialectic, but we note that in rhetoric too the corruption has to do with the

"choice" of the speaker, with what he or she is "out after" from the start. The point, as we will see, is that in rhetoric, where not the mere believability of an opinion or *doxa* is at stake, as it is in dialectic, but rather *to pithanon*, what is trustworthy and convincing, validity hinges most of all on the *êthos* or character of the speaker (compare 1356a11–13).

4. We note the original, nontechnical use of *dialegesthai* as "talking things through" in characterizing the kind of existential and nondemonstrative arguments going on here, when it is said at 63d that such "talking things through" might, in the guard's opinion, be so stimulating as to make a double or triple dose of the hemlock necessary and hence Socrates should "talk as little as possible" (ὡς ἐλάχιστα διαλέγεσθαι).

5. Gadamer highlights for us the dramatic importance of this shift in the scene and the interlocutors (see DD 30).

6. See the *Theaetetus* 164e and 169c and Gadamer, IGPAPh 40. The *Republic*, book 6, makes clear, of course, that even the mathematician's *apodeixis ex hupotheseôs* or demonstration from a hypothesis in the form of "Let [*estô*] X be Y" falls short of a reasoning from an *archê* or noetically intuited first principle, a reasoning, namely, which "does not take hypotheses as its starting points and principles [τὰς ὑποθέσεις ποιούμενος οὐκ ἀρχὰς] but takes them, for what they really are, stepping stones and springboards, as it were, in order that one might proceed up to the anhypothetical and to the first principle of everything, and take hold of it [ἵνα μέχρι τοῦ ἀνυποθέτου ἐπὶ τὴν τοῦ παντὸς ἀρχὴν ἰών]" (511b). Here in the *Republic* this ultimate reasoning from true, anhypothetical first principles is called dialectic; Aristotle will make clear, however, that only this is *apodeixis haplôs* or demonstration strictly speaking (see *An. Post.* 2.19 and chapter 5 below).

7. In his "The Origin of the Artwork" Heidegger speaks of the nature of art as poetry (*Dichtung*, literally, "thickening"), and, then, of poetry as the "endowment of truth" (*die Stiftung der Wahrheit*) (*Holzwege* [Frankfurt, 1963 ff.], p. 62). This "endowment," in turn, is then said to be a giving (*Schenken*), a grounding (*Gründung*), and a beginning (*Anfangen*). The point of this odd language is actually quite straightforward: the original poetic word does not merely signify, or even copy in sound, something whose being is already established for us. Rather, it first endows the thing with its being by "calling" it the name it gives to it. Only such naming lets us see, or better, hear things for what they "are."

Gadamer, who does not share Heidegger's concern to rise above our "everyday" experience, but who, instead would remain within it, can make this point in a rather less rarified way. In *Truth and Method* he speaks of the "speculative structure of the speech event," which, he says is displayed not only the the poet's way of talking but also in our everyday talk, whenever anything "comes to be spoken of anew" (*neu zur Sprache kommt*) (WM 446). At these moments we get to see, as if in a speculum or mirror, what something really "is" for the first time.

8. Gadamer points out that it is not by chance but by design that the one who raises this objection is not named. Plato wants to emphasize that none

of those present *could* have raised it, for in distinguishing contraries as such from contrary things, it presupposes the advance that Plato makes over the Pythagoreans in "separating" the noetic numerical order of existent things from the latter. Pythagoreans, it will be remembered, still took numbers to be existent things just like any other (see DD 35).

9. Gadamer writes that

> there could hardly have ever been an interpreter of Plato who could not see that this proof of the ontological realtionship of idea, life, and soul, as marvelous as it might be, is incapable of demonstrating anything more than the character of the universal *eidê*, Life and Soul.
>
> The thesis which I am seeking to establish here is that actually Plato himself did not expect this fact would escape anyone. . . . As convincing as the discussion might have been, the conclusion is drawn that the proofs are not sufficient and that one must continue to test their premises insofar as is humanly possible. (DD 36)

10. I have reworked materials for this section used in a different context in my "Tensions in the Phaedrus: Dialogue and Dialectic, Speech and Writing," in *Plato's Dialogues: The Dialogical Approach*, ed. R. Hart and V. Tejera (Lewiston, N.Y., 1997), pp. 169–200.

11. The exposition here will rely extensively on E. Havelock's *Preface to Plato* (Cambridge, Mass., 1963), in particular, chapter 7, "The Oral Sources of the Hellenic Intelligence," pp. 115–33; chapter 8, "The Homeric State of Mind," pp. 134–44; chapter 11, "Psyche or the Separation of the Knower from the Known," pp. 197–214; and chapter 12, "The Recognition of the Known as Object," pp. 215–33. However, I read Havelock with Heideggerian eyes, as it were; for what Havelock has to say about orality and literacy takes on new significance if it is correlated with Heidegger's account of the shift in the understanding of being (*das Sein*) that occurs with Plato, a shift from being as coming to pass, to being as static presence. See, in particular, Heidegger, *Platons Lehre von der Wahrheit* (Bern, 1947).

12. As noted previously, I use the admittedly cumbersome "narrative historical" to render Heidegger's rather more ordinary word *geschichtlich*. The point is that *die Geschichte* in German means both history and story. In this regard, then, one can read Heidegger with Havelockian eyes, and see that the temporality of particular existent beings, their *Geschictlichkeit* or "historicity," correlates with the way we *talk* about them, correlates, that is, with their "narrativity" when we, like Homer, come to tell the oral tale of them.

13. Significantly, the expression *prohairesis tou biou* occurs in the rhetor Demosthenes (see 23.142, 58.56), for, as we know, in the *Rhetoric* Aristotle uses the word *prohairesis* precisely in order to differentiate the sophist from the dialectician and, similarly, to differentiate the sophistical rhetor, who has chosen the sophistical life, from the honorable rhetor. See *Rhet.* 1355b17–21 and note 3 above.

14. See Gadamer on Plato and the *dunamis tôn onomatôn*, or "potential of word names" to mean the opposite of themselves (WM 384–85).

15. In regard to a word name's bestowing being on a thing and first making it what it is, we think today, perhaps, only of the ancient traditions of naming children. Thus, in regard to naming Odysseus, Autolycus says to Euryclea (*Odyssey* 19.406–9)," Give him the name that I say [τίθεσθ' ὄνομ', ὅττι κεν εἴπα]: since I have come here hateful [ὀδυσσάμενος] to many . . . , so shall his name be the eponym 'Hateful' [τῷ δ' 'Οδυσεὺς ὄνομ' ἔστω ἐπώνυμον]." In the oral, narrative historical understanding of speech, however, this naming and calling into being was universal and extended to everything. Thus, we could say, with Heidegger, that in drawing upon speech as they have heard it from their predecessors, the ancient poets name the "world" and "endow" it with its being: "Insofar as speech first names what is, this naming first lets what is come to be spoken of in words and brings it into appearance" ("Vom Ursprung des Kunstwerkes," in *Holzwege,* p. 60; see also *Holzwege,* p. 62, on poetic "endowment" and note 7 above. The point, one largely unnoticed once writing has displaced orality and language is thought of as as system of signs, is that how we speak of things first establishes the framework in terms of which we can think of them. Like other narratives at the origins of other cultures, Homer's poems, for instance, "set up" the "world" of the Greeks and "ground" how they understand themselves and their world.

16. Compare Gadamer on mathematics as a paradigm for overcoming sophistical techniques of conflation and confutation (IGPAPh 17–19).

17. See Havelock: "it can fairly be generalized that the saga considered from the standpoint of a later and more sophisticated critique is essentially the record of an event-series, of things-happening, never of a system of relations or of cause or of categories and topics" (*Preface to Plato,* 173). Compare also Walter J. Ong, *Orality and Literacy* (New York, 1982), pp. 36–57, on the characteristics of oral syntax, specifically, to name a few of these, that it is "additive rather than subordinative," "aggregative rather than analytic," "redundant or 'copious,' " "close to the human lifeworld"—Is "lifeworld" taken from Husserl and Heidegger?—"empathetic and participatory rather than objectively distanced," "situational rather than abstract." In what follows here the task will be to show, first, that precisely these characteristics of orality are the characteristics of *rhetoric* that Plato would have eliminated with the new "art" of rhetoric proposed in the *Phaedrus,* and, second, that this announced project notwithstanding, he in fact perpetuates these very same characteristics of orality in the dialogue itself, taken as a whole.

18. As we will see in section 4.2.2, in his "Plato's Pharmacy" (in *Dissemination,* trans. Barbara Johnson [Chicago, 1981], pp. 61–172) Jacques Derrida fails to specify just which "writing" it is, namely the writing down of orality, that Plato would displace with Socratic dialogue. Consequently, Derrida's essay overlooks the primacy and importance of another type of writing, found in mathematics, for Plato's new model of argumentation, namely *apodeixis* or demonstration. Nor does Derrida see the tension and contradiction in Plato's reliance on this writing and simultaneous recurrence to Socrates' oral argumentation in question and answer.

19. Again, see Ong, *Orality and Literacy*, pp. 37–41, on the additive, aggregative, copious style characteristic of orality.

20. For the four kinds of opposites (*antitheseis*), contradictories (*antiphaseis*), contraries (*enantia*), having-lacking (*hexis-steresis*), and correlatives (*ta pros ti*) see Aristotle, *Topics* 2.8.113b ff. and chapter 3 above. In the *Metaphysics*, and under the heading of *antikeimena*, literally, "things lying over against each other," Aristotle adds to this list "extremes, such as those in processes of generation and destruction" and "things that are not susceptible of being simultaneously present in something that admits of either one separately" (1018a–20 ff.). As we have seen, arguments whose premises are derived from any one of these are to be "placed" under the "topic" of difference, but they are all rooted in the antiphonal sequence of the Greek *men* . . . *de*, "on the one hand, this, . . . (whereas, but, however), on the other hand, that."

21. Ong rightly points out that the French structuralist tradition, including Derrida, fails necessarily to recognize the inappropriateness of Plato's criticism of orality as unstructured. For "Oral cultures," Ong writes, "had no sense of language as 'structure.' They did not conceive of language by analogy with a building or other object in space," and, he continues, "Architecture had nothing to do with language and thought. For 'structuralism' it does, by ineluctable implication" (Ong, *Orality and Literacy*, p. 169). In extending this argument I would say that French sturcturalists can *see* structures in orality only by a retrojection from their own exaggerated culture of literacy, which misleads them into thinking of all language, even speech, as spatially distributed marks. (After all, in what other language but French, with its suppression of original sounds and consequent multitude of "silent" letters and even syllables, would the peculiar inversion of the *dicté* be necessary, in which students are required to translate back into writing a "text" read to them out loud?) Speech and voice, however, are not seen on a surface, but heard over time.

22. One could ask, to use the customary language of *literary* rhetoric, if the "schemata" or "syntactical" "figures" of speech that "Lysias" employs here are not ultimately spatial and visual arrangements too, rather than acoustical and temporal sequences. Must not his "schema" of "antithesis," his favored "on the one hand, this . . . on the other, that" *structure*, be thought of spatially as "this over here vis à vis that over there"? After all, "schema" and "figure" are visual, not acoustical, in origin, and "syntax" means how things are "placed" (*tithemena*) "together" (*sun*). Moreover, "antithesis" means "placing" (*tithenai*) things "over against" (*anti*) each other. And is not the same spatialization true of his "parallelism," which figure refers to things lying "alongside" (*para*) "one another" (*allelôn*)? Certainly, by the time these turns of speech are named "schemata," they are in fact being thought of spatially and understood in a retrojection from writing. Still, even if the literary names we traditionally use for them obscure the fact, they are originally ways of phrasing what one says aloud in voice or *phônê*, for instance, in "antithesis," in rising intonation for the first phrase and falling intonation for the second, and for that reason we have chosen anti*phony* to replace antithesis. Originally, then, these envisionable

"structural" "figures" of speech are acoustical and temporal sequences, and are not visual and spatial at all. Hence, in analyzing the phrasing of "Lysias's" speech in terms of a later literary rhetoric's "arrangement"—*diathesis* actually means "disposition" or "layout"—and "schemata," we would be guilty ourselves of a literary, optical distortion of original, acoustical orality. As Thomas Cole points out in his excellent *The Origins of Rhetoric in Ancient Greece* (Baltimore, 1991), such retrojections upon the oral past from a "rhetoric," the idea of which was conceived only with Plato and Aristotle and after the ascendance of writing, have led to all kinds of distortion.

23. Compare the *Gorgias* 503d–504a:

> For is it not so that the good man, who also speaks with regard to what is best, does not just say what he says arbitrarily, but instead looks to something he has in view [ἀλλ' ἀποβλέπων πρός τι]? So too, all the others who make things. In looking to their own work, each applies whatever he applies to his work, not selecting it arbitrarily but selecting it, instead, in order that what he is working on might have a certain form [εἶδός τι σχῇ]. For example, you might look at the painters, the house builders, the ship builders, and all the other makers of things, whichever one of these you wish, and see just how each positions each thing that he positions, and how he constrains each one to fit properly and harmonize with the other until the whole thing is put together [συστήσηται] in an ordered composition. And as it is with these makers of things, so it is, too, with the others of whom we were now speaking, those whose concern is the body, trainers and doctors: in some way or other they order the body and put it together [συντάττουσιν].

24. In this regard, too, the *Gorgias* is instructive. At 452e "Gorgias" defines rhetoric precisely as convincing (*to peithein*) by speeches in the law courts or in political councils, where the issue is either the just and unjust or the good and bad. Rhetoric, then, emerges as a "producer of conviction" (*peithous demiourgos*) (453a). At 253d, however, a distinction is made between the "convincing argument" of the rhetor and the "convincing argument" of one who teaches (*didaskei*), and the latter is called instructional conviction (*pistis didaskalikê*) at 453e–454a, even though it is said to concern such mathematical things as odd and even numbers, which are never the objects of conviction but only of instruction. The lines here are blurred, but that "conviction" has ceased to mean convincing someone to decide for a course of action and now really means instruction to an insight, that is, not conviction at all, becomes clear in the distinction made at 454c–d between having learned something (*mathekenai*) and having been merely convinced of it (*pepisteukenai*), and when it is said that the former engenders learning (*mathêsis*) whereas the latter engenders mere conviction (*pistis*) or, at 454e, that the one kind of "convincing" "provides conviction without insight but the other, science" (τὸ μὲν πίστιν παρεχόμενον ἄνευ τοῦ εἰδέναι, τὸ δ' ἐπιστήμην). Here, too, it seems, the new rhetoric should be modeled on mathematical instruction.

For all his differences with Plato and Platonism in regard to rhetoric, Aristotle, too, sometimes seems to take the transformation of rhetorical argument into scientific demonstration, and of conviction produced by persuasion into insight produced by instruction, as his ultimate aim; with him, if not already with Plato, the paradigm of demonstration becomes canonical (see the *Posterior Analytics*). Hence, we find, even in his *Rhetoric*, passages like this:

> The convincing argument is a demonstration of a kind, for we are persuaded most of all whenever we assume something to have been demonstrated. The rhetorical demonstration is the enthymeme, and this is, so to speak, simply the most powerful of convincing arguments [ἡ δ' πίστις ἀπόδειξις τις, τότε γὰρ πιστεύομεν μάλιστα ὅταν ἀποδεδεῖχθαι ὑπολάβωμεν, ἔστι δ' ἀπόδειξις ῥητορικὴ ἐνθύμημα, καὶ ἔστι τοῦτο ὡς εἰπειν ἁπλῶς κυριώτατον τῶν πίστεων]. (1355a5–8)

25. Compare Heidegger on *Befindlichkeit* or, literally, the way one "finds oneself feeling" (*sich befindet*), SZ §29, "Being-There as the Way One Finds Oneself Feeling" (*Das Da-sein als Befindlichkeit*)," pp. 134–40, and §30, "Fear as a Mode of How One Finds Oneself Feeling" (*Die Furcht als ein Modus der Befindlichkeit*), pp. 140–42. See also section 2.2 above.

26. As we have noted in our discussion of *Stimmung* and *Befindlichkeit* in section 2.1, instead of Plato's *hesuchia* and *scholê*, Heidegger, in referring to Aristotle's *Metaphysics* 1.2.982b22 ff., cites the very similar *rhaistonê* and *diagôgê*, "ease" and "just passing time," as the affective disposition prerequisite for theoretical discourse: "Even the purest *theôria*, however, has not transcended affect altogether. For in its 'looking-at-something,' even that being which is now merely present-on-hand displays itself purely, as 'the way it looks,' then only when *theôria*, in *quiet* lingering with it—in *rhaistônê* and *diagôgê*, can let it come to the fore" (SZ 138). The point here is the necessary disengagement and detachment from the practical, existential world of convincing ourselves and others, in our taking counsel with each other, to decide on a course of action. It remains for us to show here that, despite his apparent turn to the theoretical and his apparent abstraction from the lifeworld of rhetorical conviction, in the end Plato does not want to induce this disengagement after all, but rather, even in the *Phaedrus*, to convince us to make an existential decision.

27. In this regard, however, see Gadamer's interpretation of Plato on language, WM 383 ff. Starting not from the *Phaedo* but from the *Cratylus*'s treatment of *onomata* or word names, Gadamer shows that in Plato the name first becomes a label or tag assigned to something that is already what it is and already has a specific form (*idea*) to it and a specific "look" (*eidos*) about it.

28. In his struggles to recover an earlier sense of *ist* or "is" before it became static presence, Heidegger is led to a variety of linguistic contortions like *west an* or "is fading in" and *west ab* or "is fading away." (The English here is considerably more natural than Heidegger's forced play on the German *anwesend* and *abwesend*, present and absent.) Heidegger makes his point most successfully,

perhaps, with Goethe's "Über allen Gipfeln *ist* Ruh," or "Over all mountain peaks *is* quiet." For contrary to the "is" of the *eidos* that is ever the same, the way quiet "is" over mountains "is" in temporally in coming to pass (see EM 68).

29. This is the central argument in the critique of rhetoric in the *Gorgias* too. See 503d ff., cited in note 23 above.

30. The *Sophist* contains a similar turn to the earlier physiological conception of *phusis* as *dunamis*:

> I say, then, that what possesses a power of some sort, whichever it might be, either to make a difference in something else, whatever its nature, or to undergo itself even the smallest change induced by the most insignificant thing, and be this just once—I say that all this *is* really. (248de)

See Aristotle, *Metaphysics* 5.4.1014b16 ff., for an account of the various senses of *phusis*, or "nature," ranging from the earlier concrete *genesis* of growing things to the later more abstract substance (*ousia*) and conceptual form (*eidos*), and Heidegger, GBM §§8–9, pp. 37–52 on *phusis* in its original and later senses.

31. Even in the later more theoretical dialogues where the task would no longer seem to be "guiding the souls" of the audience, this practical rhetorical task sometimes still does obtain. Hence, the recalcitrant "Philebus," for example, cannot be the interlocutor in the dialogue named for him, rather it must be the very much more tractable "Protarchus." It is also clear that the desired rhetorical effect of even these dialogues can only be achieved if they are reenacted vocally. Thus, we find the "Athenian" even saying in *The Laws* that the dialogues themselves are to be the new drama:

> For in looking back over the speeches we have been going through from this morning until now—and not without a touch of the divine spirit—these seemed to me to have been spoken above all like a kind of poetry. . . . For more than all the speeches I have learned *or heard*, be they *spoken* in poetry or merely spilled out, ours struck me as being the most appropriate and the most fitting for youths *to hear*. (811c–d; emphasis added)

And at 817b he concludes, "we ourselves are the poets of tragedy at once the most beautiful and the best that there can be" (see DD 71).

32. In fact, in the *Theaetetus* it is said, not without a touch of irony, that even sterile souls are to be "matched" with the appropriate, that is, sophistical, speakers:

> But at times, Theaetetus, when somehow they do not seem to me to be pregnant and I know they do not need me, in all good will I even court them for someone else, and to speak in the presence of God, I hit quite proficiently upon those from whose society they might profit. I have given many of them over to Prodicus, and many to still other wise and oracular men [σοφοῖς καὶ θεσπεσίοις ἀνδράσι]. (151b)

33. To be sure, the argument of this passage (244c–246a) oscillates between a demonstration by universal classes of things—"*All* soul is immortal," and so forth—and the "physiological" account, announced ahead of time at 245c, of what, by nature, can happen to *a* soul and what *a* soul does (see note 30 above); but, roughly, the demonstrative logic here would seem to be (1) What moves itself never ceases to move; soul moves itself; therefore soul never ceases to move. What never ceases to move is immortal; soul never ceases to move; therefore soul is immortal. Or, again, (2) what moves itself is ungenerated; soul moves itself, therefore soul is ungenerated. What is ungenerated is indestructible and immortal; soul is ungenerated; therefore soul is indestructible and immortal.

In applying his hermeneutical approach to Plato's *Timaeus* Gadamer alerts us to that dialogue's similar "shifts from the narrative, to the expositional mode of discourse," inattention to which has caused, he maintains, insoluable problems for Tayor, Cornford, Crombie, and others (DD 160; see also 177). These shifts, for instance, the shift to the expositional mode from 48a to 68e in the *Timaeus,* go together, he points out, with a shift in the intended audience for what is being said, namely from those who can only follow a story to " 'you' who are mathematically trained and who can therefore follow the *logic* of the argument" (171). (See also p. 178: "you mathematicians who can follow the account given.") I would add that such a shift in the *Phaedrus,* at least, is also a shift from the rhetorical-convincing to the instructional and, hence, from argument as a *pistis* or convincing argument for listeners who might hear its exhortation, to argument as *apodeixis* or demonstration for onlookers who might see its point.

34. In contrast with the emphasis in the *Rhetoric,* book 1, chapter 1, on the enthymeme as a "demonstration of a kind" and as the "most powerful of convincing arguments" (κυριώτατον τῶν πίστεων) (1355a8), at 1.2 Aristotle, as we know, asserts that of the three *pisteis* or "convincers," *logos, êthos,* and *pathos, êthos* might even be said to be the most powerful (κυριότατην ἔχει πίστιν τὸ ἦθος) (1356a13). In my view, this assertion is much more than a concession to the practical necessity of having to argue before people who cannot follow an extended *logical* argument (Compare the opposed view of J. Sprute in *Aristotle's Rhetoric,* pp. 117–22). Rather, in displaying here a characteristic but sometimes contradictory predilection for pre-Platonic thought, Aristotle recurs here to the original idea of argument, not as demonstration to detached onlookers (*theôretes*), but as exhortation of engaged hearers (*akouontes*), "there," "in the world," to an existential decision. Thus, we find at 1.3.1358a36–1358b6 that it is a hearer (*akroatês*) at whom the speech is aimed and that this hearer either is one who only looks on (*theôron einai*), or is a judge who decides about what was done in the past, in judicial rhetoric or, in consultative rhetoric, what is to be done in the future. Only in the case of "showoff" rhetoric, then, can the hearer withdraw from his or her practical engagement in the situation and afford theoretical detachment. Now, once this shift is made from logical demonstration for observers back to original argument for a hearer who must decide, *êthos,* the character of the speaker, does indeed become again the principal way to earn

the conviction *and trust—pistis,* after all, means both—of the audience. The point, already established in our examination of the *Phaedo,* is that in the end Plato, too, recognizes the "predominance" of *êthos* in producing the effect he intends for his dialogues, namely conviction to decide on an existential choice, not instruction.

35. As we will see in the next section, Plato's condemnation of writing as a "poison" (*pharmakon*) that invades the interior of thought, all the while he would depend on the paradigm of "the writing in the soul," is the theme of Derrida's "Plato's Pharmacy."

36. It could be argued, of course, that the *Meno* exemplifies for us how Socratic dialogue of question and answer can be used to induce the "recollection" (*anamnêsis*) of static eidetic relationships, namely the relationships to each other of "double area," "square," and "square built on the diagonal of another square," and the like, none of which are "susceptible of being otherwise than they are" and all of which are beyond indeterminacy and questionability (see *Meno* 82b ff.). The salient thing about this example, however, is that the question-and-answer dialogue here serves only to disabuse the interlocutor of misconceptions about how to double the area of a particular square, for instance, by doubling its side, and once dialogue has served this propedeutic function it gives way, at 84c ff., to Socrates' "pointing out" (*apodeiknunai*) the solution to the problem to someone looking on. From this point on the "questions" are only to check whether the interlocutor is able to follow the steps of the demonstration. Furthermore, this "aporetic" dialogue deliberately leaves indeterminate and questionable just how such a demonstration could possibly "teach" someone such an indeterminate and questionable thing as what virtue is, much less make him or her virtuous. Indeed, it "concludes" with the *question* whether virtue and, *a fortiori,* justice and decency are the sort of things that can be "taught" at all. Here, too, then, a theoretical *aporia* ultimately clears the way for the dialogue to revert to a practical, rhetorical exhortation to choose the life of virtue.

37. Heidegger alerts us to such nondemonstrative modes of speaking as prayer: "This [i.e., the apophantic] mode of making plain, in the sense of pointing something out and making it visible," he says, "is not proper to every kind of 'speech.' A pleading (*euchê*), for example, makes something plain too, but in another way" (SZ 32).

38. I refer here to the English translation, "Plato's Pharmacy," which appeared in Derrida, *Dissemination,* pp. 61–171 (PPh.) For a similarly daring and provocative Plato reading, this time of the *Timaeus,* one should also consult Derrida's *Khôra* (Paris, 1993). One should not overlook that, as extravagant as his expositions may seem, they are in fact based in knowledgeable, careful, and close reading of the texts. Few if any of his followers match him in this regard.

39. Heidegger's words are *früher, anfänglich,* and *ursprünglicher.* Although I draw upon Heidegger extensively here, this section is not intended as an explication or even application of any of his specific works. However, my uses of Heideggerian themes to elaborate the *Phaedrus* should be compared with

Heidegger's own treatment of the dialogue, PS 308–51. Here I would only point out that Heidegger continues to find Plato's attack on sophism support for his own efforts to break through the "everyday," "mediocre" ways of understandings of things bandied about in our "everyday" chatter with each other.

40. Though other works of Eric Havelock's have followed on the subject of the transition from orality to literacy in Greece, his *Preface to Plato* remains, in my view, the most interesting philosophically. It points out the differences in the oral-acoustical and literate-visual experiences of reality or being and argues convincingly that the transition from the ontology of Homer to the ontology of Plato presupposes a shift from the oral-acoustical to the literate-visual. Still, there is also a modernist tendency evident in Havelock's treatment of Plato as some sort of advance over Homer, and in his consequent failure to see what might have gotten lost with the transition in Plato from orality to writing. On this last count Heidegger's critique of the "metaphysical" turn in Plato is superior, even if Heidegger, too, persists in reading the pre-Platonic philosophers as well as Plato from a literary-visual perspective. See *Vom Wesen der Wahrheit* (GA 34) (Frankfurt, 1988) for Heidegger's early (1931–32) reading of the *Republic* and *Theaetetus.*

41. We should keep in mind that originally *logos* had a computational sense of a "reckoning up," as in *logizesthai,* meaning to calculate; hence, its ready serviceability for mathematics. It is easy to see, however, how *logos* derived from *legein,* meaning "to gather," as combined with *eirein,* meaning "to string together," could come to mean a "recounting" or "telling" of a story, and then a "speech."

42. John Stewart, for one, has recognized the inadequacies of any account of language as a system of signs to actually account for what happens in our everyday exchanges with each other, and he, too, has sought to recover the prioity of aural-oral communication in sound. See his scholarly and innovative *Language as Articulate Contact: Toward a Post-Semiotic Philosophy of Communication* (Albany, 1995). However, like Gadamer and Heidegger, on whom he builds extensively, Stewart, in moving beyond the account of language as representation in signs, fails to move beyond, or better said, back behind, the account of language as constitutive of a world that we *see* and *understand* "at a distance" (Heidegger, borrowing from Kierkegaard: *auf Abstand*), and, hence, he fails to move back behind our "talking things through" theoretically, in dialectic, to rhetoric's original existential exhortations "there" "in the world" to decide upon and choose a course of action. The title's "articulate contact" thus promises more than is delivered. One might have hoped that the "contact" would be interpreted, not as some sort of neutralized "linguistic transaction" in "coming to an understanding" of how things stand, but rather as a somatic, physical encounter in which the voiced sound of what we say to each other affects and moves us. Put another way, it is one thing to come to a detached articulate understanding of how things stand, but quite another to feel, hear, and obey or disobey what another has said.

43. Some years ago Gadamer pointed out to some of his former students that Derrida, in reading *Gegenwart* as "presence," does not hear the intrinsic

nonpresence to self of the *Warten auf das, was uns entgegen kommt,* which the German word *Gegenwart* contains, the "waiting for that which is coming toward us." The thought is Heideggerian, to be sure, and not something Husserl was likely to have had in mind either when he used such related expressions as *Gegenwärtigung* and *Vergegenwärtigung.*

44. Heidegger's *Being and Time* (SZ) can be read as a phenomenological exposition of the temporality of human existence and of the concomitance of being and not being in any human being which follows from this temporality.

45. See Heidegger, *Vorträge und Aufsätze* (Pfüllingen, 1954), "Bauen, Wohnen, Denken," pp. 145–62, and "Das Ding," pp. 163–81. See also Heidegger, "Der Ursprung des Kunstwerkes," in Holzwege, pp. 7–68.

46. See Heidegger, *Platons Lehre von der Wahrheit.*

47. See Gadamer, "The Model of Plato's Dialectic," WM 344–51, and "The Logic of Question and Answer," pp. 351–60.

48. See Derrida, *Of Grammatology* (Baltimore, 1974), pp. 9–10.

49. See Havelock, pp. 146–51.

50. We note, in this regard, that not all of Theuth's literary inventions are to be rejected. After all, among his other discoveries, the games of draughts and dice are not listed first here, rather, as Derrida conveniently overlooks, numbers, calculation, geometry, and astronomy (274d), and these Pythagorean sciences, all of which presuppose a break with the oral tradition and a turn to the graphic and diagrammatical, figure prominently in Plato's own educational curriculum (see *Rep.* 510c–d, 525b–527d).

51. See Havelock, *Preface to Plato,* "*Psyche* or the Separation of the Knower from the Known," pp. 197–214, and "The Origin of the Theory of Forms." pp. 254–75. Perhaps this is the place to point out that written words, which we see and read, afford us a distance and dispassion that the spoken words we hear do not, for what we look at does not envelope and involve us in a way that voiced sound does. The point here is made *e contrario* by musicology: for if we would not be enveloped and involved in the voices we hear, and if we are to evade undergoing the *pathos* or "feel" of them, we need only envision them diagrammatically. We need only translate our auditory experience into visual experience; we need only tran*scribe* the sound that we hear into "notes" on a score that we read and comprehend. This is why Plato lays such stress on training in harmony in the *Republic* (see 531a–c): instead of hearing melodies and being caught up in them we should learn to see and know (*eidenai*) the proportions (*logoi*) that obtain among the notes that we hear. And despite his reference elsewhere to the *pathos tôn logôn,* Plato makes just such a "musicological" move in the *Phaedrus* too, a move from hearing and undergoing the tone of what is said to envisioning the diagrammatic structure of it.

52. See Gregory Nagy, "The Name of Achilles," *The Best of the Achaeans* (Baltimore, 1979), pp. 69–83.

53. Ultimately New Testament scholars of the interpretive or hermeneutical school, for example, Raymond Brown, Robert Karris, et al., who see the meaning of New Testament narratives as evolving with every interpretation rather than as

historically fixed, presuppose just this point, to which the "new questers" for the historical Jesus, D. Crossan for one, seem wholly oblivious.

54. I have used, with slight modifications, W. R. M. Lamb's translations of Agathon's speech. See the Loeb edition of the *Symposium* (Cambridge, 1967) p. 161. However, for reasons that will become evident momentarily, I have not found his translations of Diotima's speech serviceable and have returned to my own.

Chapter 5

1. Martin Heidegger, *Logik* (GA 21) (Frankfurt, 1976), and *Heraklit* (GA 51) (Frankfurt, 1979).

2. What shifts in this continuous concern is Heidegger's understanding of the origin of this opening up of things for us. From an inititial ambivalence about this, say, in the *Basic Concepts of Metaphysics* (GBM), the origin seems at one point—in the *Introduction to Metaphysics* (EM), for instance—to have gravitated to the frightening (*deinos*) action of *Dasein*'s violent projection of itself: "The human being," we read there, "does violence, not aside from, and along with, other things, but solely in the sense that on the basis of, and in, his violence-activity he uses violence against the overpowering violence [of what is on the whole]. . . . [H]e is τὸ δεινότατον, the most violent—violently active in the midst of overpowering violence" (EM 115). But then, with the collapse of this, and Heidegger's own disastrously hybristic Promethean-Nietzschean project of the 1930s (see the notorious *Die Selbstbehauptung der Deutschen Universität* [Frankfurt, 1990]), it becomes being's fate for us (*Seinsgeschick*), of which we are receptive, and which we do not enact but undergo. See, for instance, in "Der Spruch des Anaximander," the transitive active play on the verb *ereignen* in "Das epochale Wesen des Seins *ereignet* das ekstatische Wesen des Da-seins (The epochale fading in of being *happens in appropriating* the ecstatic fading in of [our] being-there)" (HW 311; emphasis added).

3. At the end of §28 of his 1925 *Platon: Sophistes* lecture course Heidegger specifies two places where Aristotle treats dialectic, namely in the *Metaphysics*, 4, 2, and in the "doctrine of the *logos*" found in the *Topics* and its actual last book, *Sophistical Refutations* (PS 203). At the same time he announces that he will pursue both these sources, the first in connection with his exposition of Aristotle's idea of *sophia* or wisdom, and the second, "in connection with the theory of *legein* in the sense of theoretical discussion of something" (id.). Unfortunately for us, however, in what follows we find only an exposition of *Metaphysics*, 4, 1–2 (pp. 208–14) and nothing about the *Topics*' "doctrine of the *logos*."

4. In *Being and Time*—and in departing from Plato's *Sophist*, 244a, "but we are now at a loss to say what being (*seiend*, ὄν) means" (SZ 1)—Heidegger would address the question of what the participle, being, *seiend*, *on*, *ens*, *existens*, means by turning to human being or human existence, namely, *Dasein* or being "there," as an instance and exemplification of being in time. For time, he will argue, is

"the possible horizon of any understanding of being at all" (id.). Now, it is clear that with this introduction of time into the question about being, not-being is also introduced and, hence, contradiction, which is to say, a conjunction of "is" and "is not." For in contrast to metaphysics' *ständige Anwesenheit* or "steady presence," what "is" temporally involves *tempora* or tenses and thus "is not" any longer what it was in the past and "is not" yet what it will be in the future. Precisely this conjunction of "is" and "is not" is characteristic of human "being" or existence.

To be sure, it might be objected that human existence at any one time "is" just what it is with no contradiction. But it is precisely this metaphysical conception of being as a sequence of static presents disjoined from pasts and futures that Heidegger wishes to circumvent. He would show, for instance, that any authentic self "is" authentic only in "not being" authentic any longer and "not being" authentic yet. Hence, its temporality makes it inevitable that it "is" authentically and inauthentically concomitantly, *zugleich,* at the same time. Aristotle's construal of physical being as simultaneous being potentially (*dunamei on*) and being actually (*energeiai on*) comes close, we might note, to putting things this way. But ultimately it fails insofar as it ends up making this Heraclitian shifting, fluvian being secondary to the primary static beingness (*ousia*) said to underlie (*hupokeisthai*) it, namely *to hupokeimenon* or "the underlying (thing)," later *substans,* "the (thing) staying underneath."

5. See in particular Gadamer, *Truth and Method,* "Sprache und *Logos* (Speech and *Logos*)" (WM 383–95).

6. The usual translation of *auto to kalon* is "absolute beauty," but to speak with Heidegger, like all translations this one reveals some things that these words mean while concealing others. In the first place, the Latinate and overly terminological "absolute" emphasizes the aspect of abstraction and separation (*ho chôrismos*) in *auto* much more than this very ordinary and natural use of the word in the Greek here warrants, and it thereby obscures lingering traces of a premetaphysical understanding of things even in Plato, whose turn to the mathematical and diagrammatic may be said to be the beginning of metaphysical abstraction in argument. (See sections 4.1 and 4.2 above for our exposition of Plato's *Phaedo* and *Phaedrus* dialogues and 4.4 on the diction and style of this passage.)

In the second place, *to kalon,* has, to be sure, an application in aesthetics that is rendered appropriately by "beauty," but even in Plato this is not its principal sense. Primarily it has to do with the decency of some thing, some person, or some action, and whether that thing, person, or action can stand the light of day. Compare the *Philebus,* 66a.

7. See, for instance, *Republic* 534b–c:

> And it is the same in regard to the good: whoever is unable in an argument to define the idea of the good by abstracting the idea of it from all else, and whoever cannot, as if in battle, go through all counterattacks [ὥσπερ ἐν μάχῃ διὰ πάντων ἐλέγχων διεξιών] and is not willed to counterargue not by

> appearances but by essential being, whoever in all these counterattacks does not ride through on an argument not to be brought to a fall [ἀπτῶτι τῷ λόγῳ]—if all this be true of him, you would not say that one so disposed has seen and knows either the good itself or any other good.

8. For example, in commenting on *Metaphysics,* book 12, chapter 1, Gadamer writes,

> That there is a quite definite sense attached to "being" (*ousia*) is made evident by what is excluded: only such being that "is" in an original [*ursprünglichen*] sense is to be the object of the exposition. Here Aristotle presupposes the distinction of the categories: there is being in the sense of "substance" to which all other assertions of being are subordinated [for example, being of a certain quality, or size, or being in a certain state, and so forth], no matter how this differentation in the senses of being that the categories represent might be thought of.
>
> But it was just such being that is "for itself" and not, like the being of any sort of properties, in relation to something else, that philosophers, with the exception of those of that day, namely the Platonists, had always been treating, that is to say, the concrete particular, and it is plain that here Aristotle, in opposition to the Platonists, wants to defend an older understanding of being [*ein älteres Seinsverständnis*]. (Gadamer, *Aristoteles: Metaphysik XII* [Frankfurt, 1948], p. 46)

9. Of course, the word *archê* has primary logical function, for the *archê* is that from which argument begins and which, therefore, is itself not grounded by argument, at least not by demonstrative scientific argument. As we will see presently (section 5.4), according to the *Topics,* 1.2, the *archê* of any science may be grounded in an-archic dialectical argument, but in the *Posterior Analytics* Aristotle does not entertain this possibility:

> If indeed scientific knowing is what we have postulated, it is necessary that demonstrative scientific knowledge be inferred from what is true, primary, immediate as well as better known, prior to, and explanatory of the conclusion drawn from it. . . . "From what is primary" means "from appropriate principles" [ἐξ ἀρχῶν οἰκείων], for I mean the same thing by "primary" and "principle" [ταὐτὸ γὰρ λέγω πρῶτον καὶ ἀρχήν]. Indeed, a principle is an immediate premise of a demonstration [ἀρχὴ δ' ἐστὶν ἀποδείξεως πρότασις ἄμεσος] and "immediate" means "that to which there there is nothing prior" (*An. Post.* 71b20–72a8).

Significantly, in the *Posterior Analytics* these logical *archai* will have the same ontological status as Aristotle's prime mover: they are eternal, necessary, being, which is not "susceptible of being otherwise."

10. As we learned in section 4.1, the task in withstanding sophistical attacks, Plato tells us, is to establish for oneself whether the consequences of the idea one

has posited are "consonant with each other or dissonant [αλλέλοις συμφωνεῖ ἢ διαφωνεῖ]" (101d); see also 100a: "and positing whatever definition I decide to be the strongest, I assume to be true such things as seem to me to be consonant with this" (ἃ δ' ἂν δοκῇ τούτῳ συμφωνεῖν).

We would add now that the *Sophist* also reveals this origin of the envisionable "dialectic" of the *genê* and *eidê*, the "kinds" and "forms," in an earlier acoustical thinking based in the experience of voice (*phônê*). The dialectician, it is argued at 253b-c, must possess a science showing "which of the kinds are consonant with which others [ποῖα ποίοις συμφωνεῖ τῶν γενῶν] and which do not accept each other." This passage is all the more striking for having been introduced by two acoustical analogies. In the first, an analogy is drawn of dialectic with the science of letters, written letters, to be sure, *grammata*, but letters which, even so, are considered here as voiced sounds insofar as "some somehow do not harmonize with each other while, on the other hand, some together" (τὰ μὲν ἀναρμοστεῖ που πρὸς ἄλληλα, τὰ δὲ ξυναρμόττει) (253a). Though the idea of *harmonia* comes from *harma* or chariot and thus originates in the joiner's art, it clearly refers here not to how letters as spatial parts can or cannot be composed in a written word, but rather to which voiced sounds can or cannot be uttered one after the other in time. In the second analogy there is not a hint of the visual-spatial at all: a comparison is drawn between dialectic and a musician's knowledge of "high and low sounds" that either "mix" with each other or do not (253b). (Plato's abstraction from primary oral and acoustical experience, and his abstraction to the theory of the secondary written and visual was, of course, the theme of our exposition of the *Phaedrus* and our critique of Derrida's misreading of this dialogue in chapter 4 above.)

11. As Gadamer points out in *Dialogue and Dialectic* (DD n.21, 106–107), sophists, for instance, Protagoras, could, by drawing particular chords in a particular circle, *make it seem* that a square area could be made (*poiemenon*) equal that of "this given circle here." Only a mathematician, who looks away from the physical particulars to the purely conceptual idea of what they are, would be immune to such deception.

12. *Bedingung der Möglichkeit,* in Kant's case, namely, immortality, freedom, and the existence of God (*Kritik der Praktischen Vernunft,* 1. Teil, 2. Buch, 2. Hauptstück, 4–6, [Stuttgart, 1961], pp. 219–40). Actually Kant's words here are "praktisch notwendige Bedingung" (necessary condition practically), and "notwendigkeit der Bedingung" (necessity of the condition) (p. 238). In other words, Kant argues, without these postulates our practical, moral reason could not function; we do (want to) reason morally; therefore, they must hold. My point is that for Aristotle the laws of noncontradiction and the excluded middle work the same way in demonstrative and even dialectical reasoning, or so it seems in *Metaphysics,* 4, at least.

13. See section 4.1.2, note 6, above on the distinction made between hypothetical and anhypothetical reasoning in the *Republic,* 511a–d. We note that Aristotle's dialectical way of proceeding here is characteristic of Aristotle's treatment of all meta-logical problems. For instance, at *An. Post.* 75b5 f. we

find—paradoxically—a splendid *dialectical* argument about demonstrative reasoning. The dialectical problem to be addressed is "is or is not all scientific knowing [*epistasthai*] the result of demonstration?" and on this occasion also, to establish his own point of view that it is *not,* Aristotle takes on the opposed arguments of those who say that it *is.* As we will see later on, in regard to the logical principle of noncontradiction we are, in fact, not dealing with intuited first principles, the *archai* of the *An. Post.* 2.19, at all, but with those first principles of science that the *Topics* tell us are arrived at through dialectic (101a36–37).

14. Aristotle's repeated use of *bebaiotatê* or "best secured" for the principle of noncontradiction (see also 1005b12 and 17), is strongly reminiscent of Plato's "with an argument not to be overthrown" (ἀπτῶτι τῷ λόγῳ) (*Republic* 534c; see note 7 above). For in both cases the associative imagery is taken from hand-to-hand combat where a firm foothold is required in order that one can "have taken a stand" (*bebekenai*) and not be thrown to the ground.

15. First, it is supremely unfortunate to have to use such a racist example as this, particularly when Aristotle himself acknowledges the easy perversion of any such reasoning *kata sumbebêkos* and would advance scientific knowing and its demonstrative argument precisely as a means of heading this off; see *An. Post.* 71b9 f., "We know an individual thing epistemically in the strict sense and not in the sophistical way by what has happened accidentally, . . ." For the intent in our returning here to original reasoning *kata sumbebêkos* is not at all to legitimize racist arguments. Rather, the point, contrary to Aristotle's hopes—and to Plato's and to the claims made by traditional analytical philosophy, as well—is that the successful defense against such sophistical arguments does not lie in the misleading appearance or "Blendwerk" of some illusory reduction of dialectical and rhetorical reasoning to demonstration; instead it must be sought, as I will try to show presently, in recovering in any discussion the character (*êthos*) of the discussants, the kind of life they have chosen for themselves, their *prohairesis tou biou,* as Aristotle likes to say (see *Metaphy.* 10004b25), and the genuineness and appropriateness of the *pathos* that each speaker wishes to communicate. If sophism, the sophism of Plato's and Aristotle's day and our own, is to be countered, *êthos* and *pathos,* I will maintain, cannot be separated from *logos* (see *Rhet.* 1356a4 f. and section 5.5 below).

Second, Aristotle's example is in the singular, literally, "the white [one] is cultured," but English, unlike Greek (and German), generally allows this kind of expression only in the plural, as in "the best and the brightest" or "the poor." We have here an indication of a progressive reification in Western languages, in which verbal processes describable in adjectival form, happenings going on, are displaced more and more by static nouns. Hence, it is easily overlooked that the "smoke," for instance, has its origin in "smoking" going on that is "smoky," and that many nouns are solidified processes and occurrences just as many verbs are, so to speak, liquified substances, for instance, "to house." In reality the apparently solid and static is soluable.

Since for the most part modern English uses no longer recognizable Latin verbal stems, say, *sist* or *sta,* compounded with no longer recognizable prepositional prefixes, *de, con, ex, in, super, sub,* and so forth, and verbal suffixes, *ens, ans,* as in in-sist-ent and even sub-sta-(a)nce, it tends to obscure and suppress the original verbal nature of its word names and to become more and more a technical language of word signs designating static beings. (Compare Heidegger's badly timed but perhaps accurate rejection of Americanism and American English, for instance, in his 1942 *Hölderlins "Der Ister"* [GA 53] [Frankfurt, 1993], 68 and 80–81.) To be sure, the verbal orgins are not quite so imperceptible in word names like the Anglo-Saxon fore-tell-ing and the German *Vor-aus-sag-ung.* Evidently, even Aristotle's Greek obscures verbality, for in seeking a static basis for our reasoning he himself overlooks that his words for substance, *ousia* and *to hupokeimenon,* actually mean be*ing* and the underly*ing.* I will say more about this presently.

16. In one of his infamous "paleologisms," so to speak, Heidegger tries to make this verbal substrate plain by speaking not of *das Wesen,* the essence, but of *Anwesen* and *Abwesen* or a thing's "phasing into" presence and "phasing out of" presence—this in criticism of metaphysics' preference for what he calls a *standige Anwesenheit* or static presentness (*ousia*). For *ständige Anwesenheit* is pure presence with precisely no absence. It is pure, timeless being with no "not yet" and no "no longer" attaching to it, and hence there is no contradiction possible in it. But any original (*ursprüngliches*) *Anwesen* always implies a concomitant *Abwesen,* just as the truth (*alêtheia*) disclosed in this kind of being implies a concomitant oblivion and obscurity (*lêthe*). Being in this case "is" always, or "ever" (*aei*), in temporal transition from not being yet, to being now, to being no longer, and hence it is inherently self-contradictory. English translators have resorted to a variety of barbarisms of their own, like "presencing" and "absencing," to render this genetic being. These seem overdone, especially when one considers that the Anglo-Saxon participial "ing" here simply doubles the participial "ens" of the Latin *prae(s)ens* and *ab(s)ens.*

On the whole I find Gadamer's a much more graceful way to take up the ontological questions Heidegger raises. As is obvious by now, I have relied heavily on Gadamer's exposition of the priority of the question over the answer in any dialectial "method" of attaining to dialectical likelihood—as opposed to the scientific "method" of attaining to demonstrative, necessary, and static truth. See especially, in this regard, *Truth and Method* (WM), pp. 368 f.

17. It is striking that in *Metaphysics,* 3, Aristotle goes so far as to distinguish demonstration—which proceeds according to the law of noncontradiction and by causality, substance (*ousia*), and the predication of those accidents intrinsic (*kath' hauta*) to substances—from dialectical reasoning from received opinions and by the topics of "sameness and difference, like and unlike, prior and posterior and all other such things" (995b5–25), this as if to imply that dialectic from received opinions and by the topics is concerned with things on an entirely different ontological level from the substances that are the concern of demonstration, and even that the law of noncontradiction applies only to the latter.

18. The entire project of Platonic philosophy may be viewed as an attempt to establish an ontological difference where, for Aristotle, one sometimes seems not

yet to exist. As we have seen, Plato wants to turn the adjective and predicate *kalon* or decent, a word name which "tells" of narrative historical being (Heidegger: *geschichtliches Sein*) as it happens to have happened, into an eponym and sign for the static essential being *auto to kalon*, or "the decent itself" (see chapter 4 above). The latter, it is assumed, can be known apart from, and prior to, any word sign we might establish for it and would thus be immune to sophistical misrepresentations of it in equivocal word names. As we will see, Aristotle's resistence to this project is most evident in his critique of the idea of the good.

19. My translation of *gemein* as "ordinary" suppresses the connotation of "vulgar" that Heidegger obviously wishes to imply here. Again, we must keep in mind why Heidegger did not pursue, as we are pursuing it, the hermeneutics of original argument: for him original argument was the "fallen" and "inauthentic" "mere talk" of those who had lost themselves to the "they" and "gone up" (*aufgegangen*) in it like smoke. We, in contrast, are taking this "ordinary knowledge" or *gemeine Kenntnis* to be *endoxa* or received opinions and are not concerned, as is Aristotle in the *Analytics*, to replace it with some sort of demonstrative "science," or even, as is Heidegger in *Being and Time*, with another knowledge that transcends its supposed inauthenticity. On the contrary, for us it is the legitimate source from which all ethical, political, and judicial reasoning derives. Importantly, Gadamer does not follow Heidegger in this rejection of the everyday world and, least of all, in Heidegger's development of this rejection into his disastrous and despicable revolutionary Prometheanism of the early 1930s, say, in his *Introduction to Metaphysics* (EM). Consequently Gadamer, quite in contrast to Heidegger, is able to validate the authority of tradition. See WM 261–69, "The Rehabilitation of Authority and Tradition."

20. It is clear that this seeing and establishing of logical relationships would be speechless and voiceless—*aneu phônês*, as Plato puts it (*Soph.* 263e)—and consequently writing, not speech, would be the the primary means of its communication. So far as this realm goes, I find Derrida's argument that in fact there never are any ideal essences here to be envisioned to begin with, but only written signs signifying written signs, *ad infinitum*, entirely convincing. See section 4.3.1 above.

21. Gadamer argues convincingly that Plato, in stripping language of its expression in audible, voiced speaking, only conceals the original "tie-in to speech" (*Sprachgebundenheit*) of any dialogue, even that of the soul with itself (WM 385; see *Soph.* 263e): "The discovery of the ideas by Plato covers up speech's own nature more fundamentally than did the sophist theoreticians, who developed their own art in the use and abuse of speech" (id.).

Against Plato, Gadamer avails himself of the Johannine theory of the incarnation of the word (*logos, verbum*) to show that the internal world finds its perfection in its spoken expression (see WM 395–404, "Speech and *Verbum*"). Our point, which builds on Gadamer's, is that for finite human beings, as opposed to a creator God, even the internal word, *ho esô logos*, is heard, not envisioned, and cannot, therefore, be the starting point and origin. Rather, it always entails an abstraction and withdrawal from the actual, voiced external word, *ho exô logos,* that we first had to hear spoken to us before we could say it to ourselves in thought. (See section 3.1 and chapter 3, note 7 above on the communal origins of any deliberation by oneself.)

Chapter 6

1. Whereas in Plato and, ultimately, even in Aristotle's case we must speak of an *e*visceration of Greek rhetoric, in a certain sense we can speak of the New Testament's "subsequent *re*visceration" of it. The New Testament Greek for "guts" or viscera is *splanchna* as in Saint Paul's "For God is my witness how I long for you in the viscera of Christ Jesus" (ἐν σπλάγχνοις Χριστοῦ Ἰησοῦ) (*Philippians* 1:8). Though startling to modern, if not postmodern, sensibilities, expressions like this are not uncommon in Paul; indeed, one might even call them characteristic. Granted, the heart (*hê kardia*) is said more often than *splanchna* to be the visceral seat of love, mercy, comfort, and so forth, but surprisingly perhaps, Paul, the supposed contemner of the flesh, is in no way averse to the more "gutsy" *splanchna.* See, for example 2. Corinthians 6:12 and Philemon 7, 12, 20.

To be sure *splanchna* is not preferred diction in traditional Greek, and thus it might seem in Paul to be merely an indicator or marker of the Hebrew *meim* and *rachamim,* which the *Septuagint* translates with *koilia* and *enkata,* respectively (see, e.g., Genesis 15:23 and 43:30). Still, we should adhere here to a hermeneutical principle which maintains that what a word has come to mean in translation is always something new and always something more than the word it translates. Hence, the translation is never just a sign or *sêmeion* for the original word translated. With Gadamer, we could say that when *meim* and *rachamim* are rendered with *splanchna,* there is both a "merging of horizons" and an "accretion in meaning": on the one hand, *splanchna* takes on new dimensions of meaning from the *meim* and *rachamim* it translates, Hebrew meanings associated with *chesed* or mercy and forgiveness, and previously unknown to Greek. On the other hand, *meim* and *rachamim* acquire a new sense once they are translated, carried over, into the Greek context of *splanchna.* After all, *splanchna* was not previously an empty sound in Greek even if its use in Paul has special Hebraic senses, and therefore its meaning continues to derive, too, from the complex of related Greek words in which it lies. It follows, then, that its meaning must be established not only by recurring to its Hebrew origins but also with recourse to the place it came to occupy in Greek when Greek was used to translate Hebrew words.

We will see in this chapter that, though *splanchna* is restricted to entrails of sacrificial animals in Homer, there is in Homer's Greek a clear correlate to the linguistic context in which Paul uses *splanchna,* namely, Homer's use of *phrenes, thumos, kardie,* on the traditional range of which Paul can draw in rendering the Hebrew *meim* and *rachamim* as *splanchna.* However, we will see, too, that this correlative context in Homer is systematically eliminated in Plato in a way that then becomes definitive for Greek argument and rhetoric following him.

Hence, any real recovery of visceral Greek rhetoric and of visceral rhetoric generally could not have been achieved solely within the Greek tradition itself. It could come, in other words, only with infusions into the Greek of ways of speaking and thinking from a very different language frame. And precisely this is what happens with the New Testament's translations into Greek from Hebrew. Indeed, Homer's language of *phrenes, thumos, kardie* is recovered only once the New Testament adapts *splanchna* and *kardia* for the purpose of evangelization and homiletics. Greek argument was visceral in Homer but was eviscerated by Plato, whose evisceration of argument Aristotle largely perpetuates. Hence, we can say that argument in Greek was "reviscerated" only by the New Testament and its invocation of *splanchna*, "guts" and viscera and the "merging of horizons" of Greek and Hebrew it thereby effected.

Saint Paul's letters, of course, are not the only places in the New Testament where this "merging of horizons" of Greek and Hebrew occurs. In the "synoptic" Gospels, Mark, Mathew, Luke, in both the stories that Jesus himself tells and the stories that the evangelists tell about Jesus, the rhetorical point is the same, namely that "those who have ears" will "hear." With regard to the stories Jesus tells, we find, for example, in the parable of the "good Samaritan" that this "foreigner" comes across the injured and unclean victim of a robbery and that, upon seeing him, "was viscerally moved" (*esplanchnisthê*) to acts of compassion and kindness (Luke 10:33). The point of the story is obviously not so much that we see theoretically "Who is a neighbor?"—this, after all, was the question that occasioned Jesus' recounting of it—but that, having heard the story, we should be brought to a similar "gut" transformation from malice to charity. For only such a transformation will allow us to turn and *hear* what we are supposed to do and then do it.

The same thing holds for the stories told about Jesus. In regard to the widow whose son had died and was to be revived by Jesus, we hear that upon seeing her Jesus himself "was viscerally moved" (*esplanchnisthê*) for her (Luke 7:13) or, in regard to the multitude on the shore, that "he saw the great crowd and was viscerally moved [*esplanchnisthê*] for them and healed their sick ones" (Matthew 14:14; see also 15:32 and Mark 8:2). And in regard to the blind men by the wayside, we hear that, "Viscerally moved" [*splanchnistheis*] for them, Jesus touched their eyes and straightaway they saw (Matthew 20:24). The homiletical point is that in hearing these stories read out loud, the listeners should similarly be viscerally moved to acts of compassion. For acts of compassion, precisely as acts of compassion, are not based in a mere thought but in a "gut" feeling, and the exhortation (*parainesis*) to perform them must accordingly be acoustical communication on a "gut" level.

Just as do the "synoptic" Gospels, Paul seeks the communication of compassion and a turning from the ways of hatred, the only difference being that his means of acoustical communication on the "gut" level are not vivid parables but rather an extraordinarily lyrical and moving phrasing such as that found, for instance, in the opening of Philippians 2—again, I cite the King James translation because of all the English translations it renders most accurately the figures with which Paul creates the cadences and rhythms needed to communicate the visceral passion of what he is saying:

> If there be therefore any consolation in Christ,
> if any comfort of love,
> if any fellowship of the Spirit,
> if any bowels and mercies, [εἴ τις σπλάγχνα καὶ οἰκτιρμοί],
> fulfill ye my joy that ye be likeminded,
>
> having the same love,
> being of one accord,
> of one mind.
>
> Let nothing be done through strife or vainglory;
> but in lowliness of mind
> let each esteem other better than themselves.
>
> look not every man on his own things,
> but every man also on the things of others.
>
> Let this mind be in you,
> which was also in Christ Jesus. (1–5)

In contrast with communication by parables, say, Nathan's (2 Samuel 12) or Jesus', here there is nothing to imagine, no picture to get, and as a result, everything to hear. We take note accordingly the classical Greek tropes Paul uses to achieve his acoustical effect: the anaphora, asyndeton, and symphony (parallelism) in "If there be . . . any consolation, if any comfort . . . if any bowels and mercies," that impell this first phrase to its culmination in the imperative "Fulfill ye my joy." We note as well the asyndeton and symphony in the parenthetical *rallentando,* as it were, of "same love," "one accord," "one mind," and then, as a developmental interlude, the three imperatives, the first two phrased antiphonally in "Let nothing be done through strife, *but* . . . let each esteem the other" and "Look not every man on his own things *but* every man also on the things of others." We note further the anaphora here of "every man . . . every man" and the antiphony (antithesis) of "own things" and "things of others." And, finally, though ultimately all this is only a prelude, we arrive at the climax of this first period, "Let this mind be in you, which was also in Christ Jesus." I call this period a prelude because the entirety of what we have heard so far is, of course, designed to issue in the grand Christological and creedal hymn of verses 6–11. Nonetheless, even the truncated version of this passage has served to make clear that only a modern, Enlightenment ear, trained, as it is, in the Platonic tradition to focus on cognitive content in rigorous exclusion of anything visceral, could be deaf to the "gut" communication here and could lose itself in trying to see theoretically the "what" in what is said. Only a modern, Enlightenment ear, that is to say, could miss the New Testament's startling "revisceration" of Greek rhetoric.

2. See Kierkegaard, *Either/Or*, part 2 (Princeton, 1987), p. 5. Kierkegaard, with his emphasis on "indirect communication," understands as well as anyone—and certainly better than Aristotle—the visceral dimension of the parable (compare *Rhet.* 1393b24–94a9 on the "fable"). He understands, this is to say, how it engages the "gut" of the one ready, not just to see the point of it, but to hear its exhortation. How adroitly he is able to use this form of argument for his own homiletical purposes is made clear by the wealth of Kierkegaard's parables collected in Thomas Oden's compilation, *Parables of Kierkegaard* (Princeton, 1978).

3. It is in just this regard that C. Perelman's rejection of Cartesian demonstration from self-evidident principles as a paradigm for argument is, despite the radical breakthrough it achieves, ultimately disappointing (see C. Perelman and L. Olbrechts Tyteca, *The New Rhetoric* [Notre Dame, Ind., 1969]). For, as he says, the theory of argumentation he will propose is "the study of the discursive techniques allowing us *to induce or to increase the mind's adherence to the theses presented for its assent*" (p. 4; his emphasis). As a consequence of narrowing his considerations of rhetoric this way, he provides, to be sure, a brilliant rehabilitation of the topical, dialectical argument, in which one person *instructs* another to see the point and *assent* to it intellectually, but he neglects completely the acoustical dimensions of argument—diction and delivery—without attention to which no one can *convince* someone else to *consent* to do something. In this omission he remains very much a part of the French *literary* tradition, for which speech is secondary to writing. See section 4.3 on Derrida, of whom the same thing may be said.

4. It is Gadamer who alerts us to the crucial importance of this dialogue, which he makes central to his own *Destruktion* of the mathematical sign, the *characteristica universalis,* as the paradigm for communication of intelligible truth, and to his own "laying bare" and "laying out" of the word name as a mirror (speculum) in which the being of a thing first becomes clear. See WM 383–95, "Speech and *Logos,*" and 432–49, "The Medium of Speech and its Speculative Structure." See also my "Plato as Impulse and Obstacle in Gadamer's Development of a Hermeneutical Theory," in *Gadamer and Hermeneutics,* ed. Hugh Silverman (New York, 1991), pp. 23–41. Despite the attention he pays to the *Laut* or sound of the word name, Gadamer's concern, like Heidegger's, remains focused on what it "makes plain" for us to *see,* or, in Greek, the *dêlôma* which the word name accomplishes when it is uttered (see WM 388–89). In contrast, our focus will be on the message the voiced word gives us to *hear.*

5. Edwards makes the point convincingly (233–36) that Achilles feels deserted by his friends in that they themselves have done nothing to resist Agamemnon's act of hubris. We note that none of the speakers addresses this issue here, and their arguments, and especially Odysseus's, thus fail not only on the level of *pathos* but *êthos* too: save for Phoenix (who may be a later insertion in the story), Achilles cannot feel the prerequisite *philia* for these fair-weather *philoi.* That a *pathos* or *Stimmung* is absolutely basic for the way Homer's heroes decide to act is made evident by the *Iliad* itself, which far from being the story of

the siege of Troy, is, of course, the story of Achilles' rage. He decides to re-enter the war only when that rage is converted into the desire to avenge Patroclus's death at the hands of Hector. The *Iliad* climaxes only when this transferred rage finally abates in the extroadinary reconciliation scene with Priam in book 24.

6. That *êthos* and *pathos* would have turned out to be intrinsic to rhetorical argument and not mere extrinsic "add-ons" was clearly signaled at the start when in chapter 2 the three *pisteis,* the three dimensions of "what serves to convince" (*to endechomenon pithanon*) (1355b26), were named equally, *êthos, pathos,* and *logos* (1356a1 f.), and all three were said, *precisely in contrast to the external, atechnoi* witnesses, torturings, and documents (1355b35–37; see also 1.15.1375a21 f.), to be *entechnoi pisteis* or an internal part of the art of rhetorical conviction provided by the speech itself (*dia tou logou porizomenai*) (1355b35 f.).

7. It is significant that we no longer make any distinction between *communication* and the *transmission* of data or imformation. Originally, to communicate something meant to establish a community of people who share in a common feeling about it, which is what Lincoln's speeches, for instance, set out to do. In the guise of "impartiality" and "objectivity," however, this central dimension of communication has been deleted, and with the result of radical individuation, isolation, and estrangement. For what has been accomplished is only an appearance of impartiality and objectivity that, in truth, pits each of us against the other in forcing us to submit to the will of a technocratic-commercial oligarchy.

8. Our own modern—and postmodern—nearly exclusive emphasis on writing and obliviousness to speech has invalidated the similar and uniquely affecting, pleonastic *lexis* of the King James Bible, here in an orally transmitted Anglican ascription drawn from Jude, 1 Peter, Paul's letters, and Revelation: "Now to God the Father, God the Son, and God the Holy Ghost, be ascribed, as is most justly due, all might, majesty, dominion, power and praise, both now and forever. Amen." To just read this silently would indeed make it seem like simpleminded reiteration of the same idea. And—to go from the sublime to the ridiculous—the same would hold for Yogi Berra's exquisite redundancy, "It's déjà vu all over again!"

9. In this section I have reworked materials used in a different context in my "From Acoustics to Optics: The Rise of the Metaphysical and Demise of the Melodic in Aristotle's Poetics," in *Sites of Vision,* ed. David Michael Levin (Cambridge, 1997), pp. 69–91. Once again, it is the young Heidegger who alerts us to Aristotle's striking ambivalence, at the beginning of the *Metaphysics,* in regard to which is the primary form of *aisthesis* or perception, seeing or hearing: having opened with the assertion that it is seeing (*horan*) that most of all makes us knowledgeable and displays to us the differences among things, Aristotle proceeds to say next, remarkably, that it is hearing, *akouein,* that distinguishes those animals that can learn, *manthanein,* from those that cannot (*Metaphy.* 980a22 f.; see also Heidegger, PS 70).

10. Gadamer alerts us to the profound significance of this expression from Aeschylus (*Agamemnon,* 177) in recurring to Aeschylus and tragedy in order to

recover the idea of experience or *Erfahrung* after Hegel's systematic elimination of it and, in fact, of all limits to consciousness. Here Gadamer picks up a theme from Heidegger, namely that any self-projection or *Sich-Entwerfen* is always limited by our having already been injected or *geworfen* into a situation not of our own making. The point, in Gadamer's terms, is that *Wirkungsgeschichtliches Bewußtsein* actively effects history but also *undergoes* its effects; hence, the term must be translated as "historically effective *and effected* consciousness." For the usefulness of Aeschylus's *pathei mathos* in making this point see WM 339, and my own HHF 175 n.9, 190, 274.

11. See *Essays on Aristotle's Poetics*, ed. A. O. Rorty (Princeton, 1992), pp. 51–72, in particular p. 67.

12. See Cyril of Jerusalem, *Mystagogical Catacheses*, 2.5, in *St. Cyril of Jerusalem's Lectures on the Christian Sacraments*, ed. F. L. Cross (Crestwood, N.Y., 1986), and cited by Kosman in Rorty, *Essays*, p. 68.

13. It is only Nietzsche, of course, who will recover the full significance of this origin of tragedy in satyr plays. See chapter 7 below and GT §7 on the satyr chorus as the soil and ground (*Boden*) from which tragedy arose (KSA 1, 55), in particular, where Nietzsche asserts that "The tragedy grew upwards upon this foundation" (id.):

> The satyr, as the Dionysian choral dancer, lives in a religious reality permitted under the sanction of myth and cult. That tragedy begins with him, that the Dionysian wisdom of the tragedy speaks out of him, is a phenomenon every bit as off-putting for us here as the development of the tragedy out of the chorus. . . . [F]aced with the satyr chorus the cultured Greek felt himself canceled and transcended. (55–56)

"The satyr chorus of the dithyramb is the saving deed of Greek art" (57).

14. Havelock's *Preface to Plato* contains some remarkable insights that would corroborate, and be corroborated by, the *Destruktion* in Heidegger of disembodied thought and, before Heidegger, in Nietzsche. Particularly useful is Havelock's chapter 11, "*Psyche* or the Separation of the Knower from the Known," pp. 197–214, in which he argues cogently that with the transition from an oral, acoustical culture to a literate, visual one the word *psuchê* shifts its meaning from the "life" of the body to the "personality," "soul," or "self" as the seat of moral decision detached from the body and removed from bodily experience. I might add that in regard to the *psuchê*, too, Aristotle involves himself in remarkable contradictions insofar as he preserves the earlier, pre-Platonic understandings of it as "life" while at the same time elaborating the Platonic psychology of disengaged contemplation.

15. Thus, Aristotle, in moving from the level of the consciousious "for him" of the tragic agent, Oedipus, to the level "for us" onlookers, foreshadows the very cancelation of experience (*Erfahrung*) that Gadamer, with his emphasis on *pathei mathos*, finds and resists in Hegel. See the "Einleitung" to Hegel's *Phänomenologie des Geistes* (Hamburg, 1952), pp. 63–75, on the distinction between the actual

experience of consciousness "for it" and the logic of that experience "for us" who are observing it, and note 4 above.

Chapter 7

1. Although he has moved in a direction somewhat different from ours, Manfred Riedel, in his *Hören auf die Sprache: Die akroamatische Dimension der Hermeneutik* (Frankfurt, 1990), pp. 330–54, has already come a long way in bringing the early Nietzsche to bear on the recovery of the original acoustical dimension of speech. Indeed, he has cited many of the Nietzsche passages to which we will recur here. Riedel, however, takes "hermeneutics" not as *Destruktion* that "lays bare" an original phenomenon in order to then "lay it out" interpretively, but as a theory of *Verstehen* or understanding of meaning; hence his concern, unlike ours, is not to ground derivative speech in the *Boden* or soil of original tonality from which it originates, but to exposit the conjunction of *Bild und Ton,* visual image and audible sound, as coequals in language's communication of meaning (see, e.g., p. 346). Thus, for him the "acroamatic" or acoustical is *a* source of knowledge (*Quelle des Wissens*) (p. 345), but not, as in our reading of Nietzsche, *the* source from which the optical and visual derives.

Accordingly, Riedel is very useful for us when it comes to uncovering the metonymic-metaphorical potential of language as a basis for reasoning and argument (see, in particular, pp. 347–48), and in this he reminds us of Gadamer's emphasis on the metaphorical "prior accomplishments" of language. He is not so useful for us, however, when it comes, with Heidegger, to uncovering the embeddedness of conceptual speech in "voicing" and tonality, of *logos* in *pathos.* (Compare SZ §29, 134–40, on the *Stimmung* as basic precondition for any opening up (*Erschließen*) of meaningfulness, even the meaningfulness of "objects" for pure *theôria.*) Thus, if Riedel does point out that "the concept is what remains when the tone has ceased to resonate and only the image is left" (p. 351), he fails to draw the radical conclusions to which Nietzsche would lead us, namely that communication by speech originates in, and depends upon, the *phônê* or tone of voice, and hence the spoken word was always much more than the visual residue left for cognitive understanding when the tone of it has faded away, just as the song that was heard was much more than the theoretical visualization of its logical relationships after it is over. Moreover, if Riedel speaks of the gestures of language (*Gestik der Sprache*) (p. 351), unlike Nietzsche, he is unable to penetrate to the "orchestral" origins of speech, to the dance or *orchê* as the physical, somatic dimension of hearing and speaking. Consequently, he misses the origin of apparent speech "acts" in speech "passions," of the *logos* or argument we "run," in the *pathê* or feelings we undergo.

2. Regrettably, much like the table of contents for this book. As we have observed, the original sense of *logos* is not "spoken utterance" but "computation." Hence, even Heraclitus is already thinking of something calculable and envisionable intellectually even if he still expects his audience to hear and not read silently what he has to say.

3. See the reference to Cyril of Jerusalem on baptism and the Eucharist in section 6.3 above. To those familiar only with the later Nietzsche's relentless attack on Christianity, with his *Der Antichrist,* for instance, any references to the rite of the Eucharist might seem wholly incongruous with the uses of Nietzsche we are making here. However, insofar as we are relying solely on the young Nietzsche (1870–72), they are, in fact, not incongruous at all. Indeed, in notes from late 1870 or early 1871 we find: "The Gospel of John [was] born out of Greek atmosphere, out of the soil [*Boden*] of the Dionysian" (7[13]; KSA 7, 139), and, later, "In the thoroughly Greek product of the Gospel of John absolute mysticism reveals itself to be born out of the mystery rites even if it gets its name and impetus from the Orient" (7 [80]; KSA 7, 156), and, finally, from 1872,

> Greek cheerfulness is the enjoyment of the will when a [certain] stage is reached. It is always reproducing itself anew: Homer, Sophocles, the Gospel of John—three stages of the same thing. Homer as the triumph of the Olympian gods over the titanic powers of horror. Sophocles as the triumph of the tragic thought and the victory over the Aeschylean rites of Dionysius. The Gospel of John as the triumph of the mystery-beatitude, of salvation. (7 [174]; KSA 7, 207)

The thought here is entirely compatible with a contemporary passage in the *Birth of Tragedy* in which Nietzsche tells us that

> [e]nchantment is the presupposition of all dramatic art. In this enchantment the dionysian enthusiast sees himself as Satyr and as Satyr, moreover, he sees the god, that is, he sees, in his metamorphosis a new vision outside of himself as the Apollonian perfection of his condition. (GT §8; KSA 1, 61–62)

It is, of course, precisely any application of such thoughts as this to the rites of Christianity that the later Nietzsche will vehemently disown in his 1886 "An Attempt at Self-criticism," but not, we note, because of their inconsistency with his earlier views, but because of his increasing concern with opposing both Christian and German Romanticism.

4. The exposition of the parable of the sower of seeds that follows this verse in Luke, given here in the King James version, makes clear just how kerygmatically devasting the loss of the sound of the word would be:

> Now the parable is this: the seed is the word of God. Those by the way side are they that *hear*; then cometh the devil, and taketh away the word out of their hearts, lest they should believe and be saved. They on the rock are they, which, when they *hear,* receive the word with joy; and these have no root, which for a while believe, and in time of temptation fall away. And that which fell among the thorns are they, which, when they *have heard,* go forth, and are choked with cares and riches and pleasures of this life, and bring no fruit to perfection. But that on the good ground are they, which in an honest and good heart, *having heard* the word, keep it, and bring forth fruit with patience. . . . Take heed therefore

> how ye *hear*; for whosoever hath, to him shall be given; and whosoever hath not, from him shall be taken even that which he seemeth to have. (8:11–15, 18)

5. Garver, whose work I find to be by far the most illuminating of the spate of recent publications on the *Rhetoric*, refers to the Second Inaugural Address in his own discussion of the indissociability of *logos*, *êthos*, and *pathos* in rhetorical argument, and in displaying just what Aristotle means when he says that people differ in regard to their decisions insofar as their *pathê* have changed (*Rhet.* 1378a19–20; see Garver, p. 115 f.). "In his Second Inaugural Address," writes Garver,

> Lincoln transforms the triumphal feelings of vindication he sees in his audience into feelings of humility. By seeing the Civil War as an instance of divine judgment, he makes us regard the losing side differently because we now will act differently toward the South. . . . As Lincoln's example shows, the passions cannot simply be interstitial tie breakers because they have other roles as well; in this case having an emotion predisposes us to see and judge in a certain way. (135)

I would only add that the change in *pathê* predisposes us not so much *to see and judge* in a certain way but *to hear and decide* for a certain course of action. For the point is that Lincoln does not want so much for his audience, as detached observers, to come to a certain point of view, as he wants them to join with him in a certain common undertaking. See chapter 2, note 7, above for my reservations about Garver's use of "judgment" to translate *krisis.* "Judgment" eliminates the willed, existential engagement of those making the decision and reduces *krisis* to a function of what Heidegger, following Kierkegaard, would call *Wissen auf Abstand*—knowing or cognition at a distance.

Furthermore, despite Garver's Nietzschean sounding reference to a "community of pleasure and pain" (p. 122), which would seem to imply communion in a *pathos* by the speaker and the members of the audience, he continues to think of the *pathê* as emotions undergone by the individuated subject. "[O]nly individuals feel emotions," he says (p. 131). In this way Garver closes himself off to the community of dance, the orchestral community of those who find themselves resonating to the same *melos* and sharing in the one *pathos* it communicates. If we listen radically enough, it is just such a community as this that Lincoln's spoken phrases engender and on which the effectiveness of his speech ultimately depends.

Once again, the early Heidegger gives us starting points to rethink the "subjective" understanding of *pathos* as private emotion, but starting points which he himself left undeveloped. In *Being and Time* he shows that "to begin with" (*zuerst*) we never have an isolated "subject" that must then find ways to get outside of its head, as it were, and "emphathize" with another isolated "subject." On the contrary, "to begin with" we always already find ourselves together with others as participants in taking care of things (*Besorgen*) in a shared world and in caring about others (*Fürsorge*) and sharing with them in the prevailing "voicing" to things or feeling (*Stimmung*). Individuation into private "subjects" comes, Heidegger points out, only in the "deficient modes" of our being-there in the world together with others, that is, only when we are no longer concerned to take care of things in the world and no longer care about others.

Unfortunately for us, however, Heidegger's preferred method of bringing the being of something to light, is to begin with its deficient modes; hence he treats the original community of feeling only in its *in*authentic forms. "The public realm, as the 'everybody's' kind of being not only has its determinate feeling; it needs a feeling and creates one for itself," he says (SZ 138), and in his view only the radically individuating feeling of *Angst* can free us our fallenness to this public realm and our dissipation in, and absorption into, its shared feelings. Contrary to Heidegger, however, one might ask if there is not such a thing as an *authentic* communion in a feeling, say, in Lincoln's "charity for all," that might free us precisely from our fallenness into community-less isolation and from our absorption into its own feelings of malice, resentment, hatred. Why, after all, do religions have chants, melodies, and rituals if not to accomplish a basic change at what Nietzsche calls the Dionysian level, a change in how the community feels?

This is not to say that the essentially isolating feelings of malice, resentment, and hatred could not easily be manipulated by a fascist demagogue who is himself consumed by them, into a bogus feeling in the audience of solidarity with all who bear the same malice, resentment, and hatred. That such solidarity is not real community is made clear, however, by the fact that such feelings of malice, resentment, and hatred presuppose the *exclusion* of those for whom they are felt, and consequently, the isolation of the speaker and audience from those they hate. The precondition of genuine community, Lincoln's reconciliation with the former enemy in the *agôn*, is completely missing here.

Index